Talking About Organization Science

Organization Science

Series Editor: Arie Y. Lewin

Books from Sage Publications, *Organization Science*, and the Institute for Operations Research and the Management Sciences

The Sage Publications **Organization Science** book series reprints expanded Special Issues of *Organization Science*. Each individual volume is based on the original Special Issue that appeared in *Organization Science*. It includes all-new introductions by the editors as well as several chapters that did not appear in the original Special Issue. These new chapters may include reprints of papers that appeared in other issues of *Organization Science*, relevant papers that appeared in other journals, and also new original articles.

The book series is published by Sage Publications in partnership with INFORMS (the Institute for Operations Research and Management Sciences) the publisher of *Organization Science*. The Series Editor is Arie Y. Lewin, the Editor in Chief of *Organization Science*.

Organization Science was founded in 1989 as an international journal with the aim of advancing the field of organization studies by attracting, then publishing innovative research from across the social sciences. The term "Science" in the journal's title is interpreted in the broadest possible sense to include diverse methods and theoretical approaches. The editors of *Organization Science* believe that creative insight often occurs outside traditional approaches and topic areas, and that the role of *Organization Science* is to be broadly inclusive of the field by helping to integrate the diverse stands of organizational research. Authors are expected to describe theoretical concepts that give meaning to data, and to show how these concepts are relevant to organizations. Manuscripts that speculate beyond current thinking are more desirable than papers that use tried and true methods to study routine problems.

Initial books in this series:

Longitudinal Field Research Methods: Studying Processes of Organizational Change
   Edited by George P. Huber and Andrew H. Van de Ven

Organizational Learning
   Edited by Michael D. Cohen and Lee S. Sproull

Cognition Within and Between Organizations
   Edited by James R. Meindl, Charles Stubbart, and Joseph F. Porac

Managing in Times of Disorder: Hypercompetitive Organizational Responses
   Edited by Anne Y. Ilinitch, Arie Y. Lewin, and Richard D'Aveni

Shaping Organization Form: Communication, Connection, and Community
   Edited by Gerardine DeSanctis and Janet Fulk

Talking About Organization Science: Debates and Dialogue From *Crossroads*
   Edited by Peter J. Frost, Arie Y. Lewin, and Richard L. Daft

For information on subscriptions to *Organization Science*, please contact INFORMS at 940-A Elkridge Landing Road, Linthicum, MD 21090-2909, 800-446-3676. For submission guidelines, contact INFORMS at 290 Westminster Street, Providence, RI 02903, 800-343-0062.

Talking About Organization Science

Debates and Dialogue From *Crossroads*

Peter J. Frost
Arie Y. Lewin
Richard L. Daft
Editors

Organization Science

Sage Publications, Inc.
International Educational and Professional Publisher
Thousand Oaks ▪ London ▪ New Delhi

For information:

Sage Publications, Inc.
2455 Teller Road
Thousand Oaks, California 91320
E-mail: order@sagepub.com

Sage Publications Ltd.
6 Bonhill Street
London EC2A 4PU
United Kingdom

Sage Publications India Pvt. Ltd.
M-32 Market
Greater Kailash I
New Delhi 110048 India

Printed in the United States of America

Library of Congress Cataloging-in-Publication Data

Main entry under title:

Talking about organization science: Debates and dialogue from
crossroads / edited by Peter J. Frost, Arie Y. Lewin, and Richard L. Daft.
      p.   cm. — (Organization science)
    Includes bibliographical references.
    ISBN 0-7619-1565-6 (cloth: alk. paper)
    ISBN 0-7619-1556-4 (pbk: alk. paper)
    1. Organization sociology.   I. Frost, Peter J.   II. Lewin, Arie Y.
    1935–   III. Daft, Richard L.   IV. Organization science (Thousand Oaks,
    Calif.)
    HM786 .T35 2000
    302.3′5—dc21   99-050409

00   01   02   03   04   05   06   7   6   5   4   3   2   1

Acquiring Editor:	Harry Briggs
Editorial Assistant:	MaryAnn Vail
Production Editor:	Astrid Virding
Production Assistant:	Cindy Bear
Typesetter:	Tina Hill
Cover Designer:	Candice Harman

Contents

Introduction   ix

PART I. DEBATES IN ORGANIZATION SCIENCE   **1**

1. Collaboration or Paradigm Shift? Caveat Emptor and the
   Risk of Romance With Economic Models for Strategy
   and Policy Research   3

   Paul M. Hirsch, Ray Friedman, and Mitchell P. Koza

2. The Myth of a Monolithic Economics: Fundamental
   Assumptions and the Use of Economic Models in
   Policy and Strategy Research   19

   William S. Hesterly and Todd R. Zenger

3. Barriers to the Advance of Organizational Science:
   Paradigm Development as a Dependent Variable   39

   Jeffrey Pfeffer

4. Style as Theory   63

   John Van Maanen

5. Mortality Reproducibility and the Persistence of Styles of Theory   83

   Jeffrey Pfeffer

6. Fear and Loathing in Organization Studies   93

    John Van Maanen

PART II. DISCOURSES ABOUT ORGANIZATION SCIENCE   **105**

7. Two Dimensions: Four Paradigms   107

    Gibson Burrell and Gareth Morgan

8. Describing Differences in Approaches to Organization Science:
Rethinking Burrell and Morgan and Their Legacy   123

    Stanley Deetz

9. From Quicksand to Crossroads: An Agnostic Perspective
on Conversation   153

    Walter R. Nord and Ann F. Connell

10. Organizational Performance as a Dependent Variable   171

    James G. March and Robert I. Sutton

11. Writing Organizational Tales: Four Authors and Their
Stories About Culture
Introduction by Dvora Yanow   179

    *Harrison M. Trice, Janice M. Beyer, Gideon Kunda,
Joanne Martin, and Linda Smircich*

12. Critical Issues in Organization Science: A Dialogue, Part 1   201

    John M. Jermier and Stewart R. Clegg

PART III. DIALOGUES AND DIRECTIONS   **215**

13. Tempered Radicalism and the Politics of Ambivalence
and Change   217

    Debra E. Meyerson and Maureen A. Scully

14. The Virtues of Closet Qualitative Research   245

    Robert I. Sutton

15. Critical Issues in Organization Science: A Dialogue, Part 2   261

    John M. Jermier and Stewart R. Clegg

16. "Soul Work" in Organizations   267

    Philip H. Mirvis

17. Bridging Academia and Business:
    A Conversation With Steve Kerr   293

PART IV. CONCLUSION   **317**

    Peter Frost, Richard L. Daft, and Arie Y. Lewin

    About the Editors   319

Introduction

A frog lived all his life in a large, deep stone well on a prosperous
farm. One day a frog from the sea paid him a visit.
    "Where do you come from?" asked the frog in the well. "From the
great ocean," he replied.
    "How big is your ocean?"
    "It's gigantic."
    "You mean about a quarter of the size of my well here?"
    "No, bigger."
    "Bigger? You mean half as big?"
    "No, even bigger."
    "Is it . . . as big as this well?"
    "There's no comparison."
    "That's impossible! I've got to see this for myself."
    They set off together. As they came over a rise and the frog from the
well saw the limitless ocean, it was such a shock that his eyes glazed, his
head was in great pain, and he fell unconscious.

Sogyal Rinpoche (1993, p. 41)

In this Buddhist story, the stone well is a metaphor for a person's perspective, understanding, or paradigm. Each person pursues life from a paradigm-well of sorts, and interprets the rest of the world through that perspective.

    In the field of organization science there are many stone wells, and it seems that people sometimes think their view is the ocean. Perhaps this would not be of concern, except that the field of organization studies has many paradigms and perspectives, and advocates of a given paradigm often seek dominance based on its limited beliefs and research habits. Organization scholars' assumptions about whether various wells exist or whether they can be brought together, may influence whether they believe the field of organization science can get to the ocean, or whether there is an ocean of unity at all.

The original purpose of *Organization Science* was to provide a voice for areas in the field that were not being expressed in major journals. *Organization Science's* purpose was to "loosen the straitjacket" of normal science by encouraging greater decentralization, pluralism, and anarchy in the journal publication process, giving voice to perspectives unheard.

The vision of *Crossroads* within *Organization Science* was to provide a forum for expressing passionate work on timely issues and ideas that build bridges, break old frames, identify flash points, and air ideas, insights, and opinions from different disciplines, so that readers have access to a variety of perspectives. Through this conjunction of ideas, new directions for research over the next decade may emerge. The world, its organizations and political systems, is changing at a breathtaking pace. The sheer pace of change has upset traditional values and approaches to managing organizations. Can the science of organizations reflect this diversity and contribute something meaningful to a larger conversation? As we reach the turn of the century, will the scientific study of the organization be seen as too narrow or as obsolete? *Crossroads* was created with the dream of publishing urgent new ways of thinking about organizations. *Crossroads* has provided the intersection for people from different constituencies who were thinking and writing about organizations in provocative and innovative ways.

This book extends the purposes of both *Organization Science* and *Crossroads,* with the express purpose of engaging readers in a conversation about flashpoints, provocative ideas, and multiple perspectives within organization science. Drawing primarily from papers published in *Crossroads,* this book displays conversations in the field about the field, so readers can talk about these ideas and encourage others to talk and listen to these perspectives.

This book contains a rich array of ideas, issues, arguments, perspectives, paradigms, and suggested prescriptions. The chapters were chosen to provide a discussion of organization science, some sense of history, of substance, of perspective, of process, and possibly of new directions. It seems especially important in our field to show how science and organization interface, particularly how the field of science can be organized to improve the quality of the work outcomes through debates and discourses. This book's ultimate mission is to contribute to the quality of science and organizational understanding being created within the field of organization science.

The book is organized into three sections, each of which represents different voices, approaches, and arguments. These sections are ordered in the

---

EXHIBIT I.1

3. DIALOGUE

Seek common ground. Build across groups and diverse positions. Integrate self with others. Pursue unity or unifying potential.

2. DISCOURSE

Articulate larger framework or system that integrates the parts. Seek relationship among elements. Introduce self into discussion.

1. DEBATE ·

Articulate position as different from others. See diversity, but focus on differences rather than similarities. Espouse own position as superior.

---

sequence of debate, discourse, and dialogue, modes of conversation that produce different, but potentially valuable outcomes. The three ways of communicating are illustrated in Exhibit I.1. As you proceed through the book you will find a widening and deepening of the arguments presented in each part. We see the three sections as evolving stages based on forms of conversation—debates, discourses, or dialogue. We see also the importance of paying attention to directions in which the field may move. We invite the reader to participate in each.

A debate is a discussion, sometimes a formal discussion about a public question, in which the positive and negative sides of an issue are advocated by opposing speakers or writers. Debate is based on opposition and argument. Each side articulates a position different from the other. People engaged in a debate see differences and focus on them, rather than on similarities or common ground. They see their own position as superior.

The debate is a traditional way of getting to the truth. Its value is in sharpening and crystallizing opposing points so that listeners or readers can decide for themselves where truth lies. The clash of debate has a history in politics and the law as a valuable tool for deciding important questions.

A discourse, as we use it here, means that the writer communicates a more comprehensive system of thought to explore all sides of an issue and to organize differences into a single framework or system. The point of a discourse is to exposit basic elements of a system, to reveal and disclose to the reader the way the parts hang together into a whole concerning the subject under discussion. Thus a discourse is not designed primarily to win the argument and to identify differences but to organize and embrace different elements into a larger structure and delineate assumptions that make known the larger structure.

Dialogue differs from both debate and discourse in the sense that its goal is to achieve shared meaning among participants. The roots of dialogue are *dia* and *logos,* which in combination can be thought of as "stream of meaning." In a dialogue, people open up to one another and suspend their tightly defended assumptions and views. A dialogue slows down the exchange so that people can hear one another at a deeper, more authentic level without defensiveness or counterattack. Rather than seeking to achieve a specific conclusion, as in a debate or discourse, dialogue seeks breadth and diversity, widening the perspectives and the conversation rather than narrowing them or excluding anything. Dialogue asks listeners to suspend judgment, to reflect on their own thoughts and feelings, to release control of the outcome, to seek deeper understanding, and to find a common ground upon which they share meaning and understanding. A dialogue is about finding an answer that brings people together rather than defining one answer as correct, as in a debate, or offering a reasoned system of thought, as in a discourse.

A direction, in our terms, is a guiding or motivating purpose, an assistance in pointing out a desired or desirable route . . . and, in some cases, a line or course along which something is moving or might move. There will likely be several directions that flow into and from any debate, discourse, or dialogue.

PART I: DEBATES

The readings in Part I adopt a debate format to crystallize the differences between economic models and behavioral approaches to strategy research and to evaluate both sides of the issues of whether organization science should be a single- versus multiple-paradigm field. These positions are well argued in the Part I chapters, with emphasis on articulating one's own position as different from and superior to the other's. As reader, think to yourself about the value received from this form of argument and what you would say as part of the conversation. How would you respond to the debaters? Can you find common ground between them?

The issues surrounding economics and paradigms are real issues that concern scholars in the field. The nature of economics and the extent to which paradigms should be narrowed and refined are of concern to many. The debates also emphasize the importance of language and writing in organization science (is writing a "side show," or is it "the main event"?). Also, you can see the intensity of emotions of the protagonists. This is likely mirrored by readers who resonate with one set of arguments or another. The debates set the scene and tone of the book. Parts II and III reinforce and expand a debate's content and tone in various ways.

PART II: DISCOURSES

The essays, conversations, stories, and expositions in this section broaden the conversation about the nature of organization science. First, these chapters attempt to resolve the key polarizations in the debate chapters by providing broader frameworks within which to organize the various perspectives. Thus each perspective becomes part of a larger landscape. Second, these chapters identify underlying assumptions among various positions. There is an element of debate in these chapters also, such as when one organizing framework is deemed superior to another.

The conversation is also expanded in Part II by the introduction of self. One's own perspective, experiences, and conditioning may play a role in how the field is interpreted and acted upon. Thus we see the perspective of "agnosticism" and the tales of three sets of authors and a commentary on them. The context of organization science is also explored by comparing the history of the U.S. positivist approach to European and other approaches to organization studies.

PART III: DIALOGUES AND DIRECTIONS

The third part is characterized by chapters that seek to build bridges and common ground across groups. Looking for unity and unifying potential suggests new directions for intellectual inquiry and research. This section is concerned with harnessing the creativity in different perspectives without continuous warfare, with talking to one another rather than past one another. In this section the term "tempered radicals" emerges rather than radicalism, and we see ways for people doing research on the periphery to bring ideas into the main stream in politically astute ways. The quantitative gatekeepers are bypassed and in so doing, qualitative and quantitative thinking are brought together. The two concluding chapters deal insightfully with community building in a way that could create a learning organization of our entire field, perhaps moving into areas of the heart and spirit as a source for connection. A mechanism that actively creates community among diverse organization science perspectives is one possibility. The other is about building bridges between academics and practitioners as suggested in an interview with a scholar-practitioner who has personally crossed several boundaries. Perhaps no one perspective has a monopoly on good ideas or wisdom. The solution to differences is to talk to one another and listen to what each has to say.

Together, these three parts of the book ultimately delve into whether there is a role for listening as well as "rightness" among scholars, whether truth can be ameliorated with love and connection, whether the monk and warrior can enhance the sage, whether we need both Gandhi and Patton in our thinking and behavior.

With respect to the frog in the well, which perspective in this book has more value for you? Can the field move forward with sharply defined argument and debate, fueled by the desire to be correct and to prove the other position wrong? Or is it better fueled by larger frameworks and perspectives that provide a context for protagonists? Or, perhaps by pursuing common ground rather than debate, seeking connection at a deeper level, collaborating rather than arguing, possibly serving a shared purpose together in community? This would mean bringing the frogs to the ocean of our shared truth, or at least getting the frogs to communicate with one another from their respective wells, seeking to understand the larger landscape and each other.

REFERENCE

Rinpoche, Sogyal (1993). *The Tibetan Book of Living and Dying.* San Francisco: Harper San Francisco.

PART I

DEBATES IN ORGANIZATION SCIENCE

The chapters in Part I are about real issues that concern scholars in the field. The chapters by Hirsch, Friedman, and Koza ("Collaboration or Paradigm Shift? Caveat Emptor and the Risk of Romance With Economic Models for Strategy and Policy Research") and by Hesterly and Zenger ("The Myth of a Monolithic Economics") grapple with the question: What is the nature of economics and can it serve a positive role in the organization sciences? The second major question is the strategic direction for the field of organization science. The set of four chapters, two each by Pfeffer ("Barriers to the Advance of Organization Science: Paradigm Development as a Dependent Variable" and "Mortality Reproducibility and the Persistence of Styles of Theory") and by Van Maanen ("Style as Theory" and "Fear and Loathing in Organization Studies") argue over whether the field of organization science should be characterized by multiple paradigms or movement toward a single overarching paradigm, similar, say, to economics? These several chapters rely on debate, logic, and persuasion as a vehicle to arrive at a "superior" truth.

As you read these chapters, consider the following questions: Do you feel affinity for one point of view over the other? If so, why? Is it about the argument itself or is it about your own preferences? What are the assumptions underlying each point of view? By identifying and understanding assumptions, sometimes common ground can be achieved.

What is the underlying motivation for each chapter? Do you feel emotions coming through the chapters? Can you sense whether an author is yearning for something better and perhaps more organized, whether an author is feeling unjustly criticized, or is threatened by unwanted constraints or limitations?

What would you say in response to each chapter? What can you add to the conversation? Finally, do you sense that these authors are frogs in a well or that they have access to a larger truth? Taking the six chapters as a group, what do you surmise is the appropriate direction for our field?

1

Collaboration or Paradigm Shift?

Caveat Emptor and the Risk of Romance With Economic Models for Strategy and Policy Research

PAUL M. HIRSCH
Kellogg Graduate School of Management, Northwestern University

RAY FRIEDMAN
Graduate School of Business, Harvard University

MITCHELL P. KOZA
INSEAD, Fontainebleau

To those who write and profess in the areas of management, entrepreneurship, and business policy: look around you, because economists, the practitioners of the Imperial Science are invading your market. If you do not rise above the merely descriptive *(sic)*, we will do to you what we did to sociologists and political scientists. (Hansen 1985, p. 10)

While such a threat may seem overdrawn to some in the area of policy studies, there are clear indications that economic analysis has risen to a prominent position in the study of business policy and strategy. Michael Porter's (1980) conception of management as the process of placing one's company in a favorable competitive niche is among the most dominant in both fields.

From "Collaboration or Paradigm Shift? Caveat Emptor and the Risks of Romance With Economic Models for Strategy and Policy Research," by Paul M. Hirsch, Ray Friedman, and Mitchell P. Koza, 1990, *Organization Science, 4*(3), pp. 87-97. Copyright © 1990, The Institute of Management Sciences. Reprinted with permission.

3

Indeed, inspired by Porter's framework, a new generation of policy scholars views industrial organization economics as the base discipline for policy research. Similarly, transaction cost economics approaches to choices about the internal structure of organizations have grown to hold a prominent place in business policy research (Williamson 1975, 1979; Ouchi 1980; Teece 1982; Leblebici 1985; Robins 1987).

These economic perspectives bring to the field clear benefits, as supplements to contributions from other disciplines as well. Compared to what policy studies has been and still is, economic analysis enjoys the benefit of parsimony. The complex tasks and skills of managers charged with the operation of entire organizations (or multifunctional units of organizations) are simplified, modeled and "explained" in terms of a few principles assuming utility maximizing behavior by rational actors, and the power of free exchange. As Heyne (1976) put it, theories of economics, "with surprisingly few exceptions, are simply extensions of the assumption that individuals choose those options which seem to them most likely to secure their largest net advantage." Other factors are either subsumed under this basic assumption of economics or assumed away. Thus, some of the more intractable, and we believe more interesting, problems of policy analysis—identifiable by such concepts as "process," "fit," "socialization," "politics," "power," "coalitions," and "uncertainty"—disappear from view.

With economics fewer and cleaner concepts have also come more hypothetical-deductive models. Hypotheses are more sharply defined, units of analysis more easily aggregated, and theories, therefore, more easily tested. Indeed, economic analysis and modeling are the implicit answer to calls for more hypothetical-deductive approaches to business policy (see, e.g., Camerer 1985). These "advantages" of economic analysis offer relief from the ambiguity with which policy studies has traditionally been associated.

Nonetheless, it is important to step back and look at the position of policy studies within business education (its market niche, so to speak) and to ask whether the very power of the assumptions held by economics may, necessarily, distract policy scholars from an important part of their mission. A significant part of that mission, we believe, is to provide what Etzioni (1987) calls a "medical" component of scholarly analysis. While the primary goal of a "pure" science is to isolate particular phenomena in order to predict them better, policy studies inherently deal with the problem of complex interactions among many factors, and the need to provide judgments or conclusions without adding the proviso "all else being equal." Under this "medical" model, judgments and experience are critical, and the concern is the life of the patient (firm, or organization). While not suggesting that business policy eschew science, *we believe it important for policy studies to explicitly retain in its domain a clear commitment to tolerating ambiguity,* and to the craft of building managerial action out of environmental and organizational uncertainty.

Key Issues

Business Policy is an eclectic field drawing on ideas and research from military strategy, political science, economics, current events, organizational sociology, and psychology. Its hallmark is the pragmatic use of an available stock of ideas rather than disciplinary purity. Given the growing influence of economics as a theoretical base of policy studies, two questions which must be asked now are: Will the economically-informed focus on competitive and market forces lead policy scholars to undervalue the complex organizational and behavioral dynamics that can make-or-break even the most economically well-informed strategic plans? And, will economic modellers be flexible enough to learn from other disciplines?

In this article we: (a) explore three implications of economics' rising stock in business policy; (b) look at the related intellectual transformation occurring in the basic academic disciplines; and (c) provide a more detailed illustration of how economic and behavioral approaches to business policy presently diverge, using the example of agency theory. We also highlight the idea that present moves toward an economic view of policy have implications for management and management education. These implications must be recognized—not because they are "wrong" in any simple sense—but because economic assumptions are so powerful and enticing that scholars and practitioners risk losing sight of what is *left out* of these models.

PROBLEMS WITH THE ECONOMIC VIEW

In the following sections, we address three cautionary implications of a potentially "pure" economics-driven research agenda for policy studies.

First, it would focus attention nearly exclusively on the field's long-standing interest in the *substantive outcomes* of policy, but at the high cost of directing attention away from its equally long-standing focus on policy *processes and implementation.*

Second, it renders ambiguous the level and unit of analysis. From an economic point of view, this is usually not the individual *firm.* Rather, it is the product or capital markets: the industry or stock price. Even when the "typical" firm is addressed, the analyst's attention is focused on the idealized average, rather than on the deviant case. Attention is directed toward being on the regression line rather than on firms above or below it on the scatterplot. As companies come to be viewed as little more than bundles of contracts and

preferably liquid assets for sale, operations management, increasingly subsumed under finance, becomes "asset management." Organizations disappear from view except as temporary portfolios.

Third, as economists' free market determinism is taken for empirical reality, management becomes irrelevant, or worse, seen only as opportunistic
actors in need of market discipline. In such models managers are substitut-
able commodities and it is very easy to just "assume a management."

In academe, economic thinking and methods are moving into allied disciplines at an impressive rate. Becker (1981, 1975) has applied economic
theorizing to the study of the family; Williamson (1981, 1975) has applied it
to the study of organizational structures; and in sociology "rational actor"
theory (Coleman 1974; Emerson 1972) is becoming institutionalized as a
subfield of the discipline. Methods employed in, although not limited to economics, such as structural equations, event history analysis, mathematical
modeling, and game theory have diffused into the scholarship and methodology of other social sciences, further displacing comparative case studies,
qualitative techniques such as in-depth interviews and (to a lesser but still
noticeable extent) the analysis of variance.

Consider the intellectual impact of the "sum" of the following developments: (1) the serious presumption that all action is rational and opportunistic—along with an accompanying set of beliefs about human nature (Hirsch,
Michaels and Friedman 1986); (2) the focus on the individual level rather
than groups or larger units as the most interesting level of analysis; (3) a style
of theorizing based on modeling the interaction of rational atoms, always
under conditions of scarcity (Kuttner 1985); and (4) a preference for deductive theorizing from abstract concepts rather than inductive reasoning from
known cases (Camerer 1985). All these are economic conceptions currently
influencing a substantial body of work in social science. While economists
should be increasingly comfortable with these developments, such moves
within general business theory, taken to the extreme, could decrease the integrative value of "policy studies" (Schon 1983).

Chester Barnard's (1938) seminal work on the chief executive inaugurated
research in business policy. Barnard identified the primary managerial tasks
faced by the chief executive, and described his approach to managerial problem solving. The field achieved a major intellectual thrust with Chandler's
(1962) work on the multidivisional form and Rumelt's (1972) test of the strat-
egy/structure hypothesis. Over the last 15 years the field has expanded into
many newer policy domains, including diversification, policy processes, and
mergers and acquisitions. While approaches to each of these topics typically
took the firm as their unit of analysis, and examined their impact on organizations and CEO's, the more recent economic approaches emphasize the
importance and domination of the market. By far the most influential recent

TABLE 1.1 Perspectives on Business Policy

Perspectives	Economics	Behavioral
1) Unit of Analysis	Investors (Stock Price)	The Organization
	Product Markets	Managers
	Formal Contracts	
2) Stages Covered	Formulation	Formulation and Implementation
	Post-Hoc Outcomes	Content and Process
3) Source of Change	Environmental Selection	Managerial Decisions
	Laws of Efficiency	Pressures to Adapt to Change

stream of research is applied industry analysis (Porter 1980, 1985), although scholarship on environmental selection (Hannan and Freeman 1976; McKelvey 1982) and the theory of the firm (cf., Barney and Ouchi 1986) also has established constituencies in departments of business administration.

What implications does economic theorizing have for Business Policy directly? To answer this question we must compare and contrast the assumptions underlying economic theory to the more behavioral traditions that are significant parts of policy studies. There are at least three important differences outlined in Table 1.1.[1]

Unit of Analysis:
The Organization or Stock Returns?

At the fundamental level of unit of analysis, the economic perspective does not see organizations, as such, as a useful focus of study. For Jensen and Meckling (1976) or Manne (1965), the organization is a bundle of assets.[2] Its pieces can be bought and sold indiscriminately, and organizational units and personnel reshuffled as mere commodities. Williamson's (1975) approach, following from Coase (1937), reinforces this view. He argues that the basic unit of analysis is the transaction. An organization is merely an amalgamation of contracts, open for renegotiation at any moment if efficiencies can be gained.[3]

Such a model of economic life is highly idealized and empirically suspect. Both workers and managers are loath to be treated like commodities, and both will act to retain organizational slack and hold the "free market" at bay. Indeed, much study has already been done showing that "survival"—not profit maximization—is the commonest approach taken by organizations (Pfeffer and Salancik 1978; Scherer 1970; Galbraith 1967).

Furthermore, factors such as loyalty, trust and cooperation have long been held crucial for organizational cooperation (Maitland, Brysen, and Van de Ven 1985; Ouchi and Jaeger 1978; Drucker 1974; Wrapp 1967). Using Williamson's own argument about the high likelihood of managers' "opportunism," one might well counter that strong ties must be established between an organization and its employees to prevent abuse. But Williamson largely fails to elaborate the "transaction costs" of distrust, dislocation, and anger generated by managing employees, or organizational units, as if they were disposable and dispensable assets. For example, the anger and waste generated by corporate takeovers cannot be incorporated into Manne's (1965) or Jensen and Ruback's (1983) stock-return analyses. Even if that were the only appropriate measure (which it is not), the long-run effects of perpetual dislocation are seldom captured in day-after, or even years-after-sale analyses of share price. Yet they are "external" to these models and declared "irrelevant," by definition.

Whether or not economists' *normative* claim that organizations are best treated as disposable assets is true, the fact is that organizational realities and the study of management are not that simple. An empirically grounded portrayal requires expanding such models to include issues and variables that now are conveniently ignored. As those who have to pick up the pieces after a corporate dismantling well know, what remains of the organization still must be managed. And in real life the political fact is that its managers, employees, customers, suppliers and communities are fighting mad. They look to the 1970's environment, when stakeholders were still recognized as having a legitimate claim on the organization, as the more proper model for corporate governance. It is interesting to note that as business policy scholars show less interest in "stakeholder" research, a new stream of finance research on corporate risk is pursuing this important issue (cf. Titman 1984; Shleifer and Summers 1987).

As a result of these differing perspectives on the relevance of the organization as a unit of analysis, and the related degree of attention paid to employee commitment and loyalty, the economic and behavioral views of business policy also differ greatly in their approaches to employee incentives. Behavioralists are concerned with long-run incentives that develop company loyalty—e.g., career ladders that provide the employee with a future in the company. On the shop floor this is represented as "seniority," and in the office by vested pensions, promotions, and stock options. The economic approach is quite the opposite. Output is optimized in that view by conceiving of all relationships as short run only, or in terms of future returns calculated at present discount rates. This applies at every level of the hierarchy, from CEO on down. If an employee serves your purposes today, "hire 'em"—if not, "fire 'em." As T. Boone Pickens put it, when "told of a worker who had been laid off after having given 30 years to his company . . . 'Given? Didn't he get paid?' " (*Time,* 1985, p. 61).

If and when Policy takes such a wholly narrow economic view of orga-nizations, there should be less need for either "strategy" or "management." Externally, firms would be restructured by Wall Street, and internally, the day could start with each employee contracting for the day's work. The field is too important and too interesting to trade in its concerns for the long-term health of the enterprise and its stakeholders and shareholders for a redefinition which reduces the sole purpose of the firm to enriching short-term investors. Business policy as a field—its texts, cases, and research—is built on the idea that organizations *are* relevant units of analysis, and that their dynamics and processes are critical. These are no less important to the outcome than the market. Firms also may be as interested in creating new markets or changing hostile environments as they are in simply adapting to them (Bower 1983).

Economists overlook these factors because their approach is normative, not empirical. They *derive* principles of behavior from *pre-given* assump-tions about rational human nature and utility functions (cf. Williamson 1975). But cases and much policy and organizational behavior research open, and often challenge the economist's "black box," by showing employee inter-actions, executive quirks, organizational screw-ups, and internal politics— up close.

Formulation or Implementation (or Both)?

Economics' market-oriented approach is commendable when analyzing the content of broad goals to be set for the corporation—i.e., in the policy "formulation" stage. There, it is appropriate to take an idealized view of orga-nizations and markets, if only to conduct thought-exercises and focus manag-ers' attention on market forces. But to do so without an awareness of the *processes* through which policy is developed and implemented is naive. An excellent example is the work of Michael Porter. While Porter's popular book, *Competitive Strategy,* has become a standard in many policy courses, it contains scarcely a single mention of strategy implementations or the pro-cesses of consensus formation necessary for policy to be effectively devel-oped. How are we to believe an organization goes through the processes of observing markets, deciding where it wants to be, and getting itself there? Not without some intra-organizational convincing, coalition building, arm twisting, and inter-organizational fighting and resistance by competitors.

To be fair, Porter's influential second book, *Competitive Advantage* (1985), attempts to correct this deficiency in the chapters on horizontal strat-egy and interrelationships; these chapters describe how an organization may produce "synergy" between organizational subunits. However, as interesting as these chapters are, they offer little advice for management and touch on people and their behavior only tangentially. Even where economists treat the problem of behavior more directly, they are constrained by their models and assumptions from considering the implications of many of the factors critical to implementation and process: equity, internal politics, leadership, meaning, communications, commitment, and other "fuzzy" phenomena. As Baker, Jensen and Murphy (1988, p. 30) have aptly noted: " . . . economic analysis can only go so far: at some point we must defer to political pressure or to behavioral notions of fairness, social responsibility, trust, or culture. We are not yet willing to throw in the proverbial towel, but admit that our economic understanding of internal incentive structures is far from complete."

Internal organizational processes, along with external resistance to new competition, are also the appropriate substance of business policy. They make execution of plans difficult, and require an awareness of the older standard elements of motivation, personal values, and leadership (Andrews 1980; Selznick 1957). An idealized focus on market competition is incomplete. Quinn (1983), Wrapp (1967) and others push this point even further. They see the entire process, combining formulation and implementation, as essentially behavioral and political.

There certainly is great value in studying formulation. But there are risks: that the many sides of this complex interactive process will be treated in isolation, to the degree that the ground rules of economic analysis preclude considerations of processes and policy implementation; that we will see formulation, content, implementation, and process as elements that can be studied too independently, with each one holding constant the core of the others.

Management Volition or Market Determinism?

The third area of conflict between economic and behavioral perspectives on policy is the concept of volition. Macro organization theory's population ecology views of organizations (Aldrich 1979; Hannan and Freeman 1977) leave little room for voluntary action (Perrow 1986). Here, even formulation is denied relevance. In a free market, only the fittest organizations are "selected" to survive. From the perspective of this sociological variant of economics (Alchian 1950), single organizations or firms cannot even take credit (or blame) for their own actions. Rather, it is entire aggregations (e.g., industries) that are "selected."[4]

While selection occurs, of course, to a degree, it is only *one* aspect of organizational change. There are many examples where organizational "exit" is politically untenable, and "voice" comes to the fore (Hirschman 1970). Railroads have never been permitted to cease operation, for example. And rather than be "selected out" by the environment, Chrysler and Lockheed managed their environments (in the 1970s) to stave off going out of business.

Overemphasizing selection leads to minimizing the theoretical importance of "enacted" environments (Weick 1976). Organizations seek to control their environment through mechanisms like interlocking directorates (Pfeffer 1972), cooptation (Hirsch 1975, 1972; Selznick 1949), or lobbying (Koza 1988); and advertising budgets and PAC contributions belie the image of businesses as simply passive actors in a free-market economy. Firms also diversify routinely into new product lines and industries. The choice of a new "production function" means that from the viewpoint of the organization the environment has changed. Recently, for example, banks have diversified into financial services and railroads have started to lay fibre optics cable in an innovative use of their right of way. By moving into new businesses firms enact new boundaries and markets.

Moreover, Hrebiniak and Joyce (1985) argued that the degree to which strategic choice is possible should be considered a *separate dimension* from environmental determinism so that "natural selection" only occurs in one subset of possible types. Levels of autonomy, interorganizational politics, and strategic learning vary a great deal. Perhaps in the "long-run" economic forces will reign, but, recalling Keynes' classic response to this argument, "in the long-run we are all dead." Economists could inform management that in the long run worldwide auto manufacture will shift to the Far East, but that provides only the broadest of guideposts for Ford Motor Co. management's decisions on retooling and reorganizing in the face of these new economic realities.

In their classic critique of the economic theory of the firm, March and Simon cautioned against treating the firm as a black box. The firm, they noted, is a complex system of functional and administrative subunits pursuing their separate interests. To ignore the effects of interest difference would be to misspecify models of organizational behavior. Today, 30 years later, organization and strategic management theories risk reinventing the production function logic of the very sort that March and Simon persuasively argued against. While in population ecology, for example, the firm is described in terms of its "form" (Hannan and Freeman 1976), or "distinctive competence" (McKelvey 1982), the focus in their applications remains on a set of resource inputs and production outputs.

While the formulation and content sides of policy studies and strategic management draw appropriately from economic theory, we caution that, taken to its logical extreme, economic theory assumes away aspects of implementation and policy formulation processes, implies lack of choice in organizational decision-making, and makes the organization as such a nonentity. "Asset management" replaces long-range planning and strategic management. The firm is considered ready for liquidation, or for sale at any moment to the highest bidder—in order to fetch the greatest immediate, one-shot value for its shareholders of the moment. Managing organizations becomes no different than managing a stock portfolio.

An Illustration: Agency Theory

The implications of an overly economistic view of organizations for policy/strategy can be further illustrated by comparing economic and behavioral approaches to corporate agency. This example is particularly relevant for current controversies about corporate takeovers and restructurings.

Since Berle and Means' (1932) famous analysis of corporate control, the issue of managerial agency has been heavily debated. While much attention in social science has historically focused on corporate responsibilities towards the community, customers and society, the most basic division now lies between shareholder profit and stakeholder equity. In part, this distinction aptly summarizes the respective biases of economic versus behavioral models of the firm, as outlined in Table 1.2.

The economic approach to corporate agency as presented by Jensen and Ruback (1983) focuses attention outside the firm. It is an investor's model. Most important from this perspective is how the stock market values the company. Based on its share price fluctuations, organizations are forced to change. "Nonperforming" management is dismissed, and business segments are reorganized to suit stockholders desire for higher share prices.

A behavioral approach, by contrast, is far more the "caretaker" management model. It directs attention more towards the inner reaches of the company, while seeking to balance the interests of multiple stakeholder constituencies. The organization is also a source of stable employment for managers and the community; they are concerned with its long-run survival as a unit, not solely with how it can raise short-term share price. Managerial behavior occurs in response to career opportunities, incentive systems, personal values, and job ladders. There is a "corporate culture," ideally permitting visibility, advancement, and slack (Thompson 1967: Thompson and Strickland 1983).

Economic analysis is identified with the market and the interests of investors, while behavioral analysis is identified with the firm and its managers. The former sees the company as a unit subsumed under the regulatory forces of the market, while the latter conceives the market as a challenge faced, and to be overcome, by the company and its people (Eisenhardt 1988). The firm is a *producer* of goods and services in one case, but is *itself* a commodity for sale in the other.

TABLE 1.2 Contrasting Agency Perspectives

	Finance Model	*Behavioral Model*
FOCUS	Outside the Firm	Inside the Company
	Valuation, Markets	Job Ladders, Incentive Systems
	Change-Oriented	Stability-Oriented (career planning bias)
REFERENTS	Investor	Manager
	Market > Company	Company > Market
	Firm as Commodity	Firm as Producer of Goods and Services
LEANING	Pro-Takeover, Noting:	Anti-Takeover, Noting:
	Shareholders Benefit	Good Managers Leave
	Shakes Up and Disciplines	
	Managements	All Bets Are Off and Morale Crashes
	Spurs Efficiencies	Total Strangers Arrive
EMPHASIS	Pre-Merger Planning	Post-Merger Cleanup
	(Financial)	(Behavioral)

Takeovers, then, are treated quite differently in each case. Economists generally favor takeover as a means to discipline managers and spur efficiency. As long as the stock goes up, utility is maximized, and the world is better off. Behavioral analysts, though, point out that psychological contracts are being broken, that talented managers will early-on seek new employment, and morale crashes as new managers, with no history in the organization, take over and personal ties and obligations are lost (Hirsch 1987). How to clean up the ensuing mess is of concern to those with a behavioral approach (in the midst of downsizings, for example, "outplacement" has become a growth industry). Economic analysts, by contrast, stick to financial plans and results, and ignore (or assume away) the damage done by the cross-fire.

We see from this example that an economic approach minimizes concern for the organizations, managers, and human choices which these activities entail. The world view presented is narrow, with a pivotal criterion for analysis and judgment becoming the firm's share price. An enormous amount, deliberately ignored by the model, is left out, to be filled in by others if they so choose. This includes: filling in the empirical gaps, and showing how individual firms actually behave; explaining what, why, and how specific organizational choices were actually made; and if and how they were implemented—or prevented from being implemented—under real-life business conditions.

Further, the pro-takeover bias in the finance model assumes that U.S. firms are less competitive in global markets than overseas firms because U.S. firms are inefficient. Its solution is to discipline managers and firms to extract slack resources and thereby lower the value added cost structure and compete more successfully in global markets. However, behavioralists point out this strategy can succeed only up to a certain point. With overseas wage rates sometimes one-fifth those of the U.S. and with the added costs of overseas procurement and transportation, U.S. firms are inevitably going to have a higher cost structure than overseas competitors down the vertical product flow. Thus, attempts to make U.S. firms more efficient by market discipline can be only partially successful. If U.S. firms cannot be fully competitive with overseas firms, they argue, then some slack resources are more reasonably viewed as the embodied capacity of firms to be flexible in the face of new environmental opportunities and threats. The fundamental problem, from the behavioralist point of view, is not how to discipline firms to focus exclusively on ever-shorter horizons of efficiency and profits (Hayes and Abernathy 1980), but rather to maximize the probability that organizational slack may be properly employed for innovation. Organizational slack offers the potential for competitive advantage.

CONCLUSION

Do recent trends towards an economic view of business policy represent collaboration or a paradigm shift? To the degree it is the former, we are enriched by the addition of new and interesting applications to the field of business policy. Economics has an obviously important and influential position and role to play in policy studies. It has expanded our understanding of a firm's strategy options and provided a vocabulary to effectively evaluate a firm's market, competitive, and technological environments. But, while economic facts cannot and should not be ignored, *we should beware of the limited focus of economists' powerful assumptions because they may preclude the possibility of collaboration with behavioral approaches, and demand a complete paradigm shift that would be unhealthy for the field.*

Such a disproportionate tilt would have profound and unhealthy implications. To the degree that a shift in the direction of assuming opportunism, individual utility maximization, and free market efficiency and determinism is required by economic approaches to policy, we do not see how the fields of business policy and/or strategic management would avoid becoming an anomalous contradiction in terms. Other voices must continue to be heard, even though economics' powerful logical coherence and all-reaching answers are tempting attractions—especially for (more behavioral) fields that are less bound together by simple assumptions, untestable "general laws," normative certainty, and mathematical models.

We hope this paper serves as a clarification and warning for behavioralists who value the contribution of economics to business policy. As collaboration, economics offers much. As a paradigm shift, we oppose abandoning the field's strong points. We must remember that our purpose is to bridge the gap between elegant theories and real world practice—that we must integrate our base disciplines and the empirical realities which they encompass. If we are to continue being of high value to colleagues, students and business, we will not trade in our traditions for just one set of disciplinary blinders. Strategy and Business Policy should continue to embody and keep track of diverse intellectual perspectives and the concrete realities they address.

NOTES

1. This table is illustrative and deliberately limited in scope. For a more inclusive treatment of different strands in policy research, see Jemison (1981).

2. Jensen's more recent work (Baker, Jensen and Murphy 1988; Jensen and Murphy 1988) shows a greater interest in modeling what goes on inside the firm.

3. In Porter's earlier (1980) work, the business is taken as the unit of analysis, but not as a *complex* organization. Rather, it is depicted as a black box which is simply placed into a field of other black boxes in such a way that, all other things being equal, it can minimize direct competitive pressures. Internal processes and interactions among people are not among Porter's major concerns.

4. In Porter's (1980/1931) original formulation, management retains a higher level of control. Population ecologists do not agree with the above characterization, but unfortunately have not persuaded us.

REFERENCES

Alchian, A. (1950). "Uncertainty, Evolution, and Economic Theory," *J. Political Economy,* 58, 211-221.

Aldrich, H. (1979). *Organizations and Environments,* Prentice Hall, Englewood Cliffs, NJ.

Andrews, K. R. (1980). *The Concept of Corporate Strategy,* Revised Ed., Irwin, Homewood, IL.

Baker, George, P., Michael C. Jensen and Kevin J. Murphy, (1988). "Compensation and Incentives: Practice vs. Theory," Working Paper 88-036, Harvard Business School.

Barnard, Chester (1938). *The Functions of the Executive,* Cambridge, MA.

Barney, J. B. and W. G. Ouchi (Eds.) (1986). *Organizational Economics,* Jossey-Bass, San Francisco.

Becker, G. (1981). *A Treatise on the Family,* Harvard University Press, Cambridge.

———— (1975). *Human Capital,* National Bureau of Economic Research, New York.

Berle, A., and G. Means (1932). *The Modern Corporation and Private Property,* Macmillan, New York.

Bower, J. L. (1983). *The Two Faces of Management,* Houghton Mifflin Co., Boston.

Camerer, Colin (1985). "Redirecting Research in Business Policy and Strategy," *Strategic Management J.,* 6, 1-15.

Chandler, Alfred D. (1962). *Strategy and Structure: Chapters in the History of the American Industrial Enterprise,* MIT, Cambridge, MA.

Coase, R. H. (1937). "The Nature of the Firm," *Economica N.S.,* 4, 386-405.

Coleman, J. S. (1974). *Power and Structure of Society,* Norton, New York.

Drucker, P. F. (1974). *Management: Tasks, Responsibilities, Practices,* Harper and Row, New York.

Eisenhardt, Kathleen (1988). "Agency Theory: An Assessment and Review," *Acad. Management Rev.,* 14, 1.

Emerson, R. M. (1972). "Exchange Theory, Part I: A Psychological Basis for Social Exchange, and Exchange Theory, Part II: Exchange Relations, Exchange Networks, and Groups as Exchange Systems," in J. Berger et al. (Eds.), *Sociological Theories in Progress,* Vol. II, Houghton Mifflin, Boston.

Etzioni, Amitai (1987). "Making Policy for Complex Systems: A Medical Model for Economics," *J. Policy Anal. and Management,* 4, 3, 383-395.

Fredrickson, J. (1984). "The Comprehensiveness of Strategic Decision Processes: Extension, Observations, Future Directions," *Acad. Management J.,* 27, 445-466.

Hannan, M. T. and J. H. Freeman (1976). "The Population Ecology of Organizations," *Amer. Sociology,* 82, 5, 929-964.

Hansen, R. G. (Winter 1985). Review of P. F. Drucker's *Innovation and Entrepreneurship-Practice and Principles,* In *Tuck Today.*

Hayes, R. and R. Abernathy (July-August: 1980). "Managing Our Way to Economic Decline," *Harvard Business Rev.,* 67-77.

Heyne, Paul (1976). *The Economic Way of Thinking,* 2nd ed., Science Research Associates, Chicago.

Hirsch, P. M. (1987). *Pack Your Own Parachute: How to Survive Mergers, Takeovers, and Other Corporate Disasters,* Addison Wesley, Reading, MA.

———— (September 1975). "Organizational Effectiveness and the Institutional Environment," *Admin. Sci. Quart.,* 20, 327-44.

———— (1972). "Processing Fads and Fashions: An Organization-Set Analysis of Cultural Industries Systems," *Amer. J. Sociology,* 77, 639-659.

———— (Fall 1986). S. Michaels and R. Friedman, (1972), " 'Dirty Hands' vs. 'Clean Models': Is Sociology in Danger of Being Seduced by Economics?" *Theory and Society.*

Hirschman A. O. (1970). *Exit, Voice, and Loyalty,* Harvard University Press, Cambridge, MA.

Hrebiniak, L. G. and W. F. Joyce (1985). "Organizational Adaptation: Strategic Choice and Environmental Determinism," *Admin. Sci. Quart.,* 30, 336-349.

Jemison, D. (1981). "The Importance of an Integrative Approach to Strategic Management Research," *Acad. Management Rev.,* 6, 4, 601-608.

Jensen, M. C. and K. J. Murphy (1988). "Performance Pay and Top Management Incentives," Working Paper 88-059, Harvard Business School.

———— and R. S. Ruback (1983). "The Market for Corporate Control: The Scientific Evidence." *J. Financial Economics,* 11, 5-50.

Koza, M. P. (1988). "Organization and Regulation: Environmental Niche Structure and Administrative Organization," in Samuel Bacharach and Nancy DiTomaso (Eds.), *Research in the Sociology of Organizations,* Vol. 6, JAI, Greenwich, CT.

Kuttner, R. (February 1985). "The Poverty of Economics," *Atlantic Monthly,* 74-84.

Leblebici, H. (1985). "Transactions and Organization Forms: A Re-analysis," *Organization Studies* 6, 2, 97-115.

Maitland, I., J. Bryson and A. Van De Ven (1985). "Sociologists, Economists, and Opportunism," *Acad. Management Rev.,* 20, 59-65.

Manne, H. (April 1965). "Mergers and the Market for Corporate Control," *J. Political Economy,* 73, 110-112.

March, James G. and Herbert A. Simon (1958). *Organizations,* Wiley, New York.

McKelvey, Bill (1982). *Organization Systematics,* University of California, Berkeley.

Ouchi, W. G. (1980). "Markets Bureaucracies and Clans," *Admin. Sci. Quart.,* 25, 129-141.

——— and A. M. Jaeger (1978). "Type Z Organization: Stability in the Midst of Mobility," *Acad. Management Rev.,* 23, 305-314.

Perrow, Charles (1986). *Complex Organization: A Critical Essay,* 3rd Ed., New York, Random House.

Pfeffer, J. (1972). "Size and Composition of Corporate Boards of Directors: The Organization and Its Environment," *Admin. Sci. Quart.,* 17, 218-228.

——— and G. Salancik (1978). *The External Control of Organizations,* Harper and Row, New York.

Porter, M. (1980). *Competitive Strategy,* The Free Press, New York.

——— (1981). "The Contributions of Industrial Organization to Strategic Management," *Acad. Management Rev.,* 6, 4, 609-620.

——— (1985). *Competitive Advantage: Creating and Sustaining Superior Performance,* Free Press, New York.

Quinn, J. B. (1983). *Strategies for Change: Logical Incrementalism,* Irwin, Homewood, IL.

Robins, James (1987). "Organizational Economics: Notes on the use of Transaction Cost Theory in the Study of Organizations," *Admin. Sci. Quart.,* 32, 68-86.

Scherer, F. (1970). *Industrial Market Structure and Economic Performance,* Rand McNally, Chicago.

Schon, D. (1983). *The Reflective Practitioner: How Professionals Think In Action,* Basic Books, New York.

Selznick, P. (1957). *Leadership in Administration,* Harper and Row, New York.

——— (1949). *TVA and the Grass Roots,* University of California Press, Berkeley.

Shleifer, A. and L. Summers (1987). "Breach of Trust in Hostile Takeovers," *NBER,* Working Paper #2342.

Teece, David J. (1982). "Toward an Economic Theory of Multiproduct Firms," *J. Economic Behavior and Organization,* 3, 36-63.

Thompson, A. A. and A. J. Strickland III (1983). *Strategy Formulation and Implementation: Tasks of the General Manager,* Revised Ed., Business Publications, Inc., Plano, TX.

Thompson, J. (1967). *Organizations in Action,* McGraw-Hill, New York.

Titman, Sheridan (1984). "The Effects of Capital Structure on a Firm's Liquidation Decision," *J. Financial Economics,* 13, 137-183.

Weick, K. E. (1976). "Educational Organizations as Loosely-Coupled Systems," *Admin. Sci. Quart.,* 21, 1-19.

Williamson, O. E. (November 1981). "The Economics of Organization: The Transaction Cost Approach," *Amer. J. Sociology,* 87, 548-577.

——— (1979). "Transaction-Cost Economics: The Governance of Contractual Relations," *J. Law and Economics,* 22, 233-261.

——— (1975). *Markets and Hierarchies,* Free Press, New York.

Wrapp, H. E. (September-October 1967). "Good Managers Don't Make Policy Decisions," *Harvard Business Rev.,* 91-99.

2

The Myth of a Monolithic Economics

Fundamental Assumptions and the
Use of Economic Models in
Policy and Strategy Research

WILLIAM S. HESTERLY
David Eccles School of Business, University of Utah

TODD R. ZENGER
John M. Olin School of Business, Washington University

In recent years strategy and policy scholars have witnessed a dramatic increase in the use of economics in their field. The emergence of economic approaches has spawned a growing debate on the role of economics in strategy and policy (Barney 1990; Donaldson 1990a, b; Bettis 1991). Joining in this debate, Hirsch et al. (1990) seek to "provoke discussion" (p. 96) by providing a strong warning in the inaugural issue of *Organization Science* to all students of strategy and policy who might be lured by the "romance of economic models":

> we should beware of the limited focus of economists' powerful assumptions
> because they may preclude the possibility of collaboration with behavioral
> approaches, and demand a complete paradigm shift that would be unhealthy for
> the field. (p. 95)

From "The Myth of a Monolithic Economics: Fundamental Assumptions and the Use of Economic Models in Policy and Strategy Research," by William S. Hesterly and Todd R. Zenger, 1993, *Organization Science, 4*(3), pp. 496-510. Copyright © 1993 by The Institute of Management Sciences. Reprinted with permission.

19

In the view of Hirsch et al., economic approaches miss the mark in the assumptions they hold about human nature, organizations and the determinacy of markets. More specifically, they criticize economics for viewing all human action as utility maximizing (p. 87) and "opportunistic" (p. 89). Moreover, they argue, economic theories dismiss most organizational concerns by treating organizations as a nonentity configured entirely by market forces. From their perspective, economic approaches make critical errors in their choice of the unit of analysis; economists view organizations as bundles of commodity-like assets to be purchased, dispensed and restructured by Wall Street. Further, managers and employees are completely interchangeable and often disposable commodities. Hirsch et al. also maintain that economic theories assume an investor's perspective which focuses attention outside the firm. Consequently, economists applaud takeovers as the preferred means of disciplining managers, yet ignore the human costs of such takeovers. By contrast, they argue the behavioral approach is a " 'caretaker' management model" that focuses on the organization's internal functions and balances multiple constituencies (p. 94). Thus, in their view, adopting an economic perspective is tantamount to ignoring the concerns, needs and interests of managers and employees.

While Hirsch et al. (p. 95) intend their paper to serve as "a clarification and a warning for behavioralists who value the contribution of economics to business policy," our fundamental concern is that their paper seeks to critique an outdated view of economics and thereby potentially incites a level of fear that we believe is unwarranted. They are right, we believe, in arguing that strategy scholars should view very cautiously economic approaches that ignore organizations, assume all human behavior as opportunistic, and adopt assumptions of hyper-rationality. Any such approaches are not likely to produce new insights for strategy and policy scholars. However, strategy scholars must understand that the economic approaches organizational and policy scholars most often adopt do not share these extreme assumptions of neoclassical microeconomic theory (see Cyert and March 1963, Nelson and Winter 1982, Moe 1984 for reviews). Indeed, policy and organizational scholars' recent interest in economic approaches, such as transactions cost economics, agency theory and evolutionary economics, can be largely credited to these theories both adopting more realistic assumptions and focusing more directly on the organization. Moreover, we differ with the conclusion of Hirsch et al. that economic reasoning views markets and humans in a way that necessarily assumes market determinism, demands an investor focus, and leads to a preference for takeovers. Assigning normative positions to economics as though it were a monolithic body of thought is mistaken and misleading. Important differences exist among economic approaches. Because of these differences, some economic approaches are both more amenable to collaboration with behavioral approaches and more useful to strategy and policy scholars than others.

Our goal is to clarify where those economic approaches of interest to strategy scholars stand on important assumptions about human behavior, organizations as a unit of analysis, market determinism and investor focus. We also seek to make clear the extent to which economics adopts a shareholder perspective. We argue that economic approaches, particularly those that fit under the general label "organizational economics" (see Barney and Ouchi 1986, Moe 1984, Hesterly et al. 1990), address fundamental assumptions in ways that are not endemically incompatible with the more behavioral approaches commonly used by strategy scholars. On assumptions about human nature, this paper examines more closely the beliefs about rationality and opportunism necessary to support the economic theories relevant to policy researchers. Regarding economic units of analysis, this paper contends that economists, particularly organizational economists, do not generally regard organizations as commodity-like asset bundles staffed by dispensable managers. To the contrary, economic approaches contribute to our understanding the need for tightly bundled organizational units staffed by long term employees. This reply further argues that economists do not universally endorse strong-form versions of market determinism that assume away the role of managers, nor are they confined paradigmatically to side with the interests of shareholders. Finally, this paper argues that economists are likely to be extremely selective in the types of takeovers they support as favorable.

ECONOMIC MODELS AND HUMAN ASSUMPTIONS

Economics has often been denounced for adopting unrealistic assumptions. Hirsch and his colleagues criticize economics for "the serious presumption that all behavior is rational and opportunistic" (p. 89). Economists clearly cling aggressively to the assumption of rationality. *Homos economicus* has been characterized as hyper-rational (Williamson 1981, p. 553), "preposterously omniscient" (Simon 1976, p. xxvi-xxvii) and as a perfect mathematician (Marschak and Radner 1972). These kind of strong-form rationality assumptions are of limited use to behaviorally-oriented policy researchers. Fortunately, not all economic theories take such unrealistic views of human nature, however. Notably, the economic models that organizational scholars most often employ adopt behavioral assumptions which differ significantly from those of neoclassical economics. For example, Williamson (1985, p. 44-47) eschews the strong form of maximizing rationality of traditional neoclassical economics and instead adopts the assumption of bounded rationality which involves limits in both information processing and computational capacity. Williamson further argues that other economic approaches such as evolutionary theory (e.g. Alchian 1950, Nelson and Winter 1982) and the Austrian school (Kirzner 1973) employ a still weaker assumption of "organic rationality." Evolutionary theorists, for example, argue that in the face of great complexity, managers resort to relatively simple decision rules and respond to the environment in a way that is "sluggish, halting, and sometimes inconsistent" (Nelson and Winter 1982, pp. 35-36, 58).

Agency theory, particularly the more mathematical principal-agent literature (for distinction see Levinthal 1988, Eisenhardt 1989), and related work in information economics, adopt a somewhat less realistic assumption of rationality. Although the approach departs from the neoclassical assumption that individuals know completely all relevant information, hyperrationality is assumed in an individual's ability to develop and respond to complex contractual mechanisms. In other words, although information asymmetries may exist, the approach assumes parties to a contract "have the cognitive competence to craft contracts of unrestricted complexity" (Williamson 1985, p. 28). Such work merits some criticism. Cognitive limits are clearly constrained. Indeed, Coase (1984, p. 231) joins in warning against the folly of assuming excessive rationality in utility maximization. He argues that modern institutional economics should "start with real institutions" and also "start with man as he is."

The real issue, however, is not whether individuals are rational, but rather in what manner they are rational. Simon (1986, p. s210) argues that psychology has no quarrel with economics' view that human beings are rational; he sees the conflict in how rationality is defined. Recent work by psychologists has begun to document the manner in which individuals are constrained in their reasoning ability (e.g., Tversky and Kahneman 1974, Hogarth 1987, Nisbett and Ross 1980). Economists, particularly principal-agent theorists, would improve the usefulness and predictive power of their models considerably by adopting more reasonable assumptions of rationality.

Hirsch et al. (1990, p. 89) also express concern that economics makes the "serious presumption" that all action is opportunistic. We strongly concur that the notion of every human act involving opportunism—deception, lying, cheating, etc.—is both offensive and unrealistic. Indeed, this assumption is an even more dismal view of humans than is typically assumed in the "dismal science." We agree that this focus on opportunism perhaps has encouraged organizational economists to neglect more benign manifestations of human nature such as altruism and loyalty (Donaldson 1990a, b). To a large degree, Williamson's use of the term opportunism and his definition as "self-interest seeking with guile" are an unfortunate choice of language. The primary function of the term is to distinguish transactions cost behavioral assumptions from the neoclassical assumptions of a world in which all parties reveal all private information. Interestingly, in many ways Williamson's definition of human behavior is more in line with implicit assumptions of organization theory in which individuals featherbed, show favoritism and generally use political power (Douglas 1990, Perrow 1986). Nevertheless, this definition, as it has been interpreted, appears to have exaggerated both the frequency and the magnitude of opportunism necessary to organizational economic theories. In terms of frequency, the necessary assumption is that not *all* individuals are fully forthcoming in disclosing information nor always trustworthy. At least some will either actively or passively withhold, distort, or disguise information. Further, self-interest seeking with guile is only the extreme form of a wide range of behaviors that damage the effectiveness of contracting. Alchian and Woodward (1988, p. 66) appear to deemphasize the role of guile and deception and take a more expansive view of what constitutes opportunistic behavior than Williamson:

> Opportunism covers more than the propensity for mutually reliant parties to mislead, distort, disguise, obfuscate, or otherwise confuse in order to expropriate wealth from one another. It includes honest disagreements . . . many business arrangements interpreted as responses to potential "dishonest" opportunism are equally appropriate for avoiding costly disputes between honest, ethical people who disagree about what event transpired and what adjustment would have been agreed to initially had the event been anticipated. (p. 66)
>   . . . it is important to recognize the forces of ethics, etiquette, and "proper, correct, reasonable, moral, etc." standards of conduct in controlling business relationships . . . (p. 77)

Economists have also become increasingly active in explaining mechanisms that induce cooperative, nonopportunistic behavior. This literature highlights the fragility of cooperation in organizations. Time horizons, reputation, evolution, uncertainty and behavioral probabilities have all been analyzed as determinants of cooperation (Heide and Miner 1992, Axelrod 1984). For instance, Hill (1990) argues that the role of opportunism as a determinant of vertical integration has been overemphasized and that the invisible hand of the market—as an evolutionary selection mechanism—favors, over time, those actors who stress cooperation and trust in their behavior. Casson (1991) has modelled the importance of culture, leadership, trust and morality to economic efficiency. His reasoning suggests that all behavior need not be trustworthy and moral for widespread honesty to be sustained. Indeed, recent economic work demonstrates an increased focus on how norms of cooperation and long term trust relations arise (Miller 1992). While such studies are far from ubiquitous, they represent an important trend.

ECONOMIC MODELS AND UNITS OF ANALYSIS

Hirsch et al. argue that because of the ambiguous unit of analysis adopted by the economic perspective, "organizations, as such" are not a "useful focus of study." They contend that economic approaches view organizations either as "bundles of assets" whose "pieces can be bought and sold indiscriminantly, and organizational units and personnel reshuffled as mere commodities" or as "an amalgamation of contracts, open for negotiation at any moment if efficiencies can be gained" (p. 90). If these are accurate characterizations of economic theories, particularly the view of organizations as disposable assets, then indeed the configuration of an organization is quite arbitrary in such theories and hence unsuited for study.

Although some economic theories indeed adopt a contractual metaphor to understand organizations, organizations are by no means characterized as bundles of disposable assets that are dismembered and reassembled with little consequence. To the contrary, in transactions cost economics for instance, organizations emerge in response to the need for long-term attachments among individuals and subunits of the organizations and to the enormous cost of continuous contract renegotiation. The presence and importance of shared knowledge, specific assets, coordination, close physical proximity and specialized skills between units engaged in exchanging information, services, technology and products lead to the bundling of organizational units within a firm. There is no prediction (nor, certainly, encouragement) of indiscriminate purchase of organizational units or their dismemberment, nor is there a prediction of continual costly contract renegotiation. If managers have correctly defined the boundaries of the organization, indiscriminate sales of organizational units should have negative consequences for firm performance because the gains from reducing the transaction costs associated with these exchanges are forfeited. Indeed, transactions costs reasoning has arguably provided the most powerful explanation for the existence of organizations.

Hirsch, Friedman, and Koza's characterization of the economic view of organizations is somewhat more appropriately leveled at agency theory, although rather than bundles of assets, the organization is viewed as a nexus of contracts (Jensen and Meckling 1976). While, as Williamson (1991) argues, the agency theory definition misses much of what is unique about the organization, viewing the organization as a bundle of disposable assets and a conglomeration of expendable managers. The theory by no means suggests that these contracts can be shuffled without penalty. Furthermore, this explicitly contractual perspective also allows for addressing phenomena at the micro, macro and strategic levels of analysis. The diversity or topics addressed by principal-agent theory includes incentives (Eisenhardt 1985, 1988), transfer pricing (Eccles 1985), organizational structure (Holmstrom and Tirole 1991), promotion (Aoki 1988), political behavior in organizations (Milgrom and Roberts 1988), and leadership (Rotemberg and Saloner 1991). Such flexibility in application is rare in an era in which scholarly work in organization and strategy research has become increasingly constrained by micro and macro "disciplinary" boundaries (Staw 1991). Nonetheless, although the agency theory view of organization has yielded considerable insight and has drawn increased empirical attention, we concur with Hirsch et al. that this economic approach may encourage an overly atomistic view of organizations that warrants some caution.

Unlike both transactions cost and agency theory, evolutionary economics (Nelson and Winter 1982) is "quite sociological" in its treatment of the organization (Perrow 1986, p. 216). This theory raises a number of propositions about economic change that are rooted in explicit propositions about organizations. Far from dismissing the organization as a unit of analysis, the evolutionary view maintains that organizations, not individuals, serve as "repositories of productive knowledge over extended periods of time" (Winter 1990, p. 273). Nelson and Winter (1982) advocate placing organizational routines—regular, predictable processes and activities (Winter 1990, p. 276)—as the basic unit of analysis. This productive knowledge is embedded within organizational routines that are often not easily articulated or imitated. Thus, organizational know-how is distinguished from individual knowledge as a topic of inquiry. This theory appears to be rather influential in the development of the increasingly popular resource-based perspective of strategic management (Grant 1992, p. 122-123). As Mahoney and Pandian (1992, p. 369-370) note, a firm's distinctive competencies or resources may be defined by the set of substantive rules and routines used by the firm.

Hirsch et al. also criticize economic approaches for disregarding the importance of employee commitment and loyalty. As they characterize the economic view, "each day could start with each employee contracting for a day's work" (p. 91). By contrast, they argue, "behavioralists are concerned with long run incentives that develop company loyalty—e.g., career ladders that provide the employee with a future in the company" (p. 91). We believe this characterization of economic approaches to be rather misleading.

Economists do tend to view the employment relationship as a voluntary contract between employer and employee. However, economists have perhaps been the most avid researchers of the economic necessity of long-term employment relationships. In 1962, Becker advanced the argument that while on the job, individuals develop unique, firm-specific human capital which employers have incentives to retain through long-term employment relationships. Arguably, the attention that Becker drew to the concept of asset specifically triggered the subsequent insights of Williamson et al. (1975), Williamson (1981), and Klein et al. (1978) that formed the primary basis for much of the work in transaction cost economics. Relations with employees and contracts with suppliers cannot be short term when specialized skills or assets are required. Economic scholars have thus explored the mechanisms through which firms encourage long-term relationships with employees (see Doeringer and Piore 1971, Williamson et al. 1975, Aoki 1988, Lazear and Rosen 1981, Akerlof and Yellen 1986). Far from treating people and assets indiscriminately, this economic reasoning explains how long-term incentives, seniority wages, and career ladders induce the long-term relationships necessary in many work settings. Economic theories have also contributed to our understanding of when mechanisms that induce long-term employment are desirable and where they are undesirable. Although agency theorists, along with organizations theorists (e.g., Staw 1980, Abelson and Baysinger 1984), might acknowledge benefits of some modest level of turnover, the "hire'em and fire'em" attitude ascribed by Hirsch et al. to work in organizational economics seems inappropriate.

Other approaches rooted in economics also reject the view of managers as commodities. While, as noted above, evolutionary theory focuses on organizations as repositories for skills and routines, this organizational focus does not mean that individual employees are consigned to commodity-like status. Individuals often serve as repositories for knowledge that is important and idiosyncratic to the organization. Moreover, such knowledge may be tacit in that it is not written down and is difficult to articulate. Nelson and Winter (1982, p. 115) argue that under these conditions, the loss of an employee damages the continuity of a routine. Castanias and Helfat (1991) have also drawn upon economic reasoning to argue that managers possess firm-specific skills that are a possible source of sustained competitive advantage for firms.

While transaction cost economics, agency theory and evolutionary economics have explicitly attempted to examine the internal workings of organizations, there is little question that economists have seriously neglected organizational behavior and policy research. We concur with others (Simon 1991, Williamson 1985, p. 402) who suggest that this is a serious shortfall of current economic work. However, consistent with our arguments above, we would assert that the origin of this neglect has very little to do with organizational economics' unit of analysis or its characterization of organization. In large part the neglect reflects economists' bias and preferences in research methods. In economics, theoretical work is seldom empirically grounded and empirical work typically involves archival databases. Both are often quite detached from the phenomena of interest. We thus concur with others who suggest that increasingly, advances in the economics of organization are likely to be made by behavioral scholars rather than economists. Policy and organizational scholars, because they are more familiar with the behavioral approaches and because they are more multidisciplinary, are thus better positioned than economists to apply organization theory to economics (Coase 1978, Williamson 1985, p. 402), and conversely, economics to organization theory (e.g., Ouchi 1980, Eisenhardt 1985, Eccles 1985). Management scholars might realize significant opportunities for contribution by exploiting their advantage in areas where economists tend to be weaker such as in survey research and theoretical work using behavioral assumptions (Hesterly et al. 1990).

DOES ECONOMICS ASSUME MARKET DETERMINISM?

Hirsch et al. (1990) argue that economic and behavioral perspectives clash over the concept of volition. They describe an economics that sees environmental (read "market") selection, not managerial action, as the source of change in organizations. Thus, economics and organizational ecology, which they view as a "sociological variant of economics" (p. 92), deny the relevance of voluntary action. This overemphasis of selection, in their thinking, leads economists to view managers as passive actors unable to alter strategy or influence environments.

We agree that voluntary action plays a necessary role in explaining strategic processes and outcomes. We concede that some economic approaches do tend to leave little room for managerial volition. In a neoclassical economic world, managers and employees are machines and costs are purely a function of technology. Furthermore, the structure-conduct-performance paradigm of IO economics suggests that industry structure, not managerial action, is the driving force in the strategic behavior of firms. As Conner (1991, p. 133) points out, this perspective tends to see firm behavior as a foregone conclusion from industry structure. However, as we argue below, the absence of management volition is not generally characteristic of other economic theories of interest to policy researchers. Further, we concur that selection, as used by economists, is underdeveloped. And, while we do not agree that economics is inherently investor-focused or pro-takeover, we do see room for clarification.

Management volition is the primary focus of agency theory. By its very title, agency theory is a theory of individual action and autonomy. The theory explores mechanisms that encourage behavior consistent and inconsistent with both the principal's and agent's desires. Indeed, this individualist orientation is seen as a limitation by those who favor a methodologically collectivist approach (Donaldson 1990a, b). Further, selection pressures are assumed to be particularly imperfect in agency theory; if selection pressures were strong all firms with managers engaging in nonshareholder-maximizing behavior would be effectively disciplined and removed. Transaction cost economics adopts a similar perspective, acknowledging managerial discretion, while arguing that selection pressures, although imperfect, encourage efficient organization (Williamson 1988a). Managers in this perspective may design and craft efficient structures, incentives and information systems, but at the same time still excessively meddle, distort information and jockey for power and influence. The more efficient organizations are likely to survive, but only in the long term. Thus, both agency and transaction cost theory recognize market imperfections, contrary to the assumptions imputed by Hirsch et al.

As organizational ecologists argue, volition and selection are not mutually exclusive. Carroll (1990) notes that much of the criticism directed towards organizational ecology has been directed towards Hannan and Freeman's (1977) strong assumption of inertia. The view that organizations are extremely inert leaves little room for managerial adaptation and volition. Two points must be considered, however. First, organizational ecologists have backed away from this strong assertion of inertia. Carroll (1990, p. 64) joins others who view selection and adaptation as either complementary (Scott 1987, p. 200-203) or interdependent (Levinthal 1991): "Short-term change among individual organizations can be primarily adaptive while long-term change in populations of organizations can be through selection." Though we find no problem with assuming both selection and adaptive processes operating simultaneously, we agree with observers such as Granovetter (1985) and Robins (1987) that efficiency-based selection may not always be prevalent even in firms. Meyer and Zucker's (1989) description of "permanently failing organizations" demonstrates that inefficient and ineffective organizations sometimes persist despite their inadequacies. As Hirsch and his colleagues point out, firms sometimes manage their environments rather than being selected out by them. Although some economic work, such as regulatory capture theory (see Scherer 1980), examines how firms manage their environments, work in transactions cost economics does on occasion fall into the trap of assuming that, due to selection pressures, what exists is efficient (Granovetter 1990). The concept of selection and its impact on organizational design remains in need of further development (Williamson 1988a).

Economics can be criticized for the way it views voluntary choice, but it clearly focuses on the study of human choice behavior (Hogarth and Reder 1986). Winship and Rosen (1988), one a sociologist and the other an economist, go so far as to suggest that it is partly *because* of economic's emphasis on individual action that it contributes to functionalist reasoning. They (Winship and Rosen 1988, p. S11) conclude that, "*If economics does anything, it provides a theory of individual behavior.*"

IS ECONOMICS INVESTOR FOCUSED?

Hirsch et al. conclude their paper by examining agency theory as an example of economics gone awry. In their view, agency theory is an investor's model in which takeovers are applauded for their ability to enhance shareholder wealth and discipline management. While an investor bias is clearly evident in theory and research that evaluates mergers and acquisitions solely on whether or not investors profit from such actions, this investor focus is not endemic to economic reasoning. Shleifer and Summers (1988), for example, examine the consequences of takeovers on stakeholders other than shareholders. Moreover, other economists have examined the consequences of ownership changes on labor (Brown and Medoff 1988, Lichtenberg and Siegel 1990), research and development (Hall 1988), and business line operating performance (Ravenscraft and Scherer 1987) among other effects. Clearly, the same economic tools used to assess the effect of ownership change on shareholder value can be used to assess the impact of ownership change on labor and other stakeholders. In part the current empirical bias reflects the ease of obtaining share price information and the relative difficulty in obtaining information on other stakeholders' fortunes.

Furthermore, even when economists adopt a shareholder perspective, this view does not necessitate a universal endorsement of takeovers. Agency theory (and the work of financial economists) yields at least three different explanations for takeovers. One view is that takeovers are displays of self-interest by managers that more often destroy value than create value for shareholder (Type I). A second explanation is that takeovers are disciplinary devices that control managerial behavior which if unchecked may destroy shareholder value and indeed may often harm the fortunes of other stakeholders as well (Type II). A third explanation is that takeovers are self-interested acts that enhance shareholder value at the expense of other stakeholders such as employers and suppliers (Shleifer and Summers 1988). This is the view of takeovers (or type of takeovers) adopted by Hirsch and his colleagues (Type III). Both economists and noneconomists alike will view these three takeover types with differing levels of support.

Empirical studies, largely by economists, suggest that takeovers and acquisitions generally destroy rather than enhance shareholder value (Type I) and thus warrant rather restrained and selective applause from both economists and behavioral scholars alike. When the time frame considered extends one to three years after a takeover, acquiring firms, on average, experience negative abnormal returns from acquisitions (Jensen and Ruback 1983, Scherer 1988, Schleifer and Vishny 1991). This was particularly true during the 1980s. This empirical finding alone, stemming from the agency tradition, suggests that economists are likely to view much takeover activity as evidence of managers' opportunistic behavior rather than as effective market discipline.

However, economists are likely to view more favorably takeovers that discipline managerial activity that destroys shareholder value (Type II). Paradoxically, managers indulging in value-destroying takeovers (Type I) may find themselves the recipient of a Type II disciplinary takeover. Further, economists are likely to view favorably disciplinary takeovers that actually dismantle conglomerations of unrelated businesses assembled through acquisition. Such conglomerations often reflect past managerial actions that have treated organizations as bundles of commodity-like assets to be bought, sold or harvested. Through disciplinary takeovers or the fear of such takeovers, unrelated business units are sold (commonly in one piece) to other organizations in more closely related lines of business. There is growing empirical evidence to suggest that much recent takeover, acquisition and merger activity has produced such reallocation (Bhagat et al. 1990, Scherer 1988, Markides 1990, Hoskisson and Johnson 1992). Thus, although many economists may discourage constraints on hostile takeovers, this position largely reflects a desire to reduce the empire-building tendencies of managers who indiscriminately purchase commodity-like organizational units. Nonetheless, there is little doubt that this form of discipline is enormously costly. The economy is served far better by managers adopting long term incentives, making wise investments in people and products, and returning to shareholders those funds that might chase poor investments. Or, in the absence of such managerial actions, the economy is served better by board members who actively step in to influence policy, adjust incentives and replace managers.

Hirsch et al. appear to assume that takeovers are primarily of Type III. They imply that, although perhaps motivated by a desire to enhance shareholder value, for the most part takeovers have devastating effects on managers, employees and other stakeholders. Hence, in adopting an investor focus, economists overlook the devastation to managers, employees, customers, suppliers and communities, the broken psychological commitments, and the bruised morale that accompany takeovers. Economists' support of disciplinary takeovers is thus an alliance with shareholders against managers and employees. Indeed, it is difficult to dispute anecdotal evidence of massive disruption to communities and employees from notable takeovers (Hirsch 1987). However, anecdotal evidence also suggests that disruptive restructurings frequently occur without direct takeover threats. Further, anecdotal evidence suggests that many ownership changes yield little alteration in the status of employees and that many others are euphorically accepted by managers.

A thorough review of the consequences of acquisitions and takeovers is well beyond the scope of this reply; however the image of vast devastation to managers and employees is not a clear conclusion from the current evidence on ownership changes. Brown and Medoff (1988), Yago and Stevenson (1986), and Kaplan (1989) all find little evidence of increased layoffs following an ownership change. However, Lichtenberg and Siegel (1990) do find evidence of employment reductions following ownership changes, although primarily white collar reductions associated with the consolidation of headquarters. Further, Bhagat et al. (1990) find evidence of layoffs (primarily white collar) in 28 of 62 hostile takeovers ($50 million or more) during 1985 and 1986, although interpreting these results is somewhat problematic without information concerning the likelihood of layoffs in the absence of a takeover. Clearly, further research investigating the consequences of takeovers and threatened takeovers is merited, since considerable theoretical and empirical disagreement remains, even among economists, concerning both the consequences of and motivation for takeovers (see Shleifer and Summers 1988, Williamson 1988b, Holmstrom 1988).

CONCLUSION

Hirsch et al. have raised important questions about economics' fundamental assumptions concerning human nature, units of analysis and market determinism. We agree that policy and strategy scholars should thoughtfully examine the assumptions implicit in the economic models they use. Further, we concur that policy and strategy scholars should examine the implications of strategic changes beyond their effect on shareholders. Nevertheless, we disagree with Hirsh, Friedman and Koza's central conclusion: that the limited focus of economists' assumptions may preclude collaboration with behavioral approaches and thus demand a complete paradigm shift for the field. Contrary to their warning, economists are becoming increasingly varied in the assumptions they assert. Thus, most simple statements about what "economists" assume are likely to be untrue for significant subareas of the field. Some economic approaches may well be incompatible with more behavioral approaches, but others are compatible. Moreover, collaboration or integration between economic and behavioral approaches appears to be on the increase. Part of the appeal of economic approaches used by strategy and policy researchers is that they are *not* like Hirsch, Friedman and Koza's mythical economic modelers who advocate a "pure economics research agenda" while not being "flexible enough to learn from other disciplines" (p. 88).

Recent developments, in institutional or organizational economics particularly, attempt to incorporate insights from other disciplines such as organization science, sociology and psychology. Economists are incorporating concepts such as networks (Williamson 1991), intraorganizational politics (Milgrom and Roberts 1988), trust (Casson (1991), and leadership (Casson 1991, Castanias and Helfat 1991) in their theory and models. Lazear's (1991, p. 89) view of the relationship between economics and psychology is becoming increasingly representative: "psychologists have concepts and data which would be useful to economists. A number of their ideas have already made their way into economics and more will follow . . ."

We do not suggest that all economists are so enlightened. Much economic work deals with issues within the strategy and policy domain but makes no reference to theory and research beyond economics. For example, Shapiro's (1989) article that equates business strategy with game theory makes no reference to the strategy field. Likewise, Jensen's (1983) article boldly proclaiming agency theory as a revolution in organization theory shows little awareness, much less appreciation, for extant organization theory and research. Much of the economic work in areas of interest that overlap those of strategy and policy researchers does employ unrealistic assumptions and is ignorant of research by organizational and policy scholars. Arguably, though, this work has not been embraced heartily by organizational and policy scholars.

Just as some economists have erred in ignoring the work of strategy and organization scholars, it is also an error for strategy and organization scholars to dismiss work in economics simply because it is economics. Such prejudice serves neither field. Hirsch and his colleagues touch upon a question central to a multidisciplinary area of inquiry such as strategy: What is the appropriate response to approaches from other disciplines? Despite our defense of some economic approaches, we do not advocate the unreserved adoption of economic models for strategy and policy analysis. Policy and strategy scholars should evaluate the validity of assumptions used, the empirical evidence behind the theories, and the prescriptive implications of economic models (see for example, Granovetter 1985, Robins 1987, Jones and Hill 1988, Perrow 1986, Putterman 1982). A fair evaluation of any model or set of models first requires unprejudiced description of the models in question. Yet, at least two deterrents hinder such unbiased description and multidisciplinary integration. On the one hand, as Barney (1990) has noted, organization and strategic studies are rife with intergroup rivalry within the field. A typical consequence of this type of rivalry is that one group stereotypes, and even misrepresents the other; such rivalry leads more to labeling than real analysis of opposing points of view, and, thus acts as an impediment to real integration within the field. We agree with Barney (1990, p. 391) that the appropriate response is constructive dialogue and conflict. The aspects of economics with implications for strategy and policy should be debated on their merits, not dismissed or even treated with suspicion because they are labeled "economics." This, of course, does not mean that all criticism of a discipline by another is rooted in intergroup rivalry. As Donaldson (1990b) has noted, many of these criticisms are rationally and substantively based. Our emphasis is on understanding first before criticizing or dismissing. While his is an ambitious task, it is a course that will take the field towards greater integration rather than segmentation.

While many economics scholars are moving toward more realistic assumptions, there are strategy and policy scholars who employ economics in their research that are worthy of emulation. Rather than unquestioningly buying into the unrealistic assumptions of traditional neoclassical economics, these scholars are using strategy and economics in a true interdisciplinary way. For example, Ouchi (1980) integrated insights from transaction cost economics with those of Durkheim. More recently, Eisenhardt's (1989) review of agency theory showed that often organization and strategy scholars using agency theory are combining it with other, more behavioral theories. This strikes us as a proper course. We are not the first to point out that organization and strategy researchers are particularly well-positioned to make advances in understanding by combining the approaches of multiple disciplines (Barney and Ouchi 1986, Eisenhardt 1989, Hesterly et al. 1990). First, strategy researchers are more likely to have received training in other social science disciplines than are economists. As a result, strategy researchers are more sensitive to sociological factors such as institutionalization (Eisenhardt 1988) and trust (Ring and Van de Ven 1992). Similarly, strategy researchers are more likely to combine their use of economic approaches with psychological concerns such as equity (Zenger 1992, Zajac 1990) or escalating commitments (Hesterly and Jansen 1993). Abundant opportunities for collaboration between behavioral and economic approaches remain unexploited.

Second, strategy researchers are more likely to be trained in a variety of research methods whereas economists are more likely to be skilled in mathematical modeling and in secondary data analysis. Historical studies (Chandler 1962), ethnographic field studies (Larson 1992), case studies such as those published at Harvard, and survey research (Zajac 1990) not only reflect the diversity of approaches typical of the field but also offer examples of management scholars undertaking collaborative research that has enriched our understanding of economic approaches as applied to strategic management issues.

Finally, the strategy and policy field is embedded in mechanisms that tend to impose a real-world orientation on scholars. One of the primary professional associations of strategy and policy scholars, the Strategic Management Society, actively seeks to balance managers, consultants and academicians in its activities. A more pervasive mechanism in raising sensitivity toward real-world concerns is the case-oriented teaching tradition in strategy and policy. Most strategy scholars regularly find themselves in the classroom, often with either MBA students or practicing managers, where their audiences demand explanations and prescriptions for specific cases. In such situations, abstract models that show little connection to real-world situations are seldom well-received. Whatever the reason, strategy and policy scholars tend to be more problem and issue-oriented than discipline-oriented. Given this orientation toward problems and issues, scholars are not likely to become enamored with elegant economic models that are irrelevant to the strategic issues faced by firms. For policy scholars, the true test of economic models is in their effectiveness in aiding these different constituencies to understand strategic issues. We concur with Hirsch et al. that an element of caution is warranted in evaluating economic models generally, however policy scholars current "romance" with selected economic theories must in part reflect a perception of enhanced understanding.

REFERENCES

Abelson, Michael A. and Barry D. Baysinger (1984), "Optimal and Dysfunctional Turnover: Toward an Organizational Level Model," *Academy of Management Review*, 9, 331-341.

Akerlof, George and Janet Yellen (1986), *Efficiency Wage Models of the Labor Market*, Cambridge, England: Cambridge University Press.

Alchian, Armen A. (1950), "Uncertainty, Evolution, and Economic Theory," *Journal of Political Economy*, 58, 211-221.

——— and Susan Woodward (1988), "The Firm Is Dead; Long Live the Firm: A Review of Oliver E. Williamson's *The Economic Institutions of Capitalism*," *Journal of Economic Literature*, 26, 65-79.

Amihud, Y. and B. Lev (1981), "Risk Reduction as a Managerial Motive for Conglomerate Mergers," *Bell Journal of Economics*, 12, 605-616.

Aoki, Masahiko (1988), *Information, Incentives, and Bargaining in the Japanese Economy*, Cambridge, England: Cambridge University Press.

Axelrod, R. (1984), *The Evolution of Cooperation*, New York: Basic Books.

Barney, Jay B. (1990). "The Debate Between Traditional Management Theory and Organizational Economics: Substantive Difference or Intergroup Conflict?" *Academy of Management Review*, 15, 382-393.

——— and William G. Ouchi (Eds.) (1986), *Organizational Economics: Toward a New Paradigm for Understanding and Studying Organizations*, San Francisco: Jossey-Bass.

Becker, Gary S. (1962), "Investment in Human Capital: A Theoretical Analysis," *Journal of Political Economy*, 70, 49-70.

Bettis, Richard A. (1991), "Strategic Management and the Straightjacket: An Editorial Essay," *Organization Science*, 2, 315-319.

Bhagat, Sanjai, Andrei Shleifer, and Robert Vishny (1990), "Hostile Takeovers in the 1980's: The Return to Corporate Specialization," *The Brookings Papers on Economic Activity: Microeconomics,* 1990, 1-84.

Brown, C. L. and J. L. Medoff (1988), "The Impact of Firm Acquisitions on Labor," in A. J. Auerbach (Ed.), *Corporate Takeovers: Causes and Consequences,* Chicago: University of Chicago Press.

Carroll, G. R. (1990), "On the Organizational Ecology of Chester I. Barnard," in O. E. Williamson (Ed.), *Organization Theory,* New York: Oxford University Press.

Casson, M. (1991), *The Economics of Business Culture: Game Theory, Transaction Costs, and Economic Performance,* Oxford England: Clarendon Press.

Castanias, R. P. and C. E. Helfat (1991), "Managerial Resources and Rents," *Journal of Management,* 17, 155-172.

Chandler, Alfred D. (1962), *Strategy and Structure: Chapters in the History of the American Industrial Enterprise,* Cambridge MA: MIT Press.

Coase, R. H. (1978), "Economics and Contiguous Disciplines," *Journal of Legal Studies,* 7, 201-211.

———— (1984), "The New Institutional Economics," *Journal of Institutional and Theoretical Economics,* 140, 229-231.

Coleman, J. S. (1986), "Social Theory, Social Research, and a Theory of Action," *American Journal of Sociology,* 91, 1309-1335.

Conner, K. R. (1991), "A Historical Comparison of Resource-based Theory and Five Schools of Thought Within Industrial Organization Economics: Do We Have a New Theory of the Firm?" *Journal of Management,* 17, 121-154.

Cyert, R. M. and J. G. March (1963), *A Behavioral Theory of the Firm,* Englewood Cliffs, NJ: Prentice Hall.

Doeringer, Peter and Michael Piore (1971), *Internal Labor Markets and Manpower Analysis,* Lexington, MA: D. C. Heath.

Donaldson, Lex (1985), *In Defense of Organization Theory,* Cambridge, England: Cambridge University Press.

———— (1990a), "The Ethereal Hand: Organizational Economics and Management Theory," *Academy of Management Review,* 15, 369-381.

———— (1990b), "A Rational Basis for Criticisms of Organizational Economics: A Reply to Barney," *Academy of Management Review,* 15, 394-401.

Douglas, M. (1990), "Converging on Autonomy: Anthropology and Institutional Economics," in O. E. Williamson (Ed.), *Organization Theory,* New York: Oxford University Press.

Eccles, Robert G. (1985), "Transfer Pricing as a Problem of Agency," in John W. Pratt and Richard J. Zeckhauser (Eds.), *Principals and Agents: The Structure of Business,* Boston, MA: Harvard Business School Press.

Eisenhardt, Kathleen M. (1989), "Agency Theory: An Assessment and Review," *Academy of Management Review,* 14, 57-74.

———— (1985), "Organizational Control: Organizational and Economic Approaches," *Management Science,* 31, 134-149.

———— (1988), "Agency- and Institutional-Theory Explanations: The Case of Retail Sales Compensation," *Academy of Management Journal,* 31, 488-511.

Granovetter, Mark (1985), "Economic Action and Social Structure: The Problem of Embeddedness," *American Journal of Sociology,* 91, 481-510.

———— (1990), Interview in Richard Swedberg, Economics and Sociology: *Redefining Their Boundaries: Conversations with Economists and Sociologists,* Princeton, NJ: Princeton University Press.

Grant, Robert M. (1991), "The Resource-based Theory of Competitive Advantage," *California Management Review,* 33 (Spring), 114-135.

Hall, B. H. (1988), "The Effect of Takeover Activity on Corporate Research and Development," in A. J. Auerbach (Ed.), *Corporate Takeovers: Causes and Consequences,* Chicago: University of Chicago Press.

Hannan, M. T. and J. Freeman (1977), "The Population Ecology of Organizations," *American Journal of Sociology,* 82, 929-966.

Heide, Jan B. and Anne S. Miner (1992), "The Shadow of the Future: Effects of Anticipated Interaction and Frequency on Buyer-Seller Cooperation," *Academy of Management Journal,* 35, 2, 265-291.

Hesterly, William S. and Erik Jansen (1993), "The Impact of Monitoring Styles and Incentive Compensation on Strategic Persistence," Unpublished Paper, University of Utah.

———, Julia Liebeskind and Todd R. Zenger (1990), "Organizational Economics: An Impending Revolution in Organization Theory?" *Academy of Management Review,* 15, 402-420.

Hill, C. W. L. (1990), "Cooperation, Opportunism, and the Invisible Hand: Implications for Transaction Cost Theory," *Academy of Management Review,* 15, 500-513.

Hirsch, P. M. (1987), *Pack Your Own Parachute,* Reading, MA: Addison-Wesley.

———, R. Friedman and M. P. Koza (1990), "Collaboration or Paradigm Shift? Caveat Emptor and the Risk of Romance with Economic Models for Strategy and Policy Research," *Organization Science,* 1, 87-98.

Hogarth, R. M. and M. W. Reder (1986), "Editors' Comments: Perspectives from Economics and Psychology," *Journal of Business,* 59, S185-S208.

Hogarth, Robin M. (1987), *Judgement and Choice* (2nd Ed.), New York: Wiley and Sons.

Holmstrom, B. (1988) "Comment on Breach of Trust in Hostile Takeovers," in A. J. Auerbach (Ed.), *Corporate Takeovers: Causes and Consequences,* Chicago, IL: University of Chicago Press.

——— and J. Tirole (1991), "Transfer Pricing and Organizational Form," *Journal of Law, Economics, and Organization,* 7 (2), 201-228.

Hoskisson, R. E. and R. E. Johnson (1992), "Corporate Restructuring and Strategic Change: The Effect of Diversification Strategy and R & D Intensity," *Strategic Management Journal,* 13 (8), 625-634.

Jensen, M. C. (1983), "Organization Theory and Methodology," *Accounting Review,* 50, 319-339.

——— and W. Meckling (1976), "Theory of the Firm: Managerial Behavior, Agency Costs, and Ownership Structure," *Journal of Financial Economics,* 3, 305-360.

——— and R. S. Ruback (1983), "The Market for Corporate Control: The Scientific Evidence," *Journal of Financial Economics,* 11, 5-50.

Jones, G. P. and C. W. L. Hill (1988), "Transactions Cost Analysis of Strategy Structure Choice," *Strategic Management Journal,* 9, 159-172.

Kaplan, S. (1989), "The Effect of Management Buyouts on Operations and Value," *Journal of Financial Economics,* 24, 217-254.

Kirzner, I. M. (1973), *Competition and Entrepreneurship,* Chicago, IL: University of Chicago Press.

Klein, B., R. G. Crawford and A. A. Alchian (1978), "Vertical Integration, Appropriable Rents and the Competitive Contracting Process," *Journal of Law and Economics,* 21, 297-326.

Larson, Andrea (1992), "Network Dyads in Entrepreneurial Settings: A Study of the Governance of Exchange Relationships," *Administrative Science Quarterly,* 37, 76-104.

Lazear, E. (1991), "Labor Economics and the Psychology of Organizations," *Journal of Economic Perspectives,* 5, 89-110.

——— and S. Rosen (1981), "Rank-Order Tournaments as Optimal Labor Contracts," *Journal of Political Economy,* 89, 841-864.

Levinthal, D. (1988), "A Survey of Agency Models of Organizations," *Journal of Economic Behavior and Organization,* 9, 153-185.

——— (1991), "Organizational Adaptation and Environmental Selection-Interrelated Processes of Change," *Organization Science,* 2, 140-145.

Lichtenberg, F. R. and D. Siegel (1990), "The Effect of Ownership Changes on the Employment and Wages of Central Office and Other Personnel," *Journal of Law and Economics,* 33, 383-408.

Mahoney, Joseph T. and J. Rajendran Pandian (1992), "The Resource-based View within the Conversation of Strategic Management," *Strategic Management Journal,* 13, 363-380.

Markides, Constantinos C. (1993), "Diversification, Restructuring and Economic Performance," Unpublished Paper, London Business School.

Marschak, J. and R. Radner (1972), *The Theory of Teams,* New Haven, CT: Yale University Press.

Meyer, M. W. and L. G. Zucker (1989), *Permanently Failing Organizations,* Beverly Hills, CA: Sage.

Milgrom, P. and J. Roberts (1988), "An Economic Approach to Influence Activities in Organizations," *American Journal of Sociology,* 94 (Supplement), 154-179.

Miller, G. (1992), *Managerial Dilemmas: The Political Economy of Hierarchy,* Cambridge, England: Cambridge University Press.

Moe, T. M. (1984), "The New Economics of Organizations." *American Journal of Political Science,* 28, 739-777.

Nelson, R. R. and S. G. Winter (1982), *An Evolutionary Theory of Economic Change,* Cambridge, MA: Harvard University Press.

Nisbett, Richard and Lee Ross (1980), *Human Inferences: Strategies and Shortcomings of Social Judgement,* Englewood Cliffs, NJ: Prentice Hall.

Ouchi, W. G. (1980), "Markets, Bureaucracies and Clans," *Administrative Science Quarterly,* 25, 129-141.

Perrow, C. (1986), *Complex Organizations: A Critical Essay,* New York: Random House.

Putterman, L. (1982), "Some Behavioral Perspectives on the Dominance of Hierarchical over Democratic Forms of Enterprise," *Journal of Economic Behavior and Organization,* 3, 139-160.

Ravenscraft, D. J. and F. M. Scherer (1987), *Mergers, Sell-offs, and Economic Efficiency,* Washington DC: The Brookings Institution.

Ring, Peter S. and Andrew H. Van de Ven (1992), "Structuring Cooperative Relationships Between Organizations," *Strategic Management Journal,* 13, 483-498.

Robins, J. A. (1987), "Organizational Economics: Notes on the Use of Transaction-Cost Theory in the Study of Organizations," *Administrative Science Quarterly,* 32, 68-86.

Rotemberg, J. and G. Saloner (1991), "Leadership Style and Incentives," Sloan School of Management, MIT, Working Paper.

Scherer, F. M. (1980) *Industrial Market Structure and Economic Performance,* Chicago, IL: Rand McNally.

——— (1988), "Corporate Takeovers: The Efficiency Arguments," *Journal of Economic Perspectives,* 2, 69-82.

Scott, W. R. (1987), *Organizations: Rational, Natural and Open Systems* (2nd Ed.), Englewood Cliffs, NJ: Prentice Hall.

Shapiro, C. (1989), "The Theory of Business Strategy," *Rand Journal of Economics,* 20, 1, 125-137.

Shleifer, A. and L. H. Summers (1988), "Breach of Trust in Hostile Takeovers," in A. J. Auerbach
    (Ed.), *Corporate Takeovers: Causes and Consequences,* Chicago, IL: University of Chi-
    cago Press.
Shleifer, Andrei and Robert W. Vishny (1991), "Takeovers in the 60's and the 80's: Evidence and
    Implications," *Strategic Management Journal,* 12, 51-59.
Simon, H. A. (1976), *Administrative Behavior* (3rd Ed.), New York: Free Press.
——— (1986), "Rationality in Psychology and Economics," *Journal of Business,* 59, s209-
    s224.
——— (1991), "Organizations and Markets," *Journal of Economic Perspectives,* 5, 25-44.
Staw, Barry (1980), "The Consequences of Turnover," *Journal of Occupational Behavior,* 1,
    253-273.
——— (1991), "Dressing Up Like an Organization: When Psychological Theories Can Explain
    Organizational Action," *Journal of Management,* 17, 805-820.
Stiglitz, J. E. (1991), "Symposium on Organizations and Economics," *Journal of Economic Per-
    spectives,* 5, 15-24.
Tversky, A. and D. Kahneman (1974), "Judgment Under Uncertainty: Heuristics and Biases,"
    Science, 185; 1124-1131.
Williamson, O. E. (1981), "The Economics of Organization: The Transaction Cost Approach,"
    American Journal of Sociology, 87, 548-577.
——— (1985), *The Economic Institutions of Capitalism,* New York: Free Press.
——— (1988a), "The Economics and Sociology of Organization: Promoting a Dialogue," in
    G. Farkas and P. England (Eds.), *Industries, Firms, and Jobs: Sociological and Economic
    Approaches,* New York: Plenum.
——— (1988b), "Comment on Breach of Trust in Hostile Takeovers," in A. J. Auerbach (Ed.),
    Corporate Takeovers: Causes and Consequences, Chicago, IL: University of Chicago
    Press.
——— (1990), "Introduction," in O. E. Williamson (Ed.), *Organization Theory,* New York:
    Oxford University Press.
——— (1991), "Comparative Economic Organization: The Analysis of Discrete Structural
    Alternatives," *Administrative Science Quarterly,* 36, 269-296.
Williamson, Oliver E., Michael L. Wachter and Jeffrey E. Harris (1975), "Understanding the
    Employment Relation: The Analysis of Idiosyncratic Exchange," *Bell Journal of Eco-
    nomics,* 24, 6, 250-280.
Winship, C. and S. Rosen (1988), "Introduction: Sociological and Economic Approaches to the
    Analysis of Social Structure," *American Journal of Sociology,* 94, S1-S16.
Winter, S. G. (1990), "Survival, Selection, and Inheritance in Evolutionary Theories of Organi-
    zation," in J. V. Singh (Ed.), *Organizational Evolution: New Directions,* Newbury Park,
    CA: Sage.
Yago, G. and G. Stevenson (1986), *Mergers and Acquisitions in the New Jersey Economy,* New
    York: Securities Industry Association.
Zajac, Edward J. (1990), "CEO Selection, Compensation, and Firm Performance: A Theoretical
    Integration and Empirical Analysis," *Strategic Management Journal,* 11, 217-231.
Zenger, Todd R. (1992), "Why Do Employers Only Reward Extreme Performance? Examining
    the Relationship among Performance, Pay, and Turnover," *Administrative Science Quar-
    terly,* 378, 198-219.
——— (to appear), "Explaining Organizational Diseconomics of Scale in R & D: Agency Prob-
    lems and the Allocation of Engineering Talent, Ideas and Effort by Firm Size," *Manage-
    ment Science.*

3

Barriers to the Advance of Organizational Science

Paradigm Development as a Dependent Variable

JEFFREY PFEFFER
Stanford University

In the sociology of science literature, few concepts have enjoyed as wide acceptance or provided as much conceptual leverage as that of the level of paradigm development. "Thomas Kuhn (1970) differentiates among the sciences by the extent to which they have a developed paradigm or shared theoretical structures and methodological approaches about which there is a high level of consensus" (Cole, 1983: 112). To this point, most, if not all, of the existing research has been devoted to operationalizing the concept of paradigm development, seeing if there really are differences in the sciences in terms of the amount of consensus, and examining the effects of paradigm development on a range of outcomes. In this article, the first part of my argument entails reviewing the evidence that (a) there are differences in the level of paradigm development across scientific fields and that (b) these differences have significant consequences for a number of important outcomes.

Given the importance and predictive power of the concept of the level of paradigm development, it is unfortunate that little attention has been given to asking why it is that some fields have more consensus than others. This is an important issue because the second part of my argument is that consensus is a necessary, although clearly not sufficient, condition for the systematic advancement of knowledge. Thus, because researchers are concerned with the development and growth of organizational science, they can benefit from understanding something about the factors associated with more or less paradigmatically developed fields. This article is far from the first to make this point. Zammuto and Connolly (1984: 30), for instance, argued that "the organizational sciences are severely fragmented and . . . this fragmentation presents a serious obstacle to scientific growth of the field."

After I have shown that paradigm development is theoretically important and that consensus is a critical precondition to scientific advancement, in the third part of my argument I address the factors that seem to affect the development of scientific paradigms in general and organizational science more specifically. In particular, I explore the dual effects of the value placed on theoretical and methodological diversity and participation. As in other contexts, there are trade-offs involved; this is not to say that the trade-offs should be made in one way rather than another, but that researchers should be conscious of them and their long-run implications for the field.

THE MEASUREMENT AND EFFECTS OF THE
LEVEL OF PARADIGM DEVELOPMENT

As originally operationalized by Lodahl and Gordon (1972), paradigm development refers to the technological uncertainty associated with the production of knowledge in a given scientific field or subspecialty. Technological certainty means that there is a wide agreement on the connections between actions and their consequences (Thompson & Tuden, 1959), or in this case, agreement that certain methods, certain sequences and programs of study, and certain research questions will advance training and knowledge in the given field. Whitley (1982: 335) noted that "the meaning, relevance, and significance of research results for theoretical goals vary in clarity and straightforwardness in different fields. Even where techniques are standardized, the overall significance and importance of results may remain vague and subject to disputes."

Measures and Indicators of the Construct

Lodahl and Gordon (1972) surveyed faculty and department chairs in 20 departments in the fields of physics, sociology, chemistry, and political science, and they asked respondents to rank seven fields (the four surveyed plus biology, economics, and psychology) on the "amount of consensus over paradigms (law, theory, and methodology)" (Lodahl & Gordon, 1973a: 192). These authors found good agreement on the rankings of the fields in terms of their paradigm development. They further found that the social scientists reported less agreement over course content, graduate degree requirements, and the content of survey courses than did those in the physical sciences (Lodahl & Gordon, 1973a: 193).

Surveying to obtain measures of consensus is time consuming: this technique also potentially measures perceived rather than actual level of consensus. Therefore, researchers have developed a number of archival or unobtrusive measures of the level of paradigm development of a field. Price (1970) suggested two measures. One is the proportion of Ph.D. graduates employed in college or university teaching. He argued that this number reflected the place of each branch of learning in society:

> In some fields, such as history and philosophy, most of the embryonic research-
> ers get their Ph.D.'s and then proceed toward some sort of career as a teacher. In
> that case society is paying for students to become teachers to beget students;
> research becomes an epiphenomenon. In the most "scientific" departments at our
> universities only about 20 percent of the Ph.D. output is fed back into education,
> and society gets for its investment . . . also the training of Ph.D.'s who become
> employed in the nonuniversity world. (Price, 1970: 5)

The second measure is the percent of references in published works that were themselves published in the preceding five years, an index that corresponds well with intuitive ideas of hard science, soft science, and nonscience.

Salancik, Staw, and Pondy (1980) reasoned that fields with highly developed paradigms, in which there was more consensus, should be characterized by more efficient communication—less time needed to be spent defining terms or explaining concepts. Lodahl and Gordon (1972: 61) had noted that "the high consensus found in high paradigm fields . . . provides an accepted and shared vocabulary for discussing the content of the field." This idea led to the use of the length of dissertation abstracts (in words), the length of dissertations (in pages), and the proportion of publications in a field that are in the form of articles rather than books (Konrad & Pfeffer, 1990) as indicators of the level of paradigm development (see also Pfeffer & Moore, 1980a).

A high degree of consensus also makes interdependent activity more possible. Thus, another indicator used by Salancik and his colleagues was the length of the longest chain of courses in a department, where a *chain* is defined as a course being a prerequisite to another course, and that course being a prerequisite to another course, and so on. The length of a course chain was highly correlated with communication efficiency, and for the seven fields measured by Lodahl and Gordon, a scale developed from these indicators correlated above .8 with the survey results (Pfeffer & Moore, 1980a: 397). The possibility of coordinating interdependent activity also means that it is easier to organize and manage the work of others on research. Lodahl and Gordon (1972) found that scientists in fields with highly developed paradigms wanted and used more graduate assistants than those in fields with lower levels of paradigm development. Thus, the preference for and use of graduate students and assistants in the research process is another indicator of the level of paradigm development.

The Effects of the Level of Paradigm Development

The level of a scientific field's paradigm development has a number of substantively important effects. Table 3.1 presents a listing of many (although certainly not all) of the consequences of the level of paradigm development. There is evidence that more highly developed fields fare better in the contest for resource allocations, both as distributed by external funding agencies and by the administration within a given college or university. For instance, Lodahl and Gordon (1973a, 1973b) found that the physical sciences were much better funded than the social sciences regarding either university funding or funding from outside sources; this finding held true when department size and quality were taken into account. Such a finding is not surprising because "policy makers and the public can be more certain of results from the more developed sciences" (Lodahl & Gordon, 1973a: 196). Pfeffer and Moore (1980b) found that the level of paradigm development affected both the amount of grants received by departments and the budget allocations to academic departments on two campuses of a large state university. Of course, because research has shown that grants and contracts are an important source of subunit power in universities (Pfeffer & Moore, 1980b; Salancik & Pfeffer, 1974), the fact that external funding advantages translate into internal funding advantages is to be expected. But Pfeffer and Moore's results indicate that paradigm development has an effect on resource allocations, even when departmental power is taken into account. Moreover, because the analysis examined changes over time, it accounted for the possibility of differences in initial funding levels due to inherent differences in the fields.

The level of paradigm development affects not only differences in the level of resource allocations but also the dispersion of such allocations. Lodahl and Gordon (1973a: 197) reported the average level of funding per faculty member in physics, chemistry, sociology, and political science for departments rated as distinguished, strong, good, or adequate plus. They found that "funding is more highly concentrated by quality levels in the physical than in the social sciences. The more distinguished physical science departments enjoy three times the overall funding of lower-quality physical science departments, while the more distinguished social science departments have only one and one-half times the overall funding of their less-

TABLE 3.1 Outcomes Affected by the Level of Paradigm Development

Resource allocations including funding levels of departments
Dispersion in funding across departments; dispersion in talent
Connection between productivity and pay
Connection between wage dispersion and job satisfaction
Connection between social ties and the National Science Foundation's grant allocations
Connection between social ties and journal publications
Connection between social ties and editorial board appointments
Governance of academic departments
Department head turnover or average tenure
Journal rejection rates
Time to publication for research
Power of fields and departments and salary paid to faculty
Working collaboratively rather than alone on research
Cross-citation practices among fields

distinguished counterparts" (1973a: 196). A study of individual reputation in these four fields revealed that "ability, like funding, is more dispersed in the social sciences" (Lodahl & Gordon, 1973a: 198). Thus, there is less concentration of both talent and resources in less paradigmatically developed fields.

Because paradigm development affects the ease and certainty of evaluating scientific research, Konrad and Pfeffer (1990) observed that in fields with more highly developed scientific paradigms, there was a greater effect of academic research productivity on pay. Pfeffer, Leong, and Strehl (1976) earlier had observed that publication was a more important predictor of both departmental prestige and prestige mobility in more paradigmatically developed fields. Beyer and Snipper (1974) reported that the quality of faculty degrees and mean research funds per faculty member were more strongly related to the quality ratings of physical science departments as contrasted with social science departments. Thus, it seems that objective measures of performance translate into status or financial rewards with more certainty in more highly developed fields. This consensus over the evaluation of scientific contributions also affects individual reactions to wage inequality. Pfeffer and Langton (in press) used the 1969 Carnegie survey of university faculty to study the effect that wage dispersion within departments had on members' job satisfaction. They found that a given level of wage inequality had less effect on members' dissatisfaction in departments in high-paradigm fields, in which there was more consensus on standards for evaluation.

If consensually shared beliefs about the nature of knowledge and methods in a field are present, such beliefs will guide decisions on grant allocations and publication. If such technological certainty is absent, decisions are more likely to be made on other, more particularistic bases. One such particularistic basis of allocating resources is sharing an affiliation with the recipient of the allocation. Pfeffer, Salancik, and Leblebici (1976) found that the National Science Foundation's grant allocations were more strongly related to institutional presence on the advisory board in fields that were less paradigmatically developed, controlling for departmental size and quality. Pfeffer, Leong, and Strehl (1977) found that institutional membership on editorial boards had a greater effect on institutional representation in journal publications the less paradigmatically developed the field, even after measures of institutional quality and size were statistically controlled. Beyer (1978) surveyed journal editors in four fields and found some evidence that particularistic criteria (e.g., personal knowledge of the author, institutional affiliation of the author, and position within a professional association) were somewhat more likely to be used in less paradigmatically developed fields.

Yoels (1974), in a study of seven scientific fields, examined the effect of paradigm development on the tendency of editors-in-chief to appoint people from the same institution to their editorial boards. He found that "the selection of editors for social science journals is more subject to the influence of 'particularistic' criteria than for physical and natural science journals" (1974: 271). Yoels's results for editorial board appointments are consistent with the study of grant allocations and journal publications: In each instance, there was evidence that similarity in institutional affiliation affected outcomes more strongly in less paradigmatically developed fields. Another study (Lindsey, 1976) examined the scholarly productivity of members of editorial boards in various journals in psychology, sociology, and social work. Editorial boards were more consistently staffed with more productive scientists in personality and social psychology than in counseling psychology, and psychology, overall, had higher quality (in terms of article publication and citations to their work) editorial board members than did sociology, which, in turn, ranked well ahead of social work. Appointments to prestigious gatekeeping positions were more highly related to scholarly contributions in subspecialties that were more paradigmatically developed. In more developed fields, more universalistic, quality-based measures were employed in allocation decisions.

The level of paradigm development is also related to governance of academic departments. For instance, Lodahl and Gordon (1973a) reported that departments in high-paradigm fields enjoyed more autonomy from the central university administration, in part because of the greater visibility and predictability of consequences of their actions (see also Beyer & Lodahl, 1976). In a study of English universities, Beyer and Lodahl (1976: 120) reported that the authority of the department chair was higher in the more highly developed physical sciences.

The turnover (or average tenure) of academic department heads is related to the department's level of paradigm development. Not surprisingly, there is more turnover, controlling for other factors, in departments with lower levels of paradigm development (Pfeffer & Moore, 1980a: Salancik et al., 1980). Paradigm development is, after all, an indicator of consensus. The greater the consensus and the greater the certainty on the connections between actions and their consequences, the less the conflict, and the less the conflict, the less either voluntary or involuntary turnover in leadership positions there will be.

Paradigm development is related to journal rejection rates. Hargens (1988) analyzed journal rejection rates for 30 scholarly journals over time, to control for the effects of space shortages as contrasted with paradigm development. He gathered data on both submissions and the number of papers published. He argued that if journal rejection rates were a function of space shortages, changes in submission rates should account for changes in journal rejection rates over time. The fact that journal submission rates had a trivially small effect on rejection rates, even though submission rates varied substantially over the period, whereas the independent effect of earlier rejection rates was strong, Hargens interpreted as impugning the claim that variations in rejection rates were caused by differences in space shortages (Hargens, 1988: 140). He concluded that "space shortages affect journals' backlogs rather than their rejection rates" (Hargens, 1988: 141). Journal acceptance rates in the physical and biological sciences were typically in the .6 and higher range, whereas in anthropology, sociology, psychology, and political science journal acceptance rates were typically .2 or lower (Hargens, 1988: 150).

Hargens also found that review times were substantially shorter in the more paradigmatically developed fields. This finding is consistent with Beyer's (1978) findings that time to publication is shorter in journals in the more paradigmatically developed scientific fields. Garvey, Lin, and Nelson (1970) studied lags in the information flow process and the transfer of information from the informal to the formal (journal publication) domain. They found that the elapsed time from the earliest report of research to publication in a journal was much shorter in the physical sciences compared to the social sciences. However, "these longer lags should not be attributed to lethargy or inefficiency on the part of individual social scientists; rather, they are lags which stem from the characteristics of the dissemination system currently functioning in the social sciences" (Garvey et al., 1970: 68). The biggest factor associated with the lag from research results to dissemination was the higher rejection rate in the social science journals. Even for articles that were eventually published in a so-called core journal, in the social sciences some 25 percent had been previously rejected by one or more journals.

Because of the greater consensus in more paradigmatically developed fields and the greater certainty of technology, collaborative research is easier to organize and accomplish in these areas. Just as communication is more efficient and course sequences can be longer in high-paradigm fields, so too is it easier to organize the activities of larger groups of people in a collaborative research venture. In exploring what affects patterns of research collaboration. Pfeffer and Langton (in press) found that the level of paradigm development was the single most important factor affecting whether or not people worked alone on research, with one or two others, or in larger group. Work can be better and more efficiently organized in the presence of greater task certainty. Whitley (1982: 337) noted that "the more predictable are task outcomes, the more work can be systematically planned outside the work process, work roles allocated on a full time basis, tasks highly differentiated and results coordinated and controlled through a formal hierarchy, with an elaborate communication system. . . . Scientific fields where task uncertainty is higher are less likely to formulate and carry out research programmes in a systematic way which directs work across employment organizations."

The level of paradigm development affects researchers' ability to take coordinated action. Beyer and Lodahl (1976: 114) argued that "faculty members who have more consensus can form stronger and more effective coalitions that those in fields rife with internal conflicts." This unity and consensus gives those departments and fields that are more paradigmatically developed more power (Pfeffer, 1992). This power, in turn, can produce higher levels of resource allocations in the form of budgets and higher faculty salaries. Although there is some evidence that within business schools, salaries are higher in fields in which there is more consensus such as finance, accounting, and production and operations management compared to fields such as management and marketing (AACSB, 1992), Moore and Pfeffer (1980) found that the level of a department's scientific paradigm development had no significant effect on faculty acceleration or deceleration in pay advancement at the University of California.

Finally, because paradigm development is associated with power, it affects patterns of citations. In a social network, one would expect to observe more communication from people in positions of lower power directed to people in positions of more power, and people who have more powerful positions should be more central in the structure. In exactly the same way, there is more tendency, when cross-citations are observed, for citations in low-paradigm fields to come from fields that are more paradigmatically developed. For instance, there are many more citations to economics in both the sociology and organizations literature than there are citations in economics to either organizations or sociology. In a 1992 computer-based search of three bibliographic files covering economics, sociology, and psychology, regarding articles addressing topics in any of these fields or organizational behavior, I found the following: in economics there are 105 articles on organizational behavior, 580 on sociology, and 315 on psychology. By contrast, both sociology and psychology files produced more than 1,000 articles referencing economics. If one examines recent issues of any of the leading organizations journals, one would find substantial citations to economic concepts such as transaction costs, efficiency wages, and agency theory, but one would be hard pressed to find a single citation to organizational articles treating these or related topics in any of the major economics journals. Baron and Hannan (in press) reported a 650 percent increase in citations to economists in the *American Sociological Review* and an 1,100 percent increase in the *American Journal of Sociology* between 1970 and 1980, but no further increase since that time. Although their major point is that there is very little impact of either economics on sociology or the reverse, they noted that "data on cross-journal citation patterns . . . show essentially no influence of the sociology journals . . . either in the late 1970s or at present" (Baron & Hannan, in press: 3).

It is evident that the level of a scientific field or academic departments' paradigm development has a number of effects that follow logically from the impact that consensus and e chnological certainty have on behavior. It is also clear that a number of these effects are substantively important. But perhaps the most important effect of paradigm development and the consensus implied by that construct is on the subsequent development of knowledge in a field.

Where Does Organization Studies Stand?

The study of organizations has numerous subspecialties, and these certainly vary in terms of the level of paradigm development. Nevertheless, it appears that, in general, the field of organizational studies is characterized by a fairly low level of paradigm development, particularly as compared to some adjacent social sciences such as psychology, economics, and even political science. In addition to the factors already noted (a high rate of citing other social sciences; low salaries compared to other business school disciplines; high rates of manuscript rejection in the major journals), many previous commentators on the field have noted its pre-paradigmatic state. Zammuto and Connolly (1984: 30) noted the low level of interconnection of materials in textbooks, an indicator of a low level of conceptual connection and interdependence. Webster and Starbuck (1988), who examined only industrial and organizational psychology rather than the field as a whole, argued that the development of knowledge was progressing slowly. They called attention to the fact that the strength of relationships reported in research on a set of topics was getting weaker over time. They also cited a study by Campbell, Daft, and Hulin (1982) that asked respondents to suggest the major research needs during the next 10 to 15 years. The 105 respondents produced some 146 suggestions, of which 106 were unique; they were contributed by only one person. Webster and Starbuck believed that this study indicated there was little consensus in the field about what were the most significant research issues.

Miner's (1984) examination of the relationship between usefulness, scientific validity, and frequency of mention by scholars for 24 theories—he found little connection among these three indicators—was prompted by his concern for the absence of a systematically developing scientific paradigm in the field. Burrell and Morgan's (1979) review of only sociological paradigms documented the theoretical diversity in the field. One might have thought, now more than 10 years after the publication of this influential work, that progress would have been made in evaluating the relative usefulness of these different theoretical foci and winnowing down the avenues to be explored. However, if anything, the field is more fragmented and diverse than it has been. Donaldson (1985) asked whether or not there can be a science of organizations. The debate over theory and method that raged in the early 1980s (e.g., Burrell & Morgan, 1979; Clegg, 1977; Donaldson, 1985) is no closer to resolution today (see, e.g. Marsden, 1993). Indeed, whether or not one wants to achieve a high level of paradigm development, to the extent that implies consensus, is itself open to dispute in the field:

> Their [Burrell and Morgan's] prescription is, in fact, a strategy for achieving plurality and diversity in organizational analysis, a guard against "dominant orthodoxies swamping promising heterodoxies and stunting the growth of innovative theoretical development (Reed, 1985: 184)." (Marsden, 1993: 99)

Proponents of functionalism, postmodernism, critical theory, realism, and many other theoretical approaches today contend vigorously in the study of organizations. Whatever else one might think of this state of affairs, it is, by definition, a state that signifies a field that is fragmented and that does not share the consensus characterizing more paradigmatically developed disciplines.

PARADIGM DEVELOPMENT AND THE ADVANCE OF KNOWLEDGE: POSITIVE FEEDBACK LOOPS

A given level of paradigm development is itself associated with processes that maintain the level of development that exits. In other words, developed fields will tend to advance more consistently and more rapidly, and less developed fields are quite likely to remain comparatively un- or underdeveloped. Fields are unlikely to change their relative positions, but how they do so is an important topic taken up later in this article. At one level, this stability is almost patently obvious. Consider how outcomes affected by paradigm development, listed in Table 3.1, are themselves likely to affect the subsequent development of knowledge in a field.

Fields that are more paradigmatically developed fare better in the contest for resources. Although at one point the National Science Board argued for compensating funding to ensure the development of disciplines in a pre-paradigmatic state, there is little evidence that this advice has been heeded and lots of evidence that in this domain, as in others, the rich get richer. As noted previously, university funding patterns magnify the external inequalities in funding in favor of more paradigmatically developed fields. These resources are not likely to be wasted. Because more developed fields receive a disproportionate share of both external and internal funding, such fields are able to mount more extensive research efforts. These more extensive and better funded research efforts are themselves, other things equal, likely to lead to a greater rate of knowledge accumulation in those fields that are already more paradigmatically developed.

Moreover, the fact that research resources and academic talent are more dispersed in less paradigmatically developed fields also has implications for the rate of development of the field. Lodahl and Gordon (1973b: 82) reported that "quality was not associated as strongly with levels of funding in the social as in the physical sciences. The result was less reinforcement of existing quality patterns." They go on to trace the implications of this resource dispersion for the development of knowledge in these already less paradigmatically developed fields:

> The present diffusion of research support may not be advantageous to the development of the social sciences in universities. It is possible that the best talents are scattered and the funds are following them, but it is also possible that social science funding is being diluted because of . . . the low visibility of consequences in the less developed sciences. (Lodahl & Gordon, 1973b: 82)

Funding may be diffused because particularistic factors operate with more effect and because there is in fact less consensus on quality evaluations in the less paradigmatically developed fields. But whatever the factors producing the results, the diffusion of both talent and research support makes the development of knowledge more difficult. Research support is diffused over a larger number of people of varying skills, so that funds are not allocated to what would necessarily be their highest and best use. And the diffusion of talent makes the benefits of interaction and collaboration more difficult to achieve.

In less paradigmatically developed fields in which there is less collaboration and in which taking coordinated action is more difficult, it is less likely that dense networks of researchers crossing university boundaries can or will emerge. There will be fewer, smaller, and less well-organized "invisible colleges." But the very absence of these more tightly integrated, cross-organizational networks makes it more difficult to resolve technical uncertainty and to develop consensus that extends across organizational boundaries. As a consequence, the very absence of consensus and the social organization it promotes makes developing more consensus and technical certainty difficult and highly problematic.

The fact that productivity is less closely tied to pay in less paradigmatically developed fields means that there is less reinforcement for producing research in these fields. Although pay is not the only, or even perhaps the most important, incentive for academics, the diminished connection between pay and productivity cannot provide less paradigmatically developed fields with an advantage in terms of incentive or motivation. Furthermore, the lower rates of manuscript acceptance and greater delays in publication also reduce the positive reinforcement of research for those in fields with less developed paradigms.

There are other effects of the higher journal rejection rates. On the one hand, an 80 or a 90 percent rejection rate means that those who are able to publish should (and do) feel comparatively advantaged, part of an elite and very select group. On the other hand, these high rejection rates mean that by far the vast majority of research effort in the field is wasted. Even if some of the rejected articles are subsequently published elsewhere, there is often more effort put forth as authors revise and rewrite the papers. For papers that are ultimately accepted by the first journal to which they are submitted, it is almost certain that the authors will experience the revise-and-resubmit process, a consequence of the lack of agreement among referees. "At most major journals in the social sciences, the overall recommendations given by reviewers of the same paper correlate only about .25" (Marwell, 1992: iii). Revising and resubmitting papers is a process that is unknown in many of the physical sciences, and it requires additional expenditure of time and effort not on advancing knowledge but on getting one's scientific results placed in the public domain. The lack of certainty in the technology that links activity to consequences means, inevitably, that much more activity will be wasted in less paradigmatically developed fields. Although there may be less wasted activity on the part of the more talented or experienced members of any academic discipline, it is nevertheless the case that a high rate of rejection speaks to a substantial waste of effort and resources—a waste much less likely to occur in fields in which there is more certainty about what to do and how to do it.

The fact that social ties and other particularistic criteria loom larger in decisions about funding, journal publication, and editorial board appointments in less paradigmatically developed fields means that there is less reinforcement provided for quality work and, instead, there is more reinforcement for engaging in political strategies of career advancement. This differential reinforcement must inevitably lead to wasted effort (from the point of view of the development of knowledge and advancement of the field) in influence activities, a point made with respect to organizational resource allocation more generally by Milgrom and Roberts (1988). Thus, the very reward system in less paradigmatically developed fields tends to divert efforts to social influence and political strategies and does not send a consistent message that productive scholarly effort is the surest way to achieve status and recognition.

The fact that coordination is more difficult in less paradigmatically developed fields and collaborative research is less likely as a consequence means that such fields will tend to lose out on the advantages of social facilitation effects, peer influence, and support in the research and teaching process. Although academic teaching and research are not identical to production work, it is likely to be the case that many of the advantages of teamwork now being discovered in other work settings also operate, at least to some degree, in academic environments. If researchers work in isolation, it is harder for them to achieve the benefits of social support and intellectual cross-stimulation.

The fact that fields with less developed paradigms are more likely to import ideas from fields with highly developed paradigms (witness the importation of economic concepts and theories into sociology, political science, and organizational behavior) means that the boundaries and domain of the less paradigmatically developed fields are more often in contest and being negotiated. A lot of boundary maintenance and definition activity occurs that would otherwise not be required. Moreover, this process, if carried to the extreme, means that the less developed field simply disappears, as it is taken over by its more developed rival. Although this is one way to develop a field of knowledge (to have its questions subsumed by another, more paradigmatically developed specialty), it is a course of development that leaves the research questions of the absorbed field not necessarily answered in the way they would have been had the field retained its boundaries and its academic integrity.

THE IMPORTANCE OF CONSENSUS FOR
KNOWLEDGE DEVELOPMENT

The preceding ideas make the point that the very effects of paradigm development work in a self-reinforcing way to maintain fields at their given comparative level of development. But a more fundamental point should be made; namely, that consensus itself, however achieved, is a vital component for the advancement of knowledge in a field. Without some minimal level of consensus about research questions and methods, fields can scarcely expect to produce knowledge in a cumulative, developmental process.

This argument is neither new nor novel. "Kuhn (1970), Polanyi (1958), Lakatos (1970), and Ziman (1968) have argued convincingly that some degree of consensus is a necessary though not a sufficient condition for the accumulation of knowledge in science or in any other type of intellectual activity" (Cole, 1983: 134). As Stephen Cole (1983: 134-135) argued:

> Accumulation of knowledge can occur only during periods of normal science which are characterized by the adherence of the scientific community to a paradigm. It is only when scientists are committed to a paradigm and take it as the starting point for additional research that progress can be made. Without agreement on fundamentals, scientists will not be able to build on the work of others and will spend all their time debating assumptions and first principles. . . . Most new and contradictory ideas prove to be of little value. If scientists were too willing to accept every unorthodox theory, method, or technique, the established consensus would be destroyed, and the intellectual structure of science would become chaotic. Scientists would be faced with a multitude of conflicting and unorganized theories and would lack research guidelines and standards.

Webster and Starbuck (1988: 95) noted that an absence of consensus about theories fostered "divergent findings and incomparable studies that claim to be comparable." They argued that theories should play a stabilizing role in the social sciences, as they do in the physical sciences, organizing the collection of data and interpretations of the world, and they should not be discarded too readily or replaced for reasons of fad or fashion. They noted:

> As much as correctness, theories need the backing of consensus and consistency. When scientists agree among themselves to explain phenomena in terms of baseline theories, they project their findings into shared perceptual frameworks that reinforce the collective nature of research by facilitating communication and comparison and by defining what is important or irrelevant. (Webster and Starbuck, 1988: 127)

Whitley (1982: 338) noted that in fields with greater task uncertainty, "local considerations and exigencies will have more impact on the nature of the work carried out and how it is done." Although local adaptation may be useful in some circumstances, it is likely to lead to proliferation of concepts and methods that make the development of knowledge difficult. As Zammuto and Connolly (1984: 32) noted, doctoral students "are confronted with a morass of bubbling and sometimes noxious literature. Theories presented are incompatible, research findings inconsistent." This lack of agreement leads to difficulties in doctoral training, including high rates of attrition, a long period of time needed to complete the degree; and problems in training doctoral students in distinguishing good from bad theory and methods.

In the study of organizations, it is almost as if consensus is systematically avoided. Journal editors and reviewers seem to seek novelty, and there are great rewards for coining a new term. The various divisions of the Academy of Management often give awards for formulating "new concepts" but not for studying or rejecting concepts that are already invented.

WHERE DOES CONSENSUS COME FROM?

Why is it that some fields are more paradigmatically developed and have more consensus than others? One answer to this question, which undoubtedly has some empirical validity, is that there are simply inevitable, irreducible differences across scientific areas of inquiry that are inherent in the very nature of the phenomena being studied and the knowledge of these different subjects. For instance, it may be that people, the subject of organizational science, sociology, and psychology, are simply more unpredictable and difficult to explain than the behavior of either light waves or physical particles or the course of chemical reactions. This answer, however, does not explain the difference in paradigm development between, for instance, economics and either sociology or organizational studies. Economic activity is activity undertaken by individuals, and there is little evidence that such activity is either more predictable or easier to comprehend than the subject matter of organizational science. Moreover, there are differences even across subspecialties of organizational studies. For example, it is my impression that population ecology is characterized by much more consensus either than the field as a whole or than most other topic domains within it. There is enormous consistency in terms of the methods used (event-history analysis, most often using the computer program RATE), the dependent variables studied, the literature that is cited, and most important, on what are judged to be the next important problems to work on (e.g., Carroll, 1988). This is the one branch of organization studies in which one can frequently hear (as I have) that it is important to get research done and published quickly, because, otherwise, in a year or so, it will be made obsolete by what other researchers are doing. This time urgency, because of the predictable advance of the domain of inquiry, is one sign of a highly developed paradigm.

As one who has been a participant-observer of business schools specifically and universities more generally for some time, it seems clear to me that consensus is, at least to some degree, created and imposed in those fields or subspecialties where it exists. It is imposed in several ways.

Cole (1983: 137-138), describing how science works generally, noted:

> One of the primary mechanisms through which consensus is maintained is the practice of vesting authority in elites. . . . Generally, the stars of a discipline occupy the main gatekeeping roles. . . . For the gatekeepers to establish consensus, they must have legitimated authority. . . . Legitimacy is granted by virtue of one's being a star. If the gatekeeper positions are filled by "average" scientists, it will be difficult for the authority exercised to be granted legitimacy.

The Academy of Management has, for good reasons, intentionally constituted itself as a representative body, and representativeness is a treasured value of the organization. Elitism is shunned. Compare the editorial boards of any of the Academy journals to the editorial board of *Econometrica,* for instance, in terms of the number of different institutions and the institutional prestige represented. Similar comparisons in the officers of professional associations will reveal the same, simple fact: that the Academy and other organizations and journals involved in the discipline of organization studies are substantially less elitist and more egalitarian, and they have spread the distribution of power much more widely than one will observe in more paradigmatically developed physical science fields or even economics. The explicit incorporation of representativeness when slates of officers or editorial board members are selected—where representativeness is defined in terms of geography, public/private college or university, field of specialization, gender, career stage and academic rank, theoretical perspective, and academic achievement—as is often done in this field, may have a number of desirable effects, but building consensus on a paradigm is not likely to be one of them.

Consensus is enforced when members of a field develop a set of methodological standards and ensure that these are consistently maintained. In the study of organizations at present, a good idea can obviate obvious empirical shortcomings. For instance, although some researchers of the effects of personality on organizational behavior adhere to methodological rigor, many authors do not (see, e.g., Davis-Blake & Pfeffer, 1989). In fields with highly developed paradigms, researchers also prefer some issues and points of view rather than others. The difference in this case is their commitment to enforce a set of research standards that are more central to the definition of science in those fields, more agreed upon, and zealously maintained.

Members of high-paradigm fields enforce both theoretical and methodological conformity. They do this by reserving the most desirable places only for those who conform to the disciplinary orthodoxy and criticizing, regardless of their power or the validity of their ideas, those who depart from the established paths. For instance, shortly after the election of Bill Clinton to the presidency in 1992, Robert Reich was appointed to the team advising the president-elect on economic policies. This appointment enraged conventional economists, and an article in the *New York Times* provides a good illustration of how a discipline maintains consensus and enforces its standards:

> Although the general approach of Mr. Reich is increasingly shared by others, his specific work has nevertheless been criticized by trained economists, mostly on the ground that he is a lawyer, not a Ph.D. in economics, and his insights lack the rigor and precision that economists provide through their training in mathematics and economic theory.
>
> That criticism has been one reason that Mr. Reich . . . has failed to get a tenured professorship at the Kennedy School, where he has been a lecturer . . . for more than a decade, under a contract renewed every few years . . . the criticism of Mr. Reich's credentials . . . has intensified with his appointment last week as chief of the economics transition team. (Uchitelle, 1992: 17)

Michael Piore (Doeringer & Piore, 1971; Piore & Sabel, 1984) holds a somewhat similar position in the discipline because of his different use of methodology and different theoretical approach. Although he is a tenured member of the economics department at MIT, many economists in private conversations maintain that he isn't really an economist—regardless of their opinion of his work—because he doesn't think like one.

Contrast these examples with organization studies. The contents of the July 1992 special issue of the *Academy of Management Review,* although perhaps an extreme example of the proliferation of theoretical perspectives ranging from feminism to conversation analysis and radical humanism, make the point that the field not only has, to use the current political parlance, a very large "tent," but a tent in which fundamentally any theoretical perspective or methodological approach is as valid as any other offer. Those who study organizations energetically seek out ideas, perspectives, and techniques from numerous allied social sciences, the humanities, economics, anthropology, political science, psychology, and with the current play given to deconstruction and conversation analysis, from linguistics and English.

My argument is, at its heart, a very simple one: A substantial amount of the variation in the level of paradigm development is a consequence of the social structure, culture, and power relations that characterize the discipline (i.e., how it is organized and the factors that create and perpetuate that organization). Here, again, there are forces at work that tend toward stability of whatever system is in place. A field in which control is concentrated in the hands of a comparatively small elite is one in which power is much more institutionalized and control by the dominant paradigm is quite likely to be perpetuated. By contrast, an area of inquiry characterized by diffuse perspectives, none of which has the power to institutionalize its dominance, is one in which consensus is likely to remain elusive and the dispersion in resources, rewards, and activity will be great.

CONCLUSION

There is evidence that disciplines can change in their level of paradigm development, in spite of the many self-reinforcing feedback loops described in this paper. When Lodahl and Gordon   972) conducted their survey, political science was the least paradigmatically developed field. But over time, actually beginning in the 1960s, political science evolved. Adopting many of the methods and theoretical assumptions of economics, political science became noninstitutional, as researchers emphasized theories that are (a) reductionist (behavior is seen as the aggregate consequence of individual action); (b) utilitarian (behavior is presumed to result from calculated self-interest); (c) functionalist (history and the passage of time tend to produce appropriate and efficient outcomes); and (d) instrumentalist (the allocation of resources and decision making are seen as the central foci of interest) (March & Olsen, 1989: 3). Those in political science have developed a much more coherent, consensually shared paradigm, and it is now probably one of the more paradigmatically developed social sciences.

This evolution may have come at a cost, at least according to some theorists. As the evolution was unfolding and the rational choice paradigm was gaining increasing preeminence, Ball (1976: 172) argued for "being tenacious in defending and tolerant in criticizing research programs." He noted that in response to Kuhn, critics "emphasized the narrowing of focus and the 'dogmatism' of 'normal science.' If that is what a normal or mature science looks like, then political scientists should want no part of it. Paradigms . . . tyrannize; and so political scientists committed to free inquiry should resist all blandishments to make theirs a 'normal' science" (Ball, 1976: 153). Ball's pleas fell largely on deaf ears as the discipline evolved in the directions already mentioned.

The question for organizational science is whether the field can strike an appropriate balance between theoretical tyranny and an anything-goes attitude, which seems to be more characteristic of the present state. Those who bemoan the present condition of presumed positivist hegemony (e.g., Marsden, 1993) need only to consider economics or political science, adjacent social sciences whose members are interested in many of the same things, to see how truly open and unstructured organizational theory really is.

It is crucial to distinguish among disagreement over (a) the substantive research questions that are considered to be important, or the goals of knowledge development in the field; (b) the ways in which relevant variables should be measured and modeled; (c) the methods used to collect and analyze relevant data; (d) the theoretical models of behavior used to guide the measurement process, to analyze the data, and to comprehend the phenomena of interest; and (e) the rules for determining which approach to each of these four domains is more or less fruitful. A field characterized by disagreements over all five areas will almost certainly be unable to make progress of any consequence. Theoretical and methodological diversity may be adaptive as long as there is some agreement over fundamental goals and on a set of rules to winnow the measures, methods, and theories on the basis of accumulated evidence. In the study of organizations, there appears to have been more agreement on these issues in the past than there is at present, when almost every aspect of the research process is contested.

A diversity in ideas and in methodology can be useful to the field as long as the diversity can be resolved at some point. The question is whether the social structure and organization of the field encourage resolution of diverse ideas or the continued particularistic advancement of separate agendas, often with explicitly political undertones. At present, I believe that the field encourages the development and advancement of differences and separate agendas rather than attempts at integration or resolution. More than 10 years ago, I (Pfeffer, 1982: 1) argued that "the domain of organization theory is coming to resemble more of a weed patch than a well-tended garden. Theories . . . proliferate along with measures, terms, concepts, and research paradigms. It is often difficult to discern in what direction knowledge of organizations is progressing." The situation has not changed, and, if anything, there are now more diversity of ideas and measures and more contention over the rules for organizational science than there were a decade ago.

Richard Marsden (1993: 101) noted:

> Paradigmatic change is not a purely cerebral affair, but depends on the outcome of political conflicts between custodians and opponents of a paradigm. Resistance to change is the norm; breakthroughs typically occur when the hegemony of the "invisible college" is broken.

But Marsden's unit of analysis needs to be extended outside the boundaries of the discipline to adjacent fields of inquiry. In this context, the contest is not just within the various branches of organizational science; it is between organizational science and related disciplines. The hegemony of the invisible college that may be broken is the hegemony of those who have fostered theoretical dissensus.

It already seems clear that the 1990s are not going to be a great decade for higher education in general or for business schools in particular. In state after state, budgets for colleges and universities are being severely constrained, and tuition, in both public and private schools, is rising rapidly. Business school applications are down some 20 percent this academic year and have fallen in the past several years, although not as dramatically. After all the articles in the popular press criticizing business schools and business education, and after the decades of truly phenomenal growth, it is scarcely surprising that the halcyon days are over.

I think we know two things about political processes: (a) power is more likely to be exercised when resources are scarce (e.g., Salancik & Pfeffer, 1974) and (b) unity of perspective and the ability to take collective action with ease provide an important source of power (Pfeffer, 1992). It seems fair to forecast that contests for resources are likely to increase in universities and in schools of administration in the coming years. It also seems reasonable to suggest that the theoretical and methodological diversity and disagreements that characterize the study of organizations are disadvantages rather than advantages in this coming struggle.

Do researchers in the organizational sciences have to become like their competitors to survive and prosper? Must they, to use a phrase of one commentator on this argument, follow the lead of economics and mutilate the phenomena they are studying in order to compete and survive?

Disagreement in theoretical approaches and even in methodology will not prove detrimental as long as there is some agreement about what the fundamental questions or issues are and as long as there are some agreed upon ways of resolving theoretical and methodological disputes. At the moment neither condition holds. There is no commitment to a unifying set of research goals or questions being pursued by varied means. There is no agreement as to whether the field should serve the powerful, presumably business and government interests, or the powerless. There is little apparent agreement about how to resolve the controversies among competing paradigms—not only disagreement about which one is correct or useful, but disagreement about how to even go about figuring this out. Because of these fundamental disagreements, debates about basic epistemological issues, even though useful at one level, never seem to produce much resolution. Rather, they are repeated periodically, often covering the same ground.

It would be interesting and useful to study the history of related fields such as political science and economics to understand exactly how paradigm consensus was achieved. My sense is that such consensus was developed by a group of individuals forming a dense network of connections and unified view, who then intentionally and systematically took over positions of power and imposed their views, at times gradually and at times surreptitiously, on the field. There seems to be nothing in the natural order of things that suggests that mathematical rigor should be valued over empirical richness or realism. Rather, the criteria, the status hierarchy, and the enforcement of rules were and are very much political processes.

Many researchers entered the field of organizations because of its theoretical and methodological openness and pluralism. But anything carried to an extreme can be harmful, and given the current climate, downright dangerous. Without a recommitment to a set of fundamental questions—perhaps pursued in a multitude of ways—and without working through a set of processes or rules to resolve theoretical disputes and debates, the field of organizational studies will remain ripe for either a hostile takeover from within or from outside. In either case, much of what is distinctive, and much of the pluralism that is so valued, will be irretrievably lost.

REFERENCES

American Assembly of Collegiate Schools of Business (AACSB). 1992. Annual salary survey: The recession hits home. *Newsline,* 22 (Winter): 1-3.

Ball, T. 1976. From paradigms to research programs: Toward a post-Kuhnian political science. *American Journal of Political Science,* 20: 151-177.

Baron, J. N., & Hannan, M. T. In press. The impact of economics on contemporary sociology. *Journal of Economic Literature.*

Beyer, J. M. 1978. Editorial policies and practices among leading journals in four scientific fields. *Sociological Quarterly,* 19: 68-88.

Beyer, J. M., & Lodahl, T. M. 1976. A comparative study of patterns of influence in United States and English universities. *Administrative Science Quarterly,* 21: 104-129.

Beyer, J. M., & Snipper, R. 1974. Objective versus subjective indicators of quality in graduate education. *Sociology of Education,* 47:541-557.

Burrell, G., & Morgan, G. 1979. *Sociological paradigms and organizational analysis.* London: Heinemann.

Campbell, J. P., Daft, R. L. & Hulin, C. L. 1982. *What to study: Generating and developing research questions.* Beverly Hills, CA: Sage.

Carroll, G. R. 1988. Organizational ecology in theoretical perspective. In G. R. Carroll (Ed.), *Ecological models of organizations:* 1-6. Cambridge, MA. Ballinger.

Clegg, S. R. 1977. Power, organization theory, Marx and critique. In S. R. Clegg & D. Dunkerly (Eds.), *Critical issues in organizations:* 21-40. London: Routledge & Kegan Paul.

Cole, S. 1993. The hierarchy of the sciences? *American Journal of Sociology,* 89: 111-139.

60   DEBATES

Davis-Blake, A., & Pfeffer, J. 1989. Just a mirage: The search for dispositional effects in organi-
zational research. *Academy of Management Journal,* 14: 385-400.
Doeringer, P., & Piore, M. 1971. *Internal labor markets and manpower analysis,* Lexington,
MA: Heath.
Donaldson, L. 1985. *In defence of organization theory: A reply to the critics.* Cambridge,
England: Cambridge University Press.
Garvey, W. D., Lin, N., & Nelson, C. E. 1970. Some comparisons of communication activities in
the physical and social sciences. In C. E. Nelson & D. K. Pollock (Eds.), *Communication
among scientists and engineers:* 61-84. Lexington, MA: Heath.
Hargens, L. L. 1988. Scholarly consensus and journal rejection rates. *American Sociological
Review,* 53: 139-151.
Konrad, A. M., & Pfeffer, J. 1990. Do you get what you deserve? Factors affecting the relation-
ship between productivity and pay. *Administrative Science Quarterly,* 35: 258-285.
Kuhn, T. S. 1970. *The structure of scientific revolutions.* (2nd ed.). Chicago: University of
Chicago Press.
Lakatos, I. 1970. Falsification and the methodology of research programmes. In I. Lakatos &
A. Musgrave (Eds.), *Criticism and the growth of knowledge:* 91-96. Cambridge, En-
gland: Cambridge University Press.
Lindsey, D. 1976. Distinction, achievement, and editorial board membership. *American Psy-
chologist,* 31: 799-804.
Lodahl, J. B., & Gordon, G. 1972. The structure of scientific fields and the functioning of univer-
sity graduate departments. *American Sociological Review,* 37: 57-72.
Lodahl, J. B., & Gordon, G. 1973a. Differences between physical and social sciences in univer-
sity graduate departments. *Research in Higher Education,* 1: 191-213.
Lodahl, J. B., & Gordon, G. 1973b. Funding the sciences in university departments. *Educational
Record,* 54: 74-82.
March, J. G., & Olsen, J. P. 1989. *Rediscovering Institutions: The organizational basis of poli-
tics.* New York: Free Press.
Marsden, R. 1993. The politics of organizational analysis. *Organization Studies,* 14: 93-124.
Marwell, G. 1992. Let's train reviewers: Editor's comment. *American Sociological Review,* 57:
iii-iv.
Milgrom, P., & Roberts, J. 1988. An economic approach to influence activities in organizations.
American Journal of Sociology, 94 (Supplement): S154-S179.
Miner, J. B. 1984. The validity and usefulness of theories in an emerging organizational science.
Academy of Management Review, 9: 296-306.
Moore, W. L., & Pfeffer, J. 1980. The relationship between department power and faculty careers
on two campuses: The case for structural effects on faculty salaries. *Research in Higher
Education,* 13: 291-306.
Pfeffer, J. 1982. *Organizations and organization theory.* Marshfield, MA: Pitman.
Pfeffer, J. 1992. *Managing with power: Politics and influence in organizations.* Boston: Harvard
Business School Press.
Pfeffer, J., & Langton, L. In press. The effect of wage dispersion on satisfaction, productivity,
and working collaboratively: Evidence from college and university faculty. *Administra-
tive Science Quarterly.*
Pfeffer, J., Leong, A., & Strehl, K. 1976. Publication and prestige mobility of university depart-
ments in three scientific disciplines. *Sociology of Education,* 49: 212-218.
Pfeffer, J., Leong, A., & Strehl, K. 1977. Paradigm development and particularism: Journal publication in three scientific disciplines. *Social Forces,* 55: 938-951.

Pfeffer, J., & Moore, W. L. 1980a. Average tenure of academic department heads: The effects of paradigm, size, and departmental demography. *Administrative Science Quarterly,* 25: 387-406.

Pfeffer, J., & Moore, W. L. 1980b. Power in university budgeting: A replication and extension. *Administrative Science Quarterly,* 25: 637-653.

Pfeffer, J., Salancik, G. R., & Leblebici, H. 1976. The effect of uncertainty on the use of social influence in organizational decision making. *Administrative Science Quarterly,* 21: 227-245.

Piore, M., & Sabel, C. 1984. *The second industrial divide.* New York: Basic Books.

Polanyi, M. 1958. *Personal knowledge.* London: Routledge & Kegan Paul.

Price, D. J. de Solla. 1970. Citation measures of hard science, soft science, technology, and nonscience. In C. E. Nelson & D. K. Pollock (Eds.), *Communication among scientists and engineers:* 3-22. Lexington, MA: Heath.

Reed, M. I. 1985. *Redirections in organizational analysis.* London: Tavistock.

Salancik, G. R., & Pfeffer, J. 1974. The bases and use of power in organizational decision making: The case of a university. *Administrative Science Quarterly,* 19: 453-473.

Salancik, G. R., Staw, B. M., & Pondy, L. R. 1980. Administrative turnover as a response to unmanaged organizational interdependence. *Academy of Management Journal,* 23: 422-437.

Thompson, J. D., & Tuden, A. 1959. Strategies, structures and processes of organizational decision. In J. D. Thompson, P. B. Hammond, R. W. Hawkes, B. H. Junker, & A. Tuden (Eds.), *Comparative studies in administration:* 195-216. Pittsburgh: University of Pittsburgh Press.

Uchitelle, L. 1992. Clinton's economics point man. *New York Times,* November 21: 17.

Webster, J., & Starbuck, W. H. 1988. Theory building in industrial and organizational psychology. In C. L. Cooper & I. Robertson (Eds.), *International review of industrial and organizational psychology 1988:* 93-138. London: Wiley.

Whitley, R. 1982. The establishment and structure of the sciences as reputational organizations. In N. Elias, H. Martins, & R. Whitley (Eds.), *Scientific establishments and hierarchies:* 313-357. Dordrecht, Holland: D. Reidel.

Yoels, W. C. 1974. The structure of scientific fields and the allocation of editorships on scientific journals: Some observations on the politics of knowledge. *Sociological Quarterly,* 15: 264-276.

Zammuto, R. F., & Connolly, T. 1984. Coping with disciplinary fragmentation. *Organizational Behavior Teaching Review,* 9: 30-37.

Ziman, J. 1968. *Public knowledge.* Cambridge, England: Cambridge University Press.

4

Style as Theory[1]

JOHN VAN MAANEN
Sloan School of Management, MIT

A small but significant portion of writing in the still expanding domain of organizational research and theory is devoted to debunking the essentialist and (allegedly) scientifically grounded ideas and programs of our peers. Some of my writing, including this effort, falls within this tradition. Debunking the would-be towers of power in our field bears a loose similarity to the work performed by voluntary firefighters. The fire of interest here is a call to draw in our topical and theoretical borders, and the intellectual incendiary is none other than Jeffrey Pfeffer whose 1992 Distinguished Scholar Address to the Organization Theory Division of the Academy of Management started a modest little blaze that was followed by my own 1993 Distinguished Scholar Address to the same group which was designed to put it out. A stroke of luck too, for what better theorist could a confessed anti-theorist wish to follow and what better foil for debunking could have been sent forward than an acknowledged desperado of the podium like Jeffrey, who courts controversy like a bear in search of honey.[2] In what follows, I recreate in writing what I first committed to speech.

Jeff's talk—later published in revised form as "Barriers to the Advance of Organizational Science: Paradigm Development as a Dependent Variable" (Pfeffer 1993a)—represents a rather shrill plea for the development of a firm and consensually approved paradigm to drive organizational theory and

From "Style as Theory," by John van Maanen, 1995, *Organization Science, 6*(1), pp. 133-143. 1995, The Institute of Management Sciences. Reprinted with permission.

research. Without much hesitation, Jeff argues that we would be wise to adopt economics as a role model for our many splendored—but unfortunately splintered—field. Economics is, after all, a proud and powerful discipline that has gone places. In a chilling segment of his address, a Stalinist purge of our low-consensus field is considered whereby we might invest authority in a few, well-published elites within our ranks who would be willing if not eager to institutionalize some topical and methodological strictures to guide our work. A high-consensus paradigm—or better yet, a Pfefferdigm—could thus be imposed. The result would be an increase in our prestige, power and pay.

The image Jeff uses to portray the field in its current state of play is pastoral but wild. There are too many of us doing too many different things. Our tangled theories do not fit neatly on any intellectual map. We do not value the systematic collection of data on a limited number of issues. Agreement across theory groups is unlikely and, given the way we structure ourselves, probably impossible; so the resources and rewards that flow from external sources to those in the field remain both modest and hotly contested. In brief, we represent something of an overgrown garden sorely in need of attention: ". . . there are thousands of flowers blooming but nobody does any manicuring or tending" (Pfeffer 1993b, p. 1). Specifically, we need to prune, pare and discard certain research topics and agendas that are, in Jeff's view, going nowhere.

I suspect I am a weed in Jeffrey's dreamtime garden. I am therefore a candidate for pruning, paring and discarding. But whether I am a tulip, wildflower or weed, I want to suggest here that this sour view of our field is—to be gentle—insufferably smug; pious and orthodox; philosophically indefensible; extraordinarily naive as to how science actually works; theoretically foolish, vain and autocratic; and—still being gentle—reflective of a most out-of-date and discredited father-knows-best version of knowledge, rhetoric and the role theory plays in the life of any intellectual community.

Jeff is not, of course, alone in suggesting that we overplay our science hand and underplay what other approaches to knowledge might teach us. Yet, just as the Enlightenment philosophers were a trifle premature in their pronouncement that science had triumphed over mere belief (doxa), those who would push for paradigmatic purity or unity in our field conveniently ignore the rhetorical elements that underpin and ultimately undermine their own efforts. More to the point, they ignore what has been called the linguistic turn (alternatively, the interpretive or textual turn) taken by a number of scholars within and across a variety of disciplines in the arts, humanities and sciences. This turn promotes language in the scheme of things and reverses the relationship typically thought to obtain between a description and the object of description.[3]

The ordinary or commonsensical view holds that the objects of the world are logically prior and thus limit and provide the measure of any description. Vocabulary, text, representation of any intendedly nonfictional sort must be constrained by fact. But as some theorists now realize (however much they may complain), language is auditioning for an a priori role in the social and material world. Moreover, it is a role that carries constitutional force, bringing facts into consciousness and therefore being. No longer then is something like an organization or, for that matter, an atom or quark thought to come first while our understandings, models or representations of an organization, atom or quark come second. Rather, our representations may well come first, allowing us to see selectively what we have described.

This reversal is visible in organizational fields and is slowly worming its way into our classrooms, meetings, literatures and theories.[4] It is, to be sure, controversial, for it suggests that taken-for-granted ideas about empirical evidence, objectivity, reason, truth, coherence, validity, measurement and fact no long provide great comfort or direction. If such concepts are language-based, they are relative, not absolute. They are therefore contestable in whatever form they appear. What drives contestation (and the resulting polarization) is of course the perception that one's discipline, sub-discipline or sub-sub-discipline is under attack. That someone else is defining the field in such a way that one's own work is being denied legitimacy. This is certainly my response to the "I'm-a-Pfeffer, you're-a-Pfeffer, wouldn't-you-like-to-be-a-Pfeffer-too" view of the world Jeff presented us with last year. But it cuts both ways. When I call into question certain narrative devices that characterize a good deal of organizational theory writings, some in my audience will applaud and feel good while others will fall silent and feel like endangered species.

My remarks—very much like Jeff's—must then be understood as moves in a language game, an understandable and necessary effort to defend my work, to create a space for what I do against what I take to be the shortsighted, overly confident and more (or less) entrenched views of others. It is in this sense that staking out a theoretical position is unavoidably a rhetorical act. Rhetoric is always with us. It is with us not only at the point of paradigmatic clashes where it is so obvious but with us everywhere and always for the simple reason that our understandings of the world are put forth in black and white, as ink on a page. Theory is a matter of words, not worlds; of maps, not territories; of representations, not realities. As much as we might like to believe that hard fact and cold logic will support our claims and carry the day, there is no escape from rhetoric: from the informal, hidden arguments carried in texts, to the figures of speech, the metaphors, the tropes and the appeals to good sense or tradition or authority made by writers to support their claims.[5]

TEXTWORK AND PERSUASION

One problem (of many) at the moment in our organizational field(s) is that
most of us are trained in a logocentric tradition of empirical science with its
count-and-classify conventions and taken-for-granted notions of progress.
We display more than a little physics envy when we reach out for covering
laws, causes, operational definitions, testable hypotheses and so forth. Our
reading practices are governed for the most part by a correspondence presumption leading us to trust text as a more or less transparent guide to the
world "out there." We cultivate and teach a writing style of nonstyle that values limited metaphor, simplicity and a formal, if not mathematical, precision.
Much of our writing is washed by a thick spray of claimed objectivity since
artful delights and forms are seen by many if not most writers (and readers) in
the field to interfere with the presentation of what is actually there in a given
social world.[6]

The result is that we elevate the "spare," "systematic," "elegant," "un-
adorned," "essential," "parsimonious" treatments of organizational life
based on concepts that are said to transcend mere textuality. How organizational worlds are represented in print is not thought to be much of an issue.
Writing is seen as a secondary or mop-up activity in our professional pursuits. This is, I think, a mistake and overlooks what might be learned if we
were to take the textuality of our organizational theories and facts more seriously: What might we learn if we were to explore the terra incognita of our
literary practices?

Such an exploration would involve the close examination of just what we
do as organizational theorists. In this regard, I follow Geertz's (1974) quite
sensible remark that if one wants to know what a science is—or, for that matter, what any scholarly field amounts to—one must begin by examining what
the people in the field do. This is a post-Kuhnian perspective on the nature of
our work and differs little from any ethnographically sensitive approach to
technical work.[7]

What we do as organizational theorists is, of course, spend enormous
amounts of time reading and writing. Some of us produce both discourse and
text we explicitly label theory whose purpose is to communicate our understandings of organization to particular audiences. Communication however
implies that we are also and necessarily concerned with persuading our readers—the more the better—that not only do we have something to say but that
what we have to say is correct, important and well worth heeding. The discourse we produce as organization theory has an action component which
seeks to induce belief among our readers. Our writing is then something of a
performance with a persuasive aim. In this sense, when our theories are well

received they do practical work. Rather than mirror reality, our theories help generate reality for readers.

How does such a reality-building process work in print? This is not a simple matter. To approach it from a textual angle requires looking at how well-received theories are written, and this means looking at—rather than through—our more persuasive writings. Putting theory in print is a literary performance; an activity involving the use of language whose methods are ways of writing through which certain identifiable reader responses are produced. The materials of such a performance are words, phrases, sentences, paragraphs, articles, books and so forth. The question at hand, then, is what literary methods—the particular compositional and performative characteristics of a text(s)—are associated with a certifiable example(s) of influential organizational theory?

THE ALLEGORIC BREACHING OF KARL WEICK

To begin to answer this question requires a specific case of persuasive theorizing. Any case might do but my strategy here is to focus on what I take to be a deviant case of theorizing, deviant in the sense that the narrative and rhetorical practices used to produce the examined body of work appear to violate some of our received and more or less unquestioned notions of just how and what organizational texts (and theories) are convincing. Alas, I must leave it to others to follow with careful readings of other—perhaps more generic or conventional—theorists in the field.

My exemplar is Karl Weick who, over the years, has produced a substantial body of work. It is a body of work I have tried to enter and understand (not always successfully). His writings have the advantage of being familiar to most readers of organization theory because so many of them are on the required reading lists of Ph.D. programs in the field and it is surely the case that students cannot consider themselves organizational scholars of any depth or breadth without having read at least some of Karl's work. My focus is on the compositional characteristics of what I take to be the more successful (i.e., persuasive) features of Karl's work. I am not indifferent to content but my purpose here is to push for a different way of understanding theory by looking at what is conventionally ignored: the textual aspects of such work.

The reception history of Karl's work is a matter of record. It has been widely reviewed, summarized, quoted, borrowed, reprinted and elaborated on. It is, in general, seen by those in and out of the organizational theory field as insightful and innovative. Reviewers characteristically praise the work but not always in the same terms or without reservation. A set of frequently used receptive epithets include terms like "subtle," "cunning," "brilliant," "wandering," "multi-faceted," "relativistic," "nonconforming," "artistic," "airy," "metaphorical," "evasive," "fragmentary," "cryptic," "evocative," and "suggestive." The issue to explore now is what compositional practices appear to produce such effects among readers?[8]

Before pushing on, however, I must say that I am not out to valorize or idolize the Weickian style, although I am most certainly a fan. My intent is to look carefully at what most of us would call a maverick style of theorizing—quite different from that celebrated by Jeffrey Pfeffer—and identify what I think is a distinctive and altogether useful way of putting theory into print. It is a way of theorizing that might well pass unnoticed if we did not look at its textual features because, at least in this case, theory and style are closely aligned. One carries the other.

In other words (my words), a good deal of the scholarly appeal of Karl Weick's writing and hence his theory rests on its more or less unique style. It is a style that combines allegory and breaching. Allegory represents the idea that a coherent spiritual or abstract (in this case, theoretical or general) message is being conveyed in writing through the narration of a most concrete set of events. It is near symbolism as a literary form but more focused and controlled. Breaching carries the idea that the writing breaks with conventional textual practices in the field in which it enters. In this case, Weick's writings stand apart from most organization theory writings in identifiable ways. Four characteristics of Karl's work back up my use of the allegoric breaching label.[9] In no particular order, they follow.

Essay Form

Weick is something of a confessed essayist. This can be seen most readily in many of his articles but is also visible in some of the chapters of *The Social Psychology of Organizing* (Weick 1969, 1979; both editions). The essay is of course a literary format more linked to art than science. By working in such a form Weick breaches the generic recognizability of normal organizational theorizing with its relentless summaries of past research, propositional chants, pachyderm-like solemnity and off-the-shelf textual forms (i.e., introduction, hypotheses, methods, findings, conclusions). Few plain writers of referential prose in organizational theory commit themselves and their readers to such a blatantly literary (artsy) style.

But Weick does so with glee and seemingly takes pride in the nonlinear possibilities of the essay form. Meanderings, detours, distractions are common in his writing. A personalized author is also put forth as is characteristic of the essay: the use of "I" and the refusal to cloak a writing in anonymity. While not obviously self-referencing (or self-effacing), it is difficult for readers to forget they are reading Weick while engaged with his work. This may well be a distinguishing feature of convincing theory texts since we stubbornly link pure theory with particular names like Perrow and March or the fashionable French like Foucault or Bourdieu. When theory becomes anonymous, it loses style and slides into a well-worn and recognizable genre such as a research report, an empirical monograph, an instruction manual, an article for a specific journal or a textbook where standard formats, topics, terminology and methods play large roles.

The essay is anything but an overtly systematic presentation of an author's views. This stylistic feature is sometimes treated as a bothersome defect by some readers, a defect that can be overcome only when others extract or cull the analytic jewels out of a messy piece of work, the jewels being the detachable theoretical contributions to be found in the work. Beginning students and textbook writers are perhaps the most likely to be both puzzled and disturbed with Weick for the apparent disorder that comes kit and caboodle with his essayist style. Yet, it is altogether possible that the lack of a system and the appearance of a tidy order in his writing is downright central to the point, purpose and value of his work.

To take an example of all this, consider a recent paper with the most Weickian title, "Cosmology Episodes in Organizations: Young Men and Fire and the Mann Gulch Disaster" (Weick 1993a). The paper is called an essay in the first sentence. A section title does not appear until page 7 (called "Sensemaking in Mann Gulch") and another five pages go by before another title appears ("Social Structure in Mann Gulch"). The last section head appears on page 15, "From Vulnerability to Resilience." Three headings, 27 pages. No ordinary introduction, no generic section titles, no obvious summary or conclusion sections and no recommendations for further research.[10] Not an atypical Weick paper. It seems the order could easily be otherwise; beginnings could be endings and vice versa. From title to last line, the order is unsettling and difficult to categorize as to its intentions.

Certainly there is a shape and pattern to this work. It is not a blob by any means but it stands some distance from the conventional writing styles. The work reads as something of a personal reflection, a meditation on a theme and is put forth in terse, highly qualified and personal prose. Moreover, the matters that occupy Weick's interest in the paper are not presented as things to which one must agree or disagree but as ideas tossed out to complicate our thinking about current problems in organizational theory (and elsewhere). Literary theorists repeatedly suggest that readers often reject argumentative thrusts or ideas presented as solid and unassailable. Weick's essays allow a reader to sense a writer struggling with an idea and trying to use that idea to come to terms with some concrete event or experience that serves as the narrative center for the writing.

In general, an elementary principle of the successful essay is precisely what Weick respects and follows in much of his work. An essay works to the extent that readers identify with the writer. And when they do, the essay will carry greater persuasive appeal than writings that force on a reader a systematic barrage of concepts, definitions, truth claims and roll call of famous names all serving to express certitude. Identification is created, in part, by revealing doubt. Who can identify with the all-knowing author? It may well be that the most persuasive style in the late 20th century is one that is informal, a little self-conscious perhaps but basically genial and pitched at creating a conversation or dialogue between equals.

Indeterminacy and Open-Endedness

A good deal of Weick's writings refuse settlement. Interpretations are left open and the world as depicted in print remains indeterminate. Weick is willfully and often amusingly paradoxical. The tactic is realized in its clearest form when Karl takes a perfectly reasonable and conventional proposition from organization theory and turns it around to see if it works equally well in reverse. In "Cosmology Episodes," Weick (1993a) reverses the altogether logical proposition that "sensemaking precedes structure" and suggests that the reverse is just as likely. He says of an organization, "as it loses structure, it loses sense" (pp. 6-7). More concretely, he observes that "this loss of organization intensified fear" (p. 14). We normally think of fear or panic as preceding a loss of organization or structure rather than the other way around.

All these claims are put forth in a hesitant, subtle and rather hypothetical mode of expression wherein the words "perhaps," "if" and "maybe" play major roles. This comes close to what could be called a Hamlet Strategy of deferring final judgment while all aspects of an event are carefully examined from a variety of perspectives. It stands in stark contrast to the dogmatic, this-is-a-that and pin-everything-down language of organization science where we are told by an author at the outset, in the middle, and at the end of a paper precisely what is being proved beyond doubt.

Another distinctive feature that comprises the indecisive and open-ended character of Weick's writings is his stringing together of ideas or propositions without connectives. The reporting style is that of montage and it runs counter to the logically dependent clauses that arrange proposition flows sequentially. For instance, Weick lists four sources of organizational resilience in his "Cosmology Episodes" paper. The four are discussed in turn and consist of (1) improvisation and bricolage; (2) virtual role systems, (3) the attitude of wisdom and (4) respectful interaction (Weick 1993a, p. 16). There is no logical order to the four. One doesn't follow from another. The list (and ensuing discussion) acts on a reader as an estranging device and the reading experience is both befuddlement and wonderment. By breaking away from an easy logic, Weick challenges the reader to figure out with him how these things go together and just what they might mean in the context of his discussion.

A question to raise at this point is whether or not an apparently coherent and tightly ordered narrative is superior to a narrative, like Weick's, full of loose ends and logical reversals? Is the simple structure superior to the complex? Reading Weick one must say no. Again, the indeterminacy of the writing allows for identification since the style seems to me to be closer to the way we readers—pallid little trolls that we are—come to terms with the world and do theory ourselves.

To write in an essayistic, highly indeterminate fashion about organizations in a field so dominated by impersonal, disciplined rhetorics is clearly a breach. But I am reminded also that sociologists of scientific knowledge, when observing the everyday work of scientists, often note scientists, in private, think not in black and white but in various shades of gray (e.g., Latour and Woolgar 1979, Garfinkel et al. 1981, Gilbert and Mulkay 1983). When pondering their work, say, in the laboratory or lounge with colleagues, they speak in a tentative, open, one-step-up, one-step-back manner in which things could always be otherwise. But when going public and putting theories into words on a page (or spoken from a platform), all shades of opinion and doubt vanish. Simons (1988, p. 48) calls this pattern "think Yiddish, speak British."

My reading of Karl's work is that much of the time he "thinks Yiddish and speaks Yiddish." As such, his style represents an assault on the unquestioned objectivity of our received notions of the world. If a celebrated theorist publicly displays a tentative and reversible stance toward the objects of his affection, these objects may not be so very objective after all. The style becomes the theory. By letting doubt into his accounts, a reader's hold on organizational reality may be loosened. Doubt multiplies and a reader is forced to credit several explanations—sometimes contradictory—for the always concrete happenings that punctuate Weickian tales. This stylistic mark is closely related to the third characteristic of much of Karl's writing.

Dialectic Reconstruction

A favored Weick technique is to take two logical opposites and show how both may be true at the same time; thus the dialectic itself is transformed. This is an obvious violation of the scientific identity principle that decrees something cannot be true and false at the same time. Karl did this with a vengeance on some work of mine, showing just how an organizational socialization process could be both formal and informal, individual and collective simultaneously (Weick 1982, pp. 394-398). He works in reverse as well, producing a dialectic from an identity. In a clever paper on educational administration, he played off the cliché "a community of scholars" to note that community endangers scholarship while scholarship prevents community (Weick 1983). Both were needed if an educational institution were to thrive, but the language we use to understand the situation is often confusing and gets in the way of the very understanding we seek.

In "Cosmology Episodes," the tactic shows up again. Specifically, Karl argues that "ignorance and knowledge" often go and grow together in organizational settings (Weick 1993a, pp. 22-23). The more knowledge that seems to be available to organizational members, the more ignorance there is among them (and vice versa). These are of course two matters we normally consider contradictory. It is a playful argument but instructive, and in a world full of seemingly insurmountable dilemmas, awards should be handed out to those who try to get past the tired either/or oppositions characteristic of formal logic.

This dialectic reconstruction is accomplished by Karl with more than a little linguistic sophistry (an approach, by the way, whose good name we should restore). It is done by reformulating the very terms used to express both ordinary and theoretical concepts. It is done through inventive language use. In words and sentences that are sometimes as cool, crisp and clear as a country creek, Weick suspends logical sequencing and pries words loose from their accustomed routines. The self-canceling paradoxes work to depict an organizational world that is in continual flux, a world that is always becoming.[11] From Cosmology Episodes: ". . . it doesn't take much to qualify as an organization. The other side of it is that it also may not take much to stop being an organization" (Weick 1993a, p. 5). There is a tentative, anti-essentialist and (moving) dialectic position being carefully staked out here and it is one that I think attracts readers because Karl's style is so consistent with his message.

Presence

All writers face the problem of how to keep their reader's attention pointed toward features of the text they deem most important. Presence is a literary tactic that serves, in part, to solve this problem. Presence is magnified by such practices as repetition, amplification, enumeration, figuration, provision of concrete details and so forth. It is something of a substitute for a formalist strategy of proof and analysis. Support for an idea or position by the use of presence means repeating it time and time again, each time with a twist, a little differently so that various shades of meaning can be discerned. Redundancy is the key. Contrasted to the spare, plain-speaking, sequential, one-thing-at-a-time simplicity of a good deal of writing in organization theory, presence is indeed an unusual textual feature.

Perhaps the best example of Karl's use of presence is found in his much cited essay "Educational Organizations as Loosely Coupled Systems" (Weick 1976). In this piece, the title phrase is virtually beaten into the reader through its repeated use in shifting contexts. Time after time, different sets of concrete particulars are invoked to exemplify loose coupling, thus giving rise to a proof of the idea's vitality through its illustrated fit to diverse circumstances. Moreover, loose coupling is put forth without an explicit singular definition, without a set of theorems, and without much detailed interpretation of a general or abstract sort. Peter Manning (1992, pp. 48-51), a respected critic and close reader of Karl's work, points out that this essay contains at least 15 different ways in which loose coupling is used. The idea is thus magnified and given importance not by analysis, but by repetition and amplification. By continually adding a new supplementary documentation for its presence, loose coupling is being particularized, not generalized.

This is not unlike Tom Wolfe's (1979) strategy for communicating *The Right Stuff* to readers. Wolfe never defines "The Right Stuff" but he repeats the phrase over and over again throughout the book, always in slightly to drastically altered conditions. Similarly, Karl gives loose coupling the quiddity it deserves by virtue of his seeming inability to precisely define it. But, in so doing, he also makes readers increasingly aware of its presence. The subtext reads that if a writer of Weick's obvious rhetorical virtuosity and talent cannot precisely express the idea of "loose coupling," how great an idea it must truly be! Oh what grandeur and power it must possess!!

The downside of presence as a rhetorical move is that its persuasive appeal will depend in large measure on the reader's experience and ability to identify with the examples provided in the text. If readers have only shallow experience or no such experience with the idea—or, worse, are unwilling to put that experience to use because they are overschooled in the *proper* way to read organization theory—language such as Karl's will fail and no connection among author, idea and reader will be made. Presence, to be convincing, requires more of readers than the joyless use of a Magic Marker to underline portions of the text. It requires imaginative readers able to put themselves into the illustrative situations that fill the text and bestow on key concepts both meaning and range.[12]

The allegoric breaching style is I think a demanding one. But for readers able and willing to put in the work, it is persuasive and rewarding. It is however a style that takes a most unaggressive stance toward reality, organizational or otherwise. As such, it represents a rather different way of doing (i.e., writing) theory than we are accustomed. An example from cultural anthropology may be useful in this regard. It comes from the pen of Dorothy Lee and tells of a far-away society:

> Among the Wintu there is a recurring attitude of humility and respect toward reality, toward nature and society. . . . I cannot find an adequate term to apply to a habit of thought that is so alien to our culture. We are so aggressive toward reality. We say "this is bread." . . We do not say as do the Wintu, "I call this bread," or "I feel" or "I taste" or "I see it to be bread." . . . The Wintu never says starkly "this is." (Lee 1959, p. 129; cited in Brown 1977, p. 24)

I think Karl would be rather comfortable among the Wintu. The lack of sharp definition, claimed objectivity, descriptive certainty and detachable conclusions mark a good deal of his work. He writes against our customary aggressive certitude toward reality, a certitude that lies at the core of the foundational, scientific pose that infects so much of organization theory. And if, as I've suggested, Karl gives us a distinctive style whose reception history indicates its persuasive character, perhaps others might experiment with its features as well. For me, many of Karl's novel writing strokes offer a promising way of doing theory, a way more in tune with current intellectual trends in many of the scholarly worlds that surround us and perhaps more in tune with the culturally blended everyday worlds in which we live.

THEORY IN CONTEXT

As a way of drawing all this to a close, I want to highlight certain implicit themes that run through my remarks. First, I have had relatively little to say about normal form organizational theorizing. By and large, I have characterized standard theoretical writings in terms of what they are not and used Karl Weick's writing to serve as an exception that draws out the rule. Part of this disregard is due to a lack of space but, more importantly, part of it is due to the annoying fact that we are to a degree blind to the ways we write unless we have in front of our face an example of another way to write. From examples of novel practices can come individual and collective experiments and perhaps as a result we can loosen up some of the writer's cramps that seem so prevalent in our field. By trying to write like everyone else (and not talking about it in public), we not only bore ourselves to tears but restrict the range of our inquires and speculations in ways that might be cheerfully applauded by Jeffrey Pfeffer.[13]

Second and relatedly, I am appalled at much of organization theory for its technocratic unimaginativeness. Our generalizations often display a mind-numbing banality and an inexplicable readiness to reduce the field to a set of unexamined, turgid, hypothetical thrusts designed to render organizations systematic and organization theory safe for science. I see in Karl Weick's unusual phrases, labels, titles, reversals, sweeps and swoops of wordplay something of a protest and an example of how to break from the frozen technical writing codes we find ourselves so often following. The message seems unmistakable. The language we use to theorize about organizations is not a symptom of the problems the field faces but is a cause of such problems. A position I think Karl would agree with is that our theories of the world are not mere reflectors of the world but makers of the world, and this is why the words we use are so terribly important. To put forth my own Weickianism: "Theorists are lost because they are blind to what words in context can teach them."

Third, the positive spin I've put on indeterminacy and open-endedness draws on the familiar Weberian distinction between formal and practical (or situational) rationality. Formal rationality, when carried into theory, is the idea that we can define decisively all relevant terms, allow for all conceivable possibilities and bundle up our understandings such that our meaning will be perfectly clear. Practical rationality emphasizes context and, when carried into theory, suggests that ambiguity is always and necessarily present. The two forms of rationality clash, for it seems to me that the more we try to be precise and exact, the less we are able to say and that the harder we try to follow a rigorous theoretical system, the more we are tempted to fill it out with uninspired observations. Semantic clarity and distinctiveness is achieved only to the extent that we allow statements to depend on the identity of the writer, that we allow the circumstances that surround discourse to enter into our considerations of what is being said, that we allow ambiguous statements to stand without question in the hope that future remarks will clarify their meaning, and so on (and on). This state of affairs recommends that we put our theories forward with an awareness of a haunting irony: To be determinate, we must be indeterminate. Perhaps by focusing on concrete particulars, by revealing our doubts and anxieties, by not trying so hard to achieve the other worldly ideals of science, our writings will be able to display our ideas with coherence enough to make them intelligible but not dress them up with an alluring but false sense of finality. *Les petits fait divers* over Pfefferdigmatic certainty (or unity).

Finally, I think it possible that if we were to move away from our apparent fascination with tidy and relatively closed intellectual systems, we might be able to develop our organizational theories in a less contentious and defensive fashion. Debate, not conversation, now rules the day. Yet there are examples—Karl Weick being one—of arranging and explicating theory in what comes close to a conversational and open fashion. It is a way of doing theory that is I think sensitive to the speaking-hearing process and, when brought into the writing-reading process, represents an inviting brand of theorizing. The object of debate is of course to overwhelm or obliterate one's opponent: to prune, pare and discard. The object of conversation is to keep it going: to plant, nurture and cultivate. In the most uncertain domain of organization theory, the latter objective seems preferable.

What I am suggesting is that since the very process of theorizing helps create the organizational properties we find in an all too real world, it is a matter far too important to be left to a small set of self-proclaimed experts with their mock science routines, images and metaphors. History is on my side for it is not always the case that persuasion is simply a matter of a few well-placed power-brokers who bludgeon opponents into submission by controlling publications, positions and resources—although it is probably still too often the case. I think a disarmament program is in order to take away certain taken-for-granted tropes that govern organizational theorizing—tropes like progress, truth and reality (singular), as well as all those terms drawn from bipolar hierarchies that privilege certain terms over others, like hard over soft, objective over subjective, perception over imagination, quantitative over qualitative and masculine over feminine.

In this light, it may well be that the most crucial questions having to do with theory development concern the ways we now carry on our work with each other. For example, how can we increase our tolerance for unorthodox approaches and, at the same time, increase the chances that we will learn from one another? What are the conditions that surround productive scholarly exchange in the field? Should debate or conversation guide the process of intellectual discussion and disagreement? Are certain institutional arrangements more likely than others to facilitate tolerance, learning and conversation? These are the kinds of questions I think we should be asking. They seem to me to be still open to discussion despite vigorous attempts like Jeffrey's to answer them once and for all. The answers—if indeed there are any—must come from the polyphonic voices that comprise our highly diverse field. We must be willing to listen to each other and to listen with respect. The goal is not to control the field, increase our prestige, run a tight ship, or impose a paradigm for self-serving or utilitarian ends. The goal is to learn from one another such that our ink-on-a-page theories and consequent understandings of organizations can be improved. Too often we forget.

NOTES

1. As I note in the text, this paper began as a speech. Arie Lewin was the first to approach me about turning the speech into a paper. Peter Frost was unflagging in his efforts to gather in the spoils—whatever they may be—for *Organization Science*. Barbara Gray, John Jermier, Linda Pike and Linda Smircich read an earlier draft of this paper and raised a number of questions which I have tried to answer. Jim Walsh (and his committee members) started the speech making and paper writing process by issuing an invitation to address the Academy of Management Annual Meetings in Atlanta in August, 1993. It was an offer I could not refuse. I am grateful to all. But I also realize that a speech and a paper are two very different performances. A speech is a live performance: "a mingling of," as Goffman (1981, p. 164) says, "the living with the read." As such, I took liberties in my talk that I dare not take here. From the podium, I felt free to embellish, to exaggerate, to improvise, to tell a joke or two, to pun around and ramble on without great concern for the niceties of written and often stilted communication on the belief that my listeners would take away the spirit of my remarks more so than my words. A good deal of editing has then gone into this talk-based paper. I have tried, however, to preserve some of the spirit of my verbal performance in the body of the paper and take up the academic slack by forcing on the reader a set of my beloved if grim endnotes.

2. The tempest in a honey pot initiated by Jeff's remarks continues. There have been two published rejoinders (Perrow 1994, Cannella and Paetzold 1994) and, from personal experience, a good deal of corridor, seminar and tavern talk about the pros and cons of paradigmatic consensus in our field(s). Most of the controversy swirls around the content, not form, of Jeff's analysis and thus stands apart from the themes I pick up in this paper. It is worth noting however that Jeff's talk (and paper) is a superb example of his own style. It is stuffed with operational definitions, testable hypotheses, appeals to scientifically grounded truths, string-cited references to supporting evidence (much of it his own), and so on. It is, I think, stylistically impressive and clearly the kind of writing he does best. Indeed, when in top form, no one does it better. This makes for something of a problem, because when Jeff breaks from the impersonal, third-person, just-the-facts format and issues a hesitant personal confession or two, the displayed lack of certainty and assumed intimacy (identification) with the reader ring hollow if not false. On paper, an uncertain Jeffrey Pfeffer is no Jeffrey Pfeffer at all. My point being that he is most convincing in genre, least convincing outside of it. The genre, however, deserves scrutiny.

3. This language-first switch produces a culturally relative version of reality and suggests that perception is as much a product of imagination as imagination is a product of perception. Reality thus emerges from the interplay of imaginative perception and perceptive imagination. Language (and text) provide the symbolic representations required for both the construction and communication of conceptions of reality and thus make the notions of thought and culture inseparable. The literature exploring and promoting this ontological gerrymandering is enormous and can be found within and across many cutting (or bleeding) edge fields, e.g., natural language philosophy, post-structural linguistics, cultural and symbolic anthropology, contemporary literary studies, semiotics, constructivist schools in sociology and psychology, etc. A summary of this literature is impossible, but a few of the works I have found accessible, influential and relevant to organizational studies include: White 1978, 1981; Rabinow and Sullivan (Eds.) 1979; Ricoeur 1976; Clifford and Marcus (Eds.) 1986; Brown 1977; Clifford 1988; Fish 1989.

4. See, for example, Daft and Wiginton 1979, Burrell and Morgan 1979, Barley 1983, Morgan 1986, Turner (Ed.) 1987, Krieger 1989, Fiol 1989, Martin 1990, Astley and Zammuto 1992, Barley and Kunda 1992, Manning 1992, Reed and Hughes (Eds.) 1992. These works are appreciative of interpretive shifts in contemporary social theory but most do not problematize

inhouse representational techniques in organizational research and theory. Two recent works that do are Kilduff's (1993) splendid deconstruction of *Organizations,* the classic March and Simon (1958) text, and the savvy reading Golden-Biddle and Locke (1993) apply to several organizational ethnographies. Both works take seriously the role rhetoric plays in the materials they examine and thus force their target texts to tell a rather different story than what their respected authors may have intended.

5. In the context of this paper, I treat rhetoric as an attempt (in writing) to persuade, alter or otherwise move readers with respect to attitude, opinion, interpretation and, most critically if least likely, action. Effective rhetorics vary by genre, of course, and style, as the distinctive (individualized) use of rhetoric, is always relevant when considering influential texts. This is not to argue that organizational research and theory is reduced to rhetoric and therefore rendered corrupt but, rather, to argue that rhetoric is inevitably a part of organizational research and theory if a work is to have any impact. For some good treatments of the role rhetoric plays in social theorizing see, for example, Gusfield 1976, 1981; Brown 1988; Davis 1971; Edmondson 1984; Nelson et al. (Eds.) 1987; Simons (Ed.) 1988; Van Maanen 1988; and, especially, Green 1988. The inspiration for much for this work is, naturally, Burke (1957, 1962).

6. The kinds of vague advice we offer students on writing provide convenient examples: "avoid logical inconsistencies," "seek empirical tests of ideas," "try to be precise," "use the standard public language and avoid the babblish elements of vernacular and jargon, academic or otherwise," and so forth. We teach that sobriety, attention to detail, balance between theory and data, care without obsession and an easy, not relentless use of metaphor are critical to the legitimation of one's work. What we conveniently ignore, of course, is that these are matters set by fashion, not natural law: by the imagery and genres available in particular periods. Someone writing today with, for instance, Whyte's (1943) organic allusions or Thompson's (1967) stark propositional inventories will not qualify as a credible organizational theorist. We gloss such matters because it blurs the distinction between rhetorical and rational persuasion. But, as I argue in the text, a strong distinction between the two is impossible to maintain. On the role of rhetoric in selected disciplines, see, for example: White 1973, Fish 1980, O'Neill 1981, Bazerman 1981, Marcus and Cushman 1982, McClosky 1985, Stocking 1992, and, in organization studies, Gergen 1992.

7. The post-Kuhnian perspective implies that inquiry and advocacy are difficult to pry apart. Close ethnographic looks at high-science fields provide wonderful examples of this interdependency at work (e.g., Lynch 1985, Latour 1987, Traweek 1988). For a contemporary, telling and quite astonishing treatment of the sociology of scientific knowledge, see Ashmore (1989).

8. This is not, by any means, an exhaustive or systematic review of scholarly reactions to Karl Weick's work. To develop and categorize reader responses to the substantial body of work Karl has produced over the past 30 or so years would be a daunting task. My point here is simply to point out that it is widely regarded—indeed celebrated—as high-grade organization theory and yet also treated as more than a little idiosyncratic and enigmatic. Uniqueness is notoriously hard to pin down, but here I try to locate it in Karl's compositional practices or writing style. There is however a danger of setting myself up as a style critic who, by some master stroke, is able to authoritatively divine and define all the persuasive elements to be found in an examined work. Readers are thus homogenized and reduced to passive subjects responding to a particular text like Skinnerian rats responding to a given stimulus. This is not my belief nor intention. Readers actively locate and create the meanings they pull from texts and different readers may respond to the same text in quite different ways. This is apparent in my list of scholarly reactions to Weick's work. There is, no doubt, a collective order to reader responses however, such that subgroups of readers could, in principle, be identified by certain of the background characteristics they bring with them to a text, characteristics that may lead them to experience the text in a

similar fashion. But, alas, this highly contingent treatment of text requires a much finer-grained analysis then is presented here. Reader response theory is developed nicely by Iser (1978, 1979), and a useful, culturally contextualized example of such theory put into service is Griswold (1987).

9. I use this label with some trepidation. Like all critics, whose unenviable job it is to pigeon-hole the work of others, I realize a single, simple tag is a dangerous way to characterize a large and diverse body of work; work that continues to develop new themes, directions and stylistic gestures. Moreover, Karl—like all good writers—works within and across different literary genres and thus restricts, modifies and amplifies his style accordingly. Stylistic purity is not being suggested here. My claim is merely that "allegoric breaching" is associated with what I take to be the most persuasive of Karl's writings and the smattering of examples I've provided in this short text are intended to be representative of these writings. His least persuasive writings, I would argue, are those that display few of the compositional features I discuss here.

10. The page numbers and textual arrangements refer to an unpublished draft of "Cosmology Episodes" I had on hand—and in mind—when working up my analysis of Karl's style. The paper has subsequently been published in *Administrative Science Quarterly* under the same title but in substantially revised form (Weick 1993b). The typescript of the published version runs 49 pages, it is no longer explicitly called an essay, the personal tone has been—to a degree—sacrificed, the number of bibliographic references has more than doubled, there are eight section heads, etc. The published version still contains the allegoric breaching style I highlight here but it is certainly less prominent than in the previous draft. Perrow (1985) would call this editorial work "asphalting": a way of flattening out the writing (and writer) and bringing a work in line—down to snuff—with current journal practices. Style, it seems, is something of an anathema to journal editors. I justify my use of the unpublished draft in this paper on the grounds that it represents a relatively undiluted (unpolluted) example of Karl's style. It also has the advantages of being both recent and short.

11. This is particularly apparent in *The Social Psychology of Organizing* (Weick 1969, 1979) whose very title signals Weick's intention to take on the then canonical text of the field, Katz and Kahn (1966) *The Social Psychology of Organizations*. The move away from structure to process, from permanence to temporality, from role taking to role making and so forth is conveyed by Weick in a loose, crazy-quilt fashion quite the opposite of the target text's tight, orderly presentation where all "variables" fit neatly into place. Impressionistic anecdotes, flights of metaphoric fancy, reprints of *New Yorker* cartoons, hand drawn graphics all contrast with propositional inventories, system diagrams and universal postulates. The solid organization of Katz and Kahn is deconstructed and reconstructed by Weick as a fluid bundle of social and cognitive practices. Read in tandem, the two texts could not be further apart in theory or style.

12. The "illustrative situations" deserve comment since Karl seems increasingly concerned with apocalyptic events and landscapes—nuclear accidents, flight decks of aircraft carriers, forest fires, air disasters. These are sites where anxieties of the white dead dawn peak and where communications fail. It is these communication failures—organizational breakdowns—that challenge Weick and thus make a good deal of his work profoundly metadiscursive as he struggles with problems of expression, style and making the inexplicable explicable through the language of theory. By working toward a flawless diction where every word is made to count, Karl is also making a tacit but powerful statement about the value of form as form.

13. I am aware that some readers may well dismiss my push for textual experimentation as bad career advise. Karl Weick can get away with it but, after all, he is tenured, venerated and skilled. Those of us lacking any one of these gifts are best advised to stick with the crowd and try to write like everyone else. Such a view strikes me as terribly shortsighted for it denies that textually aware and thoughtful students can both acknowledge talent and learn from its display. It also

denies that readers—including journal editors and reviewers—are moved by graceful, innovative writings that are attentive to such literary matters as rhetoric, presence, voice and imagery. Indeed, my point throughout this paper has been to link persuasion to style and style is anything but institutionalized. Like language itself, scholarly writing practices are not cast in stone. Marshalling one's tropes to go in unconventional ways may be difficult and perhaps lonely, but it is by no means everywhere and always unwelcome.

REFERENCES

Ashmore, M. (1989), *The Reflexive Thesis,* Chicago, IL: University of Chicago Press.

Astley, W. G. and R. Zammuto (1992), "Organization Science, Managers and Language Games," *Organization Science,* 3, 443-460.

Barley, S. (1983), "Semiotics and the Study of Occupational and Organizational Cultures," *Administrative Science Quarterly,* 28, 393-413.

——— and G. Kunda (1992), "Design and Devotion: Surges of Rational and Normative Ideologies of Control in Managerial Discourse," *Administrative Science Quarterly,* 37, 363-399.

Bazerman, C. (1981), "What Written Knowledge Does: Three Examples of Academic Discourse," *Philosophy of the Social Sciences,* 11, 361-387.

Brown, R. H. (1977), *A Poetic for Sociology,* Cambridge, UK: Cambridge University Press.

——— (1988), *Society as Text,* Chicago, IL: University of Chicago Press.

Burke, K. (1957), *A Philosophy of Literary Form,* New York: Vintage.

——— (1962), *A Grammer of Motives and a Rhetoric of Motives,* Columbus, OH: Ohio State University Press.

Burrell, G. and G. Morgan (1979), *Sociological Paradigms and Organizational Analysis,* London, UK: Heinemann.

Cannella, A. A., Jr. and R. L. Paetzold (1994), "Pfeffer's Barriers to the Advance of Organizational Science: A Rejoinder," *Academy of Management Review,* 19, 2, 331-341.

Clifford, J. (1988), *The Predicament of Culture,* Cambridge: MA: Harvard University Press.

——— and G. E. Marcus (eds.) (1986), *Writing Culture,* Berkeley, CA: University of California Press.

Daft, R. L. and J. C. Wiginton (1979), "Language and Organization," *Academy of Management Review,* 4, 179-192.

Davis, M. S. (1971), "That's Interesting! Toward a Phenomenology of Sociology and a Sociology of Phenomenology," *Philosophy of Social Science,* 1, 304-344.

Edmondson, R. (1984), *Rhetoric in Sociology,* London, UK: Macmillian.

Fiol, C. M. (1989), "A Semiotic Analysis of Corporate Language," *Administrative Science Quarterly,* 34, 2, 277-3.

Fish, S. (1980), *Is there a Text in this Class?,* Cambridge, MA: Harvard University Press.

——— (1989), *Doing What Comes Naturally: Change Rhetoric and the Practice of Theory in Literary and Legal Studies,* New York: Oxford University Press.

Garfinkel, H., M. Lynch and E. Livingston (1981), "The Work of a Discovering Science Construed with Materials from the Optically Discovered Pulsar," *Philosophy of the Social Sciences,* 11, 131-158.

Geertz, C. (1974), "From the Native's Point of View," *Bulletin of the American Academy of Arts and Sciences,* 28, 27-45.

Gergen, K. J. (1992), "Organization Theory in the Postmodern Era," in M. Reed and H. Hughes (Eds.), *Rethinking Organization,* London, UK: Sage, 207-226.

Gilbert, G. N. and M. Mulkay (1983), *Opening Pandora's Box*, Cambridge, UK: Cambridge University Press.

Goffman, E. (1981), *Forms of Talk*, Philadelphis, PA: University of Pennsylvania Press.

Golden-Biddle, K. and K. Locke (1993), "Appealing Work: An Investigation of How Ethnographic Texts Convince," *Organization Science*, 4, 595-616.

Green, B. S. (1988), *Literary Methods and Sociological Theory*, Chicago, IL: University of Chicago Press.

Griswold, W. (1987), "The Fabrication of Meaning," *American Journal of Sociology*, 92, 1077-1117.

Gusfield, J. (1976), "The Literary Rhetoric of Science," *American Sociological Review*, 41, 16-33.

———— (1981), *The Culture of Public Problems*, Chicago, IL: University of Chicago Press.

Iser, W. (1978), *The Act of Reading*, Baltimore, MD: Johns Hopkins University Press.

———— (1979), *Prospecting: From Reader Response to Literary Anthropology*, Baltimore, MD: Johns Hopkins University Press.

Katz, D. and R. L. Kahn (1966), *The Social Psychology of Organizations*, New York: Wiley.

Kilduff, M. (1993), "Deconstructing Organizations," *Academy of Management Review*, 18,13-31.

Krieger, S. (1989), "Research and the Construction of Text," in N. Denzin (Ed.), *Studies in Symbolic Interactionism*, Vol. 2, Greenwich, CT: JAI Press, 167-187.

Latour, B. (1987), *Science in Action*, Milton-Keynes: Open University Press.

———— and S. Woolgar (1979), *Laboratory Life*, Beverly Hills, CA: Sage.

Lynch, M. (1985), *Art and Artifact in Laboratory Studies*, London, UK: Routledge and Kegan Paul.

Manning, P. K. (1992), *Organizational Communication*, New York: Aldine de Gruyter.

March, J. G. and H. A. Simon (1958), *Organizations*, New York: Wiley.

Marcus, G. E. and D. Cushman (1982), "Ethnographies as Text," *Annual Review of Anthropology*, 25-69.

Martin, J. (1990), "Deconstructing Organizational Taboos: The Suppression of Gender Conflict in Organizations," *Organization Science*, 1, 339-359.

McCloskey, D. N. (1985), *The Rhetoric of Economics*, Madison, WI: University of Wisconsin Press.

Morgan, G. (1986), *Images of Organizations*, Newbury Park, CA: Sage.

Nelson, J. S., A. Megill and D. N. McCloskey (Eds.) (1987), *The Rhetoric of the Human Sciences*, Madison, WI: University of Wisconsin Press.

O'Neill, J. (1981), "The Literary Production of Natural and Social Science Inquiry," *Canadian Journal of Sociology*, 6, 105-120.

Perrow, C. (1985), "Journaling Careers," in L. L. Cummings and P. Frost (Eds.), *Publishing in the Organizational Sciences*, San Francisco, CA: Jossey-Bass, 220-230.

———— (1994), "Pfeffer Slips," *Academy of Management Review*, 19, 191-194.

Pfeffer, J. (1993a), "Barriers to the Advance of Organizational Science: Paradigm Development as a Dependent Variable," *Academy of Management Review*, 18, 599-620.

———— (1993b), "An Interview with Jeffrey Pfeffer," *Organization and Management Division Newsletter*, Winter, 1, 5.

Rabinow, P. and A. Sullivan (Eds.) (1979), *Interpretive Social Science*, Berkeley, CA: University of California Press.

Reed, M. and M. Hughes (Eds.) (1992), *Rethinking Organization*, London, UK: Sage.

Ricoeur, P. (1976), *Interpretation Theory: Discourse and the Surplus of Meaning*, Fort Worth, TX: Texas Christian University Press.

Simons, H. W. (Ed.) (1988), *The Rhetorical Turn*, Chicago, IL: University of Chicago Press.

Stocking, G. W. (1992), *The Ethnographer's Magic,* Madison, WI: University of Wisconsin Press.

Thompson, J. D. (1967), *Organizations in Action,* New York: McGraw-Hill.

Traweek, S. (1988), *Beamtimes and Lifetimes,* Cambridge, MA: Harvard University Press.

Turner, B. (Ed.) (1987), *Organizational Symbolism,* Berlin, Germany: de Gruyter.

Van Maanen, J. (1988), *Tales of the Field,* Chicago, IL: University of Chicago Press.

Weick, K. (1969). *The Social Psychology of Organizing,* Reading, MA: Addison-Wesley, 2nd ed., 1979.

——— (1976), "Educational Organizations as Loosely Coupled Systems," *Administrative Science Quarterly,* 21, 1-19.

——— (1982), "Management of Organizational Change among Loosely Coupled Elements," in P. Goodman (Ed.), *Change in Organizations,* San Francisco, CA: Jossey-Bass, 375-408.

——— (1983), "Contradictions in a Community of Scholars: The Cohesion-Accuracy Trade-off," *The Review of Higher Education,* 4, 253-267.

——— (1993a), "Cosmology Episodes in Organizations: Young Men and Fire and the Mann Gulch Disaster," Unpublished Manuscript, University of Michigan.

——— (1993b), "Cosmology Episodes in Organizations: Young Men and Fire and the Mann Gulch Disaster," *Administrative Science Quarterly,* 39, 628-652.

White, H. (1973), *Metahistory,* Baltimore, MD: Johns Hopkins University Press.

——— (1978), *Tropics of Discourse,* Baltimore, MD: Johns Hopkins University Press.

——— (1981). "The Value of Narrativity in the Representation of Reality," in W. J. T. Mitchell (Ed.), *On Narrative,* Chicago, IL: University of Chicago Press.

Whyte, W. F. (1943), *Street Corner Society,* Chicago, IL: University of Chicago Press.

Wolfe, T. (1979), *The Right Stuff,* New York: Farrar, Straus and Giroux.

5

Mortality, Reproducibility, and the Persistence of Styles of Theory

Graduate School of Business, Stanford University

It seems somehow appropriate that Peter Frost's letter sending me a draft of John Van Maanen's (1995) article should have been dated November 7, 1994. For on November 8 we witnessed, at least in the United States and particularly in California, the culmination of a season of political campaigns notable for their viciousness and appeal to emotion rather than reason. Frost's (1995) characterization of Van Maanen's article as "less restrained than we are used to" was an understatement.

John is nothing if not a master of rhetoric, and his comment on my paper employs tried and true rhetorical devices. This includes contrastive pairs (Atkinson 1984), in this instance, implicitly Weick and a style of theory that "rests on its more or less unique style" (p. 135) versus Pfeffer, a presumed apologist for (if not an example of) "a logocentric tradition of empirical science with its count-and-classify conventions" and "more than a little physics envy" (p. 134). Van Maanen's article also follows Edelman's (1964, p. 124) description of political speech as "a ritual, dulling the critical faculties rather than awakening them. Chronic repetition of clichés and stale phrases that serve simply to evoke a conditioned uncritical response is a time-honored

From "Mortality, Reproducibility, and the Persistence of Styles of Theory," by Jeffrey Pfeffer, 1995, *Organization Science, 6,* pp. 681-686. © 1995, The Institute of Management Sciences. Used with permission.

habit among politicians and a mentally restful one for their audiences." Van Maanen promotes a caricature of normal science and reinforces its protagonists' unacceptability with emotion-laden adjectives (shrill, sour, vain, autocratic, insufferably smug, orthodox, and naive, among many others).

Finally, Van Maanen employs perhaps the most time-honored tradition in political language: saying one thing while doing the other (Edelman 1964). For even as Van Maanen venerates dialectic reconstruction and bemoans either/or reasoning, he couches the theoretical issues that distinguish his approach from mine as being mutually incompatible; for instance, description either following from objects or being prior to recognizing those social objects. And, even as he bemoans contention and defensiveness, he plays word games with my name, uses provocative language, and notes that "My {John's} remarks . . . must then be understood as . . . an understandable and necessary effort to *defend* my work" (1995, p. 134, emphasis added). Having not attacked nor even mentioned either him or his work in my earlier article, the need to defend same, while complaining about defensiveness, seems peculiar.

Van Maanen's particular article aside, what has surprised me in the time since I first gave my talk and my article appeared is the emotion it has aroused. I am surprised because, as I will describe below, the issues raised are scarcely unique to organization studies, being contested, albeit with occasionally less vitriol, in several adjacent fields such as strategic management, political science, and even economics. Moreover, the points I made seem scarcely controversial with respect to their empirical foundations and probably not even in the logic of the argument, as I hope to demonstrate shortly.

The intent of my talk and paper was to encourage us to take a concept— paradigm development—whose effects on a number of outcomes had been well-studied and to ask, both in general and with respect to organization studies in particular, what determined the level of paradigm development that characterized a field or subdiscipline; why is it that some fields seem to exhibit more consensus than others? It seemed useful to also explore the implications of paradigmatic consensus for fields that exist in a world of increasingly scarce resources, but that interest was secondary to trying to understand the source of paradigmatic differences: not between physics and organization studies, but between political science, or strategic management, or economics, and organization studies.

The claims of others (e.g., Canella and Paetzold 1994, p. 337) to the contrary, it remains the case that organization studies is very much at risk for experiencing some of the same processes that have occurred in related social sciences: namely, a domination by an economistic, rational choice perspective that relies on methodological individualism, neglects institutional context or detail, relies on rational choice/actor models, and postulates agency theory-like (opportunistic, self-interest seeking) assumptions about human behavior. I happen to believe that such a theoretical approach is both substantively incorrect and managerially harmful (Pfeffer 1994, Ch. 4). I remain concerned that as some of us create an interesting intellectual sideshow about presumed paradigmatic imperialism, we have failed to notice the main event: the growing influence of rational choice, economics-like theory on organization studies.

DO DEVELOPED PARADIGMS TRIUMPH?

What do the data indicate about changing intellectual orientations in fields? Here political science has much to teach us. Although the field of political science was once dominated by "institutional analysis, behaviorist methods, and group-based pluralist theory" (Green and Shapiro 1994, p. 2), today rational choice theory reigns supreme. In 1992, rational choice theory accounted for almost 40 percent of the articles published in the *American Political Science Review,* the discipline's leading journal (Green and Shapiro 1994, pp. 2-3). Moreover, "the advent of rational choice theory has recast much of the intellectual landscape in the discipline of political science" (Green and Shapiro 1994, p. 3); "its proponents are highly sought by all major American political science departments" (Green and Shapiro 1994, p. 2), and "press editors eagerly pursue half-completed manuscripts by practitioners in the field" (Ordeshook 1993, p. 74). Rational choice theory deduces the microfoundations of behavior from assumptions about incentives, constraints, and the calculations individuals make when confronted with incentives, constraints, and information about both. In political science, rational choice includes game theory. In organization science, it would include transaction cost economics and agency theory, both of which deduce, often using some kind of formalism, propositions about behavior from assumptions of economizing on the part of rational actors facing incentives and constraints.

In their compelling critique of rational choice theory, Green and Shapiro pose an apparent paradox: although rational choice theory has grown enormously in importance and stature within political science, "the stature of rational choice scholarship does not rest on a readily identifiable set of empirical successes" (1994, p. 5). Green and Shapiro (1994, p. 6) note that "the case has yet to be made that these models have advanced our understanding of how politics works in the real world." Why should a subfield grow from being virtually nonexistent in 1957 to being one of the largest (if not the largest) subspecialty in just 25 years without actually accounting for empirical observations of politics in non-trivial ways? I would argue because of the paradigmatic consensus that gives rational choice a competitive advantage over its theoretical rivals in political science that lack such consensus.

Is what happened in political science being replayed in organization science? In 1975, the year in which Williamson's (1975) first book-length exposition of transaction costs reasoning appeared, and the year before the appearance of Jensen and Meckling (1976), not surprisingly, there was little citation of economics in organizational journals; just 2.5% of the articles in *Administrative Science Quarterly* and 0% of the articles in the *Academy of Management Journal* cited economics or economists. By 1985, just ten years later, the proportions had grown to 30% in *ASQ* and 10% in *AMJ*. By 1993, the proportion of articles citing economics had risen to 40% in *ASQ* and 24% in *AMJ*. Although citations are not the only indicator of the growth of a way of doing organizational analysis, the pattern is informative and the parallels to the growth of rational choice in political science are striking.

One can also look *within* organization science to see what can be accomplished by subfields that have consensus on methods and subject matter and, most importantly, because of that consensus are efficient in training graduate students and others and developing a technology that makes scholarship more predictable and more readily accomplished. Two such subfields, although there are clearly others, are behavioral decision theory and population ecology. Over the years, behavioral decision theory has virtually taken over one of the major journals: what used to be called *Organizational Behavior and Human Performance* is now *Organizational Behavior and Human Decision Processes,* and there has been a corresponding shift in its content over time. In the case of population ecology, in the six issues of *Administrative Science Quarterly* from September 1992 through December 1993, of 32 published articles, 5, or 15.6%, were ecological approaches to organizational analysis. It is not likely that 15.6% of the field's scholars are ecologists. But these results are precisely what one would expect from the argument that theoretical consensus and coherence produces more efficient and effective research programs resulting in disproportionate impact and publication.

Even the field of economics itself holds some lessons about disciplinary evolution and the power of paradigmatic consensus. Economics did not start out in its present form or with its current analytic apparatus. Parker (1993, p. 155) noted that 30 of the 50 founders of the American Economic Association were ordained ministers, and the association was founded in 1885 as "a progressive counterweight to what its members saw as the social Darwinism then emerging in the social sciences" (1993, p. 154). Parker's review of methodological disputes within the discipline suggests that:

> While excess abstraction would seem to be a recent complaint, rooted in the
> heavy reliance on mathematics since World War II, the criticism is more than a

century old. A recent review . . . of methodological disputes among American economists begins its survey in 1860 and counts no fewer than 80 examples of basic . . . debates before 1900. (Parker 1993, p. 154)

In ways very similar to Green and Shapiro's critique of rational choice theory in political science, Parker (1993) documents both the failures of modern economic theory to account for empirical reality in nontrivial ways, and also documents the various mechanisms that have been employed to develop and maintain dominance over the discipline by that style of theory. Readers troubled by my modest expression of concern about theoretical profusion in the organizational sciences should read Parker's (1993) documentation of how serious theoretical hegemony is achieved and maintained.

The field of strategic management provides yet another context in which to observe the struggle over paradigms and paradigm consensus. On one side of the debate, arguing for more theoretical and methodological orthodoxy, are, among others, Camerer (1985) and Montgomery et al. (1989). These authors bemoaned the confusion about concepts, failure to do proper empirical testing, and the absence of cumulation or as much progress in knowledge as they would like. Camerer (1985, p. 1) advocated "the deductive use of mathematics and economic concepts." Taking the other side of the debate are people such as Mahoney (1993), who argued for pragmatism and above all, pluralism. Although it is too early to tell precisely how this debate will play itself out, there are certainly significant advances being scored by game theory and industrial organization economics.

Thus, there is suggestive evidence from adjacent social sciences that theoretical perspectives characterized by formalism and a deductive methodology often are able to achieve dominance, even when their empirical contributions are minuscule. The fact of theoretical domination in the presence of modest results makes the power of that style of theory all the more evident; after all, any theory can succeed if it is actually useful and empirically insightful. It is a much bigger challenge to prevail in the face of modest or few accomplishments. Moreover, there is evidence that many of these same theoretical trends are currently visible in organization science, with a growing importance of the same rational choice models and perspectives that first achieved dominance in economics and then political science.

WHY STYLES OF THEORY PREVAIL

Embedded in Van Maanen's illuminating discussion of Karl Weick's work is a way of understanding why work of that type (to the extent John's description of it is accurate), however much we may admire its insight, richness, lucidity, virtuosity, creativeness, and style, is inevitably disadvantaged in the marketplace of ideas. Ideas and writing have a finite lifetime and their authors most certainly are mortal. Great ideas may last in the collective consciousness longer than ideas of less originality or power, but nevertheless, citations are almost invariably time dependent. As authors retire from the scene, the only way their work and ideas can be maintained is to have others pick them up and develop them or carry them forward. Even contemporaneously, it is probably useful to have more rather than fewer students and colleagues doing work related to one's own. Influence is not simply a numbers game, but numbers certainly count.

How easy or difficult it is to recruit others to furthering one's intellectual efforts or to pick up one's intellectual torch is not independent of the style of one's work. Van Maanen uses the writing of Karl Weick as an exemplar, "a distinctive and altogether useful way of putting theory into print" (Van Maanen, p. 135). In describing Weick's writing, he argues that it has four qualities. First, it is essayistic in form, filled with "meanderings, detours," and "distractions" (Van Maanen, p. 136). Second, the writing is characterized by indeterminacy and open-endedness. Weick's writings "refuse settlement," they are "amusingly paradoxical," and Karl writes "stringing together . . . ideas or propositions without connectives" (Van Maanen, pp. 136-37). Third, Weick often takes two logical opposites and shows how both may be true at the same time, or, working in reverse, produces a dialectic from an identity (Van Maanen, p. 137). Finally, Weick keeps the reader's attention through presence—by enumerating, amplifying, and repeating ideas—always, however, in slightly different form. Salancik's description (1977, p. xiii) of Weick's development and writing about the enactment process is instructive:

> I described several difficulties that I thought readers would have with some of
> his ideas and pointed out some places where a hint of definition to enactment
> was emerging and could be expanded. When I later went through his revision,
> I noticed that he had carefully deleted nearly every sentence that I alluded to.
> From this experience, I concluded, "To define enactment is to miss the point
> about it."

How easy would it be for others to employ Weick's style, or even to build on his work? Although being elusive in one's definitions and non-linear in one's thinking may make for more interesting, intellectually challenging, or engaging reading, it is almost certainly not a prescription for having one's work extended, replicated, or adopted by others as part and parcel of their own research program. Similarly, paradox and meandering are also not likely to make it easy or perhaps even likely for others to build on those meanderings and extend the paradoxical line of thought. This is not to say that the linear, list-like, normal science-type writings that Van Maanen eschews are somehow intrinsically superior. It is simply an ecological argument; the ability to readily reproduce gives ideas (just as it does other forms) survival value.

Technology matters a lot in the ability of ideas or theories to develop adherents, which is why theories that come to have widespread use and currency often, although not always, have associated technologies that render their use easier. Three examples illustrate the point. Population ecology, in its study of the dynamics of birth and death over time, virtually requires a methodology for analyzing qualitative outcomes (such as the birth or death of an organization, or its change from one structural form or strategy to another) over time. Hannan and Tuma's (1979) development of event-history analysis and the software to implement that analysis was clearly essential in making it easier for others to adopt and implement their theoretical framework.

In the early 1980s, network concepts of organizations and social structure were diffuse and unorganized. Burt (1980, p. 79) noted:

> Anyone reading through what purports to be a "network" literature will readily perceive the wisdom of Barnes' (1972) analogy between that literature and "a terminological jungle in which any newcomer may plant a tree." A loose federation of approaches . . . is currently referenced as network analysis.

Burt's subsequent attempts to advance his particular conception of sociological analysis relied not only on the publication of his ideas (Burt 1980, 1992) but perhaps more importantly on his developing a network analysis program, "Structure," that he continues to update and refine and give away *free* to any who ask. Burt understands quite well that if he can influence the technology, the methodology by which social networks are analyzed, he is well on his way to exercising influence over the conceptual frameworks and ideas that are employed in such analyses as well.

Nor is this concern with technology limited to quantitative sociology. Heritage (1984, p. 233) noted that "conversation analysis has developed into a prominent form of ethnomethodological work and has come to exert a significant influence—both methodological and substantive—on a range of social science disciplines . . . its growth and diversification have become very extensive." Sacks (1984, p. 26), one of the founders of the method, was explicit in his concern with making ethnomethodological research replicable and with developing a technology that could be taught to others:

> When I started to do research in sociology, I figured that sociology could not be an actual science unless it was able to handle the details of actual events, handle them *formally*, and in the first instance, be informative about them in the direct

ways in which primitive sciences tend to be informative, that is, that *anyone else can go and see whether what was said is so.* (emphasis added)

Boden (1994) has an excellent review of the debate between organizational perspectives that emphasize structural constraint and those that emphasize the role of human agency and how conversation analysis, both in its methods and ideas, can help integrate this false dichotomy. But again, the important point is that a technology for analysis exists that helps others learn both the substance and method of an approach to social analysis and permits replication and extension.

Van Maanen's comment emphasizes the effect of writing on the reader, and particularly, its persuasive quality. Without denying the importance of persuasion, one must recognize that for writing to be influential, it must suggest not only what to do in general terms but how to go about doing it in very specific terms. That is why the development of replicable, teachable, transferable concepts and methods id helpful, to put it mildly.

SOME CONCLUDING THOUGHTS

Reviewing the development of the so-called Austrian school of economics, Foss and Knudsen (1993, p. 19) concluded that "there has to be some balance between the generation of new theoretic alternatives and the selection among them." Variation by itself, without mechanisms of selection and retention, is insufficient for the development of knowledge. They cited March (1991) who noted that organizations need to strike a balance between exploration and exploitation, and argued for an optimal amount of pluralism:

> We . . . conclude that disciplines characterized by a too low as well as too high degree of theoretical pluralism will be confronted with a string of specific problems. (Foss and Knudsen 1993, p. 20)

Among the problems affecting too-pluralistic disciplines are an inability to make good choices among competing theories resulting in disciplinary fragmentation and a consequent inability to effectively generate and absorb new knowledge.

Mone and McKinley (1993, p. 293) have documented the existence of a "uniqueness value" in organization studies and some of its consequences for the discipline:

> We suggest that the uniqueness value has contributed most directly to the undesirability of replications and, consequently, fewer extensions to or refuta-

tions of previous research are published. Yet . . . the rapid rate of innovation spawned partially by the uniqueness value is not necessarily strengthening our understanding of or knowledge concerning organizations . . . paradigmatic specialization, reduced integration, and information overload can occur more easily.

Some might say it is a matter of taste or style as to how much consensus a field should have, or how such consensus gets produced. What I have argued here is that, at least looking comparatively and historically, that does not seem to be the case. For very understandable reasons, possessing consensus on approaches, ideas, and perhaps most importantly, methods, provides advantages in enlisting others to one's theoretical perspective and being productive in the sense of acquiring journal space, legitimacy, and other resources. Although we may value the laissez-faire, let-a-thousand-flowers-bloom spirit that currently pervades organization studies, we should not delude ourselves that our freedom from constraint comes without some costs, or that our ability to indulge whatever particular intellectual tastes or styles we hold dear is guaranteed to last forever.

Perhaps most importantly, readers should not spend too much time or effort simply debating the points of my original article. Once again, Edelman (1971, p. 17) says it well:

Adversary role playing serves to bring valued benefits to the adversaries; and the most valued of these have little to do with the publicized symbolic goals; rather, they take the form of the achievement of an identity which will be cherished and defended.

In this instance, the issues of how and under what conditions paradigmatic consensus develops and the consequences of such consensus can and should be empirically studied. This is a debate that would benefit from having more light and less heat.

REFERENCES

Atkinson, M. (1984), *Our Masters' Voices,* London, England: Methuen.
Barnes, J. A. (1972), *Social Networks,* Reading, MA: Addison Wesley Modular Publications, 26, 1-29.
Boden, Deidre (1994), *The Business of Talk,* Cambridge, England: Polity Press.
Burt, R. S. (1980), "Models of Network Structure," in A. Inkeles, N. J. Smelser, and R. H. Turner (Eds.), *Annual Review of Sociology,* Vol. 6, Palo Alto, CA: Annual Reviews, 79-141.
———— (1992), *Structural Holes: The Social Structure of Competition,* Cambridge, MA: Harvard University Press.

Camerer, C. (1985), "Redirecting Research in Business Policy and Strategy," *Strategic Management Journal* 6, 1-15.

Canella, A. A., Jr. and R. L. Paetzold (1994), "Pfeffer's Barriers to the Advance of Organizational Science: A Rejoinder," *Academy of Management Review,* 19, 331-341.

Edelman, M. (1964), *The Symbolic Uses of Politics,* Urbana, IL: University of Illinois Press.

——— (1971), *Politics as Symbolic Action,* Chicago, IL: Markham.

Foss, N. J. and C. Knudsen (1993), "Pluralism and Scientific Progress in Economics," Working Paper, Institute of Industrial Economics and Strategy, Copenhagen Business School, Copenhagen, Denmark.

Frost, P. (1995), "Crossroads," *Organization Science,* 6, 1, 132.

Green, D. P. and I. Shapiro (1994), *Pathologies of Rational Choice Theory: A Critique of Applications in Political Sciences,* New Haven, CT: Yale University Press.

Hannan, M. T. and N. B. Tuma (1979), "Methods for Temporal Analysis," in A. Inkeles, J. Coleman, and R. H. Turner (Eds.), *Annual Review of Sociology,* Vol. 5, Palo Alto, CA: Annual Reviews, 303-328.

Heritage, J. (1984), *Garfinkel and Ethnomethodology,* Cambridge, England: Polity Press.

Jensen, M. C. and W. H. Meckling (1976), "Theory of the Firm: Managerial Behavior, Agency Cost and Ownership Structure," *Journal of Financial Economics,* 3, 305-360.

Mahoney, J. T. (1993), "Strategic Management and Determinism: Sustaining the Conversation," *Journal of Management Studies,* 30, 173-191.

March, J. G. (1991), "Exploration and Exploitation in Organizational Learning," *Organization Science,* 2, 1-19.

Mone, M. A. and W. McKinley (1993), "The Uniqueness Value and Its Consequences for Organization Studies," *Journal of Management Inquiry,* 2, 284-296.

Montgomery, C. A., B. Wernerfelt, and S. Balakrishnan (1989), "Strategy Content and the Research Process: A Critique and Commentary," *Strategic Management Journal,* 10, 189-197.

Ordeshook, P. C. (1993), "The Development of Contemporary Political Theory," in W. A. Barnett, M. J. Hinich, and N. J. Schofield, Cambridge, England: Cambridge University Press.

Parker, R. (1993), "Can Economists Save Economics?" *American Prospect,* 13, 148-160.

Pfeffer, J. (1993), "Barriers to the Advance of Organizational Science: Paradigm Development as a Dependent Variable," *Academy of Management Review,* 18, 599-620.

——— (1994), *Competitive Advantage Through People,* Boston, MA: Harvard Business School Press.

Sacks, H. (1984), "Methodological Remarks," in J. M. Atkinson, and J. C. Heritage, *Structures of Social Action: Studies in Conversation Analysis,* Cambridge, England: Cambridge University Press, 21-27.

Salancik, G. R. (1977), "Preface," in B. M. Staw and G. R. Salancik (Eds.), *New Directions in Organizational Behavior,* Chicago, IL: St. Clair Press, ix-xiv.

Van Maanen, J. (1995), "Style as Theory," *Organization Science,* 6, 1, 132-143.

Williamson, O. E. (1975), *Markets and Hierarchies,* New York: Free Press.

6

Fear and Loathing in Organization Studies[1]

Sloan School of Management, MIT

Rhetoric is the master-word for this reply to a reply and my main point is simply that like it or not we live in a rhetorical world. This is a conclusion that is inevitable once we remove literal meaning as a restraint on what we say (or write) because this first-step down the interpretive path contains all the others. This is not to say I put forth my reply without restraint—such a condition is unimaginable—but merely to signal that the restraints that are in place are not fixed but flexible, subject always to alteration through persuasive appeals.

That said, let me turn to the prickly pages of Pfeffer's "Mortality, Reproducibility and the Persistence of Styles of Theory." In this piece, I am portrayed as something of a villain for refuting certain arguments in Pfeffer (1993) that now appear to him to be *"scarcely controversial* with respect to their empirical foundations and probably not even [controversial] in the logic of the argument" (Pfeffer 1995, p. 682, emphasis and parenthesis mine). Given his remarks about our "too-pluralistic" field and the advantages he attributes to paradigm consensus, such a statement strikes me as either disingenuous or na‹ve. But, whatever the case, it does present an explicit and easily identifiable move in our respective language game and as such falls neatly into the argumentative web I spin here.

From "Fear and Loathing in Organization Studies, by John van Maanen, 1995, *Organization Science, 6,* pp. 687-692. © 1995, The Institute of Management Sciences. Reprinted with permission.

This essay is my brief answer to why Jeff's position is so very controversial (and so very wrong). I must admit however to feeling serious readers may very well anticipate my arguments for they are largely rehashings of points I put forth in "Style as Theory" (Van Maanen 1995). But, be that as it may, one always yearns for the last word in the academic blood-sport called debate.[2] And, more to the point, I find the challenge issued in Jeff's reply to be as appealing as his scholarship is appalling. So into rhetorical politics I again plunge.

NO EXIT

In the first few paragraphs of Jeff's response, I am taken to task for utilizing an emotionally laden, explicitly political, heated-up, purple and provocative language. We are told that Peter Frost's characterization of my article as " 'less restrained than we are used to' *was an understatement*" (Pfeffer 1995, p. 681; emphasis mine). Guilty as charged. Yet the phrase "less restrained" is a sneaky one and when it is used as an opprobrium to reasoned discourse and used as a broadside to undercut arguments that are otherwise ignored, a reader must surely wonder why a "more restrained" piece of writing is to be preferred? This is indeed an odd complaint since Jeffrey initiated this skirmish in the first place in a pitch hardly designed to be placating. Are we not allowed to be annoyed—and show it? And, if annoyed, must we resort to the impersonal, formulaic and dull discourse so loved by journal editors? My response was, after all, published in a forum called *Crossroads* where some of the pinched constraints of the "scientific article" are supposedly lifted.

Perhaps the application of the label "less restrained" suggests just how impoverished, stiff, sanitized and humorless our scholarly discourse has become; in Perrow's (1985) memorable term, "asphalted." Are only terms associated with calm reason and cool calculation to be found in print? Must our passions be put forth impassionately, our interests displayed with disinterest, our personal views given impersonally, our selective use of facts cloaked by scientific ideals of a century long past?

On the surface then this is a most stilted critique. For one thing, comedy, parody, satire, travesty, farce, jest and irreverence of all kinds are regular attendants in the service of persuasion and reality construction. Unusual phrasings, word play, puns, fresh analogies and metaphors, stylistic signatures of all sorts offer to invert the order of things, to unsettle accepted modes of thought, to render the taken-for-granted world a little topsy-turvy, a point I made with respect to some essays by Karl Weick though apparently a point missed completely by Jeff. The work such writings accomplish can be corrosive of dogma and thus protect consciousness and thought. The wholesale disparagement (and ban) of those genres and styles that seek to inform as well as to amuse, jibe, startle and otherwise stand apart from the taken-for-granted, technocratic language of the field is perhaps the real threat presented by Jeff's cranky response that elevates reproducibility, consensus and dogged perseverance above insight, creativity and principled tolerance for ideas not easily slipped into a paradigm file.

Below the surface however lurks a more serious matter. Jeff implies that my speech is somehow infected with a rhetoric that is absent from his own. This is a kind of argument much beloved by keepers of the scientific flame. It is also apparently of great attraction to Jeff for a reader can almost hear him chortle as he plunks it down with an attitude that it is a point so irrefutable, so rock solid that no one can get around it. Despite Jeff's smugness and intellectual *chutzpah,* it is a point easily dislodged. In a nutshell, there is no form of speech, argument, representation that is free from rhetoric. Every scientist or scholar, regardless of field, relies on common devices of rhetoric: On metaphors; on premises left unargued; on word games; on invocations of authority (Nelson et al. 1987, p. 32); on appeals to the "good sense" of readers; on using forms of evidence that sometimes ignore the concerns, backgrounds and resources available to readers; on political correctness (or its intentional violation); on purposely undefined or vague concepts; on strategic silences and the use of bland euphemisms; on tricks of writing masquerading as reason (e.g., "it is evident . . ."); and on and on (and on).

Standing behind an anti-rhetorical stance is often a powerful elitism associated with paradigmatic certainty. For those in possession of such certainty (and the clout they assume their due), any break in the institutionalized forms of discourse is seen as a regrettable descent into rhetoric. The anti-rhetoric crowd would have it that they use a neutral, transparent language uncolored by any personal or partisan agendas. Language marked by personal reference and preference, for example, or language that calls attention to itself via stylistic gesture is thus polluted by a treacherous subjectivity, by individual agendas and desires that distort whatever facts are communicated. This is the kind of language that makes one, in Jeff's phrase, a "master rhetorician." By rejecting flourish, style, unconventional phrasing and formats for a "natural" language of temperance and studied indifference, a writer becomes a reliable, trustworthy and (more or less) objective reporter of the way things are. An elegant ploy to be sure. But, in these textually sophisticated days, it is a ploy all too familiar and no longer carries great force.[3] To accept a sharp distinction between rhetorical and non-rhetorical speech is to trade in our late twentieth century understandings of language and language use for those of the seventeenth century.

In brief, the contemporary argument—which can be traced from the icy mountain tops of universal reason and clear-eyed objectivity to the steamy valleys of socially-embedded knowledge and negotiated meanings—is that one is never free from rhetoric. Even the most unpreposing, flat, minimalist, just-the-facts, Plain Jane prose proclaims itself as rhetoric as clearly as charged, stylistically innovative, loud, colorful, Calamity Jane prose. The whole range of intended or unintended ornament in speech—from zero to ten—is equally rhetorical, equally deep, equally superficial. When anti-rhetorical types hear this argument they are likely to regard it as another rhetorical trick designed to take us down that slippery slope to anarchistic relativism. And when the friends of rhetoric hear claims of language transparency, they too suspect dishonesty, though not necessarily a dishonesty marked by foresight and malice.[4] And so it goes, an endless round of accusation and counteraccusation in which truth and honesty are claimed by all. There is no escape.

The question is of course what rhetoric will prevail? Is path analysis always more persuasive than a moral argument? Is a controlled experiment more persuasive than an ethnography? Do soft, vague theories invariably lose out in the end to hard, precise ones? I doubt it. While these are often audience-specific matters, competing truth claims come down to rhetorical contests as I demonstrate by moving to the contest at hand.

I have three lines of criticism to open up. The first concerns the normative or moral grounds of Jeff's arguments. This is akin to a critical theorist's perspective and raises a few (of many) questions as to whether or not our synthetic, rather rag-tag and multiple paradigm field of organizational studies would be well served working toward (or in) paradigmatic consensus. My second set of concerns requires a quick but close look at a few of the meanings—intended or not—to be extracted from Jeff's response and thus necessitates something of a literary or deconstructive tale of his text. My third line of critique is to challenge and deny the reality of the so-called objective world Jeff tries to argue into existence. Here I challenge several propositional truths and validity claims put forth in his reply.

NORMATIVE IMPLICATIONS

Jeff seems to live in a Hobbesian world where power equals knowledge. Certainly success—as indicated by journal space, recruitment of students, tenure slots and so forth—is given most weight as the measure of a paradigm's worthiness. Matters of value, creativity, appeal, scope, paradigmatic change and innovation are given short shrift. It is a most utilitarian perspective and curiously mimics the very self-seeking premises of approaches he otherwise claims to find limiting. Paradigmatic consensus may provide blissful relief from the ambiguity and contentiousness of our field and (arguably) protect us from threatened take-over attempts by the barbarians at our gates, but the costs in scholarly and human terms of achieving such a state are not much considered.

We do get some hints at what a cozy but suffocating world paradigm consensus might be through the examples Jeff provides of those organizational studies subfields he considers fine-tuned, fit and successful: behavioral decision theory, population ecology, network analysis and so forth. Here the words and phrases he uses to describe these areas are most revealing of the kind of scholarly world that appears to exist behind paradigmatic consensus; a world Jeff would have us emulate. Consider just a few: "domination (of a field)" (p. 682), "efficient in training graduate students" (p. 683), "scholarship more predictable" (p. 683), "taken over (major journals)" (p. 683), "more efficient and effective research programs" (p. 683), "theoretical hegemony" (p. 683), "ability to readily reproduce" (p. 684), "technology for analysis" (p. 685), and "replicable, teachable, transferable concepts and methods" (p. 685). This is a call for the industrialization of scholarship, not its advancement. It is a call to further stratify our field by narrowing the legitimate research topics, theories and methods as deemed appropriate by those who build and articulate the chosen paradigm.

This of course begs the questions of how and why such a consensus could be brought about in the first place? How would we go about "enlisting others" to the cause? Just how draconian the measures to be taken to achieve a paradigm consensus can be inferred by the sense of urgency Jeff introduces into his story: *The economists are coming! The economists are coming!* If we are to survive, any number of worlds and activities will have to be curtailed or excluded and there is apparently no time to waste. Thus it seems to Jeff that what looks to me like a broad and healthy field—a loosely-knit community that is not standing still but changing its shape through growing numbers of active researchers who are exploring new territories, sharing their findings and projects with one another in an expanding number of books and journals, meeting regularly in small and large groups to explain, debate, proselytize— is really a field in poor health. Such widespread professional activity apparently disperses the power and authority that would otherwise be centralized under a paradigmatic banner and needed to go toe-to-toe, eyeball-to-eyeball with the economists and others of like ilk.

In simple moral terms, the idea that we should somehow look toward paradigmatic consensus for our salvation is wrong. Even if such a world were possible (which it is not, see below), it would be a most uncomfortable place to reside. It would be a world with little emancipatory possibilities, a world with even tighter restrictions on who can be published, promoted, fired, celebrated, reviled than we have now. *Sturm und Drang und Tenure.* The image of a large research community characterized by the kinds of traits Jeff associates with paradigm consensus is that of a clean California research park where nothing is out of place and all is governed by a corporate logic focused on productivity, competitive advantage and the good old bottom line. This is not scholarship. On normative grounds alone, paradigm consensus can be rejected.

AUTHORIAL STYLE

Jeff seems to look out on our field as if he were on the bridge of a battleship moving toward action at flank speed. However the enemies it seems are not those of rational choice persuasion or necessarily dreaded economists for their assumptions and approaches are hardly criticized at all (save one sentence on p. 682). Indeed, rat choice as a paradigm is put forward to be admired for its clockwork efficiencies and single-minded aims and methods. It is ironic that we must mimic the opposition in order to survive even though we are told the results of their grand theories are trivial.[5]

Across the several research fields (and subfields) that Jeff associates with paradigmatic consensus, certain features are common: Formalism, operationalism, methodological canons, deductive models, apparent theoretical coherence with a stress on theory testing, and a restricted range of topically legitimate issues. These features are presumably keys to a paradigmatic consensus and all the material and social benefits it will provide. That it just so happens Jeff's own research work is largely of the same sort is apparently a mere coincidence and unworthy of mention. The call for paradigm consensus may be then a call for a Pfeffer-digmatic research community so reduced in scope that its borders are those of Palo Alto.

Such a reading is possible because Jeff maintains a strategic silence on matters of critical importance to his program. Like consensus, the term paradigm is central to his concerns but it is undefined and unmarked.[6] It stands as a glossed, generic and misty signifier. At best, we can pick up clues as to what kind of paradigm he has in mind (and favors) only from the narrow range of examples he presents. Nothing is said of course about other currently powerful intellectual movements such as the anti-theory of postmodernism which, as a movement, is far more important and visible as it sweeps through the social sciences, the humanities, the arts than, say, conversational analysis or behavioral decision theory. What of the interpretive or linguistic swings taking place in many fields including our own? What of the loose, eclectic and ramshackle character of institutionalization theory whose lack of heavy-handed theoretical discipline may be part of its appeal and, in the long run, the key to its success? Without definition or exemplary specification we are left holding the end of a question mark like the handle of an umbrella.

We know of course that one of the most common tactics of elite groups of all sorts is to refuse to discuss—to label as uninteresting or vulgar—issues that are uncomfortable for them. I argued that theory makes its way in intellectual communities (and beyond) as much by its style as by its theoretical claims, logic, sweep, empirical evidence or methodological strictures. My points are not countered by Jeff. Some of them are incorporated into his story—*sotto voce*—through his linking of "styles of theory" (what we might call research genres) to social influence. But, alas, Jeff fails to consider both the reception of texts and the audience specificity of such reception(s).

Could it be that the very rhetoric of, say, organizational economics—with its familiar reductionism, abstract character, mathematical simplicity, worries about self-seeking, guile and lack of trust—is what accounts for its appeal in this society?[7] Does rational choice theory have appeal because it is individualistic, technically neat and apparently easy to grasp, use and publish? Is this success or scandal? How well does such work travel? My point is simply that Jeff's analysis ends at precisely the point where it should begin. Why (and where) do certain "styles of theory" achieve prominence (for a time)? Even if we were to accept Jeff's strange argument that "(Weick's) insight, richness, lucidity, virtuosity, creativeness and style is *inevitably* disadvantaged in the market place of ideas," (p. 684, emphasis mine), what are we to make of it beyond its claimed inevitability? This is the rhetoric of naturalization and essentialism applied to the social world of reading, interpretation and meaning. It is not persuasive.

PROPOSITIONAL TRUTHS

Consider now the evidence Jeff presents in support of his theories. Are his arguments backed up by data we can trust? All data are of course imperfect and selective but here I think we have an extreme case that is easy to dismantle. Four points, made hastily, will suffice.

First, the matter of theoretical coherence. Economics is presented as an exemplar of paradigmatic consensus. This, to adopt McCloskey's (1983, p. 494) tribal categories, should quickly be communicated to the Chicago modernists, the NYU Austrians, the Massachusetts Marxists, the Berkeley neoclassicists and the Texas institutionalists. If Jeff is worried about an agency theory or transaction cost take-over in organizational studies, perhaps we should enlist a few economic purists to whom such approaches are a hoot. Nor is it the case that in-house squabbles and theoretical disputes lead to a fall. Anthropology is a convenient example of a diffuse and multiparadigm field. It has been in "crisis" for more than a decade. It lives contentiously with its cultural, social, symbolic, material, political and economic anthropologies as well as its anthropologies of religion, work, family, medicine and so forth. Yet it is growing in both numbers and influence. The "discipline" has a gaggle of celebrated names, is at the leading and bleeding edge of social science, and finds its ideas taken up in history, cognitive science, literary studies, philosophy as well as the applied arts of education, social work, marketing, urban planning, even nursing. Crisis it seems can be a cash cow.

Second, the matter of citations rates and take-overs. Several journals, even leading ones, do not make a field. Do we really believe that the increased number of population ecology papers appearing in *ASQ* in 1992 and 1993 represents "disproportionate impact" (p. 683) independent of journal policy presumably influenced by the editor during this period, pop ecology crusader John Freeman? Is the apparent "capture" of a journal by behavioral decision theorists as suggestive (and alarming) as Jeff indicates? Measuring disciplinary or field "domination" by citation rates in one or two journals over a short period of time is imaginative but fanciful. Paradigms rise and fall and a move in either direction is not necessarily a measure of scholarly worth or value.

Third, the issue of Karl Weick's influence. Jeff asks "how easy would it be for others to employ Weick's style or even to build on his work?" (p. 684). With no data whatsoever, he answers in the negative. This is bullshit! *The Social Psychology of Organizing* is one of the field's major works and in the 25 or so years since its publication, it has changed the language we use in talking about organizations. An admiring book reviewer noted recently that the book remains his top candidate for ferocious, desert island reading: "a wonderful rattlebag of ideas . . . that on rereading you see things you haven't seen before" (Colville 1994, p. 222). Enactment, equivocality, interpretive systems, casual maps are concepts that are part of our working vocabulary. Some ideas may turn out to be loopy, others solid, but they attract attention and make us think. There is no paradigm here but enormous influence.

Finally, the matters of technology and method. Jeff argues that "for writing to be influential, it must not only suggest what to do in general terms but how to go about it in very specific terms" (p. 685). This perspective would have it that Freed Bales (and his mechanical interaction counters) is more influential than Erving Goffman or that the ubiquitous Gert Hofsteader (and his power distance scales) is more influential than Clifford Geertz. Goffman and Geertz provide no method manuals, offer no technology but their writings continue to mesmerize students. Jeff considers a very limited—within paradigm—kind of influence; a sort relatively unconcerned with creativity, insight, opening up new ways to think and see. Even if technical refinements increase the attractiveness of a research program, this hardly indicates substantive progress or knowledge accumulation. Matters of technical development and method are embedded within paradigms and cannot, by definition, advance or change them.

WHAT NOW?

To bring this to a close, I think it highly unlikely any paradigm will trump or unite our field. Various research programs guided by adventurous theories both old and new will wax and wane and we should welcome such programs (if only to combat them). These are deprovincialized times in social science (and elsewhere) and, as a result, organizational analysis is contentious and difficult. Paradigmatic competition has been the norm for 50-odd years but it is becoming more intense as schools of thought multiply and our numbers grow. Put bluntly, we are quite likely to be in each other's faces more than ever. The question is what to do about it?

In "Style as Theory," I suggested that learning to cope with and perhaps learn from one another is a most critical matter. We cannot conjure up a paradigm of sufficient appeal to voluntarily unite the organization studies community. Nor can we legislate or impress into existence the paradigmatic unity Jeff longs for. On the other hand, it is pernicious and beside the point to suggest we stick to our own claustrophobic ways with each of us camped by our own totem pole. We need ways of talking across research programs and theoretical commitments. Weick's elevates style in his writings through his almost Flaubertian obsession for *le mot juste* and, as a result, attracts readers from many paradigmatic camps. Less eloquently, this debate between Jeff and me provides another way of talking across paradigms (about paradigms). Other possibilities are open as well.

Jeff thinks our fencing about form and discourse is a "sideshow." I think it a main event. Arguably, there may be a few short-run instrumental advantages associated with the paradigmatic unity of the sort that Jeff identifies. But to seek these ends is to admit that the owl of Minerva has taken wing. To me the wager Jeff puts to us is intuitively clear. We are offered a degree of clout at the expense of open (and disorderly) inquiry. Style, breadth, theoretical and methodological innovation are impedance factors, not aims if we place our bets with Jeff. This is not an attractive wager. It is one we should energetically—with heat—refuse.

NOTES

1. The usual suspects helped me in drafting this response. The lineup includes Peter Manning, Gideon Kunda, Bob Thomas, Colleen McCallion, Lotte Bailyn, John Jermier, John Weeks and a number of participants in several seminars who were subjected to my take on the issues raised in this debate. I am sure few if any would take the same stance and spin as I do in this paper but they nonetheless pushed me to position myself. I am grateful.

2. As a genre of public discourse in an open community, debate is a cornerstone. And it is in this genre of thrust and parry that Jeff and I write (and talk). Debate is often energized by the taste

of victory of course and much postdebate conversation turns on just who "won" and "lost." But, I would argue that a goal of equal if not greater importance is simply to enhance understanding of the issues under contention in the community at large. In theory, readers or listeners (though not necessarily the participants to a debate who are often smothered by convictions not fully shared by others) should gain a better grasp of the issues at stake if ideas are tested, argued, refuted than if they are left unchallenged.

3. Had Jeff pursued Edelman (1964, 1971) in more depth he would have discovered that even explicitly anti-political language can be and is used as a rhetorical front to disguise highly political aims; a tactic made much use of by so-called political outsiders who would have us believe that their agendas are above mere politics. To label my language as "political" and his (by implication) as "reasoned and scientific" is simply a move in our argument and an appeal to the audience to swallow a false distinction without thinking. Both of us are equally political in trying the persuade our readers. Gusfield (1976) is a must read in this regard.

4. The friends of rhetoric across several disciplines who make the above argument far more eloquently than I include White (1973), Edmondson (1984), Nelson et al. (1987), Simmons (Ed.) (1988), and Fish (1989). For an illuminating essay on the role of rhetoric in organization studies, see Gergen (1992).

5. Could it be that the triviality (of findings) is related to the structural and disciplinary features of those social science paradigms Jeff more or less honors as having achieved consensus? Perhaps such a matter is not explored in the original paper or in the response for good reason since it would be deadly as a rallying cry for paradigm consensus.

6. Jeff is in good company on this matter. Kuhn (1964) uses the term paradigm in a variety of ways. When pressed by critics on the issue, he responded by saying in his 1970 postscript that there were three broad ways the term could be defined in his work but he favored one more than the others: paradigm as exemplar. Using the term paradigm to refer to shared examples suggests that it is a matter more likely to be insinuated than fiercely taught with lots of rules to obey and authorities to respect. My reading of Jeff's use of the term is that he is more comfortable with the definitions Kuhn rejected: paradigm as structure and/or paradigm as discipline.

7. On this matter, I have a theory. Many social scientists in the U.S.—like the general population—are rather absolutist about American values and ideals; to somehow equate them with human nature and proper conduct and thus treat social theories that deviate from individualistic, pragmatic, self-seeking, egalitarian assumptions as perverse. In the comparative context of world ethnology and history, such assumptions may well be uncommon, perhaps eccentric. But, for us, they are part of the air we breathe. The appeal of certain economic theories, rational choice theory, behavioral decision theory and many others is then a highly contextual (and cultural or subcultural) matter. Mauro Guillèn (1994) has wonderful stories to tell about the cross-cultural appeal—or lack thereof—carried by several highly visible and, for a time, widely accepted (in this country) management theories.

REFERENCES

Colville, I. (1994), "Searching for Karl Weick and Reviewing the Future," *Organization,* 1, 218-224.

Edelman, M. (1964), *The Symbolic Use of Politics,* Urbana, IL: University of Illinois Press.

—— (1971), *Politics as Symbolic Action,* Chicago, IL: Markham.

Edmondsun, R. (1984), *Rhetoric in Sociology,* London, UK: Macmillan.

Fish, S. (1989), *Doing What Comes Naturally: Change, Rhetoric and the Practice of Theory in Literary and Legal Studies,* New York: Oxford University Press.

Gergen, K. J. (1992), "Organization Theory in the Postmodern Era," in M. Reed and H. Hughes (Eds.), *Rethinking Organization,* London, UK: Sage, 207-226.

Guillèn, M. (1994), *Models of Management,* Chicago, IL: University of Chicago Press.

Gusfield, J. (1976), "The Literary Rhetoric of Science," *American Sociological Review,* 41, 16-33.

Kuhn, T. (1964), *The Structure of Scientific Revolutions,* Chicago, IL: University of Chicago Press, 2d ed. 1970.

McCloskey, D. N. (1983), "The Rhetoric of Economics," *Journal of Economic Literature,* 21, 481-517.

Nelson, J. S., A. Megill and D. N. McCloskey (Eds.) (1987), *The Rhetoric of the Human Sciences,* Madison, WI: University of Wisconsin Press.

Perrow, C. (1985), "Journaling Careers," in L. L. Cummings and P. Frost (Eds.), *Publishing in the Organizational Sciences,* San Francisco, CA: Jossey-Bass, 220-230.

Pfeffer, J. (1993), "Barriers to the Advance of Organizational Science: Paradigm Development as a Dependent Variable," *Academy of Management Review,* 18, 599-620.

——— (1995), "Mortality, Reproducibility, and the Persistence of Styles of Theory," *Organization Science,* 6, 680-686.

Simmons, H. W. (Ed.) (1988), *The Rhetorical Turn,* Chicago, IL: University of Chicago Press.

Van Maanen, J. (1995), "Style as Theory," *Organization Science,* 6, 1, 132-143.

White, H. (1973), *Metahistory,* Baltimore, MD: Johns Hopkins University Press.

PART II

DISCOURSES ABOUT ORGANIZATION SCIENCE

The chapters in this section represent a shift in conversation toward moving beyond the polarities in Part I. In Part II, the chapters talk about organization science in a broader context, its history and grounding, and ways to interpret voices from different perspectives. The chapters in this section reflect essays, conversations, stories, and expositions of what authors from different perspectives believe to be the nature of organization science and how scholars come to know it. As you read the first two chapters, reflect back on the debates and see where the respective chapters fit in the proposed frameworks. The Burrell and Morgan ("Two Dimensions: Four Paradigms") framework has had great impact on the field, yet frameworks can be both liberating and restraining. The Deetz framework ("Describing Differences in Approaches to Organization Science: Rethinking Burrell and Morgan and Their Legacy") proposes an alternative conceptual scheme. In some sense there is a flavor of debate in this discussion, but the first two chapters are both designed to resolve some of the key polarization's inherent in the debate chapters.

The third chapter, by Nord and Connell ("From Quicksand to Crossroads: An Agnostic Perspective on Conversation"), proposes an agnostic perspective that suggests there is no external, knowable reality that scholars can agree on. Instead of looking at differences, they propose finding commonalities and in so doing reveal something of themselves, knowing that individuals' values, opinions, and hypotheses emanate from their own backgrounds. Bridges among self-aware scholars may enable communication across traditional boundaries.

In the remaining chapters in this part, we see different stories by several different authors studying organizations and organizational culture and how the "self" links with organization, text, and reader to create different realities ("Writing Organizational Tales: Four Authors and Their Stories About Culture," Yanow, Trice and Beyer, Kunda, Martin, and Smircich). We examine, through the eyes of March and Sutton, another take on tales of the field as they focus on the complexities of doing organizational research, asking in a sense: "What's a scholar to do?" ("Organizational Performance as a Dependent Variable"). Finally, the interview between John Jermier and Stewart Clegg ("Critical Issues in Organization Science: A Dialogue, Part 1") probes into deeper assumptions about the underlying nature of the field as a way to interpret scholarly view within a larger context.

In this section, you may want to think about the following questions: How does the self and one's personal experience, particularly in a positivist environment, influence one's perspective on organization science? Can people within one perspective be expected to understand and appreciate scholarly work from a seemingly opposite perspective? If you were a part of a conversation with these authors, to which arguments would you especially listen? What would you like to say in response? And finally, can you find common ground among the diverse chapters that follow?

7

Two Dimensions

Four Paradigms

GIBSON BURRELL
School of Industrial and Business Studies, University of Warwick

GARETH MORGAN
Schulich School of Business, York University, Toronto

In the previous two chapters we have focused upon some of the key assumptions which characterise different approaches to social theory. We have argued that it is possible to analyse these approaches in terms of two key dimensions of analysis, each of which subsumes a series of related themes. It has been suggested that assumptions about the nature of science can be thought of in terms of what we call the subjective-objective dimension, and assumptions about the nature of society in terms of a regulation-radical change dimension. In this chapter we wish to discuss the relationships between the two dimensions and to develop a coherent scheme for the analysis of social theory.

We have already noted how sociological debate since the late 1960s has tended to ignore the distinctions between the two dimensions—in particular, how there has been a tendency to focus upon issues concerned with the

NOTE: Text referring to other chapters in Gibson and Morgan (1979) has been replaced with ellipses.

subjective-objective dimension and to ignore those concerned with the regulation-radical change dimension. Interestingly enough, this focus of attention has characterised sociological thought associated with both regulation
and radical change. The subjective-objective debate has been conducted
independently within both sociological camps.

Within the sociology of regulation it has assumed the form of a debate
between interpretive sociology and functionalism. In the wake of Berger and
Luckmann's treatise on the sociology of knowledge (1966), Garfinkel's work
on ethnomethodology (1967) and a general resurgence of interest in phenomenology, the questionable status of the ontological and epistemological
assumptions of the functionalist perspective have become increasingly
exposed. The debate has often led to a polarisation between the two schools
of thought.

Similarly, within the context of the sociology of radical change there has
been a division between theorists subscribing to "subjective" and "objective"
views of society. The debate in many respects takes its lead from the publication in France in 1966 and Britain in 1969 of Louis Althusser's work *For
Marx*. This presented the notion of an "epistemological break" in Marx's
work and emphasised the polarisation of Marxist theorists into two camps:
those emphasising the "subjective" aspects of Marxism (Lukács and the
Frankfurt School, for example) and those advocating more "objective"
approaches, such as that associated with Althusserian structuralism.

Within the context of the sociologies both of regulation and radical
change, therefore, the middle to late 1960s witnessed a distinct switch in the
focus of attention. The debate *between* these two sociologies which had characterised the early 1960s disappeared and was replaced by an introverted dialogue *within* the context of each of the separate schools of thought. Instead of
"speaking" to each other they turned inwards and addressed their remarks to
themselves. The concern to sort out their position with regard to what we call
the subjective-objective dimension, a complicated process in view of all
the interrelated strands, led to a neglect of the regulation-radical change
dimension.

As a consequence of these developments, recent debate has often been
confused. Sociological thought has tended to be characterised by a narrow
sectarianism, from which an overall perspective and grasp of basic issues are
conspicuously absent. The time is ripe for consideration of the way ahead,
and we submit that the two key dimensions of analysis which we have identified define critical parameters within which this can take place. We present
them as two independent dimensions which resurrect the sociological issues
of the early 1960s and place them alongside those of the late 1960s and early
1970s. Taken together, they define four distinct sociological paradigms
which can be utilised for the analysis of a wide range of social theories. The

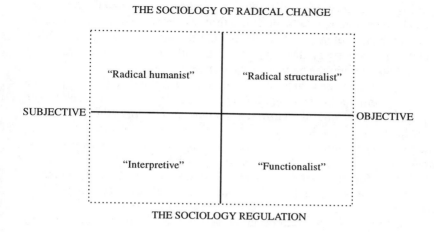

Figure 7.1. Four Paradigms for the Analysis of Social Theory

relationship between these paradigms, which we label "radical humanist", "radical structuralist", "interpretive" and "functionalist", is illustrated in Figure 7.1.

It will be clear from the diagram that each of the paradigms shares a common set of features with its neighbours on the horizontal and vertical axes in terms of one of the two dimensions but is differentiated on the other dimension. For this reason they should be viewed as contiguous but separate—contiguous because of the shared characteristics, but separate because the differentiation is, as we shall demonstrate later, of sufficient importance to warrant treatment of the paradigms as four distinct entities. The four paradigms define fundamentally different perspectives for the analysis of social phenomena. They approach this endeavour from contrasting standpoints and generate quite different concepts and analytical tools.

THE NATURE AND USES
OF THE FOUR PARADIGMS

Before going on to discuss the substantive nature of each of the paradigms, it will be as well to pay some attention to the way in which we intend the notion of "paradigm" to be used.[1] We regard our four paradigms as being defined by very basic meta-theoretical assumptions which underwrite the frame of reference, mode of theorising and *modus operandi* of the social theorists who operate within them. It is a term which is intended to emphasise the commonality of perspective which binds the work of a group of theorists together in such a way that they can be usefully regarded as approaching social theory within the bounds of the same problematic.

This definition does not imply complete unity of thought. It allows for the fact that within the context of any given paradigm there will be much debate between theorists who adopt different standpoints. The paradigm does, however, have an underlying unity in terms of its basic and often "taken for granted" assumptions, which separate a group of theorists in a very fundamental way from theorists located in other paradigms. The "unity" of the paradigm thus derives from reference to alternative views of reality which lie outside its boundaries and which may not necessarily even be recognised as existing.

In identifying four paradigms in social theory we are in essence suggesting that it is meaningful to examine work in the subject area in terms of four sets of basic assumptions. Each set identifies a quite separate social-scientific reality. To be located in a particular paradigm is to view the world in a particular way. The four paradigms thus define four views of the social world based upon different meta-theoretical assumptions with regard to the nature of science and of society.

It is our contention that all social theorists can be located within the context of these four paradigms according to the meta-theoretical assumptions reflected in their work. The four paradigms taken together provide a map for negotiating the subject area, which offers a convenient means of identifying the basic similarities and differences between the work of various theorists and, in particular, the underlying frame of reference which they adopt. It also provides a convenient way of locating one's own personal frame of reference with regard to social theory, and thus a means of understanding why certain theories and perspectives may have more personal appeal than others. Like any other map, it provides a tool for establishing where you are, where you have been and where it is possible to go in the future. It provides a tool for mapping intellectual journeys in social theory—one's own and those of the theorists who have contributed to the subject area.

In this work we intend to make much use of the map-like qualities of the four paradigms. Each defines a range of intellectual territory. Given the overall meta-theoretical assumptions which distinguish one paradigm from another, there is room for much variation within them. Within the context of the "functionalist" paradigm, for example, certain theorists adopt more extreme positions in terms of one or both of the two dimensions than others. Such differences often account for the internal debate which goes on between theorists engaged in the activities of "normal science" within the context of the same paradigm.[2] . . .

Our research suggests that whilst the activity within the context of each paradigm is often considerable, inter-paradigmatic "journeys" are much rarer. This is in keeping with Kuhn's (1970) notion of "revolutionary science." For a theorist to switch paradigms calls for a change in meta-theoretical assumptions, something which, although manifestly possible, is not often achieved in practice. As Keat and Urry put it, "For individual scientists, the change of allegiance from one paradigm to another is often a "conversion experience", akin to *Gestalt*-switches or changes of religious faith" (1975, p. 55). When a theorist does shift his position in this way, it stands out very clearly as a major break with his intellectual tradition and is heralded as being so in the literature, in that the theorist is usually welcomed by those whom he has joined and often disowned by his former "paradigm colleagues." Thus we witness what is known as the "epistemological break" between the work of the young Marx and the mature Marx—what we would identify as a shift from the radical humanist paradigm to the radical structuralist paradigm. At the level of organisational analysis, a distinct paradigm shift can be detected in the work of Silverman—a shift from the functionalist paradigm to the interpretive paradigm. . . .

Before we progress to a review of the four paradigms, one point is worthy of further emphasis. This relates to the fact that the four paradigms are mutually exclusive. They offer alternative views of social reality, and to understand the nature of all four is to understand four different views of society. They offer different ways of seeing. A synthesis is not possible, since in their pure forms they are contradictory, being based on at least one set of opposing meta-theoretical assumptions. They are alternatives, in the sense that one *can* operate in different paradigms sequentially over time, but mutually exclusive, in the sense that one cannot operate in more than one paradigm at any given point in time, since in accepting the assumptions of one, we defy the assumptions of all the others.

We offer the four paradigms for consideration in these terms, in the hope that knowledge of the competing points of view will at least make us aware of the boundaries within which we approach our subject.

THE FUNCTIONALIST PARADIGM

This paradigm has provided the dominant framework for the conduct of academic sociology and the study of organisations. It represents a perspective which is firmly rooted in the *sociology of regulation* and approaches its subject matter from an *objectivist* point of view. Functionalist theorists have been at the forefront of the order-conflict debate, and the concepts which we have used to categorise the sociology of regulation apply in varying degrees to all schools of thought within the paradigm. It is characterised by a concern for providing explanations of *the status quo, social order, consensus, social integration, solidarity, need satisfaction* and *actuality*. It approaches these general sociological concerns from a standpoint which tends to be *realist, positivist, determinist* and *nomothetic.*

The functionalist paradigm generates regulative sociology in its most fully developed form. In its overall approach it seeks to provide essentially rational explanations of social affairs. It is a perspective which is highly pragmatic in orientation, concerned to understand society in a way which generates knowledge which can be put to use. It is often problem-orientated in approach, concerned to provide practical solutions to practical problems. It is usually firmly committed to a philosophy of social engineering as a basis of social change and emphasises the importance of understanding order, equilibrium and stability in society and the way in which these can be maintained. It is concerned with the effective "regulation" and control of social affairs.

. . . [T]he approach to social science characteristic of the functionalist paradigm is rooted in the tradition of sociological positivism. This reflects the attempt, *par excellence,* to apply the models and methods of the natural sciences to the study of human affairs. Originating in France in the early decades of the nineteenth century, its major influence upon the paradigm has been through the work of social theorists such as Auguste Comte, Herbert Spencer, Emile Durkheim and Vilfredo Pareto. The functionalist approach to social science tends to assume that the social world is composed of relatively concrete empirical artefacts and relationships which can be identified, studied and measured through approaches derived from the natural sciences. The use of mechanical and biological analogies as a means of modelling and understanding the social world is particularly favoured in many functionalist theories. By way of illustration consider, for example, the work of Durkheim. Central to his position was the idea that "social facts" exist outside of men's consciousness and restrain men in their everyday activities. The aim was to understand the relationships between these "objective" social facts and to articulate the sociology which explained the types of "solidarity" providing the "social cement" which holds society together. The stability and ordered nature of the natural world was viewed as characterising the world of human affairs. For Durkheim, the task of sociology was to understand the nature of this regulated order.

Since the early decades of the twentieth century, however, the functionalist paradigm has been increasingly influenced by elements from the German idealist tradition of social thought. . . . [T]his approach reflects assumptions

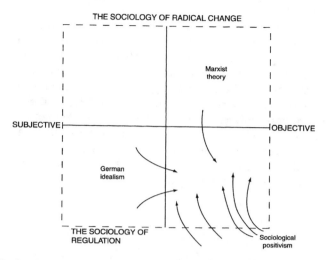

Figure 7.2. Intellectual Influences Upon the Functionalist Paradigm

about the nature of social science which stand in opposition to those of socio-logical positivism. As a result of the work of such theorists as Max Weber, George Simmel and George Herbert Mead, elements of this idealist approach have been utilised within the context of social theories which have attempted to bridge the gulf between the two traditions. In so doing they have forged theoretical perspectives characteristic of the least objectivist region of the paradigm, at its junction with the interpretive paradigm. Such theories have rejected the use of mechanical and biological analogies for studying the social world and have introduced ideas which place emphasis upon the importance of understanding society from the point of view of the actors who are actually engaged in the performance of social activities.

Since the 1940s there has been also an infusion of certain Marxist influ-ences characteristic of the sociology of radical change. These have been incorporated within the paradigm in an attempt to "radicalise" functionalist theory and rebuff the general charge that functionalism is essentially conser-vative and unable to provide explanations for social change. These attempts underwrite the debate examined in the previous chapter as to whether a theory of "conflict" can be incorporated within the bounds of a theory of "order" to provide adequate explanations of social affairs.

Put very crudely, therefore, the formation of the functionalist paradigm can be understood in terms of the interaction of three sets of intellectual forces, as illustrated in Figure 7.2. Of these, sociological positivism has been the most influential. The competing traditions have been sucked in and used within the context of the functionalist problematic, which emphasises the essentially objectivist nature of the social world and a concern for explanations which emphasise "regulation" in social affairs. These cross-currents of thought have given rise to a number of distinctive schools of thought within the paradigm, which is characterised by a wide range of theory and internal debate. By way of overview, again somewhat crudely, Figures 7.3 and 7.4 illustrate the four paradigms in terms of the constituent schools of sociological and organisational theory which we shall be exploring later on. As will be apparent, most organisation theorists, industrial sociologists, psychologists and industrial relations theorists approach their subject from within the bounds of the functionalist paradigm.

THE INTERPRETIVE PARADIGM

Theorists located within the context of the interpretive paradigm adopt an approach consonant with the tenets of what we have described as the *sociology of regulation,* though its *subjectivist* approach to the analysis of the social world makes its links with this sociology often implicit rather than explicit. The interpretive paradigm is informed by a concern to understand the world as it is, to understand the fundamental nature of the social world at the level of subjective experience. It seeks explanation within the realm of individual consciousness and subjectivity, within the frame of reference of the participant as opposed to the observer of action.

In its approach to social science it tends to be *nominalist, anti-positivist, voluntarist* and *ideographic.* It sees the social world as an emergent social process which is created by the individuals concerned. Social reality, insofar as it is recognised to have any existence outside the consciousness of any single individual, is regarded as being little more than a network of assumptions and intersubjectively shared meanings. The ontological status of the social world is viewed as extremely questionable and problematic as far as theorists located within the interpretive paradigm are concerned. Everyday life is accorded the status of a miraculous achievement. Interpretive philosophers and sociologists seek to understand the very basis and source of social reality. They often delve into the depths of human consciousness and subjectivity in their quest for the fundamental meanings which underlie social life.

Given this view of social reality, it is hardly surprising that the commitment of the interpretive sociologists to the sociology of regulation is implicit rather than explicit. Their ontological assumptions rule out a direct interest in the issues involved in the order-conflict debate as such. However, their standpoint is underwritten by the assumption that the world of human affairs is

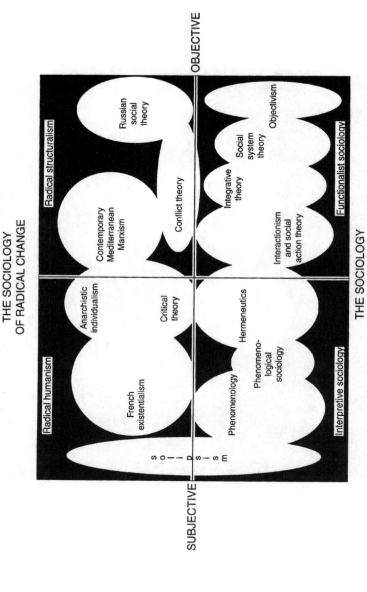

Figure 7.3. The Four Sociological Paradigms

115

116

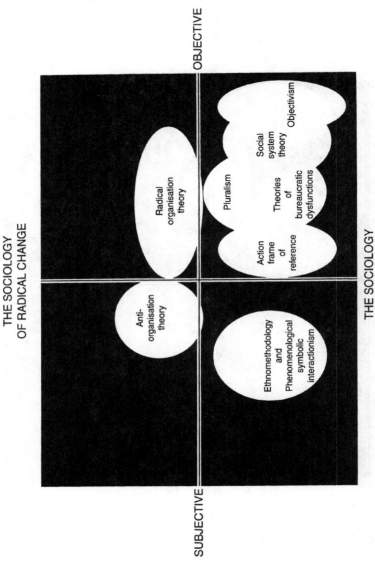

Figure 7.4. The Main Schools of Organisational Analysis

cohesive, ordered and integrated.The problems of conflict, domination, contradiction, potentiality and change play no part in their theoretical framework. They are much more oriented towards obtaining an understanding of
the subjectively created social world "as it is" in terms of an ongoing process.

Interpretive sociology is concerned with understanding the essence of the
everyday world. In terms of our analytical schema it is underwritten by an
involvement with issues relating to the nature of *the status quo, social order,
consensus, social integration and cohesion, solidarity* and *actuality*.[3]

The interpretive paradigm is the direct product of the German idealist tradition of social thought. Its foundations were laid in the work of Kant and
reflect a social philosophy which emphasises the essentially spiritual nature
of the social world. The idealist tradition was paramount in Germanic
thought from the mid-eighteenth century onwards and was closely linked
with the romantic movement in literature and the arts. Outside this realm,
however, it was of limited interest, until revived in the late 1890s and early
years of this century under the influence of the so-called neo-idealist movement. Theorists such as Dilthey, Weber, Husserl and Schutz have made a
major contribution towards establishing it as a framework for social analysis,
though with varying degrees of commitment to its underlying problematic.

Figures 7.3 and 7.4 illustrate the manner in which the paradigm has been
explored as far as our present interest in social theory and the study of organisations is concerned. Whilst there have been a small number of attempts to
study organisational concepts and situations from this point of view, the paradigm has not generated much organisation theory as such. As will become
clear from our analysis, there are good reasons for this. The premises of the
interpretive paradigm question whether organisations exist in anything but a
conceptual sense. Its significance for the study of organisations, therefore, is
of the most fundamental kind. It challenges the validity of the ontological
assumptions which underwrite functionalist approaches to sociology in general and the study of organisations in particular.

THE RADICAL HUMANIST PARADIGM

The radical humanist paradigm is defined by its concern to develop a *sociology of radical change* from a *subjectivist* standpoint. Its approach to social
science has much in common with that of the interpretive paradigm, in that it
views the social world from a perspective which tends to be *nominalist, anti-
positivist, voluntarist* and *ideographic*. However, its frame of reference is
committed to a view of society which emphasises the importance of over-
throwing or transcending the limitations of existing social arrangements.

One of the most basic notions underlying the whole of this paradigm is that the consciousness of man is dominated by the ideological superstructures with which he interacts, and that these drive a cognitive wedge between himself and his true consciousness. This wedge is the wedge of "alienation" or "false consciousness," which inhibits or prevents true human fulfilment. The major concern for theorists approaching the human predicament in these terms is with *release* from the constraints which existing social arrangements place upon human development. It is a brand of social theorising designed to provide a critique of the *status quo*. It tends to view society as anti-human and it is concerned to articulate ways in which human beings can transcend the spiritual bonds and fetters which tie them into existing social patterns and thus realise their full potential.

In terms of the elements with which we have sought to conceptualise the sociology of radical change, the radical humanist places most emphasis upon *radical change, modes of domination, emancipation, deprivation* and *potentiality*. The concepts of *structural conflict* and *contradiction* do not figure prominently within this perspective, since they are characteristic of more objectivist views of the social world, such as those presented within the context of the radical structuralist paradigm.

In keeping with its subjectivist approach to social science, the radical humanist perspective places central emphasis upon human consciousness. Its intellectual foundations can be traced to the same source as that of the interpretive paradigm. It derives from the German idealist tradition, particularly as expressed in the work of Kant and Hegel (though as reinterpreted in the writings of the young Marx). It is through Marx that the idealist tradition was first utilised as a basis for a radical social philosophy, and many radical humanists have derived their inspiration from this source. In essence Marx inverted the frame of reference reflected in Hegelian idealism and thus forged the basis for radical humanism. The paradigm has also been much influenced by an infusion of the phenomenological perspective deriving from Husserl.

. . . [A]part from the early work of Marx, interest remained dormant until the 1920s, when Lukács and Gramsci revived interest in subjectivist interpretations of Marxist theory. This interest was taken on by members of the so-called Frankfurt School, which has generated a great deal of debate, particularly through the writings of Habermas and Marcuse. The existentialist philosophy of Sartre also belongs to this paradigm, as do the writings of a group of social theorists as widely diverse as Illich, Castaneda and Laing. All in their various ways share a common concern for the release of consciousness and experience from domination by various aspects of the ideological superstructure of the social world within which men live out their lives. They seek to change the social world through a change in modes of cognition and consciousness.

Figures 7.3 and 7.4 again provide a somewhat rough and ready summary of the manner in which this paradigm has been explored in terms of social theory and the study of organisations. . . . [T]he writers who have something to say on organisations from this perspective have laid the basis of a nascent *anti-organisation theory.* The radical humanist paradigm in essence is based upon an inversion of the assumptions which define the functionalist paradigm. It should be no surprise, therefore, that anti-organisation theory inverts the problematic which defines functionalist organisation theory on almost every count.

THE RADICAL STRUCTURALIST PARADIGM

Theorists located within this paradigm advocate a *sociology of radical change* from an *objectivist* standpoint. Whilst sharing an approach to science which has many similarities with that of functionalist theory, it is directed at fundamentally different ends. Radical structuralism is committed to *radical change, emancipation,* and *potentiality,* in an analysis which emphasises *structural conflict, modes of domination, contradiction* and *deprivation.* It approaches these general concerns from a standpoint which tends to be *realist, positivist, determinist* and *nomothetic.*

Whereas the radical humanists forge their perspective by focusing upon "consciousness" as the basis for a radical critique of society, the radical structuralists concentrate upon structural relationships within a realist social world. They emphasise the fact that radical change is built into the very nature and structure of contemporary society, and they seek to provide explanations of the basic interrelationships within the context of total social formations. There is a wide range of debate within the paradigm, and different theorists stress the role of different social forces as a means of explaining social change. Whilst some focus directly upon the deep-seated internal contradictions, others focus upon the structure and analysis of power relationships. Common to all theorists is the view that contemporary society is characterised by fundamental conflicts which generate radical change through political and economic crises. It is through such conflict and change that the emancipation of men from the social structures in which they live is seen as coming about.

This paradigm owes its major intellectual debt to the work of the mature Marx, after the so-called "epistemological break" in his work. It is the paradigm to which Marx turned after a decade of active political involvement and as a result of his increasing interest in Darwinian theories of evolution and in political economy. Marx's basic ideas have been subject to a wide range of interpretations in the hands of theorists who have sought to follow his lead.

Among these Engels, Plekhanov, Lenin and Bukharin have been particularly influential. Among the leading exponents of the radical structuralist position outside the realm of Russian social theory, the names of Althusser, Poulantzas, Colletti and various Marxist sociologists of the New Left come to mind. Whilst the influence of Marx upon the radical structuralist paradigm is undoubtedly dominant, it is also possible to identify a strong Weberian influence. As we shall argue in later chapters, in recent years a group of social theorists have sought to explore the interface between the though of Marx and Weber and have generated a distinctive perspective which we describe as "conflict theory". It is to this radical structuralist perspective that the work of Dahrendorf belongs, along with that of other theorists such as Rex and Miliband.

Figures 7.3 and 7.4 again provide a general overview of the schools of thought located within the paradigm. . . . In British and American sociology the radical structuralist view has received relatively little attention outside the realm of conflict theory. This paradigm, located as it is within a realist view of the social world, has many significant implications for the study of organisations, but they have only been developed in the barest forms. . . .

EXPLORING SOCIAL THEORY

So much, then, for our overview of the four paradigms. . . . seek to place flesh upon the bones of this analytical scheme and attempt to demonstrate its power as a tool for exploring social theory.[4] Hopefully, our discussion will do justice to the essentially complex nature of the paradigms and the network of assumptions which they reflect, and will establish the relationships and links between the various perspectives dominating social analysis at the present time. . . . [T]he general principles and ideas discussed in the work as a whole clearly have relevance for the exploration of a wide variety of other social science disciplines. The scope for applying the analytical scheme to other fields of study is enormous but unfortunately lies beyond the scope of our present enquiry. However, readers interested in applying the scheme in this way should find little difficulty in proceeding from the sociological analyses . . . to an analysis of the literature in their own sphere of specialised interest.

NOTES AND REFERENCES

1. For a full discussion of the role of paradigms in scientific development, see Kuhn (1970). In his analysis, paradigms are defined as "universally recognised scientific achievements that for a time provide model problems and solutions to a community of practitioners" (p. viii). Para-

digms are regarded as governing the progress of what is called "normal science", in which "the scientist's work is devoted to the articulation and wider application of the accepted paradigm, which is not itself questioned or criticised. Scientific problems are regarded as puzzles, as problems which are known to have a solution within the framework of assumptions implicitly or explicitly embodied in the paradigm. If a puzzle is not solved, the fault lies in the scientist, and not in the paradigm" (Keat and Urry 1975, p. 55). "Normal science" contrasts with relatively brief periods of "revolutionary science", in which "the scientist is confronted by increasingly perplexing anomalies, which call into question the paradigm itself. Scientific revolution occurs when a new paradigm emerges, and becomes accepted by the scientific community" (ibid., p. 55).

We are using the term "paradigm" in a broader sense than that intended by Kuhn. Within the context of the present work we are arguing that social theory can be conveniently understood in terms of the co-existence of four distinct and rival paradigms defined by very basic meta-theoretical assumptions in relation to the nature of science and society. "Paradigms," "problematics," "alternative realities," "frames of reference," "forms of life" and "universe of discourse" are all related conceptualisations although of course they are *not* synonymous.

2. Some *inter*-paradigm debate is also possible. Giddens maintains "that all paradigms . . . are mediated by others" and that within "normal science" scientists are aware of *other* paradigms. He posits that: "The process of learning a paradigm . . . is also the process of learning what that paradigm is not" (1976, pp. 142-4).

Interestingly, he confines his discussion to the mediation of one paradigm by another one. We believe that a model of *four* conflicting paradigms within sociology is more accurate and that academics' knowledge of "scientists" within the other three paradigms is likely to be very sketchy in some cases. Relations between paradigms are perhaps better described in terms of "disinterested hostility" rather than "debate".

3. The notion of need satisfaction derives from the use of a biological analogy of an organism and plays no part in interpretive sociology.

4. The sociological concerns of recent years have resulted in a number of works which have aimed to chart a path through the social science literature by reducing the variables of sociological analysis to a number of key dimensions. Those of Dahrendorf (1959), Wallace (1969), Gouldner (1970), Friedrichs (1970), Dawe (1970), Robertson (1974), Keat and Urry (1975), Strasser (1976) and Benton (1977) all readily come to mind. In a sense our work adds to this literature. Had space permitted, we would have liked to demonstrate the precise way in which the schemes proposed by these various authors all fall, in a partial way, *within* the bounds of the scheme developed here.

REFERENCES

Althusser, V. L. (1975), *Social Analysis: A Marxist Critique and Alternative*. London and New York: Longman.

Benton, T. (1977), *Philosophical Foundations of the Three Sociologies*. London: Routledge and Kegan Paul.

Berger, P. L. and Luckmann, T. (1966), *The Social Construction of Reality*. New York: Doubleday.

Dahrendorf, R. (1959), *Class and Class Conflict in Industrial Society*. London: Routledge and Kegan Paul.

Dawe, A. (1970), "The Two Sociologies," *British Journal of Sociology,* 21, pp. 207-18.

Friedrichs, R. W. (1970), *A Sociology of Sociology*. New York: Free Press.

Garfinkel, H. (1967), *Studies in Ethnomethodology.* Englewood Cliffs, NJ: Prentice Hall.
Giddens, A. (1976), *New Rules of Sociological Method.* London: Hutchinson.
Gouldner, A. W. (1970), *The Coming Crisis of Western Sociology.* London: Heinemann.
Keat, R. and Urry, J. (1975), *Social Theory as Science.* London: Routledge and Kegan Paul.
Kuhn, T. S. (1970), *The Structure of Scientific Revolution* (2nd ed.). Chicago: University of
    Chicago Press.
Lukács, G. (1971), *History and Class Consciousness.* London: Merlin. (First published 1923).
Robertson, R. (1974), "Towards the Identification of the Major Axes of Sociological Analysis,"
    in J. Rex, ed., *Approaches to Sociology.* London: Routledge and Kegan Paul.
Strasser, H. (1976), *The Normative Structure of Sociology.* London: Routledge and Kegan Paul.
Wallace, W. L. (1969), *Sociological Theory.* London: Heinemann.

8

Describing Differences in Approaches to Organization Science

Rethinking Burrell and Morgan and Their Legacy

STANLEY DEETZ
Department of Communication, Rutgers University

When Gibson Burrell and Gareth Morgan wrote *Sociological Paradigms and Organisational Analysis,* I doubt that they, or anyone else, would have anticipated the widespread impact or resultant contestation that their four-paradigm grid would have. Many grids had appeared before in sociology and after in organizational studies, but none have gained the almost hegemonic capacity to define the alternatives in organizational analysis (see Pfeffer 1982, Astley and Van de Ven 1983, Rao and Pasmore 1989, Hirschman and Holbrook 1992, Power and Laughlin 1992, Latour 1993).

I believe that there are reasons for this significant influence beyond the clarity of presentation and exhaustive compilation of literature. When the grid and discussion were published in 1979, those of us doing alternative work readily embraced it for it gave each of us a kind of asylum. While some of us were uncomfortable with the dimensions and philosophical analysis, we happily accepted the newfound capacity to present ourselves to mainstream critics as doing fundamentally different, but legitimate, kinds of research and began to work on concepts and evaluation criteria within our now-produced-as different and unitary communities. Many of those doing more mainstream

From "Describing Differences in Approaches to Organization Science: Rethinking Burrell and Morgan and Their Legacy," by Stanley Deetz, 1996, *Organization Science, 7,* pp. 191-207. © 1996, The Institute of Management Sciences. Reprinted with permission.

work also found it appealing since, as I will argue, the dimensions used to produce the grid reproduced the world as viewed from the mainstream tradition thus reaffirming that tradition and providing a "safe" understanding of the developing alternatives. Further, the separate but equal pluralism implicit in Burrell and Morgan's conceptualization could be used by the dominant "functionalists" to protect themselves from growing criticism (the isolationist strategy noted by Reed 1985). They, too, would have a safe and separate place.

But as organizational science and research agendas have continued to evolve, problems with the Burrell and Morgan grid have become more pressing. First, the grid has been used to reify research approaches; and second, and more importantly, its dimensions of contrast obscure important differences in current research orientations and lead to poorly formed conflicts and discussions.

While not primarily a result of the original analysis, the four-paradigm solution has often led to quick categorizations and to debates around paradigm commensurability (Jackson and Carter 1991; Willmott 1990, 1993) and appropriate use of the different paradigms (Hassard 1991, Parker and McHugh 1991). Some of these problems and debates arise from the tendency to reify concepts, especially in educational programs and materials. The Burrell and Morgan grid can easily produce four classified things given object status, rather than providing two lines of differentiation that draw attention to important differences in research programs. Burrell and Morgan invite reification by claims of paradigmatic incommensurability, by staying at the level of theory and reconstructed science, and by accepting Kuhn's loose conception of paradigms. The dimensions can be used as a way of focusing attention rather than as a means of classification, but few writings have done so. One purpose of this essay is to fight the tendency to reduce conceptions to categories or reduce sensitizing concepts to definitions (see Deetz 1992, ch. 3; Sandelands and Srivatsan 1993).

But my main concern here is not paradigm commensurability nor reification but rather the dimensions of contrast themselves. A deeper and more interesting understanding of contemporary research practices and debates is possible by focusing on other dimensions. The question is not: Are these the right categories or who fits in each? But: Are these differences that make a difference? Do these dimensions provide insight into genuine differences in research programs? I hope to aid rethinking the differences and similarities among different research approaches, hopefully making our conflicts and discussions more productive rather than simply replacing four boxes with four different boxes.

In line with modern discourse theory, conceptions are always contests for meaning (see Epstein 1988; Deetz 1992, ch. 5). Language does not name objects in the world; it is core to the process of constituting objects. The appearance of labeling or categorizing existing objects is derived from this more fundamental act of object constitution through language. The world can be constituted in many ways, depending on alternative systems of valuing. The most significant part of this contest for object constitution is the capacity to enact the lines of distinction producing some things as alike and others as different. Only secondarily is the contest over the positive or negative valence ascribed to the produced things. For example, feminist writers for years have shown how male dominance is maintained by the dominant group's ability to define the dimensions of difference and position themselves at the positive end of each dimension (see Treichler 1989, Weedon 1987). Marginalized groups, following this analysis, are defined as "the other" thus acquiring an identity and valued functions but only as given by the opposition pole in the dominant group's conceptual map (e.g., "emotionally supportive" rather than "rational" or "private" rather than "public"). They acquire a type of autonomy but only in a language/conceptual game not of their own choosing. In accepting the state of "other" they have little self-definition, and the game is stacked (see further, Bourdieu 1984, 1991).

In an analogous way, I believe that Burrell and Morgan largely accepted the conceptual distinctions from sociological functionalism and its supporting philosophy of science. From this dominant conception, they merely asked who else is "other" and, from this position, in what ways are they "other." Burrell and Morgan performed a political intervention as they spoke on behalf of the oppositions, the negative terms, the "others" of "sociological functionalism." But, functionalism retained definitional authority. In contrast to their analysis, each identified marginalized paradigmatic group would have defined its difference from the dominant functionalist conceptions differently, if each had had definitional authority. This positioning, as I have suggested, partly accounts for the rapid acceptance of the Burrell and Morgan grid into the mainstream of management science.

Further, this move protected functionalist researchers from the most damning critiques (and ones they would not understand) in favor of their preferred battles (e.g., between objectivity and subjectivity). At the same time, the most innovative of the new researchers found it now even more difficult to express what they did since they had to use a language in which their meanings did not fit. They had to choose between misrepresenting themselves clearly through Burrell and Morgan or representing themselves well but being considered obscure or bad writers. Thus, the effect was to normalize the emerging research paradigms favoring rather traditional directions even within them. For example, as will be shown in more detail, when Burrell and Morgan provided "interpretive" work with the "subjective" ascription (even if now positively valued) they, perhaps unwittingly, tended to favor cultural studies that focused on member's meanings which were more subject to management control. At the same time the "objective" ascription protected "functionalist" studies from a thorough analysis of their hidden values and sources of subjectivity, as if they might be too objective—a preferred flaw—rather than too subjective—a flaw they would not understand. Similarly, the many critical theorists with strong suspicions of humanist philosophies suddenly found themselves either conceptualized as radical humanists or invisible (lost in some hole in paradigmatic space). The Frankfurt school's attack on the subjective domination in science all too often got lost in the radical humanist conception.

My point is not that Burrell and Morgan were representationally wrong in the presentation of management science (for there are many representationally "right" schemes and surely the nearly 20 years since their work has led to many changes), but their conceptions continue to foster less interesting and productive conflicts and developments than are possible. Further, the grid revisions have been insufficiently radical. Most of the revisions of Burrell and Morgan begin, as did they, with a philosophy of science based in representational views of language and a subject-object dualism. This is why as others suggest new dimensions of contrast they nearly always retain some form of the subjective-objective dimension (see Kavanagh 1993 for development; and for examples: Pfeffer 1982, Astley and Van de Ven 1983, Hirschman and Holbrook 1992, Latour 1993). Furthermore, functionalist researchers appear to collapse the regulation-change dimension to the subjective-objective one. Perhaps it is not Burrell and Morgan's or other authors fault, but a political agenda is quickly (mis)understood as simply another "subjective" position. The processes of differentiation in mainstream functionalist sociology must be abandoned before more challenging differentiations are possible and alternative research programs can be given a full complementary role in organizational science. There are better differentiations available to us already (Rao and Pasmore 1989) and I believe that a more general set of differentiations can be developed here.

Before I suggest new dimensions of contrast, I should situate myself. My work, like that of many of the new research programs, has sought to work out the significance of the "linguistic turn" in modern philosophy for organizational analysis and practice (see Deetz 1992, 1994b, d, 1995). My disciplinary interests are in the constitutive moves of discourse in organizations rather than in psychological, sociological, or economic theories of organizational behavior (Deetz 1994c). In regard to research I am interested in how organizational science is practiced—how research representations are produced, disseminated, and used rather than their truth or reconstructed justifications. In this conception, paradigms are produced and reproduced in discursive practices of unity and separation. Paradigms are incommensurable as they strive to maintain coherence, but are commensurable to the extent that they encounter the ultimately indeterminant outside world. Communication across paradigms is both possible as different groups try to build a world together, but yet incomplete in that every determination is partial (one-sided and unfinished). Following this position through, what makes social research programs different from each other is the degree of participation they favor in the interaction with other research programs, research subjects, and the wider society and the moves they make toward closure or indeterminacy in those interactions. This will form the bases for the dimensions suggested.

In my development below, I will privilege programmatic differentiations rooted in what I will develop as a dialogic perspective. What Burrell and Morgan called "functionalist" research will thus be implicitly represented as an "other." In doing so, both the lines of division and the arguments that extend from this can be redrawn. "Functionalist" style work can be reclaimed as legitimate in specifiable ways as reunderstood from dialogic conceptions. Nondialogic research programs will not be seen as alternative routes to truth, but as specific discourses which, if freed from their claims of universality and/or completion, could provide important moments in the larger dialogue about organizational life. The test of my suggested differentiations is not whether they provide a better map, but whether they provide an interesting way to talk about what is happening in research programs.

THE BORING AND MISLEADING
SUBJECTIVE-OBJECTIVE PROBLEM[1]

The most problematic legacy of Burrell and Morgan's analysis is the perpetuation of the subjective-objective controversy. Since the underlying conceptions are still widespread, a little "flogging of the dead horse" seems advisable (see for development, Natter, Schatzki and Jones 1995). Subject-object dualism is as old as Western theoretical writings (at least as reconstructed in the modern period). The discourse of "functionalist" researchers (or what is organized as such in Burrell and Morgan) as well as that of many humanists and interpretivists reproduces a basic psychological distinction between an interior and exterior world. Phenomena can either be interior or exterior. And, the research process itself is seen as directed by either the interior (thus subjective) or exterior (thus objective).

The subjective-objective distinction performs political functions by constraining the conception of science and creating hierarchies of research programs based on the same faulty logic as the distinction itself. Codified, and often quantitative studies, continue to get the privileged "objective" label and positive association to the natural sciences since, in the interior-exterior relation, they claim a double (both method and phenomenon) exterior. "Interpretivists" acquire the "subjective" (implying personal and/or particularistic) label since they claim a double hermeneutic (an interpretation of an interpreted world). While, like many marginalized groups, interpretivists may try to reverse the valence of the ascription or even claim a type of objective science, the presence of a host of social and institutional conditions reproduce the hierarchy (for example, university promotion processes that count the number of publications or journal review processes that emphasize specific types of methodological rigor over others or other criteria). The problem is the ascription, not the valence. Little is gained if subjectivity is good and objectivity bad, the same limitations remain. Three of them are most evident.

First, the meaning of the objective-subjective labels is already socially contrived. Not only is the subject-object split a cultural conception rather than a natural fact, the "objective" practices are those that Husserl (1962) and others (see Apel 1979, Bernstein 1984) have shown to be the most "subjective." While widely misunderstood, from the start the primary critics of positivism found the natural science model to be too subjective, not too objective. In so-called "objective" research, concepts and methods are held a priori, are unknown projections of researchers' own ways of encountering the world, constitute the world as observed without ownership or critical reflection, and are not subject to the "objection" of the outside toward possible alternatively constituted worlds (see Deetz 1973 for further development). Both functionalists and humanistic psychologists missed the point, as did Burrell and Morgan.

What warrants exploration is the subjectivity and implicit desire to dominate others and nature, rather than the objectivity, of the "objective" research programs. Probabilistic and law-like claims are artifacts of a particular peer group shared language game or set of constitutive activities. Questions of determining which problems to study, the relevancy of findings, and the translation back to the subject's world have always posed constitutive and value-laden issues at the very heart of any "objective" research that intends to have a social effect (Gergen 1978). The control orientation of much "objective" research (see Hamnett et al. 1984) can be seen as the domination of a particular group's desires over and against existing communities and the natural environment. A point well made by Harding (1991). In both respects, in practice so-called "interpretivists" and others often labeled as "subjective" often have the better claim to objectivity through the way they allow alternative language games and the possibility of alternative constructions arising from existing communities denying both research community conceptions and preferred methods as privileged and universal. Thus, I treat the claim of objectivity or subjectivity as a rhetorical move in a research program's system of justification rather than as a useful descriptive label. My point is not that all research is both subjective and objective nor to decide which are which. As argued below, subjectivity and objectivity are simply not very interesting ways of thinking about research program differences (see Bernstein 1984; Natter, Schatzki and Jones 1995).

Secondly, the subjective-objective conception, rather than describing a meaningful difference, reproduces a neo-positivist philosophy of science and obscures the nature of other research programs. While few claim to be a positivist anymore (given more than 50 years of critique), the retention of the discourse of the subject-object split (even given 100 years of critique) leaves most researchers still practicing a kind of neo-positivism, whether subjective humanists or hardcore abstracted empiricists. There is a reason that this conception will not go away: the subjective-objective distinction affords identity protection and privileges for powerful groups, both in the academy and other organizations. In many ways, interpretivists gain as much identity and group stature in their oppositional identity as do the functionalists.

A growing discourse of organization researchers explicitly denies the subject-object (interior/exterior) split through different concepts of language and experience and through demonstrating the abstract and politically motivated conception of the difference (e.g., Cooper 1989, Willmott 1990). Without a metaphysical separation between subjects and objects, objectivity and subjectivity occupy a different discursive space. The philosophical distinction between subjectivity and objectivity is widely challenged by nonwestern groups. And its refutation is core to the twentieth century writers (e.g., Husserl, Heidegger, Wittgenstein), who in developing a "linguistic turn" in philosophy, have served as inspiration for many of the "nonfunctionalists" organizational researchers (including many feminists, critical theorists, poststructuralists, postmodernist, and labor process theorists). Such research programs are not at a different place on the subjective-objective continuum; the dualism itself is disputed (see Willmott 1990, 1993 for a similar point). As language replaces consciousness as central, theories of discourse and representational practices replace philosophies of science based on subject-object, idealist-realist, rationalist-empiricist, or similar contrasts. Any attempt to classify these new research programs on the subjective-objective dimension of Burrell and Morgan does an injustice to their conceptions and practices and leads to distorted understandings.

Thirdly, the retention of the conception of subject-object separation has led to the continuation of rather misleading conflicts and equally misleading presumed relations between so-called qualitative and quantitative research. The association of qualitative research with the subjective label collapses the distinction between purely impressionistic musing and rigorous interpretive work and differences between studying practices or meanings. Further neo-positivist researchers accepting dualism (whether called interpretivists or functionalists) often reduce the difference in qualitative and quantitative research to different ways to collect data and, thereby, retain the dream of triangulation as if different research programs simply provided additive insights into the same phenomenon. This hides the real conflict. More important than data collection techniques are the questions asked and the intent of analysis. At root, what the research is trying to do is different. The modes of analysis do not work from different points of view on the same thing; they are producing and elaborating in the act of researching different phenomena for different reasons.

The qualitative-quantitative difference could be retained if "functionalist" researchers recognized that their "natural" objects of a presumed external world are "produced" objects for temporary methodological convenience and interpretivists saw that their "natural" objects of another's social world are emergent and interactionally formed, but in neither case does the private/subjective experience of one or the other influence more strongly. They simply enter at different places and in different ways. Both kinds of objects are socially shared, historically produced, and general to a social group. Since both can accept objects as constituted as if they were given in nature (as in any "realist" description) rather than to explore their constitution, positivist conceptions and assumptions are not unique to "functionalist" researchers but are often present for interpretivists also. Quantitative research itself could be greatly improved if freed from pretenses of functionalist ontology. Many human questions admit of numerical answers, and these answers should be good ones. But when codification, counting, and statistical reduction are separated from the full process of constituting objects, determining problems and influencing communities, when only one slice of the research process is claimed as science, research loses relevance and critical parts of the process are not investigated. The subjective-objective conception contributes to this problem.

STRIKING NEW DIFFERENCES

Accepting the "linguistic turn" (thus locating research differences in discursive moves and social relations rather than procedures and individuals) gives us a more contemporary look at alternative research programs in organization science. Two dimensions of contrast will be developed here. The first dimension focuses on the origin of concepts and problem statements as part of the constitutive process in research. Differences among research orientations can be shown by contrasting "local/emergent" research conceptions with "elite/a priori" ones. The second dimension focuses on the relation of research practices to the dominant social discourses within the organization studied, the research community, and/or wider community. Research orientations can be contrasted in the extent to which they work within a dominant set of structurings of knowledge, social relations, and identities (a reproductive practice), called here a "consensus" discourse, and the extend to which they work to disrupt these structurings (a productive practice), called here "dissensus" discourse (see Deetz 1994c, 1995). I see these dimensions as analytic ideal types in Weber's sense mapping out two distinct continua. While categories of research programs are derivatively produced by the dimensions, the intent here is to aid attention to meaningful differences and similarities among different research activities rather than classification.

Local/Emergent-Elite/A Priori

The key questions this dimension addresses is where and how do research concepts arise. In the two extremes, either concepts are developed in relation with organizational members and transformed in the research process or they are brought to the research "interaction" by the researcher and held static through the research process—concepts can be developed *with* or applied *to* the organizational members being studied. This dimension can be characterized by a set of paired conceptions which flesh out contrasts embedded in the two poles. Figure 8.1 presents an array of these contrasts. The choice of and stability of the language system is of central importance since the linguistic/conceptual system directs the statement of problems, the observational process itself in producing objects and highlighting and hiding potential experiences, the type of claims made, and the report to external groups.

The elite/a priori pole draws attention to the tendency in some types of research programs to privilege the particular language system of the researcher and the expertise of the research community as well as hold that language system constant throughout the research process.[2] Such research tends to be heavily theory driven with careful attention to definitions prior to the research process. The experiences of the researched become coded into the researcher's language system. Demands of consistency and/or reliability require changes in the conceptual system to take place outside of rather than in the research process. Whether intentional or not, the conceptual system of the researcher is considered better or more clearly represents what "really" is the case than that of everyday people and seeks generality beyond the various local systems of meaning. In privileging a language system there is further a tendency to universalize and justify such moves by appeals to foundations or essentialist assumptions. Research claims, thus, are seen as freed from their local and temporal conditions of production. In most cases these research approaches follow an enlightenment hope for producing ratio-

Figure 8.1 Characterizations of the Local/Emergent-Elite/A Priori Dimension

Local/Emergent	Elite/A Priori
Comparative communities	Privileged community
Multiple language games	Fixed language game
Particularistic	Universalistic
Systematic philosophy as ethnocentric	Grounded in hoped for systematic philosophy
Atheoretical	Theory driven
Situationally or structural determinism	Methodological determinism
Nonfoundational	Foundational
Local narratives	Grand narrative of progress and emancipation
Sensuality and meaning as central concerns	Rationality and truth as central concerns
Situated, practical knowledge	Generalizable, theoretical knowledge
Tends to be feminine in attitude	Tends to be masculine in attitude
Sees the strange	Sees the familiar
Proceeds from the other	Proceeds from the self
Ontology of "otherness" over method	Epistemological and procedural issues rule over substantive assumptions

nal knowledge not constrained by tradition or particular belief systems of the researcher or researched. The produced knowledge is treated as progressive or reformist in conception leading to increased capacities or well-being. The more functionalist (or what I will call "normative") versions openly proclaim "objectivity" and value neutrality based on the shared language game and research methods and tend to overlook the positions of their own community or alliances with other groups. The more critical versions quickly note the presence of values and distortions in normative work and hold out the hope for a better, purer form of knowledge based in processes that include more interests and means of analysis in the work.

The local/emergent pole draws attention to researchers who work with an open language system and produce a form of knowledge with less lofty claims. Central to their work is the situated nature of the research enterprise. Problem statements, the researcher's attention, and descriptions are worked out as a play between communities. The theoretical vocabulary carried into the research activity is often considered by the researcher as a first cut or guide to getting started constantly open to new meanings, translations, and redifferentiation based on interactions in the research process. The knowledge form is more often one of insight rather than truth. Such insights may be particularistic regarding both time and place even though the emerging analytic frame is designed to aid in the deeper understanding of other particular settings. Cumulative understanding happens in providing stories or accounts which may provide insight into other sites rather than cumulative universal aspiring claims. The research attends to the feelings, intuitions and multiple forms of rationality of both the researched and researcher rather than using a single logic of objectification or purified rationality. The study is guided more by concept formation than concept application. The "otherness" of the other (the way people and events exceed categories and classifications of them) is sought by the researcher to force reconception and linguistic change. This is considered more valuable than the identification and naming of pre-conceived traits, attributes, or groupings. Objectivity, to the extent that it is considered at all, arises out of the interplay and the constant ability of the researched to object and correct. The researcher is more a skilled collaborator in knowledge production than an expert observer. Such a position is expressed well by those engaged in various forms of participatory research (see Reason 1994, Whyte 1991).

Focusing on the origin of concepts and problems using a dimension of "local/emergent-elite/a priori" allows three advantages. Firstly, it acknowledges linguistic/social constructionism in all research positions and directs attention to whose concepts are used in object production and determination of what is problematic (see Deetz 1973). Secondly, the focus on the origin of concepts helps distinguish fundamentally different kinds of knowledge. Elite/a priori conceptions lead more to the development of "theoretical codified" knowledge, a kind of "book" knowledge or "knowing about." Local/emergent conceptions lead more to the development of "practical" knowledge, a kind of "street wisdom" or a "knowing how." Thirdly, re-conceptualizing this dimension allows us to more easily see that both the application and discovery of concepts can demonstrate implicit or explicit political alliances with different groups in society. For example, to the extent that organizational researchers' concepts align with managerial conceptions and problem statements and are applied a priori in studies, the knowledge claims are intrinsically biased toward certain interests as they are applied within the site community (Mumby 1988). The knowledge claims become part of the same processes that are being studied, reproducing world views, personal identities, and fostering particular interests within the organization (see Knights 1992).

Consensus-Dissensus

The "consensus-dissensus" dimension draws attention to the relation of research to existing social orders. Consensus or dissensus should not be understood as agreement and disagreement but rather as presentation of unity or of difference, the continuation or disruption of any prevailing discourse. See Figure 8.2 for conceptualization of this dimension. This dimension is similar to Burrell and Morgan's use of the traditional sociological distinctions between an interest in "change" or "regulation," but enables some

Figure 8.2 Characterizations of the Consensus-Dissensus Dimension

Consensus	Dissensus
Trust	Suspicion
Hegemonic order as natural state	Conflicts over order as natural state
Naturalization of present	Present order is historicized and politicized
Integration and harmony are possible	Order indicates domination and suppressed conflicts
Research focuses on representation	Research focused on challenge and reconsideration (representation)
Mirror (reflecting) dominant metaphor	Lens (seeing/reading as) dominant metaphor
Validity central concern	Insight and praxis central concern
Theory as abstraction	Theory as opening
Unified science and triangulation	Positional complementary
Science is neutral	Science is political
Life is discovery	Life is struggle and creation
Autonomous/free agent	Historically/socially situated agent
Researcher anonymous and out of time and space	Researcher named and positioned

advantages. Principally, the change-regulation distinction tended in most usages to assume the presence of a coherent dominant group or orders, and the primary conflict initiating change was class conflict. While many researchers do use a similar analysis of managerial or company domination, the more pressing "critical" concerns of the day are the ways dominant discourses (though often disorganized and disjunct) place limitations on people in general including managers and limit the successful functioning of organizations in meeting human needs. The problem is not group against group, but rather the suppression of parts of the human being and the presence of destructive control processes, technocracy, consumerism, careerism, environmental destruction, and exclusive concern with economic growth (see Abercrombie et al. 1980, Mumby and Putnam 1992, Alvesson and Willmott 1995, Heckscher 1995). And further, the processes of domination are less often seen today as macro-sociological and more often as routine micropractices in the work site itself (Knights and Willmott 1989, Deetz 1994a, d). The focus on discursive rather than group relations aids the understanding of domination and its reproduction.

The consensus pole draws attention to the way some research programs both seek order and treat order production as the dominant feature of natural and social systems. With such a conception, the primary goal of the research is to display a discovered order with a high degree of fidelity or verisimilitude. The descriptions hope to "mirror" entities and relations that exist outthere in a relative fixed state reflecting their "real" character. Language is treated as a system of representations, to be neutralized and made transparent, used only to display the presumed shared world. Existing orders are largely treated as natural and unproblematic. To a large extent through the highlighting of ordering principles, such orders are perpetuated. Random events and deviance are downplayed in significance in looking at norms and the normal, and attention is usually to processes reducing deviance, uncertainty, and dissonance. In most cases where deviance is itself of attention it tends to be normalized through looking at the production of deviant groups (i.e., other orders). Conflict and fragmentation are usually treated as system problems, and attention is given to how orders deal with them in attempts at maintenance.

The dissensus pole draws attention to research programs which consider struggle, conflict, and tensions to be the natural state. Research itself is seen as inevitably a move in a conflictual site. The existing orders indicate the suppression of basic conflicts and along with that the domination of people and their full variety of interests. Research aims at challenging mechanisms of order maintenance to reclaim conflicts and tension. The nonnormative aspects of human conduct and extraordinary responses are emphasized along with the importance of largely random and chance events. Rather than language naming and describing, researcher conceptions are seen as striking a difference, de- and re-differentiating experience (see Martin 1990, Cooper and Burrell 1988, Cooper 1989, Weedon 1987, Deetz 1992). The "mirror" gives way to the "lens" as the metaphor noting the shifting analytic attempt to see what could not be seen before and showing the researcher as positioned and active. For dissensus style research, the generative capacity (the ability to challenge guiding assumptions, values, social practices, and routines) of an observation is more important than representational validity (see Gergen 1978, Rorty 1989). The research is, in Knights' (1992) sense, "anti-positive." Dissensus work does not deny the significance of an ordered observed world, rather, it takes it as a powerful (and power filled) product and works to break objectifications to show fuller potential and variety than is immediately apparent. For example, consensus orientations in cultural studies seek to discover the organizational culture or cultures. Dissensus orientations show the fragmentation inherent in any claim of culture and the work required for site subjects to maintain coherence in the face of this as well as subjects' own forms of resistance (see J. Martin 1990, 1992; Smircich and Calás 1987; Calás and Smircich 1991). Consensus orientations apply role and identity classifications and relate them to other variables. Dissensus orientations see identity as multiple, conflictual, and in process.

While these differences can be characterized clearly in abstraction, in continuous time every consensus arises out of and falls to dissensus, and every dissensus gives away to emerging (if temporary) consensus. The issue is not the ultimate outcome desired nor likely but rather which part of this flow through time is claimed in the research process. For example, while critical theorists clearly seek a social consensus which is more rational, their research tries to produce this through the creation of dissensus in place of dominant orders. For example, ideological critique in the critical theory conception of the negative dialectic is to reclaim conflict and destroy a false order rather than produce a new one. Thus, I place them on the dissensus end. Critical theories differ from many dialogic or "post-modern" positions primarily in whether dissensus is produced by the use of elite understandings and procedures (as in Habermas 1984, 1987; Mumby 1987; Kunda 1992; or several essays in Alvesson and Willmott 1992) or in a deconstructive process whereby elite conceptions are unmasked to allow organizational activities to be given multiple and conflicting descriptions within particular sites (Laclau and Mouffe 1985, Martin 1990, Calás and Smircich 1991, Linstead 1993, Kilduff 1993). The dialogic outcome requires a constant dedifferentiation and redifferentiation for the sake of demythologizing and enriching natural language and consequently opening to reconsideration the most basic and certain experiences of everyday life.

PARADIGMS LOST, ORIENTATIONS STILL

The grid produced from these two dimensions still provides a spatially and visually convenient four-discursive space solution (hence we should always be easily reminded of its arbitrary and fictive character); see Figure 8.3. I will describe these as different discourses to note a way of articulating arguments and engaging in research practices rather than a means of reconstructive self-naming. Each discourse provides an orientation to organizations, a way of constituting people and events in them, and a way of reporting on them. I hope that this also leads us to think about which discourse is being used or how it is joined with others rather than pigeonholing specific authors. Figure 8.4 provides sketchy prototypical descriptions of each research orientation related to a dozen dimensions of interest shaping research programs in organization science.

Calling these discourses paradigms would be a mistake for several reasons. First, each of these four discourses, which are provisionally held apart for viewing, are filled with internal conflict and strife—including theory debates, moments of incommensurability, dilettantes, and tyrants. Second, the edges are not demarcated. Most researchers and teachers do not cluster around a prototype of each but gather at the crossroads, mix metaphors, borrow lines from other discourses, and dodging criticism by co-optation. Often practicing researchers happily move from one discourse to another without

Figure 8.3. Contrasting Dimensions From the Metatheory of Representational
Practices

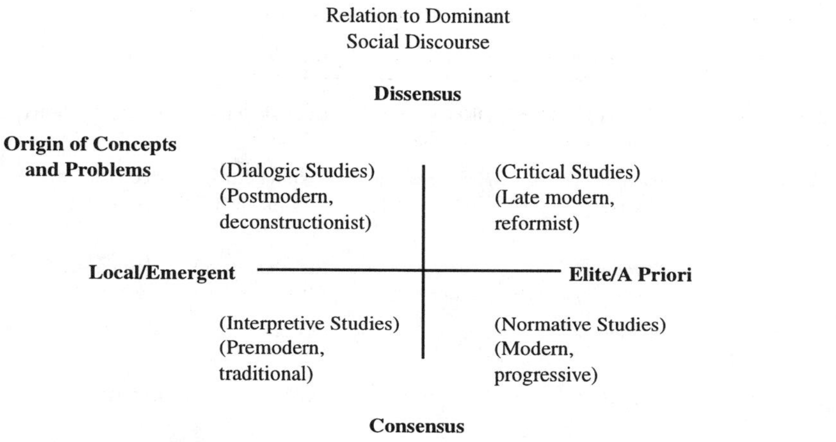

Relation to Dominant
Social Discourse

Dissensus

**Origin of Concepts
and Problems**   (Dialogic Studies)   (Critical Studies)
                        (Postmodern,   (Late modern,
                        deconstructionist)   reformist)

Local/Emergent ————————————————————————————|———————————————————— **Elite/A Priori**

                        (Interpretive Studies)   (Normative Studies)
                        (Premodern,   (Modern,
                        traditional)   progressive)

Consensus

SOURCE: Adapted from Deetz, *Communication Yearbook 17*, p. 592. © ICA. Reprinted by permission.

accounting for their own location. They operate like other organizational
members borrowing on discourses that suit their immediate purposes and the
fashions of the moment (see Deetz 1994d). There are certainly more and less
serious plays across the lines, but the issue is not crossing but the seriousness
of the play. And third, the discourses are not themselves sealed off from each
other. They pose problems for each other and steal insights across the lines.
For example, the philosophical fights between Habermas and Gadamer,
Habermas and Lyotard, Habermas and Luhmann, Foucault and everybody,
have left their traces in each one's work. From these struggles, the various
organization research programs based in these works have gained enriched
conceptions of power, knowledge, agency, and political action (see Mumby
and Putnam 1992, for example).

   Provisional ordering of discourses is not to police the lines, but to provide
a view of the social resources from which researchers draw and an understanding of the stock arguments used by those who do police the lines. The
ideal types aid the understanding of differences that matter that are hard to see
in the flow of research activity. The discursive orientation here hopes to provide insights with words which differentiate research activities and justifications before they are merely captured by the category named and become part
of the commerce of research. Clarifying the tendencies in specific types of
research positions helps clarify debates and the relation of different groups to

Figure 8.4 Prototypical Discursive Features

Issue	Discourse			
	Normative	*Interpretive*	*Critical*	*Dialogic*
Basic goal	Law-like relations among objects	Display unified culture	Unmask domination	Reclaim conflict
Method	Nomothetic science	Hermeneutics, ethnography	Cultural criticism, ideology critique	Deconstruction, genealogy
Hope	Progressive emancipation	Recovery of integrative values	Reformation of social order	Claim a space for lost voices
Metaphor of social relations	Economic	Social	Political	Mass
Organization metaphor	Marketplace	Community	Polity	Carnival
Problems addressed	Inefficiency, disorder	Meaninglessness, illegitimacy	Domination, consent	Marginalization, conflict suppression
Concern with communication	Fidelity, influence, information needs	Social acculturation, group affirmation	Misrecognition, systematic distortion	Discursive closure
Narrative style	Scientific/ technical, strategic	Romantic, embracing	Therapeutic, directive	Ironic, ambivalent
Time identity	Modern	Premodern	Late modern	Postmodern
Organizational benefits	Control, expertise	Commitment, quality of work life	Participation, expanded knowledge	Diversity, creativity
Mood	Optimistic	Friendly	Suspicious	Playful
Social fear	Disorder	Depersonalization	Authority	Totalization, normalization

them. For example, the interpretive, critical, and dialogic critiques of normative research are quite different. Normative researchers who are accustomed to making arguments against subjectivity and traditionalism simply miss the point of each of these critiques; they often reduce them to abstract and confused presentations of what they think "opponents" should be saying rather than concrete but different arguments from what they expected.

Further, while most researchers are not purists, their work carries assumptions and responsibilities which are central to understanding and evaluating their work, but are rarely explicit in study reports. For example, many feminists' writings carry a general sympathy with the conceptual and analytic power of dialogic research programs, while they still wish to have a political agenda that requires critical preconceptions which assume social divisions and gender-based domination to be general (see Fraser and Nicholson 1988, Flax 1990). Such works (e.g., Martin 1990, 1994) can be classified as dialogic, but the ethical and political character of many of these studies can not be justified easily with dialogic conceptions alone. The distinctions developed in this essay can help display the tensions and the resources from which such researchers draw to conduct and justify their work.

This can further be shown using my own work as an example. I often draw on conceptions from critical and dialogic writings. For me, critical theory conceptions of ideology and distorted communication provide useful sensitizing concepts and an analytic framework for looking for micro-practices of control, discursive closure, conflict suppression, and skewed representation in organizational sites. But rarely are these conceptions closely tied to the full critical theory agenda. They require considerable reworking in specific sites, and the results of my studies aim more at finding and giving suppressed positions and means of expression than realizing an ideal speech situation or reaching a purer consensus (see Deetz 1994b, in press a, b). What is important is not whether I am a late-modern critical theorist or a dialogic postmodernist, but rather the meaning and implications of concepts that I draw from these two competitive research orientations. My degree of consistency is of less interest than how I handle the tension and whether the two conceptual resources provide an interesting analysis of intervention. When I submit a study report for publication. I should not have to answer to "normative" study criteria nor preform group membership rituals of purification based on some categorization. But I carry special responsibilities. I must answer to some criteria based on some community agreement. But when conflictual communities are involved I assume a greater responsibility to justify the work and explicitly deal with the tensions. Rarely do I have the page space to reconstruct the entire philosophy of science supporting choices I made in the work, especially in enough detail to satisfy reviewers with a firm and/or singular philosophy of science of their own. Some clarity and general understanding in alternative research orientations provide guidance and accountability or at least a common stock of material for building and evaluating new arguments in these cases.

In an ideal research program we might identify a complementary relation among research orientations, each asking different questions at different moments and each at the moment answering the specific criteria of an orientation. This might operate as kind of rotation among incompatible orientations without any being simply a prelude or supplement to another. For example, my work relies much on a conception of discursive closure where cooperative decision making is hampered by arbitrary limits enacted in the discussion (see Deetz 1992, pp. 187 ff.). As a *critical* researcher I must show how these closures are intrusions of power relations usually based in or supporting social divisions which lead to distorted communication and a false consensus. My study appeals to reason, logical analyses, and a coherent demonstration. As a *dialogic* researcher I see these closures as the suppression of conflicts and see my own concern with consensus and appeals to reason as acts of closure.

My analysis is now judged by the way indeterminacy is allowed to reemerge and the compelling quality of recovered claims and voices. But at another moment yet, I may well pose *normative* questions: What means of closure are used most often? Who uses them? When are they used? Can people be taught to avoid them? A study designed to answer such questions now appeals to standards of definition, measurement, sampling, and data analysis. And further yet, there are *interpretive* concerns: What sense do these discursive moves have in a community? To what ends are they used? How are they self understood and justified? What are their actual consequences in specific circumstances? Interpretive research standards are now relevant. One can easily see how such a rotation through orientations might be constant and productive without in any sense losing the separation and tension, but precisely because of them. Yet, to be honest, few research programs are treated this way and most researchers, like myself, follow their own lines of interest, commitments, and training which leads to the eclipse of questions and concerns from other orientations. The point is still for the researcher to be clear about what type of questions or claims drive the work at any particular time and how the work addresses the standards and criteria appropriate to that kind of work.

Some basic understanding of alternative research orientations enables short-hand accounts and helps distinguish intentional and/or productive ambiguities from careless and/or unproductive ones. As a reviewer I am often frustrated by nonreflective mixing of metaphors and conceptions in submitted essays. Often the claims made would require a different kind of study based on different assumptions and research activities. Partly I think this arises from authors trying to anticipate reviewer needs for normative type generalizations while being committed to a nonnormative research orientation, but it also comes from inattention to what makes different kinds of research different. Clearly a balance must be struck between (1) reifying research orientations through simplistic grids and subsequent over-characterizations and rigid standards or (2) having each study try to be totally self-justifying and cut loose from any community. While I do not think that there is any easy way out of this tension between committing new type 1 or type 2 errors, having good dimensions of contrast and good characterizations helps. I hope that these might be useful. A very brief sketch of the four orientations may aid further in highlighting differences and similarities in these community discourses along the suggested dimensions of difference (for development, see Alvesson and Deetz, in press).

The Discourse of Normative Studies

The researchers producing this discourse have been described as methodological determinists, functionalists, covering law theorists, or simply practicing the variable analytic tradition. This discourse is still largely dominant in North American organizational research and in applied organizational research throughout the world. It is reconstructed and well justified in Donaldson (1985). I describe this discourse as "normative" to emphasize the centrality of codification, the search for regularity, normalization of experience, and a strategic/directive control orientation (see Deetz 1973, Hollway 1984). Conceptions of operationalization, "objectivity," and law-like relations are merely the most obvious form of practice. The research practices mirror 19th century conceptions of the natural sciences often involving the most recent advances in operationalization, hypothesization, statistical reduction, and pattern "recognition" processes. Conventional practices and methodological determinism have in most cases replaced any strong allegiance to the positivist philosophy of science that grounds many of the methods and assumptions. The "objects" constructed by the practices of this science are given qualities of constancy and permanence as if given specific attributes by nature. The combination of a priori conceptions and focus on consensus leads the artifacts of these practices to be described as facts.

The discourse is decisively modern in Gergen's (1992) sense, and the knowledge is considered positive, cumulative and progressive. A grand narrative of emancipation is shaped by a commitment to make a better world through discovery of fundamental processes and the increase of production (Lyotard 1984). The organization is usually treated as an existing object produced for instrumental ends, usually making money, though some conception of the invisible hand makes that goal well integrated with other social goals of development and widespread availability of goods and services.

This discourse is most present in classical management theories, theories of leadership, contingency theory, most other systems theories, and other places more completely described by Burrell and Morgan in their discussion of "functionalist." But it is also clearly present in those advocating the management of culture (e.g., Schein 1992, Deal and Kennedy 1982) through their conception of culture as a variable or object to be strategically deployed (see Barley, Meyer, and Gash 1988 on the normative co-optation of cultural research). Many of those working with new conceptions of organizations as "post-modern" (rather than postmodern approaches, Parker 1992) have a discourse primarily structured in a normative fashion (e.g., Bergquist 1993). Many Marxist studies utilize normative themes. Most academic Marxist works depend on privileging particular social communities and employ economic and structural explanations based on normative conceptions. Lenin's embracing of scientific management was in no way inconsistent. Within managed economies, the managerial elite group giving rise to the concepts is quite different, of course, from the managerial elite accepted by most Western European and North American studies. Elite planning and strategic management are generally highly dependent on this discourse (see Knights and Morgan 1991, Knights 1992).

The Discourse of Interpretive Studies

For interpretive researchers the organization is a social site, a special type of community which shares important characteristics with other types of communities. The emphasis is on a social rather than economic view of organizational activities. Traditional methods of studying communities are seen as especially useful. The discourse often draws on traditional and premodern themes (Gergen 1992). This is not to suggest a focus on the past as much as a concern with those aspects of life which have not yet been systematized, instrumentalized and brought under the control of modernist logics and sciences. Interpretive studies accept much of the representational and consensual view of science seen in normative writings but shift the relation between theoretical conceptions and the talk of the subjects under study. People are not considered to be objects like other objects, but are active sense makers like the researcher. Theory is given a different conception and different role here. While theory may provide important sensitizing conceptions, it is not a device of classification nor tested in any simple and direct manner. The key conceptions and understandings must be worked out with the subjects under study. Research subjects can collaborate in displaying key features of their world. But like normative research the pressure is to get it right, to display unified, consensual culture in the way that it "actually" exists. The report is to display convincingly a unified way of life with all its complexities and contradictions.

Most researchers use ethnography, phenomenology, or hermeneutics in a rigorous way as the principal means of study. Studies are usually done in the field and are based on a prolonged period of observation and depth interviewing. The interest is in the full person in the organization; thus, social and life functions beyond the work process are considered. The workplace is seen as a site of human activity, one of those activities being "work" proper. The expressed goal of interpretive studies is to show how particular realities are socially produced and maintained through norms, rites, rituals, and daily activities. In much of the writings a clear preservationist, communitarian, or naturalist tone exists. It moves to save or record a life form with its complexity and creativity that may be lost to modern, instrumental life or overlooked in it. Gergen (1992) describes the romantic sense of this discourse with its depth and connection to the inner life. Cultural studies in organizations are interpretive to the extent that they have not been captured by normative, modernist co-optations (see Barley, Meyer, and Gash 1988; Enz 1992). Most interpretivists have taken culture to be an evocative metaphor for organizational life, rather than a variable or thing that an organization has (Smircich 1983; Frost et al. 1985, 1992).

Gradually, many researchers doing interpretive work have began to question the logic of displaying a consensual unified culture and have attended more to its fragmentation, tensions, and processes of conflict suppression (Martin 1992, Frost et al. 1992). And similarly, much more attention has been paid to the politics of representation and the role of the report author (Clifford and Marcus 1986, Marcus and Fischer 1986).

The Discourse of Critical Studies

Critical researchers see organizations in general as social historical creations accomplished in conditions of struggle and domination, a domination that often hides and suppresses meaningful conflict. Organizations are largely described as political sites; thus, general social theories and especially theories of decision making in the public sphere are seen as appropriate (see Deetz 1992, 1995). While commercial organizations could be positive social institutions providing forums for the articulation and resolution of important group conflicts over the use of natural resources, distribution of income, production of desirable goods and services, the development of personal qualities, and the direction of society, various forms of power and domination have lead to skewed decision making and fostered social harms and significant waste and inefficiency. Either explicit or implicit in critical work is a goal to demonstrate and critique forms of domination, asymmetry, and distorted communication through showing how social constructions of reality can favor certain interests and alternative constructions can be obscured and misrecognized. If these can be overcome, conflicts among different interests can be reclaimed, openly discussed, and resolved with fairness and justice. The research aims at producing dissensus and providing forums for and models of discussion to aid in the building of more open consensus. Of special concern are forms of false consciousness, consent, systematically distorted communication, routines, and normalizations which produce partial interests and keep people from genuinely understanding, expressing, or acting on their own interests (Alvesson and Deetz, in press; Alvesson and Willmott 1992; Mumby 1988). Of the four orientations, critical studies have the most explicit set of value commitments and most direct attention to moral and ethical issues. With this, much of the discourse has a suspicious and therapeutic tone, but also a theory of agency which provides an additional activist tone. People ca and should act on these conditions through improved understanding as well as access to communication forums.

Studies have focused both on the external relations of organizations to the wider society, especially the social effects of corporate colonization, rationalization of society, and the domination of the public sphere, and on the internal relations in terms of the domination by instrumental reasoning, discursive closures, and consent processes (see Vallas 1993, Deetz 1992). Critical studies include a large group of researchers who are different in theory and conception but who share important discursive features in their writing. They include Frankfurt school critical theorists (see Alvesson and Willmott 1992, for examples; Czarniawska-Joerges 1988; Mumby 1988; Alvesson 1987), conflict theorists (Dahrendorf 1959, Lehman and Young 1974), structurationists (Giddens 1984, 1991), some versions of feminist work (e.g., Harding 1991, Pringle 1988), and most doing recent versions of labor process theory (Braverman 1974; Burawoy 1979, 1985; Knights and Willmott 1990). While not necessarily so, in practice researchers working from the later, more explicitly political and moral writings of Foucault engage in a critical discourse (see Knights 1992).

The Discourse of Dialogic Studies

I have chosen the term "dialogic" rather than the more obvious "postmodernist" to organize this discourse because it attends to key features of this work and because of the growing commercial use of the term "postmodern," which makes it increasingly difficult to distinguish between realist assumptions about a changing world (a postmodern world which as well could be postindustrial, post-Fordist, or ad hoc) and a postmodern or dialogic discourse which denies realist assumptions (Parker 1992, Alvesson and Deetz, in press). The term also makes it easier to include older theories like Bahktin's (see Shotter 1993, Tyler 1988). Their themes include focusing on the constructed nature of people and reality, emphasizing language as a system of distinctions which are central to the construction process, arguing against grand narratives and large-scale theoretical systems such as Marxism or functionalism, emphasizing the power/knowledge connection and the role of claims of expertise in systems of domination, emphasizing the fluid and hyper-real nature of the contemporary world and role of mass media and information technologies, and stressing narrative/fiction/rhetoric as central to the research process. Examples of writings including this discourse include: Hawes (1991), Martin (1990), Calás and Smircich (1991), Mumby and Putnam (1992), Knights (1992), Burrell (1988), and several of the essays in Hassard and Parker (1993).

Dialogic studies focus on the fragmentation and potential disunity in any discourse. Like critical studies the concern is with asymmetry and domination, but unlike the critical studies' predefinition of groups and types of domination, domination is considered mobile, situational, not done by anyone. Group and personal identity cannot be seen as fixed or unitary. The attention is to reclaim conflicts suppressed in everyday life realities, meaning systems, and self conceptions and the enhancement of local forms of resistance. Fixed conceptions give way to the appeal of that beyond conception, the "otherness" of the world and other (B. Martin 1992, Linstead 1993). Rather than critical theory's reformation of the world they hope to show the partiality (the incompletion and onesidedness) of reality and the hidden points of resistance and complexity (Martin 1990, 1994; Smircich and Calás 1987). In place of an active political agenda and the often utopian ideals therein, attention is to the space for a continually transforming world by recovery of marginalized and suppressed peoples and aspects of people.

PLURALISM AND COMPLEMENTARITY

The intent here has not been to display definitively new groups or to record self-defined groups, rather I hope to have better displayed differences that give some insight into different discourses in organization studies today, displaying some of the ways that they are alike and different. Burrell and Morgan provided a great service by clearly expressing alternatives to the dominant "functionalist" tradition. For deeply embedded, and often uncontested, in functionalist/normative studies has been the acceptance of a managerial bias in conception of the organization and articulation of organizational goals. The justification for this approach to research has often been grounded in a conception of corporations and management as a kind of value-neutral tool which scientific study can improve without direct attention to the uses to which this tool has been applied. With such a conception, scholarly concern could be narrowed to the perfectibility of the tool. To the extent that this conception has been useful, organization studies have enhanced the effective use of resources and fulfillment of human needs.

Many researchers are now questioning this "tool" version of organizations and research, claiming that researchers missed much regarding the nature and effects of modern organizations, and insufficient attention was given to their numerous social and political functions. With the presence of continued environmental destruction, economic instabilities, growing social inequality, and increased awareness of the diversity of social groups, more researchers (e.g., Alvesson and Willmott 1992) and managers (e.g., the development of the World Business Academy) are following Burrell and Morgan in reconsidering the values and social effects of the so-called "neutral tool" and dominant forms of research. Understanding our alternatives requires understanding both the relation of conceptions to the various social stakeholders and the relation of research discourse to dominant social discourses. Thinking through these relations helps provide an opening for discussion.

Despite all the differences and tensions within any display of competitive research traditions, the problems and injustice of classification has to be balanced with the gains of clearly saying that different research programs have different goals and assumptions and require different forms of evaluation. As argued, the relations among these alternatives are not well thought in exclusionary, pluralistic, supplementary, or integrative terms. Each orientation creates a vision of social problems and tries to address them. Different orientations have developed specific ways of answering the types of questions they pose and do not work terribly well in answering the questions of others. The choice of orientation, to the extent that it can be freed from training histories and department/discipline politics, can probably be reduced to alternative conceptions of social good and preferred ways of living. This grounds theory and method debate in a moral debate that is neither terribly common nor explicit in organization science, but can be made clearer when research is considered as a set of interaction processes producing identifiable social discourses. Studies need to be understood and evaluated on their own terms but should also appeal to larger social needs where both the needs and means of accomplishment are contested. Understanding their form of discourse helps.

I, like many others, sometimes wish we were all multilingual, that we could move across orientations with grace and ease, but this type of Teflon-coated multiperspectival cosmopolitan envisioned by Morgan (1986) or Hassard (1991) is often both illusionary and weak (see Parker and McHugh 1991). Good scholars have deep commitments. Multiperspectivalism often leads to shallow readings and uses of alternative orientations since unexamined basic assumptions have unexpected hidden qualities. Some scholars are more multilingual than others, but doing good work within an orientation still must be prized first. A tenuous balance between tentativeness and commitment is probably a sign of maturity of any scholar. Struggling with understandings and having arguments across programs of work are important, but the outcome is well conceived in neither synthetic (integrative) nor additive (pluralistic, supplementary) terms. Complementarity of forms of research questions and procedures is probably better (see Apel 1979, Albert et al. 1988). Not everyone needs to do each, but each has to be fostered both by giving space and taking their concerns and arguments seriously, seriously enough and with enough understanding to debate and make demands on all groups for justification and clarity of purpose.

Any research group dominating over time becomes inward looking, isolated from the problems of the larger society, and filled with blinders and trained incapacities. Its acts of perpetuation exceed its attempts at social service, its prophets become priests. Similar to most societies, marginalized research groups have had to learn two systems—their own and the dominant one—and dominant groups only one (Collins 1986). As we gradually learn socially the positive effects of diversity—beyond "separate but equal" *and* integration—organization science can also benefit from better discussions. This does not mean that we each should automatically find other groups' issues and procedures interesting or helpful, nor should we believe that all of them are. But let us make our claims and the relation between our claims and procedures clearer so objection and conflict can be on those grounds rather than impose traditional problem statements and methods on those doing something else. In doing so, the ultimate point is not in arguing it out to get it right, but to reclaim the suppressed tensions and conflicts among the many contemporary stakeholders to negotiate a life together based in appreciation of different and responsive decision making.

NOTES

1. This section is revised from an earlier discussion that appeared in Deetz 1994c.

2. "Elite" is a loaded word, and I am uncomfortable with the negative connotations; but the word works precisely because it draws attention to privileging practices. Academic discourse growing out of the enlightenment is itself privileged in many regards, and it is hard to do either critical theory or normative science very long before you either implicitly or explicitly purport to be more rational, insightful, or knowing than those being studied. The enlightenment legacy provides a defining role for the intellectual and science, which is largely taken on by normative and critical researchers (i.e., the expert role for normative work, the leadership role for critical

research). To say that they take a stance as an elite is not to claim, however, that they are elitist, though some may be. The opposite given to elite here is local. I suspect that the better term would be "across place and time privilege," but that is too awkward.

REFERENCES

Abercrombie, N., S. Hill and B. Turner (1980), *The Dominant Ideology Thesis,* London, UK: Allen & Unwin.

Albert, M., L. Cagan, N. Chomsky, R. Hahnel, M. King, L. Sargent and H. Sklar (1986), *Liberating Theory,* Boston, MA: South End Press.

Alvesson, M. (1987), *Organizational Theory and Technocratic Consciousness: Rationality, Ideology, and Quality of Work,* New York: de Gruyter.

————— and S. Deetz (in press), "Critical Theory and Postmodernism Approaches to Organization Studies," in S. Clegg, C. Harding and W. Nord (Eds.), *The Handbook of Organization Studies,* London: Sage.

————— and H. Willmott (Eds.) (1992), *Critical Management Studies,* London, UK: Sage.

————— and ————— (1995). *Making Sense of Management: A Critical Analysis,* London, UK: Sage.

Apel, K.-O. (1979), *Toward a Transformation of Philosophy,* G. Adey and D. Frisby (trans.), London, UK: Routledge & Kegan Paul.

Astley, W. and A. Van de Ven (1983), "Central Perspectives and Debates in Organizational Theory," *Administrative Science Quarterly,* 28, 245-273.

Barley, S., G. Meyer and D. Gash (1988), "Cultures of Culture: Academics, Practitioners and the Pragmatics of Normative Control," *Administrative Science Quarterly,* 33, 24-60.

Bergquist, W. (1993). *The Postmodern Organization: Mastering the Art or Irreversible Change,* San Francisco, CA: Jossey-Bass.

Bernstein, R. (1984), *Beyond Objectivism and Relativism,* Philadelphia, PA: University of Pennsylvania Press.

Bourdieu, P. (1984), *Distinctions: A Social Critique of the Judgement of Taste,* Cambridge, UK: Cambridge University Press.

————— (1991), *Language and Symbolic Power,* Cambridge, MA: Harvard University Press.

Braverman, H. (1974), *Labor and Monopoly Capitalism,* New York: Monthly Review Press.

Burawoy, M. (1979), *Manufacturing Consent,* Chicago, IL: University of Chicago Press.

————— (1985), *The Politics of Production: Factory Regimes under Capitalism and Socialism,* London, UK: Verso.

Burrell, G. (1988), "Modernism, Postmodernism and Organizational Analysis 2: The Contribution of Michel Foucault," *Organization Studies,* 9, 221-235.

————— and G. Morgan (1979), *Sociological Paradigms and Organizational Analysis,* London, UK: Heinemann.

Calás, M. and L. Smircich (1991), "Voicing Seduction to Silence Leadership," *Organization Studies,* 12, 567-602.

Clifford, J. and G. Marcus (Eds.) (1986), *Writing Culture: The Poetics and Politics of Ethnography,* Berkeley, CA: University of California Press.

Collins, P. (1986), "Learning from the Outsider Within," *Social Problems,* 33, S14-32.

Cooper, R. (1989), "Modernism, Postmodernism and Organizational Analysis 3: The Contribution of Jacques Derrida," *Organization Studies,* 10, 479-502.

————— and G. Burrell (1988), "Modernism, Postmodernism and Organizational Analysis: An Introduction," *Organization Studies,* 9, 91-112.

Czarniawska-Joerges, B. (1988), *Ideological Control in Nonideological Organizations,* New York: Praeger.

Dahrendorf, R. (1959), *Class and Class Conflict in Industrial Society,* Stanford, CA: Stanford University Press.

Deal, T. and A. Kennedy (1982), *Corporate Cultures,* Reading, MA: Addison-Wesley.

Deetz, S. (1973), "An Understanding of Science and a Hermeneutic Science of Understanding," *Journal of Communication,* 23, 139-159.

——— (1992), *Democracy in the Age of Corporate Colonization: Developments in Communication and the Politics of Everyday Life,* Albany, NY: State University of New York Press.

——— (1994a), "The New Politics of the Workplace: Ideology and Other Unobtrusive Controls," in H. Simons and M. Billig (Eds.), *After Postmodernism: Reconstructing Ideology Critique,* Thousand Oaks, CA: Sage Publications, pp. 172-199.

——— (1994b), "The Micro-politics of Identity Formation in the Workplace: The Case of a Knowledge Intensive Firm," *Human Studies,* 17, 23-44.

——— (1994c), "The Future of the Discipline: The Challenges, the Research, and the Social Contribution," in S. Deetz (Ed.), *Communication Yearbook 17,* Thousand Oaks, CA: Sage, pp. 565-600.

——— (1994d), "Representative Practices and the Political Analysis of Corporations," in B. Kovacic (Ed.), *Organizational Communication: New Perspectives,* Albany, NY: State University of New York Press, pp. 209-242.

——— (1995), *Transforming Communication, Transforming Business: Building Responsive and Responsible Workplaces,* Cresskill, NJ: Hampton Press.

——— (1996a), "Discursive Formations, Strategized Subordination, and Self-surveillance: An Empirical Case," in A. McKinlay and K. Starkey (Eds.), *Managing Foucault: A Reader,* London, UK: Sage, in press.

——— (1996b), "The Business Concept, Discursive Power, and Managerial Control in a Knowledge-intensive Company: A Case Study," in B. Sypher (Ed.), *Case Studies in Organizational Communication,* 2d ed., New York: Guilford Press, in press.

Donaldson, L. (1985), *In Defense of Organizational Theory: A Reply to Critics,* Cambridge, UK: Cambridge University Press.

Enz, C. (1992), "The Culture of Social Science Research," in P. Frost and R. Stablein (Eds.), *Doing Exemplary Research,* Thousand Oaks, CA: Sage.

Epstein, C. (1988), *Deceptive Distinctions,* New Haven, CT: Yale University Press.

Flax, J. (1990), *Thinking Fragments: Psychoanalysis, Feminism, and Postmodernism in the Contemporary West,* Berkeley, CA: University of California Press.

Fraser, N. and L. Nicholson (1988), "Social Criticism without Philosophy: An Encounter Between Feminism and Postmodernism," *Theory, Culture & Society,* 5, 373-394.

Frost, P., L. Moore, M. Louis, C. Lundberg and J. Martin (Eds.) (1985), *Organizational Culture,* Thousand Oaks, CA: Sage.

———, ———, ———, ———, and ——— (Eds.) (1992), *Reframing Culture,* Thousand Oaks, CA: Sage.

Gergen, K. (1978), "Toward Generative Theory," *Journal of Personality and Social Psychology,* 36, 1344-1360.

——— (1992), "Organizational Theory in the Postmodern Era," in M. Reed and M. Hughes (Eds.), *Rethinking Organization,* London, UK: Sage, pp. 207-226.

Giddens, A. (1984), *The Constitution of Society,* Berkeley, CA: University of California Press.

——— (1991), *Modernity and Self-identity: Self and Society in the Late Modern Age,* Stanford, CA: Stanford University Press.

Habermas, J. (1984), *The Theory of Communicative Action, Volume 1: Reason and the Rationalization of Society,* T. McCarthy (trans.), Boston, MA: Beacon.

————— (1987), *The Theory of Communicative Action, Volume 2: Lifeworld and System,* T. McCarthy (trans.), Boston, MA: Beacon Press.

Hamnett, M., D. Porter, A. Singh and K. Kumar (1984), *Ethics, Politics and International Social Science Research,* Honolulu, HI: East-West Center and University of Hawaii Press.

Harding, S. (1991), *Whose Science? Whose Knowledge?* Ithaca, NY: Cornell University Press.

Hassard, J. (1991), "Multiple Paradigms and Organizational Analysis: A Case Study," *Organization Studies,* 12, 275-299.

————— and M. Parker (Eds.) (1993), *Postmodernism and Organizations,* London, UK: Sage.

Hawes, L. (1991), Organising Narratives/Codes/Poetics, *Journal of Organizational Change Management,* 4, 45-51.

Heckscher, C. (1995), *White-collar Blues: Management Loyalties in an Age of Corporate Restructuring,* New York: Basic Books.

Hirschman, E. and M. Holbrook (1992), *Postmodern Consumer Research,* London, UK: Sage.

Hollway, W. (1984), "Fitting Work: Psychological Assessment in Organizations," in J. Henriques, W. Hallway, C. Urwin, C. Venn and V. Walkerdine (Eds.), *Changing the Subject,* New York: Methuen, pp. 26-59.

Husserl, E. (1962), *Ideas: General Introduction to Phenomenology* W. Gibson (trans.), London, UK: Collier-Macmillan.

Jackson, N. and P. Carter (1991), "In Defense of Paradigm Incommensurability," *Organization Studies,* 12, 109-127.

Kavanagh, D. (1993), "Metatheoretical Frameworks in Management Research," Unpublished paper presented at the British Academy of Management Annual Conference, Milton Keynes, UK, September.

Kilduff, M. (1993), "Deconstructing Organizations," *Academy of Management Review,* 18, 13-31.

Knights, D. (1992), "Changing Spaces: The Disruptive Impact of a New Epistemological Location for the Study of Management," *Academy of Management Review,* 17, 514-536.

————— and G. Morgan (1991), "Corporate Strategy, Organizations, and Subjectivity: A Critique," *Organization Studies,* 12, 251-273.

————— and H. Willmott (1989), "Power and Subjectivity at Work: From Degradation to Subjugation in Social Relations," *Sociology,* 23, 535-558.

————— and ————— (Eds.) (1990), *Labour Process Theory,* London, UK: Macmillan.

Kunda, G. (1992), *Engineering Culture: Control and Commitment in a High-tech Corporation,* Philadelphia, PA: Temple University Press.

Laclau, E. and C. Mouffe (1985), *Hegemony and Socialist Strategy,* W. Moore and P. Cammack (trans.), London, UK: Verso.

Latour, B. (1993), *We Have Never Been Modern,* New York: Wheatsheaf.

Lehman, T. and T. Young (1974), "From Conflict Theory and Conflict Methodology," *Sociological Inquiry,* 44, 15-28.

Linstead, S. (1993), "Deconstruction in the Study of Organizations," in J. Hassard and M. Parker (Eds.), *Postmodernism and Organizations,* London, UK: Sage.

Lyotard, J.-F. (1984), *The Postmodern Condition: A Report on Knowledge,* G. Bennington and B. Massumi (trans.), Minneapolis, MN: University of Minnesota Press.

Marcus, G. and M. Fischer (Eds.) (1986), *Anthropology as Cultural Critique,* Chicago, IL: University of Chicago Press.

Martin, B. (1992), *Matrix and Line: Derrida and the Possibilities of Postmodern Social Science,* Albany, NY: State University of New York Press.

Martin, J. (1990), "Deconstructing Organizational Taboos: The Suppression of Gender Conflict in Organizations," *Organization Science,* 1, 339-359.

———— (1992), *Cultures in Organizations: Three Perspectives,* Oxford, UK: Oxford University Press.

———— (1994), "The Organization of Exclusion: Institutionalization of Sex Inequality, Gendered Faculty Jobs and Gendered Knowledge in Organizational Theory and Research," *Organization: The Interdisciplinary Journal of Organization, Theory and Society,* 1, 401-431.

Morgan, G. (1986), *Images of Organizations,* Thousand Oaks, CA: Sage.

Mumby, D. (1987), "The Political Function of Narrative in Organizations," *Communication Monographs,* 54, 113-127.

———— (1988), *Communication and Power in Organizations: Discourse, Ideology, and Domination,* Norwood, NJ: Ablex.

———— and L. Putnam (1992), "The Politics of Emotion: A Feminist Reading of Bounded Rationality," *Academy of Management Review,* 17, 465-486.

Natter, W., T. Schatzki and J. P. Jones III (1995), *Objectivity and Its Other,* New York: Guilford Publications, Inc.

Parker, M. (1992), "Post-modern Organizations or Postmodern Organization Theory?" *Organization Studies,* 13, 1-17.

———— and G. McHugh (1991), "Five Tests in Search of an Author: A Response to John Hassard's 'Multiple Paradigms and Organizational Analysis,' " *Organization Studies,* 12, 451-456.

Pfeffer, J. (1982), *Organizations and Organizational Theory,* London, UK: Pitman.

Power, M. and R. Laughlin (1992), "Critical Theory and Accounting," in M. Alvesson and H. Willmott (Eds.), *Critical Management Studies,* London, UK: Sage, pp. 113-135.

Pringle, R. (1988), *Secretaries Talk,* London, UK: Verso.

Rao, V. and W. Pasmore (1989), "Knowledge and Interests in Organizational Studies: A Conflict of Interpretation," *Organization Studies,* 10, 225-239.

Reason, P. (1994), "Three Approaches to Participative Inquiry," in Y. Lincoln and N. Denzin (Eds.), *Handbook of Qualitative Research,* Thousand Oaks, CA: Sage, pp. 324-339.

Reed, M. (1985), *New Directions in Organizational Analysis,* London, UK: Tavistock.

Rorty, R. (1989), *Contingency, Irony and Solidarity,* Cambridge, UK: Cambridge University Press.

Sandelands, L. and V. Srivatsan (1993), "The Problem of Experience in the Study of Organizations," *Organization Studies,* 14, 1-22.

Schein, E. (1992), *Organizational Culture and Leadership,* 2nd ed., San Francisco, CA: Jossey-Bass.

Shotter, J. (1993), *Conversational Realities: The Construction of Life through Language,* Thousand Oaks, CA: Sage.

Smircich, L. (1983), "Concepts of Culture and Organizational Analysis," *Administrative Science Quarterly,* 28, 339-358.

———— and M. Calás (1987), "Organizational Culture: A Critical Assessment," in F. Jablin, L. Putnam, K. Roberts and L. Porter (Eds.), *Handbook of Organizational Communication,* Thousand Oaks, CA: Sage, pp. 228-263.

Treichler, P. (1989), "What Definitions Do: Childbirth, Cultural Crisis, and the Challenge to Medical Discourse," in B. Dervin, L. Grossberg, B. O'Keefe and E. Wartella (Eds.), *Rethinking Communication,* Newbury Park, CA: Sage, pp. 424-453.

Tyler, S. (1988), *The Unspeakable: Discourse, Dialogue, and Rhetoric in the Postmodern World,* Madison, WI: University of Wisconsin Press.

Vallas, S. (1993), *Power in the Workplace: The Politics of Production at AT & T,* Albany, NY: State University of New York Press.

Weedon, C. (1987), *Feminist Practice and Poststructuralist Theory,* Oxford, UK: Basil Blackwell.

Willmott, H. (1990), "Beyond Paradigmatic Closure in Organizational Enquiry," in J. Hassard and D. Pym (Eds.), *The Theory and Philosophy of Organisations,* New York: Routledge.

——— (1993), "Breaking the Paradigm Mentality," *Organization Studies,* 14, 681-719.

Whyte, W. (Ed.) (1991), *Participatory Action Research,* Thousand Oaks, CA: Sage.

9

From Quicksand to Crossroads

An Agnostic Perspective on Conversation

WALTER R. NORD
ANN F. CONNELL
Department of Management, University of South Florida

"... early in life, ... I discovered that one of the unpardonable sins, in the eyes of most people, is to go about unlabelled. The world regards such a person as the police do an unmuzzled dog, not under proper control. I could find no label that would suit me, so, in my desire to range myself and be respectable, I invented one; and, as the chief thing I was sure of was that I did not know a great many things that the _____ists and the _____ites about me professed to be familiar with, I called myself an agnostic." (T. H. Huxley, quoted from Bibby 1967, p. 109)

The purpose of this paper is to facilitate conservation, in the sense of Rorty (1980), among organization scientists and also between organization scientists and others. Towards this end we explore some philosophical issues and their implications for conversation, call attention to several commonalities among human beings, and define key terms associated with these commonalities. Our primary objective is to consider an experience, the Sense Of Accurate Reception (SOAR), that appears to underlie many conversations

---

(including the subjective-objective debate) and to explore ways for organization scientists to achieve this experience.

PHILOSOPHICAL ISSUES, VALUES, AND DEFINITIONS

The Subjective-Objective Debate Reconsidered

Few would deny the value of debate and conflict in scholarly endeavors. Of course, not all debates are equally valuable, and previously productive debates may reach a point of decreasing (or even increasingly negative) marginal utility. We suggest that the debate in organization science between "objectivists" and "subjectivists" regarding the nature of reality (henceforth, "the debate") has reached such a point.

"The debate" was shaped by such prominent scholars as Burrell and Morgan (1979), Morgan and Smircich (1980), Astley (1985), Pinder and Bourgeois (1982), and Donaldson (1985); recent papers by Astley and Zammuto (1992) and Donaldson (1992) demonstrate that this debate continues to divide us. As agnostics, we suggest it may be time to bypass "the debate," at least in its present form.

Positions and Values

Despite its long history, agnosticism may be a novel position to many modern social scientists. Consequently, we describe it briefly before discussing our values regarding a core process in organization science—conversation.

Agnosticism. In philosophic terminology, an agnostic is one who denies or doubts the possibility of ultimate knowledge in some area of study. The word was coined by Thomas Huxley (Bibby 1967, p. 109), although the basic agnostic issues were outlined centuries earlier by the ancient Skeptics, beginning with Pyrrho of Elis (ca. 365-275 B.C., see Stough 1969).

Our agnostic position with regard to "the debate" is: *we do not know* and cannot envision any way to find out which, if any, point on Morgan and Smircich's (1980) continuum between subjectivism and objectivism is correct. Chuang Tzu's (fourth century B.C., 1968) observation that he did not know if he was a man who had dreamed previously he was a butterfly, or if he was presently a butterfly dreaming that he was a man, captures this position well. Popper (1956, p. 82) put it more directly: ". . . the doctrine that the world is my dream . . . is irrefutable," and ". . . realism is also irrefutable."[1]

As agnostics, we are not asserting that the nature of "reality" can *never* be ascertained, since we do not know what new information might become available. Moreover, we are not saying any particular ontological or epistemological position is wrong—in fact, we are glad to entertain most any position on a temporary, as-if-true basis, in order to pursue and learn from a particular line of thought.

Values Regarding Conversation. Two values are fundamental to our position. First, we value conversation or discourse. We enjoy it for its own sake and have experienced other benefits as well (e.g., ideas about organization science, the ability to make hollandaise sauce, a sense of communion with others). Whether these outcomes are subjective constructions, reality-based truths, or something else, we experience them as benefits of conversation. Second, we are biased toward cooperative styles of conversation in general and for organization science in particular.

Obscured Commonalities Among Organization Scientists

Re-examining conversation among organization scientists, in the light of the agnostic position and our values about conversation, reveals several commonalities that are shared by seemingly incompatible approaches. While the various perspectives represented in "the debate" are not all mutually exclusive (Gioia and Pitre 1990, Lee 1991, Tsoukas 1991), "the debate" has highlighted differences and incompatibilities. For example, Morgan and Smircich (1980) focused on contrasts among various approaches along the subjective-objective continuum, and Donaldson (1992) posed a polarity— positivism vs. anti-positivism.

Focusing on differences often obscures commonalities. Important similarities may become apparent only when a "counterparadigm" (Sjoberg and Cain 1971), i.e., a perspective that makes contrasting background assumptions, is introduced. Agnosticism, a time-honored philosophical position, can provide a useful counterparadigm for viewing "the debate."

Two questions frequently involved in "the debate" are: "Is there an external, knowable reality?" and "What role do human beings play in constructing what they take to be reality?" The agnostic counterparadigm highlights two commonalities that impact efforts to deal with those questions.

First, *all* the debaters appear to share a basic assumption—that knowledge regarding those questions is available to human beings. Each debater claims either to know an answer(s) or at least to be able to rule out certain proposed answer(s). The second commonality appears to be shared by all people, not just the debaters: everything that any of us considers to be knowledge is *experienced as patterns* in separate streams of consciousness. ("Stream of consciousness" is defined below under *Definitions of Key Concepts.*) So far, no one has demonstrated a way to bypass personal patterns of consciousness, in order to obtain direct information about "reality." Of course, we can obtain verification from others for patterns, but we cannot get outside our streams of consciousness to determine that those other people actually exist. Furthermore, even if we could, we would still have no way to achieve certainty that the verifying messages we received were the same as the messages those other people had sent. In other words, patterns about patterns are still patterns.

In view of these considerations, it may be useful to think of patterns of consciousness as constituting a limit to human knowledge, at least at this time. What we mean by "limit to knowledge" is illustrated by physicist Robert Jastrow's (1977) statement:

> If [the big bang theory] is valid, the astronomer must say to his colleagues who still pursue their inquiries into the past: you may go this far, and no farther; you cannot penetrate the mystery of creation. (p. 3)

This perspective leads us to view the subjective-objective debate as moot. Consequently, to the degree it is a barrier to conversation, we would like to bypass it and focus our attention on conversation itself and on a *third* commonality, derived not from the agnostic view but from observation.

We have noticed that, despite the lack of *absolute certainty* about success in communication, most people seem to perform activities (e.g., repeating their own statements; asking, "You know what I mean?"; requesting clarification; and paraphrasing) aimed at achieving some *sense of* successful communication. This sense of successful communication is central to our thesis. However, before taking a close look at it and discussing methods of achieving it, we need to define some key terms.

Definitions of Key Concepts

Five concepts are central to our perspective.

Stream of Consciousness. Stream of consciousness refers to the ever-shifting tapestry of sensations, memories, imaginings, ideas, feelings, symbols and combination thereof that constitutes human, moment-to-moment awareness.[2] This stream itself may be a dream, a socially-constructed movie, a reflection of reality, some alternative as yet not conceived by human imagination, or some combination of the above. Again, being agnostic, we do not know and do not know how to find out.

Our approach asks each person to accept one stream of consciousness, namely her or his own, as given. In taking this step, you do not need to assume that any other beings except yourself have consciousness, or even that any other beings exist. It is possible that the configurations you think of as other people are conscious beings. However, they could also be zombies (see Dennett 1991), androids or alien-induced hypnotic illusions. Although we speak of streams of consciousness other than your own (e.g., those of the authors and of other readers), we invite you to consider them simply as patterns in your own consciousness.

Patterns of Consciousness. The sensations, memories, ideas, fantasies, feelings, and symbols which constitute your stream of consciousness are called "patterns of consciousness," or simply "patterns." These patterns include all aspects of conscious experience—the experiences of hearing a symphony, hearing a single note, speaking a word, thinking about a paradigm, and remembering the fragrance of honeysuckle all qualify as patterns of consciousness. The configurations representing other human beings also qualify as patterns of consciousness. So does the configuration representing your "self." Similarly, the various categories Morgan and Smircich (1980) used to punctuate the subjective-objective continuum (e.g., "reality as a social construction," "reality as a concrete process," etc.) are patterns.

Context. Context is the collection of other patterns in which a specified pattern is embedded in an individual stream of consciousness. The collection of patterns designated as context for a given pattern depends on the situation. The various contextual patterns in which other patterns are embedded can be assigned names. A sentence might be called the "textural context" of a word. Your collection of patterns representing books, articles, lectures and discussions about organization science might be called the "institutional context" of this article (for you).

Sense That a Pattern Is Being Sent. The sense that a pattern is being sent refers to any of the following experiences: (1) the sense of expressing a pattern to another, (2) the sense of receiving a pattern from another, and (3) the sense of observing someone send a pattern to or receive a pattern from another. The pattern may be sent by means of one or more media such as print, gesture, touch, an art form, or even possibly extrasensory perception.

SOAR (Sense Of Accurate Reception). SOAR is defined as *the sense that the pattern received is the same as the pattern sent.* It is a pattern of consciousness and may *accompany* or *follow* the experience of a receiver, sender or observer that a pattern is being sent. (Please remember that the terms "sender," "receiver," and "observer" designate patterns of consciousness; they do not necessarily imply *actual* people *out there*. For you, the reader, the locus of these patterns is assumed to be your own stream of consciousness.) The receiver's experience of SOAR is analogous to that referred to in radio communications as "message received and understood" or *"roger."* The sender experience is one of "the receiver understands" or "she gets it," an experience which sometimes evokes the slang expression, *"bingo."* An observer may also experience "bingo" when sensing that the receiver understands the message.

Some elaboration about what SOAR does not mean may help locate our view.

First, SOAR is not all or none. It may be felt regarding some parts of a pattern and not others, and the degree of experienced certainty about accurate reception may vary. To increase the degree of experienced certainty, a sender and/or a receiver may use definitions (operational, conceptual, ostensive), questions, paraphrasing, repetitions, demonstrations, pictures or other aids.

Second, SOAR can be a formal judgment, such as a student's careful assessment that she understands an assigned book chapter, or it can be a nebulous feeling, such as vague empathy with someone's description of a frustrating day. Any type of message, a lecture, a flow chart, a gift, or the absence of a gift, can provide the basis for SOAR.

Third, we use "SOAR" instead of "intersubjectivity" because intersubjectivity can refer to agreement between two people about an external object. We wish to avoid the objectivist implications of assuming an external object and even of assuming a second consciousness. SOAR is nothing more than a pattern in *one* stream of consciousness. Its presence does *not* allow us to conclude that the message even existed, much less that the message received was actually the same as the one sent.

Fourth, in pursuing SOAR, you may use signals much as one does in a popular children's game, "hot potato, cold potato." However, when you strive for SOAR, you are both asking and answering the questions. You ask yourself, "Is the message sent the same as the message received?" and you signal yourself, "yes" or "no." These signals lead you to keep communicating with your perceived partner, until you either achieve a desired degree of certainty or else give up. At a later time, you may experience new patterns that either confirm or disconfirm the earlier SOAR. Again, however, these results are themselves merely patterns, not evidence of "objective" accuracy.

Fifth, SOAR does not imply a sense that the receiver *agrees with* or *believes* the message. It merely indicates a sense that the receiver *understands* the message.

Sixth, shared meanings or shared cultural assumptions are not necessary for SOAR. Since SOAR is a personal experience, it can occur in the absence of relevant shared assumptions. For example, if you say something in English to a non-English-speaking person, your words are unlikely to trigger shared meanings. Nevertheless, if you *assume,* however erroneously, that the receiver understood your message, you still experience "she got it" or "bingo."

Seventh, a "supernatural" or "paranormal" experience may or may not entail SOAR. So long as there is the *sense of a message accurately received,* such as Joan of Arc's belief that she heard voices telling her to save France, the experience qualifies as SOAR.

Eighth, is SOAR desirable? On the basis of our values, it often is. We enjoy SOAR for its own sake. Further, even if life is a dream, within that dream there seem to be rewards associated with SOAR, whether we are preparing dinner, reading, or making love.

Finally, is SOAR always desirable? Certainly not! When watching a television commercial, we usually have minimal interest in SOAR. When brainstorming, attempts to achieve SOAR often interfere with creativity. However, in conversations about organization science, we often do desire frequent, complete and personally-convincing experiences of SOAR.[3]

SOAR: A CROSSROAD
FOR ORGANIZATION SCIENTISTS?

As stated earlier, each person, regardless of philosophical position, appears to be isolated within his own stream of consciousness; nevertheless, each appears to strive for a sense of accurate communication. The contenders in "the debate" may all share this common goal, although they may differ about how to achieve it. For example, the realist may respond "roger" when a "clear" operational definition is advanced. The subjectivist may experience "roger" when multiple meanings of a text are made apparent through deconstruction. We propose that the experience of SOAR can be viewed as a common aim and consequently can be a crossroads for all the different contenders.

Some Dynamics of SOAR

The pursuit of SOAR may be viewed as a two-person dance *within* your stream of consciousness. In this dance, the *pattern that you experience* as your "self" interacts iteratively with the pattern *that you experience* as coming from your partner. Even when you use a recording medium such as writing, the process can be described as an iterative one in your stream of consciousness, as you produce successive versions of a manuscript, and successive manuscripts, using feedback from a multitude of partners. Satisfactory performance of this dance can require skill, artistry, and persistence.

Whether you are a sender or a receiver, each step in the pursuit of SOAR (isolating patterns to be expressed, coding them in symbols, sending patterns, receiving patterns, decoding, and checking for accuracy) can influence you to revise patterns involved in the message—and other patterns as well.

Weick's (1979, p. 5) question—"How can I know what I think until I see what I say?"—illustrates the changes in consciousness that may accompany the transmission of patterns. Such shifts suggest a complement to the Heisenberg uncertainty principle. Observation can alter the phenomenon, as Heisenberg postulated, and it also can alter the observer.

From Traditional Scientific Conversation to SOAR

Our "discovery" of SOAR stems from Nord's efforts with Art Brief (Brief and Nord 1990) to define "work." Every attempt to develop a suitable definition resulted in a sense of being mired in "conceptual quicksand."

Stepping in Quicksand. What *is* work? In a sense, when composing this sentence, we were "working." The activity was related to our earning a living, which is perhaps the most common theme in definitions of work (Brief and Nord 1990). However, we wrote it on an August Sunday—a time we experienced as leisure. "Fun" captures our subjective experience far better than does "labor," "toil" or other synonyms for "work." However, had we written the sentence for a committee report, "toil" or "labor" might have been accurate labels. If even identical activities can be experienced so differently, using the same term for both can be problematic.

Many other terms commonly used in organization studies present similar problems. Some examples are: "family" and its components, such as "mother" (Hoffman 1986), "performance" (Campbell and Pritchard 1976), "innovation" (Nord and Tucker 1987), "laboratory and field research" (Campbell 1986) and "science." We have trouble achieving SOAR using the above words, because they elicit many, sometimes conflicting, patterns in us.[4]

Influential scholars have suggested that the above problem emerges when "everyday" experience and discourse contaminate science. Francis Bacon (Spedding, Ellis and Heath 1860/1962), for example, sought ways ". . . to correct the ill complexion of the understanding itself, which cannot but be tinged and infected, and at length perverted and distorted, by daily and habitual impressions" (p. 173). Centuries later, Durkheim suggested that scientists abandon all concepts derived from common usage and replace them with new, better-defined terms (Levine 1985).

For organization science, several major problems are associated with this proposal. First, reaching and sustaining agreement about definitions is difficult. Second, the definitions themselves would presumably be couched in common-discourse terms, with their multiplicity of meanings and temporal variations; consequently, the new vocabulary would have a shaky foundation. Even an operational definition that is universally accepted within a specific verbal community at a specific time does not automatically prevent confusion. The term "punishment," for example, while operationally defined and widely used in the operant-conditioning community, has always fared poorly. Problems associated with "punishment" have been so severe that Yulevich and Axelrod (1983, p. 380) branded it a "bad influence" on scientific investigation and added that it ". . . should never have been granted permanent status in the first place." Perhaps the most significant disadvantage to the elimination of common-usage, multiple-meaning terms, however, is that they can be invaluable in organization science discourse (see Daft and Wiginton 1979).

Stepping out of Quicksand. Whereas the distinction between ordinary and scientific terminology does little toward achieving SOAR, distinguishing between multiple-pattern terms (i.e., terms associated with more than one basic meaning in a given context) and single-pattern terms is most helpful. Common-discourse words, such as "work," tend to be multiple-pattern terms. Seemingly scientific or professional words or phrases can be *either* single-pattern or multiple-pattern. For example, "repression," which entails "turning something away, and keeping it at a distance, from the conscious," (Freud 1915/1957, p. 147) appears to be a single-pattern term, as does "positive reinforcer," defined by Skinner (1953) in terms of stimuli that are followed by an increase in frequency of response. In contrast, "Narcissistic Personality Disorder," like many categories in the *Diagnostic and Statistical Manual of Mental Disorders,* is clearly multiple-pattern.[5]

What we call conceptual quicksand does not arise either from the use of ordinary discourse or even from the use of multiple-pattern terms, per se. It arises from *the use of multiple-pattern terms as if they are single-pattern terms.* This is a major source of the problems with "work."

Therefore, we do not need an entirely new vocabulary to achieve SOAR. What we need are methods for designating the specific pattern or patterns we wish to transmit and for ruling out competing or confusing patterns. Such methods already exist.

AIDS TO ACHIEVING SOAR

We consider three aids to achieving SOAR in verbal communication: careful designation of patterns, inclusion of useful context, and deriving new patterns. Then we explore potential contributions of nonverbal media to the achievement of SOAR in organization science.

Careful Designation of Patterns

Our experiences with conceptual quicksand led to further consideration of ways to designate patterns. Three approaches emerged: definitions of terms, ruling out unwanted patterns and sensitivity to connotations.

Definitions of Terms. Several types of definitions (e.g., ostensive, conceptual, operational) can be helpful in designating a desired pattern or patterns, even if you do not consider such patterns to be reflections of an external reality. As Popper (1956, p. 145) observed, ". . . it seems to me that within methodology we do not have to presuppose metaphysical realism."

Ruling out Unwanted Patterns. SOAR can be fostered by explicitly ruling out patterns you do not mean to send. In this context, it appears useful to extend Pinder and Bourgeois' (1982, p. 651) guideline, ". . . metaphors and other tropes should be differentiated from identities, equivalences, isomorphisms, or formal definitions for which they might be mistaken," to apply to any pattern which could be mistaken for another.

Sensitivity to Connotations. Since they are part of the constellation of patterns associated with a term, connotations can affect SOAR. Uses of the term "narcissism" provide examples of the confusion connotations can engender. In addition to the multiple patterns of meaning *denoted* by its definition, "narcissism" *connotes* selfishness. As a result, "narcissism" can be used to convey a personal insult, masked by medical or scientific objectivity. If either a receiver or "a sender" ignores the difference between a personal insult and a nonangry use of a psychiatric term, SOAR can be difficult to achieve. Analogously, many of the problems with "punishment" may stem from its connotations of coercion and/or cruelty. Sometimes a term's connotations can be so strong that the only way to avoid them is to avoid the term.

Inclusion of Useful Context

Many of the common-usage terms that lead to conceptual quicksand entail problems of context. "Mother" is an example. Hoffman (1986) observed that while a woman who worked outside the home was statistically deviant a few decades ago, this is not the case today. Further, while mothers were once the primary providers of child care, by the end of the 1980s, primary providers were increasingly drawn from the ranks of older siblings, grandparents (or even great-grandparents)[6] and professional workers.

The achievement of SOAR often seems to require both the provision of supplementary context and also explicitness in ruling out unwanted context.

As stated above, your own stream of consciousness is the immediate context for a pattern you send. The ongoing stream of consciousness attributed to your receiver provides the context in which the patterns you send will become enmeshed. Either you or your partner may need to learn more about the other's context—maybe even to the extent of learning her idiosyncratic language.[7]

Third, treating possible motives of the sender as part of the context can aid in achieving SOAR. For example, Lieberson (1992) observed that many current controversies associated with "the debate" (e.g., "attacks on positivism" and "undue emphasis on the deductive process") "are essentially conflicts between interest groups, each pushing to advance its own distinctive concerns and seeking symbolic recognition" (p. 2). More generally, political agendas may underlie the use of the word "science," because of the status and legitimacy this term conveys.

Organization scientists, thanks largely to prompting from those on the subjective side of "the debate," seem to be increasingly concerned with providing adequate context. Current interest in thick description (Ryle 1949, Geertz 1973), as exemplified in ethnography and phenomenology, provides support for this point. Similarly, advocacy of narrative styles (e.g., Van Maanen 1982, Calás and Smircich 1988) that provide more layers of detail than traditional methods like questionnaires, has increased. The greater use of semiotics also enhances sensitivity to context by discovering ". . . the conventions, the codes, which make meaning possible" (Calás and Smircich 1988, p. 204) and by revealing the mutual determination of meanings and structures (see Barley 1986, 1990).

Deriving New Patterns

It sometimes appears that existing patterns need to be revised or replaced before SOAR can be achieved. In this section, we describe two steps in deriving new patterns: intimacy with the topic and switching lenses or turning the kaleidoscope.

Intimacy With the Topic. Deep immersion in a substantive problem is generally assumed to contribute to good research. (See Campbell, Daft and Hulin's 1982 discussion of "research milestones" in I/O psychology.) This immersion can include familiarity with patterns advanced by others (e.g., "in the literature") as well as those gained from personal experience. Too often, in our view, students of organizations underemphasize the latter.

Switching Lenses or Turning the Kaleidoscope. Kuhn (1970) invoked the lens metaphor to illustrate how scientists, guided by different paradigms (larger patterns or contexts, in our terms), see quite different patterns in the same subject matter. While the realist position associated with the lens metaphor may be valid, the agnostic position suggests the value of adding another metaphor—that of the kaleidoscope.[8] Just as the image of switching lenses can represent the changing of patterns in the *realist* schema, the image of turning a kaleidoscope can represent the changing of patterns in the *subjectivist* schema, since the patterns of a kaleidoscope may be internally generated with minimal dependence on information from outside. Turning a kaleidoscope can: (1) dislodge old patterns, (2) generate new patterns and (3) foster awareness that numerous configurations are possible.

A scientific breakthrough may occur when someone, usually after thorough acquaintance with specific subject matter, looks through a new lens or turns the kaleidoscope and happens upon an especially meaningful or useful pattern. (The new pattern may spark a scientific revolution in the sense of Kuhn, or a very subtle, barely noticeable shift in an old pattern.)

Much has been written about generating new patterns. Weick (1979), for example, pointed out the value of speculation in generating ideas. Campbell, Daft and Hulin (1982) summarized numerous ways to promote divergent thinking (e.g., synectics, systematic restructuring). They also stressed the contribution of interdisciplinary contact to the development of new frameworks. McGrath, Martin and Kulka (1982) pointed to the value of an "ecumenical attitude" that would induce organizational scientists to learn about (though not necessarily employ) one another's methods. Linguistic analysis, exemplified by deconstruction, is another way of turning the kaleidoscope. According to Martin (1990), deconstruction ". . . focuses on suppressed conflicts and multiple interpretations of a text in order to undermine all claims to objective 'truth'." Whatever their source, new patterns often can facilitate SOAR where it was previously difficult to achieve.

Beyond Language

So far, we have focused on verbal conversation through written and oral media. SOAR also may be approached through other forms of expression such as film, photographs, flow charts, and music. The use of film by social scientists often has been limited by a realist position which views the filmmaker as simply receiving, recording, and arranging pictures of the "real world." Worth (1981) demonstrated the value of another perspective. Believing that the patterns communicated by the camera are a function of the consciousness of the photographer, Worth encouraged members of the Navaho tribe to express their own meanings in their own films. According to Worth, if *we* make films of Navahos, the films will inevitably be about *us*. For us to learn most effectively about their patterns, *Navahos* need to make the movie. Meyer (1990, p. 3) discussed ways that nonverbal data (e.g., pictures, diagrams, flow charts and computer-generated graphics) add to the patterns researchers see, because ". . . informants often possess more copious and meaningful information than they can communicate verbally."

REFLECTIONS

Several reflections seem appropriate at this point. The first two look backwards; the others contemplate the road ahead.

Looking back, we see that our recommendations, based on an agnostic framework, appear to intersect with those of people from widely-varying philosophical positions. Some of our ideas fit with the feminist deconstructionist work of Calás and Smircich (1990) and Martin (1990) and also with the writings of Hulin and Campbell, whom we view as more objectivist (see Campbell, Daft and Hulin 1982). All emphasize the importance of context and of moving outside the existing literature to look through a new lens and/or turn the kaleidoscope.

Also, we realize that our perspective does not preclude discussing what some call "accumulation of knowledge." In our terms, what you take to be "accumulated knowledge" is a pattern of consciousness that encompasses what you perceive others have passed on to you. Like other patterns, it is dynamic. It emerges through the formation, transformation, acceptance, rejection and forgetting of many constituent patterns. These patterns are judged by reviewers, teachers, consultants and other "gate keepers" according to the degree that, despite perceived flaws, the patterns are or are not worth sharing with others. Frequently in this process, the patterns are reformulated.

Looking forward, we would like to use the framework offered here to discuss some vital issues regarding the development, selection and retention of patterns in organization science. For one thing, we want to explore the utility of cooperative conversation for the field as a whole. We also want to consider some major substantive issues often associated with "the debate" (e.g., the effects of socialization and ideological hegemony upon patterns of consciousness) outside the context of that debate.

Finally, we desire conversation about criteria for choosing which patterns of consciousness to entertain, explore, discuss and act upon. There are many possible criteria: "truth" in the traditional sense of "correspondence with reality"; non-traditional views of "truth" (e.g., Rorty 1989); Habermas' (1971) "interests"; advancement of personal goals (e.g., less depression, better health, and meaning in life [Seligman 1991]); and spiritual or aesthetic values. Descriptive, comparative and normative treatments of these and other criteria are needed. We suggest SOAR as a crossroads at which people of different orientations can meet to discuss such topics.

NOTES

1. John Jermier (personal communication 1992) has pointed out that perhaps solipsism and ontological agnosticism are not taken seriously, because their proponents *act as if* an external world exists, for example, by staying out of the path of speeding locomotives. If people are reasoning this way, however, their rejection is misguided, because they do not take into account the experiences of many that dream pain can be as noxious as waking pain and that motivation to avoid dream consequences can be as intense as that to avoid waking consequences. In a nightmare of being advanced upon by a speeding locomotive, a person will typically strive to avoid being hit.

2. According to Dennett's (1991, p. 111) multiple drafts model of consciousness, "all varieties of perception—indeed, all varieties of thought or mental activity—are accomplished in the brain by parallel, multitrack processes of interpretation and elaboration of sensory inputs." Our use of "stream of consciousness" simply refers to conscious experience and does not imply that only one track is operational at a time.

3. We wish to thank Linda Smircich for calling our attention to the overlap between our approach and reader-response criticism. A major distinction is that, unlike many reader-response critics, we never consider the text itself, only patterns of the text in reader consciousness or in writer consciousness.

4. Leading scholars have pointed to similar problems with other fundamental concepts. Miner (1975) expressed concern about the word "leadership" and Kimberly (1976) about organization "size." Child (1973) observed, "The present use of the organization structure is . . . probably too gross and indiscriminate" (p. 185). McGrath (1984) demonstrated the problems of defining a group in a way which differentiates members from non members unambiguously.

5. The *Diagnostic and Statistical Manual of the American Psychiatric Association III* (1987, p. 351) defines "Narcissistic Personality Disorder" as:

> a pervasive pattern of grandiosity (in fantasy or behavior), lack of empathy and hypersensitivity to the evaluation of others, beginning in early adulthood and present in a variety of contexts, as indicated by at least *five* of the following [nine characteristics] . . .

Since there are 126 ways to combine five out of nine items, it is difficult to identify one specific pattern, as Wink's (1991) "Two Faces of Narcissism" illustrates.

6. Personal communication, Hilda C. Rosselli 1990.

7. Perhaps it would be useful to think about empathic or active sending as well as active listening (see Rogers 1961). For both sending and receiving, success may require a long sequence of trials and errors.

8. Others have also suggested using the kaleidoscope metaphor to guide inquiry. The first person we know of to do so was Tuchman (1962). Her use of this metaphor differs from ours in that she appears to view history as made up of "little bits" that get rearranged. A more recent use of the kaleidoscope metaphor can be found in Salipante and Bouwen (1991), who suggested it can serve as a tool for helping people understand conflict.

REFERENCES

American Psychiatric Association (1987), *Diagnostic and Statistical Manual of Mental Disorders* (3rd ed.), Washington, D.C.: American Psychiatric Association.

Astley, W. G. (1985), "Administrative Science as Socially Constructed Reality," *Administrative Science Quarterly,* 30, 497-513.

———— and R. F. Zammuto (1992), "Organization Science, Managers, and Language Games," *Organization Science,* 3, 443-460.

Barley, S. R. (1986), "Technology as an Occasion for Structuring: Observations on CT Scanners and the Social Order of Radiology Departments," *Administrative Science Quarterly,* 31, 78-108.

———— (1990), "Images of Imaging," *Organization Science,* 1, 220-247.

Bibby, C. (Ed.) (1967), *The Essence of T. N. Huxley: Selections from His Writings,* New York: St. Martin's Press.

Bourgeois, V. W. and C. C. Pinder (1983), "Contrasting Philosophical Perspectives in Administrative Science," *Administrative Science Quarterly,* 28, 608-613.

Brief, A. P. and W. R. Nord (1990), *The Meanings of Occupational Work,* Lexington, MA: Lexington Books.

Burrell, G. and G. Morgan (1979), *Sociological Problems and Organizational Analysis,* London: Heinemann Educational Books.

Calás, M. B. and L. Smircich (1988), "Reading Leadership as a Form of Cultural Analysis," in J. G. Hunt, B. R. Baliga, H. P. Dachler, and C. A. Schriesheim (Eds.), *Emerging Leadership Vistas,* Lexington, MA: Lexington.

———— and ———— (1990), "Thrusting Toward More of the Same with the Porter-McKibbin Report," *The Academy of Management Review,* 15, 698-705.

Campbell, J. P. (1986), "Labs, Fields, and Straw Issues," in E. A. Locke (Ed.), *Generalizing from Laboratory to Field Settings,* Lexington, MA: Lexington Books.

———— and R. D. Pritchard (1976), "Motivation Theory in Industrial and Organizational Psychology," in M. D. Dunnette (Ed.), *Handbook of Industrial and Organizational Psychology,* Chicago: Rand McNally.

————, J. P., R. L. Daft, and C. L. Hulin (1982), *What to Study. Generating and Developing Research Questions,* Beverly Hills: Sage Publications.

Child, J. (1973), "Predicting and Understanding Organization Structure," *Administrative Science Quarterly,* 18, 168-185.

Chuang Tzu (1968), *The Complete Works of Chuang Tzu,* Burton Watson (Trans.), New York: Columbia University Press.

Daft, R. L. and J. C. Wiginton (1979), "Language and Organization," *Academy of Management Review,* 4, 179-191.

Dennett, D. C. (1991), *Consciousness Explained,* Boston: Little, Brown and Company.

Donaldson, L. (1985), *In Defence of Organization Theory: A Reply to the Critics,* Cambridge: Cambridge University Press.

———— (1992), "The Weick Stuff: Managing Beyond Games," *Organization Science,* 3, 461-466.

Freud, S. (1957), "Repression," in *The Complete Works of Sigmund Freud,* Strachey and Freund (Trans.), 14, London: Hogarth.

Geertz, C. (1973), *The Interpretation of Cultures,* New York: Basic Books.

Gioia, D. A. and E. Pitre (1990), "Multiparadigm Perspectives on Theory Building," *The Academy of Management Review,* 15, 584-602.

Habermas, Jurgen (1971), *Knowledge and Human Interests,* Jeremy J. Shapiro (Trans.), Boston: Beacon Press.

Hoffman, L. W. (1986), "Work, Family, and the Child," in M. S. Pallak and R. O. Perloff (Eds.), *Psychology and Work: Productivity, Change, and Employment,* Washington, D.C.: American Psychological Association.

Jastrow, R. (1977), *Until the Sun Dies,* New York: Warner Books.

Kimberly, J. R. (1976), "Organizational Size and the Structuralist Perspective: A Review, Critique, and Proposal," *Administrative Science Quarterly,* 21, 571-597.

Kuhn, T. S. (1970), *The Structure of Scientific Revolutions* (2nd ed.), Chicago: University of Chicago Press.

Lee, A. S. (1991), "Integrating Positivist and Interpretive Approaches to Organizational Research," *Organization Science,* 4, 342-365.

Levine, D. N. (1985), *The Flight from Ambiguity: Essays in Social and Cultural Theory,* Chicago: The University of Chicago Press.

Lieberson, S. (1992), "Einstein, Renoir, and Greeley: Evidence in Sociology," *American Sociological Review,* 57, 1-15.

Martin, J. (1990), "Deconstructing Organizational Taboos: The Suppression of Gender Conflict in Organizations," *Organization Science,* 1, 339-359.

McGrath, J. E. (1984), *Groups: Interaction and Performance,* Englewood Cliffs, NJ: Prentice Hall.

———, J. Martin, and R. A. Kulka (1982), *Judgment Calls in Research,* Beverly Hills: Sage Publications.

Meyer, A. (1990), "Visual Data in Organizational Research," *Organization Science,* 2, 218-236.

Miner, J. B. (1975), "The Uncertain Future of the Leadership Concept: An Overview," in J. G. Hunt and L. L. Larson, (Eds.), *Leadership Frontiers,* Kent, OH: Kent State University.

Morgan, G. and L. Smircich (1980), "The Case for Qualitative Research," *Academy of Management Review,* 5, 491-500.

Nord, W. R. and S. Tucker (1987), *Implementing Routine and Radical Innovations,* Massachusetts: D. C. Heath and Co.

Pinder, C. C. and V. W. Bourgeois (1982), "Controlling Tropes in Administrative Science," *Administrative Science Quarterly,* 27, 641-652.

Popper, K. (1956), *Realism and the Aim of Science,* Totowa, NJ: Rowman and Littlefield.

Rogers, C. R. (1961), *On Becoming a Person,* Boston: Houghton Mifflin.

Rorty, Richard (1980), *Philosophy and the Mirror of Nature,* Oxford: Basil Blackwell Ltd.

——— (1989), *Contingency, Irony and Solidarity,* New York: Cambridge University Press.

Ryle, G. (1949), *The Concept of Mind,* New York: Barnes & Noble.

Salipante, P. and R. Bouwen (in press), "The Social Construction of Grievances: Organizational Conflict as Multiple Perspectives," in K. Gergen and P. Dachler (Eds.), *Towards a Relational Theory of Organizations,* Beverly Hill, CA: Sage Publications.

Seligman, Martin (1991), *Learned Optimism,* New York: Knopf.

Sjoberg, G. and L. R. Cain (1971), "Negative Values, Countersystem Models, and the Analysis of Social Systems," in H. Turk and R. L. Simpson (Eds.), *Institutions and Social Change: The Sociologies of Talcott Parsons and George C. Homans,* New York: The Bobbs-Merrill Co., Inc.

Skinner, B. F. (1953), *Science and Human Behavior,* New York: Macmillan.

Spedding, J., R. L. Ellis, D. D. Heath (Eds.), (1860/1962). *The Works of Francis Bacon,* London: Longman and Co.

Stough, C. (1969), *Greek Skepticism: A Study in Epistemology,* Berkeley: University of California Press.

Tsoukas, H. (1991), The Missing Link: A Transformational View of Metaphors in Organizational Science, *Academy of Management Review,* 16, 566-585.

Tuchman, B. W. (1962), *The Guns of August,* New York: Macmillan.

van Maanen, J. (1982), "Field Work on the Beat," in J. van Maanen, J. M. Dabbs Jr., and R. R. Faulkner, *Varieties of Qualitative Research,* Beverly Hills, CA: Sage Publications.

Weick, K. E. (1979), *The Social Psychology of Organizing* (2nd ed.), Reading, MA: Addison-Wesley.

Wink, P. (1991), "Two Faces of Narcissism," *Journal of Personality and Social Psychology,* 61, 590-597.

Worth, S. (1981), *Studying Visual Communication,* Philadelphia: University of Pennsylvania Press.

Yulevich, L. and S. Axelrod (1983), "Punishment: A Concept That Is No Longer Necessary," in M. Hersen, R. M. Eisler, and P. M. Miller (Eds.), *Progress in Behavior Modification,* 14, New York: Academic Press, 355-382.

10

Organizational Performance as a Dependent Variable

JAMES G. MARCH
*Scandinavian Consortium for Organizational Research,
Stanford University*

ROBERT I. SUTTON
Haas School of Business, University of California

PROBLEMS IN STUDIES OF PERFORMANCE

In studies of organizations, performance sometimes appears as an independent variable, but it is more likely to appear on the left-hand side of the equation as a dependent variable.[2] This emphasis is most explicit in the field of organizational strategy, which is often defined as having organizational performance as its primary focus, but the idea that performance is to be predicted, understood, and shaped is commonplace throughout the field. Such a posture is also embraced as a code of proper behavior. The second sentence in the Academy of Management Code of Ethical Conduct is: "Our professional goals are to enhance the learning of students, colleagues, and others and to improve the effectiveness of organizations through our teaching, research, and practice of management" (Academy of Management 1995, p. 573).

Efforts to fulfill the implicit promise of the code, the hopes of managers, the logic of performance improvement, and the ambitions of students of organizational adaptation encounter a fundamental complication, however: identifying the true causal structure of organizational performance phenomena on

From "Organizational Performance as a Dependent Variable," by James G. March and Robert I. Sutton, 1997, *Organization Science, 8,* pp. 698-705. Copyright © 1997, The Institute of Management Sciences. Adapted with permission.

the basis of the incomplete information generated by historical experience is problematic. Students of organizational performance rarely exercise experimental control over predictor variables. They rely instead on analyses of observations made of naturally occurring events. As a result, they confront problems of finding adequate archival data and of soliciting and interpreting the accounts of informants. These records of naturally occurring histories of organizational performance are notoriously difficult to interpret. Any observation-based organizational history is rife with resolute ambiguities that can frustrate the efforts of statistical and interpretive imagination to identify causal links among historical events.

THE EMPEROR'S CLOTHES

Most studies of organizational performance are incapable of identifying the true causal relations among performance variables and other variables correlated with them through the data and methods they normally use. Although there are studies that mitigate these shortcomings, the emperor of organizational performance studies is for the most part rather naked. New enthusiasms succeed old ones, but the process often appears to be less one of gradual accumulation of knowledge than of intellectual drift stimulated by competition for scholarly reputation.

The questionable status of studies in which organizational performance appears as a causally dependent variable is not a secret. The difficulties in identifying causes of performance differences are common knowledge, part of the most basic training in the field (Staw 1975, Lenz 1981). As a result, the more intriguing part of this history is not the fact that the performance emperor has no clothes, for that is hardly "news." Rather it is the impressive persistence in making inferences about organizational performance histories that are so conspicuously and so generally known to be suspect.

A standard response to these persistencies has been to assume a failure of intelligence, standards, or training. Remedies of better research recruitment and training, better reviewing of journals, better consciousness of the problems have been pursued. These efforts have had very little impact. A steady flow of studies making questionable interpretations of performance evidence continues. Even though almost everyone knows that the emperor has no clothes, few people talk about that fact, and many of the same people who note the emperor's nakedness nevertheless discuss the tailoring of his suits. Since the journals involved are serious, peer-reviewed journals and the researchers are serious, well-trained researchers, the pattern reflects the field and cannot be attributed exclusively to particularistic inadequacies of specific journals or individuals.

This suggests that properties of the research context, rather than individual ignorance or journal incompetence, may be primary contributors to this curiosity. For example, the research context, particularly in the United States, provides numerous barriers to the kind of richly detailed, multiple-site, long historical studies using in-depth scholarly analyses and complex models that might yield data more appropriate to the task. Such studies are inconsistent in important ways with short-term research funding practices, rules for reputation accumulation among researchers, and the normal expectations of professional journals and publishers. The kind of persistence, attention to complexity, and delayed gratification required for a thoroughly informed and theoretically sophisticated study of the historical development of an organization has to be seen as an unusual achievement (Padgett and Ansell 1993).

Such contextual restrictions on the kind of research that is likely may provide partial explanations for the failure to improve organizational scholarship in directions that are well-known to be needed. Those elements of context do not, however, explain the gap between accepted standards of inference and assertions about causes of variations in performance. To understand the latter inconsistency it is necessary to examine some features of the organizational and social context of organizations research.

Many organizational researchers, and particularly those prone to making assessments of the factors affecting performance, are employed by professional schools. Aspiring managers, engineers, and other professionals who attend these schools presume that they are being groomed to create conditions for organizations, and people and groups within them, to perform better than others and better than in the past. Researchers secure compensation and attention as consultants to organizations, as lecturers to organizational audiences, or as authors of books providing suggestions for improving organizational performance. These occasions and constituencies provide funding and legitimacy to organizational researchers. They encourage researchers to create and espouse speculations about predicting and controlling performance outcomes. And their enthusiasm for speculation about performance differences seems largely unaffected by a long history involving the continuous overturning of old enthusiasms with new ones. In such a climate, it is not overly surprising that organizational researchers become courtiers of a naked emperor.

At the same time, many organizational researchers are linked to academic institutions and professions, systems that are less immediately concerned with improving performance and more concerned with attention to standards of research and inference that mark research institutions of distinction. They produce and review papers for professional journals, talk to colleagues in the language of inferential method, and serve as judges of the adequacy of research. These occasions and constituencies also provide funding and legitimacy to organizational researchers, but their expectations are different. They encourage researchers to question simple causal stories of performance and retrospective accounts of history. Academic researchers become not only the courtiers of a naked emperor but also keepers of a sacred faith in the methods of scholarship, systematic inference, and defensible interpretations of history.

In the tradition of such dilemmas, conflicts between these two perspectives are often "solved" by separating the two contexts. In academic institutions, one can find a culture of advice givers who tell stories about the things that affect organizational performance to people involved in trying to produce improved performance. These advice givers are ordinarily quite disconnected from serious research on organizations and quite unconcerned about research standards, as are their patrons. One can also find a culture of research workers who tell stories to each other about why one cannot make inferences about causality from correlational and retrospective studies. These research workers are ordinarily quite disconnected from the immediate problems of management and quite unconcerned about organizational performance improvement, as are their patrons. In most American universities, the two cultures are protected from each other by the semi-permeable barrier that divides professional schools from schools of arts and sciences. The buffer allows the two cultures to avoid confronting the implications of their incompatibility.

In and around professional schools, however, and particularly in the United States, this simple separation is made more difficult. The soldiers of organizational performance and the priests of research purity often occupy not only the same halls but also the same bodies. These students of organizations inhabit both cultures and cannot easily achieve the delicate pleasures of consistency that are granted to their more fortunate colleagues who reside exclusively in a world of performance concerns or exclusively in the core realms of academe. The two-culture solution is supplemented by a more localized two-sidedness in which individuals and individual institutions announce that it is not possible to make valid inferences, yet simultaneously proclaim them; or adopt the paraphernalia of scholarship without much attention to their assumptions. In a schizophrenic tour de force, the demands of the roles of consultant and teacher are disassociated from the demands of the role of researcher.

WHAT'S A SCHOLAR TO DO?

It is easy to bemoan a state of affairs in which students of organizations are driven both to proclaim scholarly standards of inferential discourse and to collaborate in subverting them in practice. The result is, in many ways, unfortunate from the point of view of scholarly traditions. It certainly calls for renewed efforts to change the context of scholarship to make it either less demanding of performance implications or more consistent with scholarly research on performance. Journals can do a better job of enforcing standards; senior scholars can do a better job of escaping the short-run research horizons learned in the course of securing tenure; funding agencies can provide more sustained support for long historical studies.

Such a call to virtue is doubtless salutary, but it ignores the extent to which there is deep social truth in simultaneously identifying factors affecting organizational performance and admitting that the identification is quite probably false. It is a cliché of speculative discourse that ideas are not to be judged solely by their empirical truth as assessed by scholarly precepts. The classical admonition to embrace beauty and justice, as well as truth, has led to a long tradition of struggle among aspirations for scholarly truth, intellectual elegance and ethical or ideological propriety. The struggle is captured poignantly in contemporary efforts to write about things such as human motivations and social power, where claims of veracity are juxtaposed with claims of human traditions and the demands of ideological correctness.

Since the earliest days of scholarship, the role of the scholar as researcher has been to pursue a vision of reality as lying outside social beliefs about that reality. The role of the scholar as part of the social establishment has been to support a social system that allows scholarship to flourish. The role of the scholar as educator has been to transform social beliefs about reality, encouraging beliefs that conform more to the understandings of scholars. The dilemma of scholarship is twofold. First, it involves finding a route between a course that is precipitous in destroying vital elements of community built on social myths and intuitive knowledge and a course that is precipitous in corrupting the integrity of scholarship. Second, it involves finding a conception of knowledge that does not discourage its pursuit, that holds out the possibility of augmenting knowledge through systematic scholarship in the face of a long history of scholarly recantations and a chronic vulnerability to nihilism.

The dilemma leads naturally to a course of collective and individual hypocrisy. Organizational researchers have often observed that organizations do not reliably connect their "talk" and their "action" (Edelman 1964, Weick 1979, Brunsson 1989). It should not be surprising that a similar pattern is found among organized research workers. Nor should the pattern be routinely condemned. When we observe that an organization justifies a decision with information that has been gathered after the decision was made, we sometimes note that the information is probably more connected to the task of confirming important social norms than to the task of making a particular decision (Feldman and March 1984). Similarly, in the present case, the tradition of honoring normatively-approved principles of scholarly inference while violating them is a way of sustaining important values. At the least, it is probably more sensible than changing the principles to match the practices, which may be the primary behavioral alternative for achieving consistency.

The simultaneous embrace of the possibility of knowledge and the difficulty of achieving it can be a form of wisdom that sustains inquiry and skepticism in healthy confrontation (Meacham 1990, Sutton and Hargadon 1996). In particular, one of the complications of personal and organizational knowledge is that there are many ways of knowing, some of them individually compelling but impossible to confirm through acceptable procedures of inference from empirical observation.[3] Confronting the conflict between what is believed and what is demonstrable threatens either the belief or the standards of demonstration in a situation in which both may be worth preserving. Maintaining a formal pretense that the belief is consistent with the evidence sustains both the belief and the sanctity of scholarly standards.

Moreover, such a resolution occurs at the collective level without necessary consciousness. Principled observers who denounce the weak inferential base of studies attempting to explain variations in organizational performance and other features of ambiguous organizational histories provide inadvertent confirmation of the questionable practices. By affirming a collective commitment to high standards of scholarly interpretation, their audit legitimizes the system they expose. At the same time, those who weave a story of the organizational determinants of relative performance secure legitimacy and resources that protect their more fastidious brethren from the practical consequences of their scruples. As has been true since the beginning, the purities of the virtuous are subsidized by the accommodations of the sinful.

Whether we accept such an apologia for the emperor's tailors and the sycophants who proclaim the fineness of imperial garments depends on how we deal with the associated pathologies. The essential point is that scholarship is probably better served by maintaining a tension between saying more than we know and understanding how little we can know, rather than by a definitive resolution of the conflict; but maintaining the tension is vulnerable to the unquestioned temptations of imagining a resolution.

One danger is that the concrete rewards from pleasing the emperor may lead us to exaggerate both the advantages of seeing his clothing and the risks involved in confirming his nakedness. If reputations and institutions are to be maintained by proclaiming insights into history and the discovery of routes to sustained performance advantage, then it may become inordinately natural to characterize the niceties of inferential clarity as dispensable scholastic pretense. The tendency of many articles with a wide range of ideological, methodological, and disciplinary prejudices to subordinate issues of inference ambiguity to issues of practical recommendations and sweeping generalizations may be a symptom of that danger. A second danger is that the terrors of claiming unjustifiable knowledge will drive us from empirical discourse into the relatively safe activities of proving theorems, contemplating conundrums, and writing poetry. The tendency of many of our best minds to eschew empirical inference for the innocently elegant worlds of mathematics, formal logic, and literary theory may be a symptom of that danger.

Partial protection from the two dangers may be provided by consciousness of the ambivalences. If we remind ourselves, from time to time, that standards of inference, like standards of imperial fashion, are more temporary approximations than eternal verities, we do not demean our allegiance to them but we reduce the risk that we will overlook the occasional beauty of cloth woven from invisible threads. And if we remind ourselves, from time to time, that what we are doing is the work of sustaining a belief in the emperor's clothes as a social mythology and a confession of weakness, we do not demean that work but we reduce the risk that we will come to believe in the emperor's clothes as a literal reality.

Ultimately, however, the pain of discomfort at failing to choose between the simultaneous imperatives of speech and silence is better endured than is the denial of either. There is no neat solution, for neatness itself would be a claim that an essential dilemma has been overcome, that virtue can be discovered and proclaimed, or that the trade-offs can be calculated and accepted. Scholarly virtue is more a struggle than an achievement, and seeking knowledge about historically ambiguous phenomena such as organizational performance is more a necessary form of disciplined self-flagellation than a pursuit of happiness.

NOTES

[1. . . .]

2. Three of the more highly regarded journals involved in publishing empirical research on organizations—the *Strategic Management Journal,* the *Academy of Management Journal,* and the *Administrative Science Quarterly*—are particularly likely to focus on performance and performance as a dependent variable. For the issues published in 1993, 1994, and 1995, we counted all articles and research notes in these journals except for editorials, editors' remarks, introductions to special issues, and essays. Whether organizational performance (or effectiveness) was examined in a paper and the role it played in the author's analysis was gleaned from the abstract. If the abstract indicated that performance (or effectiveness) was considered but it was not clear whether it was portrayed as an independent variable, dependent variable, both, or in some other way (e.g., as only a control or intervening variable), we examined the text and tables to classify it. In these three years, these three journals published 439 articles and research notes. Performance appeared as a variable in 124 (28%) of the abstracts of those articles, 88 times as a dependent variable only, 15 times as an independent variable only, 13 times as both, and 8 times in some other capacity. At the other extreme, we counted only 7 (7%) of 98 articles published in *Organi-*

zation Studies in the same three-year period as having performance as a variable cited in their abstracts (five of those with performance as a dependent variable only). *Organizational Behavior and Human Decision Processes* and *Organization Science* locate themselves between the two extremes. Performance appeared as a variable in the abstracts of 57 (16%) of the 355 articles published in those journals over the same three years, 42 times as a dependent variable only, 5 times as an independent variable only, 8 times as both, and 2 times in some other capacity.

3. The idea of multiple ways of knowing goes back at least to Plato and keeps resurfacing, particularly in the hands of those who would challenge established epistemologies, thus is a useful, generic claim of exemption from recognized rules of intelligent inference. In the present case, the distinction is not between different kinds of scholarly traditions, each of which claims specialized capabilities for making knowledge assertions, but between the procedures of scholarship and the procedures of ordinary comprehension. The argument in favor of ordinary comprehension is, however, similar to the argument in favor of deviant scholarship in that it depends on the assumption that it provides variety. Since any established mode of thought tends to become less exploratory as it becomes more effective, variety is useful even though any particular idea generated from ordinary comprehension, like any particular idea generated by deviant scholarship, is likely to be inferior.

REFERENCES

Academy of Management (1995), "Academy of Management Code of Ethical Conduct," *Academy of Management Journal,* 38, 573-577.

Brunsson, N. (1989), *The Organization of Hypocrisy,* Chichester, U.K.: Wiley.

Edelman, M. (1964), *The Symbolic Uses of Politics,* Urbana, IL: University of Illinois Press.

Feldman, M. S. and J. G. March (1981), "Information in Organizations as Signal and Symbol," *Administrative Science Quarterly,* 26, 171-186.

Lenz, R. (1981), "Determinants of Organizational Performance: An Interdisciplinary Review," *Strategic Management Review,* 2, 131-154.

Meacham, J. A. (1990), "The Loss of Wisdom," in R. J. Sternberg (Ed.), *Wisdom: Its Nature, Origins, and Development,* Cambridge, U.K.: Cambridge University Press.

Padgett, J. F. and C. K. Ansell (1993). "Robust Action and the Rise of the Medici, 1400-1434," *American Journal of Sociology,* 98, 1250-1310.

Staw, B. M. (1975), "Attribution of the 'Causes' of Performance: An Alternative Interpretation of Cross-Sectional Research on Organizations," *Organizational Behavior and Human Performance,* 13, 414-432.

Sutton, R. I. and A. Hargadon (1996), "Brainstorming Groups in Context: Effectiveness in a Product Design Firm," *Administrative Science Quarterly,* 41, 685-718.

Weick, K. (1979), *The Social Psychology of Organizing,* 2nd ed., Reading, MA: Addison-Wesley.

11

Writing Organizational Tales

Four Authors and Their Stories About Culture. Introduction

DVORA YANOW
Department of Public Administration,
California State University, Hayward

The title of this collection of short essays derives from *Tales of the Field* (Van Maanen 1988). In it, John Van Maanen argues that researchers' writings are "tales"—that is, constructions—rather than objective reports or "mirrors," to use Richard Rorty's (1979) term, of the external social world. Van Maanen writes there about ethnographies, but the point holds for social scientific (and scientific) writing in general. A text—used here in the sense of "the subject matter of a discourse" (*American Heritage Dictionary* 1979, p. 1332, 5b) and not "textbook"—ethnographic or otherwise, is a means of (re)presentation.

In our words, in authored texts, we engage in what Nelson Goodman (1978) called "world-making." To quote Van Maanen: "A culture or a cultural practice is as much *created by the writing* . . . as it determines the writing itself" (p. 6, emphasis added). In other words, culture "is made visible only through its representation" (p. 3); it is "created . . . by the active construction of a text" (p. 7).

This is a point of view that is quite different from seeing books and articles as "mirrors" of reality. We use Van Maanen's title here suggestively—it serves as a jumping off point—to pose a contrast between two views of academic writing: as *science* and as *narrative*. As science, writing is seen as

179

mirror-making, as capturing and reflecting exactly what the organizational scientist (in our case) observes in looking outside herself. As narrative, writing is seen as creating and telling a tale, a story, a construction: it reflects the particular lens or theory or way of seeing that is the author's.

What this means for our subject, organizational culture, is that from the view of texts as science, the question to ask is: What *is* organizational culture? And in this view each text makes an argument, sometimes explicitly, sometimes implicitly, that it has the right answer to the question, that it has captured precisely what constitutes organizational culture, what its elements and variables are, what it can do, how it can be used.

From the view of texts as narrative, however, we must ask a very different question: What tale or story of organizational culture has the writer told or constructed? To see academic writing as authored texts shifts the focus from what is observed external to the author and reflected in her book, to the characteristics of the author's way of looking. In this view, there is and can be no single, universally applicable, "right" theory of organizational culture. There can only be knowledge filtered through the position or "situation" of the author (his family and communal background, education, training, experience, gender, race/ethnicity, religion, class: whatever has been formative in creating that person's point of view) and the situation of the organization being studied. Moreover, every "text" attempts to convince the reader of the veracity of its author's particular way of world-making; and methodological choices, such as what constitutes data and how to use the data, bolster that attempt.

This set of essays originated in a symposium at the August 1993 meeting of the Academy of Management in Atlanta (cosponsored by the Organization and Management Theory and Research Methods Divisions and the Managerial and Organizational Cognition Interest Group). It includes four authors who have actively constructed three texts—three worlds—of organizational culture. The three books reflect the diversity of contemporary organizational culture thinking. They include *The Cultures of Work Organizations,* Harrison Trice and Janice Beyer's (1993) textbook with illustrations from many organizations; *Engineering Culture: Control and Commitment in a High-Tech Corporation,* Gideon Kunda's (1992) ethnographic study of a single organization; and *Cultures in Organizations: Three Perspectives* by Joanne Martin (1992), which marries textbook elements with extended illustrations drawn from interviews in one organization.[1] The authors have been asked to address the question: What is the nature of the tale that you have told/created in your book? We use tale, story, narration, representation interchangeably in these essays, but all focus on the active role of the writer in creating the culture she/he presents to us.

This is not to say that readers do not have a role in creating meaning. Reader-response theory (see Iser 1989, for example) criticizes earlier theories that argued that the meaning of the text lay in its author's intentions or that meaning was to be found in the text alone. Instead, readers are seen to bring their own context (experience, background, and so forth) to their reading and to be, themselves, active constructors of meaning. For one view in this approach, meaning is created in the interaction among author, text, and reader, that is, in the writing *and* in the reading. We will not explore this idea here, but it underlies Linda Smircich's comments as a reader of these texts. She has been asked to give her reading of what the authors have narrated.

One final word: Space limitations do not permit a complete exposition of these books. Each is a full and unique telling of organizational culture. Each stands on its own and deserves careful reading.

NOTE

1. The decision was made to include authored books but not edited collections of multiple authored essays (e.g., recently published books by Gagliardi 1990 or Turner 1989). The selection was intended to suggest the variety of the kinds of tales that authors write, rather than to single out any of the books (or any of those not included) for criticism or praise. Other books could well have been chosen (e.g., Ingersoll and Adams [1992] as an example of what Linda Smircich calls a cultural analysis of organizational life).

That proved, unfortunately, not to be the final word. I and many others were greatly saddened to learn of Harry Trice's death—he was hit by a car—on December 5, 1994. He had a long and productive career, moving recently into an active post-retirement phase. Indeed, the book discussed here is one of two published after he retired from the New York State School of Industrial and Labor Relations at Cornell. It was a pleasure for me to work with him on several occasions, including this symposium. We shall miss the wisdom that he brought to our field from a lifetime engaging cultural and anthropological matters.

Writing Organizational Tales:
The Cultures of Work Organizations

HARRISON M. TRICE
JANICE M. BEYER

Department of Management, College of Business Administration,
The University of Texas at Austin

The meta-theme of this book is integration of diverse perspectives on culture and on organizations. In this book, we bring together various cultural perspectives, main-stream theories of organizations, and empirical work from various social science disciplines on cultural phenomena in organizations. The inclusiveness of our approach allows us to tell many stories about organizational cultures.

We built our stories about workplace cultures around two prominent, largely anthropological themes about the nature of culture. Both themes carry important messages about what cultures are *not* as well as what they are. The first of these themes, as formulated by Max Weber and refined by Clifford Geertz, says that culture is *not* a phenomenon locked up in people's heads, but rather embodied in a collection of observable, public symbols. In this theme, symbol is a generic term for a variety of cultural forms through which emotionally-charged belief systems or ideologies are expressed and enacted. Both ideologies and cultural forms develop as people struggle with the uncertainties of their existence. Human beings lack the genetic programming that helps most other animals to behave in predictable ways that promote collective survival. Instead, humans have a relatively open nervous system that permits individuals to behave in many different ways. Through ideologies and cultural forms, cultures provide much of the additional guidance human beings need to collectively survive, adapt, and adjust to life's inevitable uncertainties.

The second theme comes from the stream of thought and work of anthropologists such as Max Gluckman, Roger Keesing, Sally Moore, Barbara Myerhoff, and Victor Turner. The story they tell is *not* one of cultural integration, solidarity, harmony, and sharedness, but rather one of paradoxes, conflicts, ambiguities, and dysfunctions intermingled with a measure of order and integration. They portray cultures as emerging to hold ever-present chaos at bay. Kenneth Burke poetically stated the essence of this theme: "Humans build their cultures, nervously loquacious, on the edge of an abyss." Since cultural ideologies and forms are inherently fuzzy, consistency, consensus, and harmony can develop in the midst of inconsistencies, ambiguities, conflicts, disruptions, double binds, and multiple meanings. Only a minimal degree of consensus and clarity about some issues is needed for collective actions to go forward. To us, these two story themes are complementary; each is incomplete without the other, but used together they help us to understand and explain complex and relatively subtle stories about life in work organizations.

Our first major story is about the multiple sets of ideologies that make up the substance of a culture and how these get expressed through workplace myths, stories, jargon, songs, metaphors, uniforms, settings, performers, humor, rituals, taboos, and rites: the cultural forms that communicate, affirm, and reinforce belief systems. We talk about how fuzzy both of these elements of culture are; sets of meanings often clash, paradoxical ones exist side-by-side. We also talk about the multivocal nature of symbols; how they can function to deliver either ideologies supporting the status quo or culture change. At the same time we include in this story descriptions of how cores of consensus seem to inevitably emerge. We explore the classical explanations of ideologies, their dysfunctions as well as functions, and their extraorganizational sources, ranging from transnational social movements to specific industries. We then tell the story of distinctive American ideologies and provide empirical examples about how they influence specific work organizations.

Our next story tells how both organizations and occupations go about socializing their members so as to achieve some measure of cultural continuity. Using rites of passage as a starting point, we trace many variations and types of socialization. In the process, we devote considerable attention to socializing agents, mid-career and late-career passages, and the likely dysfunctions of socialization efforts.

Our third story is about how subcultures inevitably emerge from sets of multiple, often conflicting, meanings that develop over time within a culture. We use occupational cultures within organizations, including managerial cultures, as a prominent instance of organizational subcultures. We focus upon occupational subcultures for three reasons: (1) because they are a prominent part of work life, but have been left out of most cultural analyses of work organizations; (2) to underscore a shift in cultural analysis from focusing on overall organizational cultures to focusing on differences that give rise to a multitude of subcultures; and (3) to set the stage for a cultural analysis of how subcultures interrelate and adapt to one another.

The cultural side of leadership is the subject of our fourth story. In it, we further develop and extend our ideas about four types of cultural leadership: that which creates, embodies, integrates, or changes cultures. We flesh out these types with extensive examples from scholarly reports and explain how various types of leadership already identified in the literature—including charismatic, transformational, institutional, consensus, and transactional leadership—fit within these types. We also point out that leadership operates both at-a-distance and face-to-face and that organizations can simultaneously have multiple cultural leaders of different types. We end this story by emphasizing the need for more attention to leadership that maintains cultures through embodiment or integration.

Our fifth story focuses on the cultural interchange between organizations and their environments. Building on institutional and resource dependence theory, we describe and illustrate the many ways that organizations import cultural elements from their environments. We then suggest that organizations also export elements of their culture in various ways, including hostile takeovers, friendly mergers, and other strategies they employ to influence their environments. The final strand of this story on the important influence that national cultures have on organizations is illustrated by looking at differences between Japanese and U.S. organizations.

Finally, after much debate and hesitation, we decided it might be useful to explore the implication of our various stories by combining them in a final story about managing cultures. This last story was necessarily complicated because we felt there were three somewhat different themes to follow: about creating, maintaining, and changing organizational cultures. Although managing culture change had previously received the most attention, most organizations are *not* engaged in drastic culture change all the time. Rather, organizations tend to alternate between periods of pronounced change and periods of relative stability. So we devoted one chapter to the relatively neglected topic of managing and maintaining cultures, and another to the more familiar topics of changing and creating cultures. We began our overall story with general considerations to be taken into account in both maintaining and changing cultures: understanding what culture is and is not, mechanisms for trying to read a specific organization's culture, and an examination of the ethical issues involved. Acting on any of the stories about an organization's culture requires an examination of the question: Are such actions ethical? We conclude that ethical issues are indeed involved, and can best be faced and answered by assessing the full range of consequences involved. Another general consideration was choosing between cultural maintenance and culture innovation.

We distilled from the relevant literature specific aphorisms about maintaining, changing, and creating cultures. These pulled together relevant data into a summary form that we hoped would convey the essence of complex sets of ideas. Different parts of these themes touch upon, for example, selecting, modifying and creating cultural forms consistent with the discovery and articulation of distinctive, new ideologies; recruiting like-minded people; capitalizing on propitious moments for change; and the cultivation of cultural leadership.

We found weaving together the diverse ideas in the cultural literature into these stories a stimulating and exciting endeavor. We hope our excitement about them is shared by our readers.

Engineering Culture:
Control and Commitment in a High-Tech Corporation

GIDEON KUNDA

Departments of Sociology and Labor Studies,
Tel Aviv University

Engineering Culture grew out of an attempt to take seriously the conceptual and methodological requirements of a cultural perspective on organizations. Briefly, the book is a critical ethnography of a large and successful high-tech corporation lauded in the popular managerial literature for its innovative post-bureaucratic "corporate culture." The corporate culture, the official story went, drove the company's employees to peaks of corporate performance and personal self-actualization. Academic views of these managerial claims fell, unsurprisingly, into two distinct camps. On the one hand (the upper one, of course) were those who participated in the construction of this grand utopian narrative: numerous texts reinforced, jargonized, and legitimated managerial claims and fed them back to ever-hungry corporate consumers of good words. On the other hand, less popular but no less persistent and no less grand, was a continuing stream of criticism of the corporation. In this view, utopian managerial claims were—as ever—no more than a disguise for malevolent managerial intentions, now in the form of tyrannical attempts to penetrate and shape employees' minds and hearts.

Despite my a priori sympathies for the latter view, no matter how platitudinous, it was on the tricky ground between these two grand narratives that I sought to position the book. To this end I asked, in the manner of the skeptical, naturalistically inclined observer, what, if any, realities lurked behind and between managerial efforts to shape culture, and how they are to be evaluated. To answer this question, the materials are presented in the traditional style of ethnographic realism. Three sections comprise the logic of investigation. First, the book documents, analyzes and attempts to organize the managerial conceptualization of the company's corporate culture (including its academic roots.) Out of the abundant managerially mandated texts which permeate the company's everyday life and make up a neverending interpretive backdrop to practical activity—tapes, slogans, speeches, newsletters, videos, fliers, manuals— the book identifies the authors and unpacks their meanings. Underlying all the verbiage, I claim, is an elaborate and highly articulated managerial ideology that presents the company as a nonhierarchic, humanistically inclined, moral collective. More crucially, the ideology constructs a distinct view of employees—I call it a member role—that prescribes not only their behavior but runs much deeper, offering elaborate scripts for their cognitive and emotional life.

The second section moves from the managerially defined textual backdrop to everyday life to the drama that unfolds before, or through it. It describes in detail the everyday interactions through which the ideology, and the member role it prescribes, is brought to life. Once again in the method of realism, a barely visible yet all-seeing ethnographic eye reports play-by-play action from boardrooms and bar rooms, labs and offices, locations where the various actors take active and passive positions vis ... vis the ideology and its requirements of them. The central theme of these rituals performances, the somewhat cynical authorial voice claims, is an unstable balance between Goffmanian role embracement and role distancing which, nevertheless, seems to trap all members in performances in which intimate layers of their selves are publicly enacted and collectively observed.

Finally, in a section which exposes the limits and limitations of realism, the book seeks to capture the experience of that elusive subject, the self. What kinds of selves, it asks, emerge in the glare of the cultural spotlight and in the shadow of its darker side? What forms of experience are constructed when experience itself becomes the target for corporate control? In this chapter answers are sought in the various organizational arenas where the self, however fleetingly, makes itself known: interviews, informal chit chat, chance encounters, office decorations, e-mail exchanges. From this somewhat impressionistic collage of materials an image of a theatrical, ironic and rather unstable organizational self emerges, a self immersed in a paradoxical world in which authenticity is at once prescribed and suspect, in which the theatrical mechanisms under-girding the construction of the self and its reality are in full view, and in which, ironically, the very genre of the text is directly challenged by its own findings.

The book does not seek to resolve this paradoxical culmination of the ethnographic logic. Rather, the text moves in two different directions. First, in the traditional manner, to conclusions, abstractions, and generalizations. The ethnographic materials are used to ask if, how, and to what end cultural engineering accomplishes normative control, and how it is to be evaluated from a moral standpoint. Thus the conclusion brings the text back into the fold, positioning it as an ethnography in the classical style: substantively, it brings an interpretive perspective to bear on some of the central theoretical concerns of students of organizations; and stylistically it is unabashedly realistic, relying on the assumed authority of the detached observer.

The conclusion is followed by a counterpunctual confessional tale designed to destabilize somewhat the comforts of realism, to preempt the expected critics of the genre (many of whom, not granting readers even the most minimal degree of sophistication, insist on belaboring the shortcomings and obvious limitations of realism over and over again), and to have some writing fun. This tale builds on the hints of impressionism already embedded in the text in order to acknowledge and explore the epistemological, practical and personal limitations of realism. I describe contextual aspects of the study with particular attention to my life circumstances at the time and the events which seemed to me to account for the shape the text assumed. These include the academic context which enabled, defined, interfered with and shaped the fieldwork; the vagaries, pains and tribulations of fieldwork in an elitist hierarchic setting whose agents viewed, on the whole, my intellectual position as "where the rubber meets the sky," and treated me accordingly; and the particular issues raised—I felt at the time, and still do today—by my Israeli background and the distinct vantage point it created for me: a sort of reverse anthropologist, studying the center and the bastions of its power from the periphery. Thus, the book ends with a personal tale, for better and for worse, hinting at the biases, limitations, and personal preferences that contributed to the book's agenda, conceptual framework, and ideological position.

What kinds of tales, then, does the book tell? The author is perhaps not the best authority on this matter: his interests, like his limitations, are quite obvious. But since asked, and since no other authority is necessarily better placed to answer such questions, I would suggest that first and foremost, *Engineering Culture* is a realistic tale (with a distinct moralistic flavor) of corporate control and its unanticipated consequences, and should be judged in these terms. If it is a story well told, the matter, as far as I'm concerned, may rest there: the trendy rhetorics of postmodernism notwithstanding, there is no shame (and some pride) in "big questions" taken seriously and straightforwardly, indeed scientifically. However, beyond this tale, for those who care to look, there are, I believe, glimpses of others: my own reading suggests that *Engineering Culture* is also a story of the moral career of my own conceptual apparatus—how, to what end, and with what results, culture "goes native"—and a (self) critical examination of the involvement, unwitting or not, of my own professional community in shaping the phenomena we study.

Finally, there is, perhaps, also an allegorical tale: how individuals can and do live with all-encompassing ideologies that attempt to shape collectives and make heavy, and potentially dangerous, demands on their members; far fetched, perhaps, but of interest, I suspect to those, who like Israelis of my generation, were raised in the shadow of deeply demanding, overt ideological constructions and who might be interested in protecting themselves from their claims.

On matters of textual interpretation, it is the readers, of course, who must ultimately assume authority: the last word is theirs. It is up to such readers, having been given fair warning of my biases, partaken of a reasonable (albeit selective) range of my observations and interpretations, and armed, one hopes, with their own relevant experiences, to decide whether and to what extent all of this is interesting and convincing. And it is for them to make of it what tale they will.

The Style and Structure of Cultures in Organizations: Three Perspectives

JOANNE MARTIN

Graduate School of Business, Stanford University

WRITING AS A STRUGGLE
FOR INTELLECTUAL DOMINANCE

Organizational culture is a topic that has brought to the surface fundamental theoretical, methodological, epistemological, and political disagreements. Such disagreements could be fruitful for this topic area and for the field of organizational studies, more broadly defined. Unfortunately, all too often, disagreements among cultural researchers take the form of a debate about which theory or method is the "one best way": an open or unspoken struggle for intellectual dominance. When opposing points of view clash openly, assumptions are laid bare and declared unwarranted or foolish and alternate viewpoints are dismissed as misguided, empirically unfounded, or irrelevant to more important questions. In other kinds of papers, only a careful reading between the lines reveals the silencing of opposing points of view, as assumptions remain unstated or unchallenged and opposing points of view are omitted, marginalized in a footnote or an aside, or declared outside the paper's focus. If culture were a topic area where quantitative methods were used by all, and if these disagreements were purely theoretical, a classic experiment or comprehensive archival study might be able to prove, conclusively, that a particular argument is false. However, because so much culture research is qualitative, such definitive empirical answers are unlikely, and so the culture debates become even less tolerant of opposing views.

Cultures in Organizations: Three Perspectives (Martin 1992) is an attempt to find alternative ways of writing about culture that are more tolerant—even expressive of—opposing views. The discussion below[1] focuses first on theoretical writing, then on writing about qualitative data, and concludes with ways of creating polyphonic cultural texts.

SEEKING AN ALTERNATIVE WAY
TO WRITE ABOUT THEORY

The book begins with a short, fierce debate among prototypical cultural researchers, illustrating how fights for dominance impede deeper intellectual

188

exchange. In the rest of the book, the rules of intellectual discourse are less like a struggle for dominance and more like a conversation. The parties to this conversation are the three conflicting theoretical perspectives that have come to dominate the cultural literature. The first of these three viewpoints is an Integration perspective that sees cultures in terms of shared values: harmony, homogeneity, and organization-wide consensus. (To the extent that conflicting meanings, subcultures, and ambiguities are discussed, they are "sideshows" to the main event or dismissed, as not part of the culture). The second is the Differentiation perspective, which focuses on inconsistencies (for example between espoused values and actual behavior), sees organizations as composed of overlapping, nested subcultures, and lets ambiguities, ironies, and ambivalence surface primarily on the boundaries where subcultures meet. The third is a Fragmentation perspective that sees ambiguity as pervasive, the defining feature of any cultural portrait; only fleeting, issue-specific affinities are found in these accounts.

In *Cultures in Organizations,* each of these three theoretical perspectives is presented in a separate chapter, in considerable detail, using the words of its advocates. Supporting empirical studies are summarized without methodological criticism. At the end of each of these chapters, after the theoretical perspective has been presented fully, major disagreements are voiced in an open manner, not trying to slip them unnoticed into assumptions, marginalia, and brief disclaimers. These three theoretical chapters (Chapters 4, 6, and 8) provide a comprehensive, critical review of much of the organizational culture research that has been produced in the last two decades. Reasons for theoretical conflict, methodological shortcomings, and differences in assumptions become evident, showing why the cultural domain has, for so long, been an arena of conceptual and empirical chaos.

The next chapter of the book (Chapter 9) offers an integrative theoretical framework that brings some order to this chaos. If one's goal is to use cultural theory to develop a fuller understanding of an organizational context, it is essential to look at the culture from each of the three perspectives in turn. Such an approach does not attempt to merge the three perspectives, so it does not distort or minimize the reasons why theoretical and methodological differences of opinion have developed. Studies supporting this three-perspective framework are briefly summarized.

SEEKING AN ALTERNATIVE WAY TO
WRITE ABOUT QUALITATIVE DATA

Cultures in Organizations intersperses these theoretical chapters with data drawn from a qualitative case study of a large, multinational corporation, labeled OZCO (e.g., Martin and Meyerson 1988). In the book, I wanted to present the OZCO data in a way which avoids the pitfalls of a conventional realistic tale, with its emphasis on authorial omniscience and the "one best" interpretation. I tried to remove my interpretations, as much as is possible, from this part of the text.

The OZCO case material is multivocal, rather than purely monophonic (that is, presented from the viewpoint of a single author). Such a minimalist textual strategy weakens the authorial role. It avoids the conventions of narrative structure and eliminates many of the rhetorical strategies that make texts elegant, foster rapport between reader and author, create false certainty, and mask over problems of generalization. The result, however, is a rather unbeautiful mosaic of quotations from OZCO employees, sorted into the three theoretical perspectives, with little interpretive or abstract linking material. These three OZCO chapters (Chapters 3, 5, and 7) were interspersed with the corresponding chapters describing the three theoretical perspectives.

This description of the book suggests that these alternative ways of writing about cultural theory and data effectively resolve the "one best way" problems outlined in the introduction to this paper. This is not the case, and the final chapter of the book (Chapter 10) makes a deeper critique of these writing strategies and offers a more innovative resolution of these writing problems.

UNDERMINING MY AUTHORITY AS AUTHOR:
A POLYPHONIC TEXT

The three-perspective framework is based on undeconstructed dichotomies which oversimplify the classification of cultural theories and position the three theoretical positions in opposition to each other. The three perspectives are categories which pigeonhole cultural studies, ignoring aspects of theory and research that straddle these boundaries or focus on other issues (the "fourth perspective problem.") Furthermore, the three perspective framework is a meta-theory (cf. Gagliardi 1991) that implicitly claims to deserve to dominate other more limited approaches to understanding cultures in organizations.

All such meta-theoretical attempts to dominate intellectual discourse ultimately fail, in part because any authorial truth claim carries "between the lines" the seeds of its own destruction (e.g., Derrida 1976). For example, although I tried to present myself as "above the fray" of the war among the perspectives, as a neutral transcriber of conflicting theoretical viewpoints and differing OZCO employees, inevitably my theoretical, personal, and political preferences shaped what I wrote and what I did not write.

In Chapter 10, I attempted to redress this balance. I discuss ways the three perspective framework silences and excludes that which does not fit these categories. I show how the OZCO material inevitably bears the mark of a transcriber who left out some material, failed to see some events, did not talk with some kinds of employees, and shaped the text by leaving out some quotations, selecting and ordering others. Even this self criticism, however, is a kind of "fable of rapport," designed to impress the reader with its honesty and self-insight.

A deeper resolution is suggested by Van Maanen's (1988) description of an "impressionist tale." This kind of narrative includes both the researcher and his or her informant(s) as individuals. A two-way dialogue replaces the omniscient, invisible writer of the traditional realist tale, revealing the author's discomfort and incomplete understanding of the culture.

In *Cultures in Organizations*, I tell a quasi-impressionist tale where my role is far from heroic, particularly in the domain that is the focus of the book. The dialogue in the anecdote comes from a taped conversation among four people: Debra Meyerson, two informants from OZCO, and myself. We met over dinner to critique the draft manuscript of *Cultures in Organizations*. We focused on the meaning of a particular cultural manifestation and in the course of the conversation, I asked a series of increasingly bewildered questions, got answers I did not anticipate, and fully exposed my lack of understanding about what this cultural manifestation meant to these cultural members. An analysis of the reasons for these misunderstandings raised a series of crucially important theoretical issues that had not previously surfaced.

This tale suggests that it is not enough to include the voices of dissenting theorists and individualized informants in a multivocal text like *Cultures in Organizations*. Cultural theory would be enriched if our texts were truly polyphonic, with informants and researchers struggling collaboratively to develop shared understandings and texts that preserve difference of opinion and ambiguity. The researcher would be just one of many authors and the role of a book editor would be a complex mixture of judge, journalist, and scholar. Such a book would be inordinately difficult to write, although some have tried. The problem is: even with the best intentions, it is nearly impossible to abnegate fully the authority of an author.

Perhaps the best resolution of this dilemma is that suggested by reader response theory: that ultimately, the power of interpretation lies with the reader. Multivocal and polyphonic books are the most likely to be open to reader interpretations not specifically intended by the author. On this note, *Cultures in Organizations* ends.

NOTE

1. This essay summarizes arguments made in *Cultures in Organizations*, particularly pp. 17, 24-27, and 193-202.

Writing Organizational Tales:
Reflections on Three Books on Organizational Culture

LINDA SMIRCICH

University of Massachusetts, Amherst

I must confess that I'm an organizational culture dropout. It's been a while since I felt much interest in reading about organizational culture. But Dvora Yanow had framed my task in an intriguing way. She asked me to comment on these three organizational culture books by Trice and Beyer, Kunda, and Martin respectively, as writings that tell stories about organizations and those who research them.

Already inherent in this framing is a view that repositions the researcher from scientist to narrator. This view understands the researcher, not as a well-placed observer-scribe using language to *mirror* the organizational reality he or she witnesses, but as someone already embedded in a language community that shapes what can be said as knowledge. As David Locke points out in *Science as Writing* (1992), "The scientific paper . . . is not a simple tale of what was done in the laboratory, not as a direct representation of research carried out, but a crafted, shaped object, formulated within rules and conventions, some spoken (or written on the backs of scientific journals) and some tacitly understood" (p. 8).

The constructed nature of knowledge doesn't begin, however, with the physical, material journal article page. Even when we go into the field to gather data, into an organization to study what is *really* going on, what is "real" to us, e.g., "leadership issues," "compensation problems," "organizational culture," has already been constituted by a prior chain of signification, a sedimentation of language, legitimated by our community. This isn't bad, it just is.

This view emphasizes the textual nature of knowledge, not just the obvious pen to paper or fingers to keyboard aspects of textuality. Rather, we're immersed in textuality and swimming in language. By positioning the panel this way Dvora moves the commentator from treating language as a tool for representing a separate reality out there to seeing language as constitutive of the realities we can know and understand. This perspective on language is already familiar to many and is actively embraced by the new sociologists of science, such as Latour and Woolgar (1979), and the cultural ethnographers who produced the book *Writing Culture* (Clifford and Marcus 1986). Cultural ethnographers in particular have had to confront the ways in which their own cultural frames have shaped what they see and say about those others they portray (Locke 1992). Dvora is suggesting that since we've already borrowed many pages from the anthropologists' books we should go along the rest of the way: to examine our constructions of organizational culture as also cultural constructions.

This is consistent with Paul Rabinow's (1986) urging that we "anthropologize the West." He suggests there is something to be gained by reconsidering our conceptions and formulations of the "real," by making exotic much of what we take for granted, and by focusing more self-consciously on the categories and concepts through which we are writing the world.

Framing the task in this way also repositions the role of the discussant. In place of a discussant whose job it is to judge the texts against the criterion of scientific adequacy, the discussant becomes explicitly a "reader." Of course, discussants have *always been* readers, but naming them so serves to remind us of the culturally contingent nature of the reading process. Because readers are always grounded in their sociocultural contexts, and their histories, they approach texts against the background of texts they've already read (and written) and which help to make them the kinds of readers they are. This repositioning requires me to acknowledge that I am not an innocent reader of these particular texts because I am already implicated in the organization culture debates.

I thought I did my organizational culture swansong in 1987, when Marta Calás and I gave a paper at SCOS called "Post Culture: Is the Organizational Culture Literature Dominant, but Dead?" Then we argued that the organizational culture literature had been pursued by some as an oppositional movement to the dominant discourses of organizational analysis, to offset the overly rationalist approaches of functionalist and positivist views in organizational theory and research. By 1987 there seemed to be a proliferating organizational culture literature, characterized by diversity of approaches, full of competing and often incompatible views. It seemed to us that functionalist, interpretivist and critical views were all speaking at the same time.

But more careful examination showed that the oppositional voices were only showing up in "special issues" of journals, and that "organizational culture" was more and more becoming part of the mainstream terminology and formuli. What had been trying to be in opposition was now in danger of incorporation into that mainstream. It was becoming "dominant," i.e., a part of the tradition—in a sense, hung there on the museum walls—just as the once outrageous impressionist and abstractionist works now hang peacefully alongside Grand Masters, having lost the capacity to provoke different questions and to help us see the world in new ways—in a sense—"dead."

Our proposal to "culture researchers" was to get out of that oppositional posture, to not try to position theirs as the "better truth" about organizational culture, but to engage instead in cultural analysis of organizational life, not analysis of organizational culture. We hoped that collectively we might stop all the arguing about what culture *really* was—an endless ontological argument—and focus instead on analyses of the processes of representation. We could get out of the "game of truth or falsity" and look at the pragmatics, poetics, politics and ethics of organizational research and theory and organizational practice. We could create a cultured organizational research, instead of researching organizational culture, to do as suggested by Rabinow and "anthropologize" organization and management theory and practice.

And so in terms of writing about organizational culture I thought I was finished. After that Marta and I went on to do work that sought to practice what we'd just preached.

Thus, as a reader of these particular texts, I bring a history of involvement with the literature. At the same time I have different relationships to the authors of these works. I've known Joanne Martin as a colleague and a friend for many years, we've shared many conversations about these topics already. The other authors I know through their writings and conference presentations. Each of them has my admiration for their many contributions to our field. These are serious scholars, each of these is a very serious book. And so, as a reader I bring to the reading task certain connections, a history and strong preferences.

There are of course many different ways to approach reading these books. It would be possible to read each from a perspective of conventional organizational science, or as exemplars of different paradigms, or from a poststructuralist perspective concerned with how they construct meanings, or from a feminist perspective concerned with issues of gender. Each of these close readings would proliferate interpretations of these books. But since there are already a number of us here offering interpretations I won't aim to do so much. Given Dvora's literary framing of the question—about tales of culture—I have read these works as types of writing and have considered the connections between *writing formats* and possible knowledges.

READING TRICE AND BEYER:
THE CULTURES OF WORK ORGANIZATIONS

The most obvious thing about this book is that it is a textbook. It's even being used at the department in Finland where I was a visiting professor. Trice and Beyer's is a story that claims not to be a story at all. They position theirs as the truth about culture in the workplace. The fact that this *is* a textbook explains why it tells the story it does and the way it does it. Textbooks are highly standardized artifacts in our culture. They are digests, compacted research and opinions, distilled for student consumption, and cultural reproduction. The textbook industry is competitive, with a lot of products on the market, lots of competition is coming from lower-cost reading packets assembled by professors, so publishers are always on the lookout for something new. Given that this is a textbook, I can't say that I am surprised by either its authoritative tone or its encyclopedic approach: these are the hallmarks of textbooks in our time and place. Institutional conditions require such stylistics.

One doesn't enter a management textbook expecting to find cultural critique. But as I read I was delighted to find moments of what I sought: moments of anthropologizing the West. Chapter 2 has an extensive section on American ideologies, it presents a discussion of American values, not in an ethnocentric way, but in a way that may help U.S. students understand themselves. Since the Finnish students are subjected to so many unreflective American textbooks they might find this a refreshing change.

This section of the book extends the discussion of ideologies into the realm of management and grounds it in U.S. history. There is a lot of history throughout this book and for me, that is its strength.

When Trice and Beyer set out to write this book they said they wanted to both integrate decades of research on culture and organizations and to unite a cultural approach with the mainstream theories of organization. I don't think this is exactly what they accomplished with their book. Instead, they offer a replacement for the exhausted subject of Organizational Behavior. Their book refashions and repackages familiar OB topics such as leadership and change, into cultural leadership and cultural change, which fit much better in these days of the "cognitive revolution." They have thus repositioned Organizational Behavior for the cognitive age.

What kind of a story is this? A story to make a space in a crowded field, a story to reclaim some glorious history to bolster the present condition, a story to relegitimate. They note that people in organizations use narratives to make sense of their experiences and express their feelings, but the authors don't apply this view to themselves. Theirs is a narrative that makes sense of some culture literature to save the field of OB, in danger of being irrelevant. Their efforts make it possible for OB to be born again as Organizational Culture, but in a new and improved, more sophisticated version. This may be all any textbook can do.

READING KUNDA: *ENGINEERING CULTURE*

Gideon's book is an ethnography, a form of writing that is in fact undergoing a great deal of review and reconsideration as critics engage the problematics of representing the other in our writings, especially as the other is capable of speaking back.

Gideon says he wants to tell a realistic tale. And from the standpoint of rhetorical strategy he writes in a way to convince us that he was there and this is what it was like. As you read you feel as if you are there overlooking the scenes, and since I was there, also in 1985, as a participant in a week long training program for new members of an experimental high commitment assembly plant, the scenes seemed very familiar.

For much of the book Gideon as author is hidden. He tells his story in the conventional way of a naturalistic account, but he brings a critical edge to his story. "Is the engineering facility a playground or a prison?" Gideon raises questions about organizations and society, and self and organizations that have almost disappeared, questions about "corporate power within the context of pluralistic, democratic society" that aren't much part of the organizational culture literature nor of the academic field of management which instead repeats its questions about person-organization fit.

For me, this is the exciting part of his text: its centering on a provocative question and his concern with societal dynamics. Given these broad interests, what's surprising to me is that Gideon draws so much on earlier theorists, such as Goffman, for his framing of the issues. Similar to Trice and Beyer, he seems desirous of connecting with a former, perhaps more glorious, time for sociology. In any case, concerns similar to Gideon's are taken up by other theorists not directly in the sociological tradition, such as Foucault (e.g., 1972, 1973, 1976) and Lyotard (1974).

Thus I see Gideon asking old and still important questions about tyranny and freedom and morality, but by adding attention to how individuals are produced as organizational subjects, they can be posed with a postmodern twist: *What kind* of people are *produced* by *strong culture companies?*

Gideon's image of human nature is consistent with that discussed by J. F. Lyotard (1984) in *The Postmodern Condition:* "A self does not amount to much, but no self is an island; each exists in a fabric of relations that is now more complex and mobile than ever before. Young or old, man or woman, rich or poor, a person is always located at "nodal points" or specific communication circuits, however tiny these may be" (1984 p. 15). The Tech story Gideon tells is one of employees who are at nodal points of many communication circuits (verbal, video, electronic) each reinforcing an image of the Tech member, each reinscribing a set of interpretations and feelings that should accompany various events or situations. For instance, there's a cultural script for burned out members, so that even the "burnee" knows how to behave, how to position himself ironically when the occasion demands. As Gideon puts it, "phenomenologically, if not concretely, people over time are submerged in a community of meaning that is to some extent monopolized by management: a total institution of sorts" (Kunda 1991, p. 224).

What kind of people are produced by strong culture corporations? Perhaps few besides Gideon care. Given unemployment rates, many people are eager for any job. The question may seem irrelevant. As Barbara Czarniawska-Joerges (1993) wrote in her review of Gideon's book, "A good recession and the whole theater will collapse." Others may feel, given the forces of global competition, that this is a question we don't have the luxury to ask.

But by asking his questions this way Kunda opens up the possibility for other questions. One doesn't have to be so interested in "strong culture" companies and whether they are playgrounds or prisons to be concerned about the meanings of organizations and work in our lives. Gideon talks about the "extra-culturals," the temporary workers on the margins of Tech, and he calls them the equivalent to the homeless (Kunda 1991, p. 225). But I think the real equivalent to the homeless are the unemployed. From Gideon's book we might be provoked to ask about "the unemployed self." Does one's self become "empty" when one is unemployed?

One of my complaints about the culture literature was that culture was becoming more a tired answer instead of an interesting question; this is definitely not so with this book.

However, I want to go back to the issue of genre and how this book is written. For most of the book Gideon is the hidden narrator. But after he concludes the story of Tech he adds a confessional appendix that tells another story—his own—about his connection to the text. Gideon knows the debates about ethnographic writing and he adds his words of warning—"Beware reader, this is my story"—all of it, not only the appendix. Being so conscious of this role in his text, Gideon could have been more reflective and more experimental and daring in his textual portrayal. He could have acknowledged the connections between his identities (Israeli man, affiliated with an engineering school, for example) and the story it was possible for him to tell and the story he chose to tell. He could have interwoven his story and Tech's, or allowed the people of Tech to add their reflections to his—as part of the main story—to have a more co-authored piece. But, of course, that would have been another story.

READING MARTIN: *CULTURES IN ORGANIZATIONS*

Joanne's book mixes genres; it's part textbook, part researcher's tale. It offers glimpses of life at OZCO but it offers glimpses into academic institutional struggles too.

Her book *could be* divided into two parts. The first section of the book ("Frameworks") stages a conversation among three competing approaches to analyzing organizational culture. Each framework is presented conceptually, exemplified with data from OZCO, and then critiqued from the standpoints of the other two. Then we turn the page, wipe the slate clean, and start the whole process over again with the new framework. This is an "etch-a-sketch" approach to writing: each drawing separate and erasable.

This first section of the book ends with a call to use all three frameworks for better representing organizational life. This would be where most authors would have stopped writing, and unfortunately I think it's where many readers will stop reading.

What follows next does not use the conventional rhetorical device of a "confessional appendix." It is instead "just another chapter." But as I see it, this chapter is Part Two of the book, what I'd call "Post Frameworks." Here is not an "etch-a-sketch" approach where you wipe the slate clean. Part 2 seems to say "throw away the slate altogether," as Joanne questions her frameworks, and the purposes of academic writing, from postmodernist assumptions.

In reading this book one may experience confusion: "What is this book about?" It doesn't provide the clarity and certainty of the textbook form, it doesn't tell a unified story as many ethnographic narratives do. It makes a different set of demands on the reader. This text traces a struggle to reconcile the irreconcilable—a struggle to move away from normativity—but it is a painful separation, for both author and reader. For me this book is exemplary and brave in the way it shows the difficulties of giving up the writing conventions of our particular community. It may inspire others to write with less author-ity.

And so, what might other jaded readers of the organizational culture literature glean from this collection of books to help in their task of writing a more cultured organizational literature? Together these books can remind us of: (1) the importance of history and historical context for our writing, research and teaching; (2) the greater possibilities for ethnography; there is room for experimentation in this form; (3) the importance of self-reflexivity in writing: being very conscious of the connection between the writer and the story she tells; and (4) the value of doubting frameworks. To write in ways that build upon these premises takes time. Writing that seeks to incorporate these practices will necessarily be done with a great deal more "contingency" and "irony" (Rorty 1989). It may indeed challenge the current "writerly" conventions of our scholarly community, reminding us again how the institutional conditions in which we "knowledge workers" labor shapes what we can "know."

REFERENCES

Calás, M. B. and L. Smircich (1987), "Post-Culture: Is the Organizational Culture Literature Dominant but Dead?" Paper presented at the Standing Conference on Organizational Symbolism, Milan, Italy.

Clifford, J. and G. Marcus (1986), *Writing Culture: The Poetics and Politics of Ethnography*, Berkeley, CA: University of California Press.

Czarniawska-Joerges, B. (1993), "Book Review of Gideon Kunda 1992 *Engineering Culture*," *Economic and Industrial Democracy*, 14, 151-160.

Derrida, J. (1976), *Speech and Phenomenon*, Evanston, IL: Northwestern University Press.

Foucault, M. (1972), *The Archaeology of Knowledge*, New York: Pantheon.

——— (1973), *The Order of Things*, New York: Vintage Books.

——— (1976), *Discipline and Punish*, New York: Vintage Books.

Gagliardi, P. (Ed.) (1990), *Symbols and Artifacts*, New York: Walter de Gruyter.

——— (1991), "Reflections on Reframing Organizational Culture," Invited presentation at the International Conference on Organizational Symbolism and Corporate Culture, Copenhagen, Denmark.

Geertz, C. (1988), *Works and Lives: The Anthropologist as Author*, Stanford, CA: Stanford University Press.

Goodman, N. (1978), *Ways of World-Making*, Indianapolis, IN: Hackett.

Ingersoll, V. Hill and G. B. Adams (1992), *The Tacit Organization*, Greenwich, CT: JAI Press.

Iser, W. (1989), *Prospecting: From Reader Response to Literary Anthropology*, Baltimore, MD: Johns Hopkins University Press.

Kunda, Gideon (1991), *Engineering Culture: Control and Commitment in a High Tech Corporation*, Philadelphia, PA: Temple University Press.

Latour, B. and S. Woolgar (1979), *Laboratory Life: The Social Construction of Scientific Facts*, Beverly Hills, CA: Sage Publications.

Locke, D. (1992), *Science as Writing*, New Haven, CT: Yale University.

Lyotard, J. F. (1984), *The Postmodern Condition: A Report on Knowledge*, Minneapolis, MN: University of Minnesota Press.

Martin, J. and D. Meyerson (1988), "Organizational Cultures and the Denial, Channeling, and Acknowledgment of Ambiguity," in L. R. Pondy, R. J. Boland, and H. Thomas (Eds.), *Managing Ambiguity and Change*, New York: Wiley, 93-125.

Martin, Joanne (1992), *Cultures in Organizations: Three Perspectives*, New York: Oxford University Press.

Rabinow, P. (1986), "Representations Are Social Facts: Modernity and Post-Modernity in Anthropology," in J. Clifford and G. E. Marcus (Eds.), *Writing Culture: The Poetics and Politics of Ethnography*, Berkeley, CA: University of California Press.

Rorty, R. (1979), *Philosophy and the Mirror of Nature*, Princeton, NJ: Princeton University Press.

——— (1989), *Contingency, Irony and Solidarity*, Cambridge, MA: Cambridge University Press.

Smircich, L. and M. B. Calás (1987), "Organizational Culture: A Critical Assessment," in F. M. Jablin, L. L. Putnam, K. H. Roberts and L. W. Porter (Eds.), *Handbook of Organizational Communication*, Newbury Park, CA: Sage Publications.

Trice, Harrison and Janice Beyer (1993), *The Cultures of Work Organizations*, New York: Prentice Hall.

Turner, B. A. (Ed.) (1989), *Organizational Symbolism*, New York: Walter de Gruyter.

Van Maanen, J. (1988), *Tales of the Field: On Writing Ethnography*, Chicago, IL: Chicago University Press.

12

Critical Issues in Organization Science

A Dialogue, Part 1

JOHN M. JERMIER
College of Business, University of South Florida

STEWART R. CLEGG
Faculty of Business and Technology, University of Western Syndey

This is a very interesting time to be a student of organization science as the most fundamental questions are being raised about the nature of both organizations and science. In a recent editorial essay, Daft and Lewin (1993) reframed *Organization Science's* mission by emphasizing its commitment to serve as a medium for communicating understanding of the paradigm shifts occurring in organizations. While not denigrating the role that normal science work can play in promoting this understanding, they reaffirmed *Organization Science's* commitment to publish work that is underwritten by alternative research philosophies, that uses creative methods, and that is presented in innovative formats. During this lengthy conversation with Stewart Clegg, we explored several philosophical and theoretical issues relevant to developing alternative approaches to organization science.

The interview had two general purposes: (1) to elicit new critical perspectives on conventional organizations and mainstream organization theory in light of the calls to rethink Marxist, feminist, and other essentialist, "emancipatory" frameworks; and (2) to reflect upon the field of organization science as it points toward social processes, namely organizations and

From "Critical Issues in Organization Science: A Dialogue," by John J. Jermier and Stewart R. Clegg, 1994, *Organization Science*, 5, pp. 1-12. Copyright © 1994, The Institute of Management Sciences. Reprinted with permission.

science, that no longer exist in the meaningful sense that once defined, bounded and even constrained them. Our discussion about critical organization theory quickly turned to Foucaultian and neo-Foucaultian concepts of power and then to some of the difficulties involved in conducting research aimed at developing a critical, emancipatory science of organizations. Our discussion of changing organizational forms and changing definitions of scientific work highlights some of the challenges and opportunities ahead as we face up to the limitations of the knowledge-producing traditions we probably have relied too heavily upon.

I chose Stewart Clegg for this interview for several reasons. One of the most important reasons is that his theoretical work on organizations has always addressed the big questions. Equally important is that in much of his work he has surfaced certain kinds of shared assumptions that many organization theorists have not even known to question. For example, in *Critical Issues in Organizations* (1977), he and David Dunkerley cut through the taken-for-granted assumptions in conventional organization theory, posing as problematic the absence of topics such as capitalism, feminism, the role of the state, and power and ideology. In *Organization, Class and Control* (1980), they provided a comprehensive critique of mainstream organization theory and began developing theoretical linkages between organizations and the political economic context. With the publication of *Class, Politics and the Economy* (1986), *Organization Theory and Class Analysis: New Approaches and New Issues* (1989), *Capitalism in Contrasting Cultures* (1990), and *Modern Organizations* (1990), the macro scope of his approach to comparative organizational studies became clear. And, of course, in *The Theory of Power and Organizations* (1979) and *Frameworks of Power* (1989), his critical reviews of the literature on power in organizations and societies provided both a synthesis of the vast multidisciplinary work in this area as well as new directions for developing alternative models of power. This brief sampling of Clegg's work suggests that he is a prodigious and substantial scholar, but also that he has used a keen sense of what is fundamental in social theory and social life in developing his contributions to thinking about organizations. For this reason, he has earned a reputation as a bold and provocative intellectual figure—an ideal subject for an interview intended to stimulate thinking about foundational issues.

In person, Stewart's erudition and passion for critically examining ideas are obvious. But, so too are his highly personable manner; his fascination with popular and countercultures (also see Boje 1993); and his self-mocking, postmodern man, national identity-crisis syndrome (few communicate with, travel to, and reside in as many places in the world as does Stewart).

In 1991, Stewart and I had a conversation while he was in Tampa that raised another interesting point relevant to this interview. In reflecting on his appointments in the School of Humanities at Griffith University and as Professor of Sociology at the University of New England (both in Australia), Stewart said that, at times, he felt like a "marginal man" vis-à-vis the European and North American organizational and management theory spheres of ideas. He made it clear that the sense of marginality came more from the nature of his appointments than from residing in Australia.

Of course, his contributions to the development of organization science and his continuing immersion in the field's dialogues and debates prevent taking the label of "marginal man" literally. But, there is a sense in which deeper awareness of the dominant culture's unrecognized assumptions and biases can be gained best by beginning analysis in the margins and then crossing boundaries (see Harding, 1991 for a discussion of "standpoint epistemology"). There are many aspects of Stewart's academic and personal biography that fit the positive image of a "boundary crosser": one who appreciates both difference *and* the way boundaries are more bridges and membranes than they are barriers (cf. Rosaldo 1989, Conquergood 1991). These factors may have something to do with Stewart's success in identifying the field's "symptomatic silences" (cf. Althusser and Balibar 1968, 1977, pp. 83-90). In any case, as I imagine will be clear from the interview text to follow, Stewart has been able to turn whatever marginalized moments he may have experienced to his own and to the field's advantage.

John: One thing I am hoping to do in this interview, Stewart, is get your opinions about the status of the varieties of critical theory, particularly as these relate to contemporary organizations and the development of organization science. With all the changes in the world, many social theorists seem to be distancing themselves from Marxist frameworks. But, where do people turn for intellectual structure to work through ideas that are based in radical concerns, even radical passions and values? Probably, the people who have been known for their work in critical organization theory have not abandoned their values, their passions, their radical concerns, but what are the ideas, the concepts, the frameworks they are moving toward? I noticed that you began to study Foucault more carefully in the early to mid-1980s. How did your critical thinking develop as you interpreted Foucault?

Stewart: It shows first in my article "Radical Revisions," published in *Organization Studies* (1989). The title was a pun. It was to be read not only as "radical revisions" but also as "revisions of a radical" and "revisions by a radical." "Radical Revisions" not only swam against the current of Marxism, but also was a significant revision of my views. It was about saying, "Look, I think the approach to power in my past work has been flawed in some respects." The key purpose of the paper was to argue for a point of unification between two streams of earlier work. If *Power, Rule and Domination* had focused upon relations of meaning in organizations and *Organization, Class* *and Control* and *The Theory of Power and Organization* had focused upon relations of production in organizations, what I sought to do in "Radical Revisions" was to argue that organizations should be seen as sites of both relations of meaning and relations of production, as arenas of radical contingency. Foucault's work stimulated this.

John: The Foucaultian influence in the paper is very apparent. But, Foucault's approach is a little opaque. In fact, it seems that Foucault provided a metaphor of power, but did not articulate very specific concepts. His view is, of course, useful in many ways, but do you see it as a radically new way to think about power? Has Foucault thoroughly reconceptualized power? I don't think his work has influenced North American organization theorists' thinking anything close to the level that it has in Europe and other places in the world. You see many people read Foucault and come away saying: "interesting metaphor, but I don't know where to go from there in theorizing power." In your view, what are some of the key ideas that come from Foucault?

Stewart: What I found interesting in Foucault was the nonessentialism in his analysis of power. One thinks of how, in his earlier work, the fixing of truth and falsehood is a result of regimes of truth, while in the later work it is tied to more concrete institutional analysis of differential regimes of penology, for instance. However, I think it's not Foucault but one of my favorite sociologists, Zygmunt Bauman, who does the best job of working from Foucaultian analysis to terms that are more applicable for organization theorists. He does it first in a book called *Memories of Class* which is an historical analysis of the formation of class society. He brings out sharply the features of regimes of disciplinary power premised upon many minute forms of routinization of procedure, or discipline. Incidentally, I think that it was this that first made me appreciate that Foucault could be read as a Weberian. Foucault, I am convinced, finds his Weberianism where Weber found so much of his: in Nietzsche. Although Foucault insisted that he was not very Weberian, I don't agree. There are many interesting commonalities between Weber and Foucault, as well as the evident differences.

In *Memories of Class,* Bauman contrasted very graphically the idea of routinized disciplinary power with the notion of sovereign power by drawing on a metaphor from Ernest Gellner. He talks of the feudal state as a dentistry state, a state that specialized in infrequent but painful extraction. The feudal notion of power adequate to this task is coercive, intrusive, violent, very often doing something to the body or to the person, but doing it infrequently. The contrast is between that and a power that doesn't need to intervene because it's so routinized, it's so structured, it's so embedded in the institutional fiber of everyday life in organizations, in hospitals, in bureaucracies, in the state, and so on. That view of power is very different from that which has been predominant in the literature.

If you look at the mainstream discussion of power in sociology and political science, and also in organization theory, there is a series of variants on models of sovereign power. Power is attributed to some sovereign subject or agency. If the theorist is a Marxist, it is the capitalist class. If they are elitist theorists, it is a ruling elite. If they are resource dependency theorists, it is those who control resource dependencies, or, if they are strategic contingency theorists, it is those who control strategic contingencies. In each case the effort is to try to track power down to concrete individuals. For organization theorists, this is somewhat bizarre because what they rarely look at is the structure of relations of domination (or what many term authority), rather begging the issue of legitimacy that always hierarchically prefigures the scene in which power gets to be represented. Very few writers look at this. Some give an account of how it is historically constituted. This is rare. If you look at the resource dependency materials, as far as I'm aware, there is no explicit discussion of the hierarchical structuring of power. Again, as far as I'm aware, there isn't such a discussion in the tradition of strategic contingencies theory. It is taken for granted. I take these as perhaps the two predominant traditions in the organizational power literature.

In studying power, Foucault is important for several reasons. First, because he dispels some errors and misconceptions that arise from the labor process debate. He stands as a corrective to a whole generation of Marxian inspired work that fetishizes the labour process and capital. Bauman observes this clearly in *Memories of Class*. Capitalists didn't sit down and think, "Aha, we have a problem of controlling the labor process" and then come up with a set of solutions adequate to the task. What they did, as institutionalist theory suggests to us they would, was mimetically adapt solutions that were already present and available in their immediate environment.

Foucault's account stresses the role of the prison and disciplinary mechanisms as the source of these mimetic solutions to too great an extent because he is focusing on the prison and punishment. As Alfred Keiser and Theodore Assad have made clear, monasteries and the military (as Dandekker has also stressed) were probably the most important sites of institutional innovation for subsequent organizational mimesis. Again, Weber had something similar to say, of course.

After Foucault, the functioning of power is not something that can be tracked simply to some sovereign subject through control of resources, whether they be resource dependencies, strategic contingencies, ruling class control of capital or ruling elite control of key positions in the bureaucratic apparatus. In fact, power is much more embedded in the interstices that normalize and routinize everyday life in organizations through performance appraisals, audits, selection mechanisms, promotion procedures, tenure mechanisms. One is not trying to describe who has the power so much as to ask where is the power, what is the power? It's a very different conception of power, one that I came to think of as starting from different premises.

John: Although Foucault ordinarily would not be thought of as a structuralist, most of your summary of Foucault sounds very much in concert with an argument developed by Blau and Schoenherr, American organization theorists who wrote *The Structure of Organizations* (1971). This argument was taken further by a political economist, Richard Edwards, in *Contested Terrain* (1979). They do a lot with rules and argue that the new forms of power reside in the institutionalization of bureaucratic rules. It's not a personal face, it's all done impersonally, in the rules. The way you interpret Foucault, it makes it sound like these are all institutionalized mechanisms. Although Foucault views power as dispersed into capillary forms, perhaps some of his emphasis is not that dissimilar from Blau and Schoenherr, or Edwards. That is, if you take disciplinary practices as rule-governed, in a general sense, and argue that all rule-governed practices have structural qualities to them.

Stewart: I'm not sure about this. There is a Weberian connection. Foucault's focus on disciplinary mechanisms is at one level a Weberian focus, but, interestingly, one also finds a similar focus in Gramsci, a Machiavellian. Gramsci is one of few writers before Foucault, with Weber and Marx, who writes about the way in which power literally inscribes itself on the body of the person in organizations. Do Blau and Schoenherr do this? Weber writes about the widespread adoption of Scientific Management, about how it nurtures a new psycho-physical apparatus in the employee, in the work. It produces a new discipline of the body. Gramsci, a few years later, makes much the same remarks when he is talking about "Americanism and Fordism" in his *Prison Notebooks.* Much of Marx's account in *Capital,* with the material taken from the "Blue Books" of the government factory inspectors, is a literal account of the violence done to the human being and body by the emerging factory system of early industrial capitalism. Foucault's conception of power is also very embodied. There are those sorts of commonalities.

There are other things that Foucault does that are important. First, he says that the concept of ideology is dead. If you have a concept of ideology, it's a conception of that which is false, one that requires that there be something that is true. Foucault implies that this means that the concept of ideology is always implicitly coupled with that of science. There is that which is science and that which is ideology. He resists application of the category of ideology as it ordinarily has been understood. Again, in terms of debates about power, that seems a very important point to make. It doesn't suggest that there is some kind of sovereign theoretical or political point or sovereign organizational mechanism that will enable one to say this is ideologically correct and that is ideologically incorrect; that this is politically true and that is politically untrue. I doubt there are grounds on which one can make those statements with the facility with which they are so often made. The implications of these views for Marxian approaches to power are that the attribution of interests to classes (or other collective actors) by an a priori model of what objective interests are is something that is neither theoretically nor empirically legitimate. Once you pull away the cornerstone of classes having essential interests and of interests being either expressed or denied, then, as I argued in *Frameworks of Power,* one pulls away the cornerstone of the whole edifice of Marxism and Marxian theory crumbles.

John: Now, when you move away from class structure, Stewart, does that mean that you're willing to accept alternative structures of stratification and identity (such as race, ethnicity, gender, sexual orientation, age or another category) as equally important in organizational analysis? That is, what is the basis for thinking through problems of structure and domination in organizations?

Stewart: I think it's an empirical matter what the structures of domination might be in organizations. However, having said that it is difficult not to see the significance of class relations, defined through relations of production. It takes a particular analytical blinkeredness not to recognize the significance of the differentially distributed ownership and control of those aspects of production relations that Marx termed the "means," and Weber the "methods," of production. While Marx focused on the relations of power Weber's focus was on relations of knowledge. It is not a choice of one or the other: analysis should be of relations both of power and knowledge.

Weber and Marx were analysts of both organization and class relations. Where do you find class relations but in organizations? That unity of focus disappeared after them and it seemed to become easier conceptually to separate class relations from organization relations. The fusion is there in Weber, it's there in Marx, with his analysis of the labor process, but it disappears afterward. In organization sociology, with few exceptions, researchers tend not to concentrate on that fusion. This is true not just of the analysis of organizations, but also the analysis of class.

John: How is it possible, then, to proceed with critique if none of the categories have any valid grounds in their own right?

Stewart: I don't think it's possible to proceed with a critique that assumes that it knows the answers before the questions have even been posed. This is what so much critique has been. Critique is so often a claim to speak from some ground of privilege about the nature of reality, the nature of phenomena. Again, I think Foucault with his insistence that we should hear the voices in the local and specific situations, that we should attend to the specific situations rather than be seeking a sovereign power that orchestrates these situations, was correct. I think he warns us against that imperialist notion of critique, even in its reflected mirror image, where it functions as a critique of imperialism.

To the extent that the notion of critique allies with essentialist positions of one kind or another, I think we should abandon that notion of critique. I don't think there is any ground from which one could presume to tell another person that what they believe or think or articulate as their world-views are "false" by some yardstick of theoretical coherence, or theoretical position immune to empirical test. I think it is very difficult to argue that there is ever any transcendent ethical or moral purpose for achieving a principled way in which the social scientist, qua social scientist, should prescribe a stance toward the big issues of life.

John: Let's see if we can make this a little more concrete. Suppose we go into an organization and we observe what appears to the researchers to be people in secondary labor market-type jobs exposed to many of the traumas often associated with the nature of that employment. Suppose we observe closely detailed (maybe even punitive and oppressive) supervision, rigidly enforced rules, monitored break times (bathroom and otherwise), hazardous working conditions, capricious work assignments, minimum wage pay and irregular employment, and many things like this. If the people in that setting do not voice disapproval with their circumstances, should the organization theorist who is researching this setting feel comfortable concluding that there is no critique or intervention possible or necessary?

Stewart: I can only answer this one indirectly. The histories of various institutional arenas and their discourses suggest that for the best of ideological motives people are capable of the worst of political action. I think Weber was correct when he said, not exactly in these words, but literally translating them into the terms of your question, that if you want the comfort of certain critique, of an absolute ethical standpoint, go and join one of the many churches out there. There are thousands of them, many diverse brand-identities, and they'll be only too glad to have you and they'll tell you what to do and they'll tell you what to think and what to critique and what not. Shop around. That's probably the most appropriate answer I can give. My answer to that question is that what may look like the well-intentioned reformism of an enlightened social scientist at a specific time may subsequently become seen as the creation of just another form of disciplinary power mechanism.

There is another substantial issue in your question, isn't there? It's the Habermasian issue of whether, in any situation, there is a genuine or a false consensus? But, that is an issue that only makes sense from the ground of a problematic that assumes that somehow or other someone is able to arbitrate between them. The question assumes that. Habermas has constructed an ideal type that is empirically a considerable distance from most forms of discourse that we might encounter. That is the point of doing it. It makes it a very ideal speech situation.

Realistically, in concrete empirical settings, people will put up with a great deal as they try to better their life-chances, not because they don't know any better, or are deluded, but because they see no more agreeable alternative under the prevailing structural conditions and see no realistic way of transforming those conditions. However, I seek to avoid judging from the ground of theoretical absolutes what's ideologically and politically correct. I don't in any conscience see why one would want to or would choose to ally with intellectual positions that could even admit that as a possibility. What if you're horribly wrong and the voice of reason that you thought you heard turned out to be wrong? It happened to Heidegger and to a whole generation of German "critical theorists." The rightwing ones, like Schmidt, didn't all flee to the United States. Some embraced Hitler and fascism.

There is another way, I think. The consequences of specific theories and policies can be displayed much more effectively by comparative analysis than by theoretical absolutism. That was the point of our arguments in *Class, Politics and the Economy*. It isn't just that we prefer social to liberal or illiberal democracy—it works better, empirically, in terms of macroeconomic outcomes, such as rates of unemployment. Of course, this is where ethics come in. It is an ethical question whether or not you want your theoretical and empirical concerns to focus on this matter or that matter, on fighting inflation first or combating unemployment. These empirical matters will not necessarily change people's political preferences, but at least they make clear what the corollaries, consequences and implications of those preferences are. So ethics enter the formulation of the questions, their answering, and the process of advocacy. What I oppose is the use of analysis that masks its ethical stance with the guise of technically neutral rationality and then advances its conclusions as if there were no alternative. Fight the TINA ["there is no alternative"] tendency. In addition, what I want to do, very much, is to avoid a situation where I would claim to speak for the voice of another with any authority: that seems an ethically indefensible thing to do. I wouldn't want others to represent my interests without consultation or to tell me what my interests are. Similarly, I wouldn't want to do that to others.

In the extreme, this discussion may seem arcane, but it has great relevance for our area. The history of organizational theory is littered with examples. The most obvious example is Mayo and the development of the counselling interview. He gave it scientific credence by rooting it in the work of the Swiss clinician, Dr. Pierre Janet. Human Relations was regarded by many as a beneficial and liberal type of intervention into the despotism of work. Today we may see things differently. Mayo developed human relations as a therapeutic cooling out of the worker, a way of not listening to the accounts that the worker proffered or of systematically reconstructing them and representing them in terms other than those in which they were produced. Certainly, lots of fine people with good liberal ideals and motives have embraced many aspects of that package, have developed them in lots of ways and have developed a whole battery, an arsenal, of human relations techniques and practices. The TQM movement, as something that seems dedicated to the production of an autopoetic subject, is a contemporary case in point of these kinds of interventions. A new kind of reflexivity, a totally reflexive loop fashioned on a one-dimensional human subject, constantly regarding themselves, their labor processes, their products and practices, from the singular auspices of zero defects as a discourse organizationally implanted into them! On the one hand it seems rather a liberal intervention, removing the need for external surveillance, but replacing it with this new form of neurotic subjectivity. It has rather an authoritarian impulse, I think, because of its one-dimensionality. From the perspective I have, I wouldn't see these as any kind of liberation. They're just another part of the network of power within which we get framed, literally and punningly. So, in a way, not to make those kinds of critiques or not to recommend those kinds of interventions is not so much an abdication of responsibility as an acknowledgement of due modesty, a responsible disinclination, an academic scrupulousness about the occupational risks of hot-gospelling Elmer Gantry's selling a Holy Grail. There, two excellent movies in one mixed metaphor!

John: So this emerging view of power and control, and perhaps even domination, seems totally dependent on the idea that unless the voices in the local settings speak clearly of injustice, or human pain and suffering, or injury, the person who is trying to understand this setting would stop short of critique and advocacy on their behalf. And this is because there is no possibility that people are ideologically manipulated?

Stewart: Well, not necessarily. One may be involved in some forms of comparative analysis. By contrasting a specific organizational setting with another specific organizational setting, one can show the consequences of different arrangements. It may be that the most useful form of critique simply is generating accounts that demonstrate the range of empirical differences that may occur. I think that we have to hold back from any position that says that by the action of the theorist we can somehow bring into being a repressed utopia. If you could somehow get rid of the mechanisms of distortion, of domination, of repression, of the non-ideal speech situation, whatever categories you use, transparency and freedom would otherwise be there. One interpretation of history seems to suggest that every time somebody has claimed to speak in the name of some other subjects, they've usually been framed up at best and fatally damaged at worst.

John: So let me see if I understand. We make comparisons. These can be very detailed and rigorous empirical studies. From research such as this, we may find differences among groups in terms of, say, disadvantage and advantage. Now, where do you go with that kind of information? You document, let's say, radical differences in income and status inequality, substantive complexity and control of work, freedom from surveillance, exposure to physical hazards, or discrimination. Who can benefit from information such as this?

Stewart: Well, it depends. Everybody has different ways of doing these things. What I do is write books, and I write articles, and I teach using the books and the articles. I know other people teach using some of the books and articles as well. The way I use them is to set up debates between students as to what they see as feasible and desirable. I try to get them to see what some implications are of what they think is feasible. It's very interesting to have a group of students, with several women in the room, for instance, talking about Japanese management. There is a dawning realization that if you're a woman in the Japanese model, you are not going to get too far: it's not necessarily the best way to go, despite everything that you may have heard. I think that can be liberating. It enables people to find their voices. You're not telling people what to think. You're simply using a range of differences to try to develop debates that have policy implications.

My interest in teaching my students is much less in terms of focusing upon organizational design in the prescriptive way in which many of our colleagues would choose to focus. I'm more interested, I guess, in trying to get students to think critically, comparatively, about issues of organizational design and to get them to see what some corollaries, consequences and implications are of various ways of institutionally framing design. One way of doing that is by using comparative materials wherever possible.

John: On the theme of comparative research studies and the possibility of advancing new forms of organizing through comparative work, let's talk about European approaches to organization studies.

Stewart: Well, I think the possibility of distinctively "European" approaches really grew out of the realization by several eminent European organization theorists of the 1960s that they only ever met each other at American Sociology Association conventions. This was both a little crazy and somewhat imperialistic. Why should their intellectual interactions be mediated through another country and its institutions? However, I don't think a single approach or something recognizably "European" ever emerged. European organization theory is an enormously heterogenous entity which changes every time there is an EGOS colloquium. From one EGOS colloquium to another there will be continuities. These continuities are given mostly by the autonomous working groups. It's heterogenous theoretically, so there isn't a single European social theory of organizations, any more than there is a single American one. There are many different kinds just as there are many different kinds anywhere else in the world. Some of them are very similar to some of those that you'd find in North America. Some of them may have different emphases. What Europe offers is a terrific opportunity for people to relate across national, cultural, linguistic, intellectual, and institutional traditions and frameworks. So its plurality, through its cross-national basis as a regular fora, is what provides it with its greatest strength. For example, the Nordic countries, in particular were influenced by the work of Emery and Trist and Trist and Thorsud and have long had a focus on organizations in terms of Tavistock social engineering, a form of progressive social tinkering of a reformist kind. In the Scandinavian countries, however, there is also a strong Stanford connection with the Stockholm Business School, the Copenhagen School of Business, the University of Bergen, particularly from Jim March and the March School of administrative rationality and foolishness. These have been very influential. In France there are several separate and very diverse research groups. Britain is characterized by a high degree of diversity also. Some of this maps easily on the U.S. scene, like the Aston studies and the kind of work that goes on around structural contingency theory. Some of it is distinctly different. Perhaps more people in the British context are less fixated on the notion of the organization and of organization theory and are more inclined to see organizations as settings in which they do social research. I think that would be true of many people around the labor process debate, for instance. The labor process debate seems a peculiarly British institution in that it's something that has taken place in Britain for about ten years or so, producing much material that has been very widely discussed in the English speaking world, except for North America where I don't think there has been a great degree of discussion of it. I know that you, John, are an exception. The labor process concerns, for obvious reasons that have to do with its critical theory lineages, are not something that one finds widely represented in the U.S. scene. It is interesting that the best known North American exponent of it is an ex-British anthropologist from the Manchester school, Michael Burawoy.

A great degree of diversity characterizes the scene and I am reluctant to generalize. From a research point of view it is much easier to do comparative research, especially within the context of evolving European Community institutions, because these institutions have funding agencies specifically concerned with the way in which different kinds of institutional arrangements structure different kinds of organizational outcomes across the national settings. From this there is a strong relevance on policy related issues, public policy and social policy. There is also a problem of the hegemonic definitions of what appropriate research into these should be that has been achieved by the economics discipline, but that is another story.

John: The point being that much organization theory has been Anglo in nature and we're only starting to see the limits of the peculiar experience, in world terms, that produced this Anglo-American bloc.

Stewart: We don't have a world organization theory. What we have is an organization theory that is principally, but not wholly, rooted in the soil, the institutions, the culture, the rhetoric, the vocabulary, the discourse, of the United States as the dominant English language nation. There is not just one set of voices in the U.S. Obviously there are many, but U.S. influence is extreme. There isn't a single world organization theory and I don't see how there ever could be one. Part of the fabric that sustains organizational life, what cultivates it, is in the literal meaning of the word, "culture." The great diversity of culture should have some impact upon the way that organizations get to be seen and get to be done. When one thinks about the richness of the methodological possibilities that organizations as culturally produced phenomena offer, the actuality of the practice of their investigation is impoverished . . . not just in comparative cultural terms. For example, we have very little work that focuses upon the symbolic landscapes that are artifactually pervasive and present in organizations. The hotel that we are sitting in has a cacophony of sound and light in what would be a peaceful foyer in most other hotels that I've ever been in outside Las Vegas. The most immediately material thing about this hotel is its cultural symbolism.

John: Formulate that a little more specifically if possible?

Stewart: Well, I think the people who have come closest are those involved in the Standing Conference on Organization Symbolism, SCOS, in Europe. There is an excellent book by Pasquale Galgiardi that contains a collection of papers from various SCOS colloquia. I think it does a great job of opening some of these aspects of the field. One exercise that I did with a group of students recently was to get them to describe their organizations to me. They started off by telling me about their organization charts. I said no, describe these organizations to me, please. What does it look like as you walk up to the door? What's the door like? Is there a lobby, is there a foyer, what does it look like? What is the physical presence of the organization?

Another thing, if you open a geography text, a book or an article in geography, there are usually lots of detailed photographs and maps of the terrain, because it helps our understanding. When was the last time you opened an organizations book and you saw lots of pictorial representations of organizations. Not graphics, but actual pictorial representations? If you are talking about the artifactual reality of organizations, then that kind of data, that kind of evidence, is enormously important. The camera is an enormously powerful research tool but I don't see it used very much by organization and management theorists.

John: What about the paint brush?

Stewart: The paint brush too, yeah, organizations in pictures and paintings. We've a wealth of data that we could begin to go with. Also cinema. One study that I think would be fascinating, would be to look at the changing representations of organizations historically in the life of the cinema. There are striking images that one could obviously deal with. The two most potent ones for modern organizations are probably Chaplin's "Modern Times" and Fritz Lang's "Metropolis," the classic German abstract expressionist movie. There are many other kinds of organizational representation as well.

I was watching one of my favorite films again the other night for about the seventh or eighth time, the great Sergio Leone's "Once Upon a Time in the West," a remarkable film on many levels, including its genre intertextuality. A large part of the narrative concerns the building of a frontier community, Sweetwater, the construction of its fabric. It's about the train. It's almost Chandlerian in its narrative structure. The train is opening up new markets, new forms of life and a new epoch centered on domesticity and consumption, represented in the character played by Claudia Cardinale. An old epoch is dying, a new one being born. Perfect for the "strategy/structure" argument. It is also a great film . . .

REFERENCES

Althusser, L., and E. Balibar (1968), *Reading Capital,* Old Woking, England: Gresham Press; (1977, 2nd Ed.).

Boje, D. M. (1993), "On Being Postmodern in the Academy: An Interview with Stewart Clegg," *Journal of Management Inquiry,* 2, 191-200.

Conquergood, D. (1991), "Rethinking Ethnography: Towards a Critical Cultural Politics," *Communication Monographs,* 58, 179-194.

Daft, R. L. and A. Y. Lewin (1993), "Where Are the Theories for the 'New' Organizational Forms? An Editorial Essay," *Organization Science,* 4, i-vi.

Harding, S. (1991), *Whose Science? Whose Knowledge? Thinking from Women's Lives,* Ithaca, NY: Cornell University Press.

Rosaldo, R. (1989), *Culture and Truth: The Remaking of Social Analysis,* Boston, MA: Beacon.

PART III

DIALOGUES AND DIRECTIONS

Part III continues to broaden and deepen the arguments about the nature of organization science. In these chapters, we see dialogue in the sense of speaking from the heart as well as from the intellect, but also a sense of new directions that our thinking and research might take.

In the first chapter, by Meyerson and Scully ("Tempered Radicalism and the Politics of Ambivalence and Change"), we find the notion of "tempered" radicalism to replace the radicalism described in Part II. Tempered radicals can hold two elements in their minds simultaneously, the current reality and their desired ideology, and are able to integrate the two. Here we see the self again, and how it becomes important in one's behavior and research. In the second chapter, about closet qualitative research ("The Virtues of Closet Qualitative Research"), Sutton implies that organization science is not a multiple paradigm field. Rather, it is dominated by quantitative positivist researchers, but qualitative researchers can do a lot to have their findings heard. Again, resolution here depends partly on the self and one's willingness to accept the tensions of existing in a world different from one's ideal, and having the courage to do something about it.

The third chapter, which is more from the interview with Clegg ("Critical Issues in Organization Science: A Dialogue, Part 2"), is about embracing diversity. The final two chapters push even farther toward community in practical and spiritual terms. The Mirvis chapter (" 'Soul Work' in Organizations") provides models for community building that suggest processes that encourage diverse thinking, yet will draw organizational scholars together. It is up to us to create ways to listen, to share ideas and information, ultimately doing so in a way that builds bridges across separate stone wells. This would indeed be a new phenomenon in organization science—embracing multiple paradigms into a single community, welcoming rather than arguing with each other, and to do so may involve a spiritual connection of sorts.

The final chapter is an interview Peter Frost had with Steve Kerr ("Bridging Academia and Business: A Conversation With Steve Kerr"). Kerr talks about building bridges between academics and practitioners. Academics do well with ideas and reflection, and practitioners innovate and get things done. Kerr himself is a tempered radical, a listener, a scholar, a practitioner. He sees the positive in all areas, understanding that no one has a monopoly on ideas or wisdom. Again we see the urging for people to talk to one another and listen to what each has to say.

The organizations that our field studies have begun a revolution toward models such as the learning organization, which involves reduction of boundaries, pulling together people, and sharing information fueled by conversations across traditional boundaries. Unity rather than separation seems to be in the forefront of contemporary organization design. Yet in some respects the field of organization science still thrives on separation—different paradigms competing for dominance. The ultimate question to consider while reading this section is whether what is good for organizations is also good for the science of organizations. Should the field begin to behave more like a true learning organization, with few boundaries and many dialogue-type conversations, or should the field of organization science continue to act as a traditional organization with separation and specialization? Following which path will direct organization science toward its own greatest contribution?

13

Tempered Radicalism and the
Politics of Ambivalence and Change

DEBRA E. MEYERSON
School of Business, The University of Michigan

MAUREEN A. SCULLY
Sloan School of Management, MIT

A woman executive can identify with feminist language that is far from commonplace in corporate life and challenges the very foundations of the corporation in which she holds office. She can also be loyal to her corporation, earnestly engaged by many of its practices and issues, and committed to a career in a traditional, male-dominated organization or profession. A male business school professor can hold an identity as a radical humanist and embrace values directly in contest with capitalist corporations. He can also be committed to his job in the business school and teach practices that, in effect, enforce the tenets of capitalist organizations. An African-American architect can identify with her ethnic community and be committed to creating a more equitable and healthy urban environment. She can also identify with a professional elite and be committed to an organization that perpetuates the decay of urban neighborhoods. These individuals do not easily fit within the dominant cultures of their organizations or professions. However, despite their lack of fit, or perhaps because of it, they can behave as committed and productive members and act as vital sources of resistance, alternative ideas, and transformation within their organizations.

These individuals must struggle continuously to handle the tension between personal and professional identities at odds with one another. This struggle may be invisible, but it is by no means rare. Women and members of minorities have become disheartened by feelings of fraudulence and loss as they try to fit into the dominant culture. Some leave the mainstream. Others silence their complaints and surrender their identities.

However, separatism and surrender are not the only options. While frustration may be inevitable, individuals can effect change, even radical change, and still enjoy fulfilling, productive, authentic careers. We write this paper about and for the people who work within mainstream organizations and professions and want also to transform them. We call these individuals "tempered radicals" and the process they enact "tempered radicalism."

We chose the name "tempered radical" deliberately to describe our protagonist. These individuals can be called "radicals" because they challenge the status quo, both through their intentional acts and also just by being who they are, people who do not fit perfectly. We chose the word "tempered" because of its multiple meanings. These people are tempered in the sense that they seek moderation ("temper blame with praise," *Webster's New World Dictionary,* 1975). In the language of physics, they are tempered in that they have become tougher by being alternately heated up and cooled down. They are also tempered in the sense that they have a temper: they are angered by the incongruities between their own values and beliefs about social justice and the values and beliefs they see enacted in their organizations. Temper can mean both "an outburst of rage" and "equanimity, composure," seemingly incongruous traits required by tempered radicals.

Tempered radicals experience tensions between the status quo and alternatives, which can fuel organizational transformation. While a great deal of attention has been devoted to issues of organizational "fit," change often comes from the margins of an organization, borne by those who do not fit well. Sources of change can give organizations welcomed vibrancy, but at the same time, the changes that the tempered radical encourages may threaten members who are vested in the status quo. Is this transformation "good for" the organization? The answer may change as standards of judgment change, for example, when an organization shifts from a stockholder to a stakeholder model. Many people ask us "what exactly" the tempered radical can change, and "how much." One dilemma for the tempered radical is that the nature and effectiveness of change actions is elusive, emergent, and difficult to gauge. The yardstick for change frequently changes metrics. In this paper, we will not focus on whether the tempered radical ultimately wins the battle for change, but rather on how she remains engaged in the dual project of working within the organization and working to change the organization. We focus on the individuals themselves, the perspectives they assume, the challenges they face, and the survival strategies they use. It is important to understand these individuals as central figures in the battle for change because if they leave the organization, burn out, or become coopted, then they cannot contribute fully to the process of change from inside.

Writing this paper is an example of tempered radicalism. We discuss our own and others' radical identities and implicitly critique professional and bureaucratic institutions. We draw from formal interviews and dozens of informal conversations with tempered radicals, first-person accounts from related literatures, and descriptions of tempered radicals in the popular press. We experiment with modes of scholarship as we attempt to weave personal narrative into our paper. The content of our stories illustrates substantive dilemmas of tempered radicalism; the form of the stories, which makes our subjectivity explicit, is an example of tempered radicalism insofar as it pushes traditional notions of social science writing and draws inspiration from feminist approaches to scholarship (e.g., Krieger 1991, Reinharz 1992).

The first section below paints a portrait of the tempered radical. The second and third sections discuss the advantages and the disadvantages of ambivalence as a cognitive and political stance. The last section describes some strategies used by tempered radicals to sustain their ambivalence and work for change.

TEMPERED RADICALISM:
THE PROCESS AND PRACTITIONERS

Tempered Radicalism

Individuals come to work with varied values, beliefs, and commitments based on multiple identities and affiliations that become more and less salient in different circumstances; they have situational identities (Demo 1992, Gecas 1982). The tempered radical represents a special case in which the values and beliefs associated with a professional or organizational identity violate values and beliefs associated with personal, extra-organizational, and political sources of identity. In the tempered radical, both the professional and personal identities are strong and salient; they do not appear alternately for special situations. In most situations, the pull of each identity only makes the opposite identity all the more apparent, threatened, and painful.

Threats to personal identity and beliefs can engender feelings of fraudulence, misalignment (Culbert and McDonough 1980), and even passion and rage (hooks 1984). These feelings can bring about change. For the tempered radical alignment and change are flip sides of the same coin. When tempered radicals bring about change, they reshape the context into one where it is a bit easier to sustain their radical identities. Untempered, this approach may alienate those in power and threaten the tempered radical's professional identity and status. The tempered radical may therefore cool-headedly play the game to get ahead, but does not want to get so caught up in the game that she violates or abandons her personal identity and beliefs. In this sense, tempered radicals must be simultaneously hot- and cool-headed. The heat fuels action and change; the coolness shapes the action and change into legitimate and viable forms.

Who Are the Tempered Radicals?

This paper has been difficult and exciting for us to write because we view ourselves as tempered radicals, struggling to act in ways that are appropriate professionally and authentic personally and politically. Both of us are feminists and radical humanists; we strongly believe in eradicating gender, race, and class injustices. We are also both faculty members in business schools and members of a discipline known as "management," although we teach about a variety of stakeholders other than managers. Both of us identify with our profession and want to advance within it. Yet we also believe that the business schools in which we work reproduce certain inequalities systematically, if unintentionally. We find ourselves in the awkward position of trying to master the norms of our profession in order to advance and maintain a foothold inside important institutions, but also trying to resist and change the profession's imperative and focus. Often people keep such feelings to themselves lest they undermine their credibility. Tempered radicalism can be lonely and silent. Nonetheless, we have learned to articulate this experience, first by talking with each other, and then by talking with, interviewing, and reading about others who have influenced us deeply. In the words of one of them:

> I've often felt that it's extremely difficult to be a critically oriented scholar within a business school and that I'd fit better someplace else on campus. Is it possible to talk about underlying values, assumptions, hopes and fears, and question the ultimate purposes of organizations when the dominant ethos is focused on the technical, the instrumentally rationale, and that defines values and purposes as outside the scope of "the problem." . . . And finally, is it possible to be a feminist and live in a business school? Can I still be me and survive in this profession? I've asked myself these questions many times. (Smircich 1986, p. 2)

Women of color in professional positions have articulated the tensions of tempered radicalism quite clearly, perhaps because their history is marked by their struggle with multiple injustices (e.g., Bell 1990, Collins 1986, Gilkes 1982, hooks 1989). Bell (1990) found that Black women professionals face significant pressure to conform to professional standards and the dominant culture of the organization as well as to live up to expectations, values, and identities based in the Black community. They must also overcome stereotypes by passing extra tests of competence and loyalty at work. Sutton (1991) describes the tension she experiences each day as an African American architect:

> With part of our selves, we work to achieve power and authority within the traditions of the dominant culture. We hoist each other toward personal success through an invincible network of friendship, economic support, mentoring, information exchange. . . . No matter how little we earn, we join the costly American Institute of Architects and make our presence felt in that organization.
>
> With another part of our selves, we reject the competitive, elitist mentality of architectural design which differentiates professionals and clients, professors and practitioners, designers and builders, and builders and users. We reject this segmentation because it reflects the segmentation that exists in the larger society between men and women, rich and poor, young and old, colored and white. (Sutton 1991, pp. 3-4)

For men of color who try to succeed within predominantly white institutions, the experience of tempered radicalism is "substantively as much a part of the minority professional in this country as baseball and apple pie" (African American law student). This same student argued:

> Struggling to get ahead in white dominated society—while struggling desperately to maintain what little we were "allowed" to develop and espouse as a black identity—has been a mainstay of the very fabric of black culture for over a century.

Gay men and lesbians who work within traditional, heterosexual institutions also experience the tensions of tempered radicalism. They must gauge how much to disclose, how much to risk, how much to trust. Those who attempt to hide their sexual orientation from colleagues report feelings of fraudulence and shame, which get exacerbated when they are accused of selling out by their more "out" gay and lesbian peers. Because gay and lesbian professionals can choose to hide their source of difference, however painfully, they face, perhaps more than any group, constant decisions about the politics of identity.

The conflicting identities faced by white heterosexual men may not be as visible, predictable, or stressful as those faced by women of all colors, men of color, or gay men and lesbians, but they certainly do exist. For example, a white man from the Boston area was coached by a colleague on how to lose his class-based accent, but was ambivalent about abandoning his working-class origins precisely because he thought he could use his managerial position to lobby for working-class employees during economic downturns. He also knew that adopting a higher class accent could help in that lobbying effort, and thus he experienced "status inconsistency" (Lenski 1954).

We speak in this paper about some of the shared experiences of tempered radicals. At the same time, we acknowledge that different groups experience different identity challenges. They undoubtedly respond with different strategies as well, using the distinctive types of insider knowledge they acquire. We hope that this paper encourages tempered radicals to share their experiences with one another and to add to the general strategies described here.

THE ADVANTAGES OF AMBIVALENCE

The dual nature of the tempered radical's identity creates a state of enduring ambivalence. In this section we detail some of the advantages of ambivalence and challenge the predominant view that ambivalence is a temporary or pathological condition to resolve (e.g., Merton 1976). Weigert and Franks (1989) summarize the sociological understanding of ambivalence:

> Insofar as ambivalence creates uncertainty and indecisiveness, it weakens that organized structure of understandings and emotional attachments through which we interpret and assimilate our environments (Marris 1975). . . . Clearly experienced emotion is an important cue to the formation of coherent inner identity (Hochschild 1983, p. 32). Without firm feelings of who we are, our actions are hesitant, halting, and incomplete. (Weigert and Franks 1989, p. 205)

"Ambivalence" stems from the Latin *ambo* (both) and *valere* (to be strong) (Foy 1985); it can be tapped as a source of strength and vitality, not just confusion and reluctance. We suggest that individuals can remain ambivalent *and* quite clear about their attachments and identities. In contrast to compromise, ambivalence involves pure expression of both sides of a dualism; compromise seeks a middle ground which may lose the flavor of both sides. Cooptation—eventually espousing only the voice of tradition—might be averted by clever compromises, but might be better fended off by the clear oppositional voices retained in a posture of ambivalence. Because both parts of a duality are represented, ambivalent responses can be more responsive to equivocal situations than compromises (Weick 1979).

The tempered radical's ambivalence resembles the experiences of marginality and biculturalism, which others have described as a tenuous balance between two cultural worlds:

> A *marginal person* is one who lives on the boundary of two distinct cultures, one being more powerful than the other, but who does not have the ancestry, *belief system,* or social skills to be fully a member of the dominant cultural group (Park 1928, Stonequist 1937). (Bell 1990, p. 463)

Like marginal people, tempered radicals experience ambivalence in three interrelated forms, each of which has its own advantages. First, and most fundamentally, tempered radicals are "outsiders within." They can access the "knowledge and insight of the insider with the critical attitude of the outsider" (Stonequist 1937, p. 155). While insider status provides access to opportunities for change, outsider status provides the detachment to recognize that there even is an issue or problem to work on. Merton (1976) described a result of this dual cognitive posture as "detached concern," where one is both objective and subjective. We suggest that the tempered radical may also experience "passionate concern," which involves dual subjectivities. Memories of being outside of the center can become a source of creativity and transformation:

> Living as we did—on the edge—we developed a particular way of seeing reality. We looked both from the outside in and from the inside out. We focused our attention on the center as well as the margin. We understood both. . . . Our survival depended on an ongoing public awareness of the separation between margin and center and an ongoing private acknowledgment that we were a necessary, vital part of that whole. . . . This sense of wholeness, impressed upon our consciousness by the structure of our daily lives, provided us with an oppositional world view—a mode of seeing unknown to most of our oppressors, that sustained us. . . . These statements identify marginality as much more than a site of deprivation; in fact, I was saying just the opposite, that it is a site of radical possibility, a space of resistance. . . . It offers one the possibility of radical perspective from which to see and create, to imagine alternative new worlds. (hooks 1984)

Second, tempered radicals can act as critics of the status quo *and* as critics of untempered radical change. Stonequist (1937) praised marginals for being "acute and able critics." In Hasenfeld and Chesler (1989, p. 519), Chesler claims that his marginality (or the ambivalence inherent in his marginality) has allowed him to be critical of the status quo: to "break away from dominant professional symbols and myths to question their validity, and to undertake innovative theory building and research. Being free of existing professional paradigms has enabled him to develop new bodies of knowledge now recognized as important to the profession." In interviews, others echoed the importance of remaining "independent." Tempered radicals may also critique a more radical approach to change. Tempered radicals have chosen to work for change from within organizations, although their career path may be as much a default, a playing out of the usual route through the education and career system, as an active political choice. In any case, because of their location, they may critique some forms of radical change for provoking fear, resistance, and backlash. Pamela Maraldo, president of Planned Parenthood, has stirred controversy among feminists by taking a tempered approach to the risks of being too radical:

> I don't believe in a strident, radical approach to things, because right away you lose many of your followers. . . . I think that "feminist" plays differently in different circles. Many people in mainstream America have vague, radical associations with the term. I do not, so I apply it easily and comfortably to myself. But I think that to present myself as a feminist would be to lose the attention early on of a lot of the important public. . . . Whatever we choose to call [feminism], the important thing is that it work. (quoted in Warner 1993, p. 22)

Third, in addition to being critics of the status quo and critics of radical change, tempered radicals can also be advocates for both. Their situation is therefore more complex than that of change agents who act strictly as critics of the status quo. As advocates for the status quo, tempered radicals earn the rewards and resources that come with commitment and (tempered) complicity, and these become their tools for change. Sutton (1991) envisions this dual posture:

> From this admittedly radicalized perspective, I imagine an alternative praxis of architecture that simultaneously embraces two seemingly contradictory missions. In this alternative approach we use our right hand to pry open the box so that more of us can get into it while using our left hand to get rid of the very box we are trying to get into. (Sutton 1991, p. 3)

Tempered radicals can and will be criticized by both radical and conservative observers. Radicals may suspect that tempered radicals' agendas are futile or retrogressive. Audre Lorde wrote, in words now famous among feminists, "The master's tools will never dismantle the master's house." Defenders of the status quo find ways to exclude suspected deviants from full entry into the institution. Jackall (1988, p. 54) quoted two managers speaking candidly about invoking group conformity pressures to silence radical voices. One said, "You can indict a person by saying he's not a team player," and the other noted, "Someone who talks about team play is out to squash dissent." Faced with pulls toward more radical and conservative stances, and with voices of uncertainty in their own heads, tempered radicals must deal with the disadvantages of ambivalence discussed in the next section.

THE CHALLENGES OF AMBIVALENCE

Despite the benefits of an ambivalent stance, a number of social and psychological forces work to persuade tempered radicals to forfeit one side of themselves or the other. Below we discuss pressures against an ambivalent stance. Most of these are forces of assimilation. We begin with a discussion of the painfulness of being seen as a hypocrite, of feeling isolated, and of being tempted to abandon the fight. We then tell a story of our own gradual co-optation from a feminist to a more mainstream research agenda. We identify from within this story several forces that can lead a tempered radical to resolve the inconsistency of her identities by trying to become an insider.

Perceptions of Hypocrisy

Tempered radicals speak to multiple constituencies, which poses the problem that they will be seen as too radical for one and as too conservative for another. An even more complex problem for a tempered radical is receiving mixed feedback from within a single constituency, particularly one she thought she understood and represented. The headline on a front page article in the *London Herald Tribune*—"[Jesse] Jackson is a Symbol to Some U.K. Blacks and Sellout to Others"—speaks to this difficulty.

> At the mention of the Reverend Jesse L. Jackson, they (a group of Black, working class "Brits") began, grudgingly at first, to show interest. "If he's gone that far," insisted one, "it must be because he's White inside." . . . "Listen, man" said a third (man), "A Black man running for president of the United States. It's important." In London's Black ghettos, Mr. Jackson is a curiosity, a symbol of success and to some, a sellout. It is the latter view, held by many of this generation of British-born Blacks, that is most worrying to those who believe, like Mr. Jackson, that the way to equality is to win power within the institution. . . . Yet few Black Britons seem to share Mr. Jackson's faith in the concept of pushing from within and some of these see him as a sellout. (DeYoung 1988, p. 1)

That some Black, working-class "Brits" viewed Jackson as a "sellout" while others viewed him as a sign of hope and change may, ironically, reflect his effectiveness as a tempered radical.

If the issue were only that some people see a tempered radical one way and others see her another way, then the tempered radical could simply manage these images separately and sequentially. Theories of managing multiple constituencies counsel letting each side see that which is most favorable to its interests (Goffman 1959). However, some people can see both images simultaneously. In this situation, tempered radicals may be accused of being hypocritical, that is, of trying to act in a situation like they are different from or better than who they in fact really are. "Liberals are particularly likely to be charged with [hypocrisy], because they are given to compromise" (Shklar 1984, p. 48). Some observers may be confused about who the tempered radical is or what she "really" stands for. Her activist friends may think she lets them take the heat from conservatives while she wins favor and the perquisites of being an insider. Her friends inside the organization may wonder if she is secretly more critical of them than she lets on.

The problem is that the tempered radical does not have a single identity that is "true" and another that is "staged." The ambiguity of having two identities may cause others to believe the tempered radical is strategically managing impressions and trying to win approval from two audiences. Once impression management is suspected, observers give less credibility to the person who appears inconsistent (Goffman 1969). Some of the tempered radicals we interviewed experienced significant stress from being labeled hypocritical or from worrying about such impressions. In the words of an anonymous tempered radical, "The worst is feeling like people who I care about think I am being fickle. I've been called a hypocrite. It stinks."

The social stigma of hypocrisy is painful. Combined with the psychological discomfort of dissonance (Bem 1972, Festinger 1964), it might drive a tempered radical to want to seek the relief of consistency and a more consonant identity. This adaptation would require forfeiting one side of her ambivalent stance or the other. We feel that most pressures point toward assimilation and surrendering the "outside" identity and commitments.

Though forces of assimilation are powerful, one tempered radical pointed out to us that we overemphasized how "easy" it was for a tempered radical to become coopted and end up fully an insider. She cautioned us that, for her and others, one of the main challenges of a professional career was to be accepted as an insider at all. The insiders were insistent on seeing her as different and on treating her as such in a variety of obvious and subtle ways. The number of help books that try to teach women how to fit in (e.g., Harrigan 1977) attests to both the appeal of learning the rules of the game and the high hurdles to succeeding.

Isolation

Perhaps a tempered radical can never go home to one community and identity or another. Tempered radicals are often lonely. A tempered radical may fear that affiliating too strongly with an identifiable group, either outside or inside the organization, may push her too close to one side and jeopardize her credibility with the other side. One tempered radical described her fear:

> In my field (forestry), if you are seen with women you are viewed as unprofessional. Real professionals talk to men about forestry, not to women about recipes. So if you talk to other women you are seen as either a lesbian or not professional. [I am] terrified to be seen with a group of women.

Given this fear, some tempered radicals become vague about their identification with various coalitions in the hopes of not threatening their legitimacy and affiliation with insiders. The feeling of isolation may cause the tempered radical to look for acceptance and companionship in the organization. Some try to prove their loyalty by conforming, sometimes emphatically, to dominant patterns of behavior or by turning on members of their outside group (Kanter 1977).

Feelings of isolation may intensify as the tempered radical advances within the organization. Ironically, just as a tempered radical approaches a higher position from which she hopes to effect change, she experiences more intensely the feelings of isolation that could pull her away from her change agenda into a position of comfortable belonging. One feminist executive reported to us that once she had become well established in a conservative organization, the few women who had been her peers along the way had dropped out, been dismissed, or been completely assimilated into the mainstream. As a relatively high-status insider (with strong ambivalence), she was structurally and institutionally closer to the center of her work organization and profession and therefore felt even more distance between her professional and personal identities. Among peers, her gender still kept her distant from male colleagues perceived as more promising candidates for further advancement. With respect to lower level employees, her high status created an awkward social and emotional distance. She hoped that junior employees with radial and idealistic beliefs would come talk to her, yet, because of her status, they did not assume she was like-minded or approachable. Because she did not advertise her outsider affinities, precisely so that she could be more effective, she experienced the pain of not being taken seriously by those whom she would have liked to reach.

Pressures of Cooptation

A number of pressures push the tempered radical away from the "outsider" piece of her identity and more fully toward the "insider" piece. The remainder of this section describes in detail the ways in which compromises can lead to cooptation. Since we experienced a variety of these coopting mechanisms over the course of this project, we tell our story as an illustration.

We began what we now call the "tempered radical" project as graduate students with a concern about the problems of feminist executives and academics. We wondered where those with the radical voices heard in the 1960s and 1970s had gone to work in the 1980s and whether they had found ways to change institutions. We were warned by faculty members that asking questions about "radical" or "feminist" change within organizations was itself radical and risky, particularly for graduate students who had not established secure positions within the academic or business communities. In addition, our identification and emotional investment threatened our perceived legitimacy as "objective" researchers. We were advised to conceive of this problem, not as a problem for feminists or radicals, but as a more general problem: effecting change from within a system. This approach would allow us to detach ourselves and, most important, avoid being labeled "radicals"—or worse, "feminists"—so early in our careers.

The advice to detach ourselves and cast the problem in the more abstract and conceptual terms of the field seemed like a reasonable compromise and like an intellectual exercise from which we might learn. We planned to come back to the feminist executive as a special case after we had developed theory about the general case. We hoped we could avoid the two painful pulls we were beginning to study: being dismissed as radicals or indefinitely deferring our true interests.

As we searched for comparable change agents inside organizations, we were presented with an opportunity to study corporate ethics officers, who were charged with implementing possibly controversial ethics programs within corporations. Corporate ethics officers, unlike feminist executives, were accessible and easy to study. Ethics programs had recently been mandated and the ethics officers were negotiating immediate change, so we seized the moment. The research involved extensive traveling, interviewing, and data analysis. We found that the topic interested academic and nonacademic audiences and could easily attract research funding. When we were asked about our research interests, it became easier for us to talk about corporate ethics programs in a vividly illustrated, theoretically compelling, and not too provocative way than to talk about the touchy subject of feminist executives. No one suggested that we try another topic or bundle this study into another research package.

Our language, audience, and ultimately our research problem gradually changed. Our study took on a life of its own and resulted in several papers about corporate ethics programs in the defense industry. This story illustrates how compromises in (1) language, (2) timing, and (3) emotional expression can lead to cooptation. We discuss each of these in detail below.

Diverse literatures dealing with change recommend using insider language to package, "sell," or legitimate a change program (e.g., Alinsky 1972, Dutton and Ashford 1993). The use of insider language may be even more essential when proposed changes intervene at a deep level to challenge the assumptions and values of the organization (Frost and Egri 1991). Catchy specifics in the language of the status quo can catalyze cooptation. For example, as our study progressed, we talked more about "corporate ethics officers" in place of internal change agents and "defense industry ethics programs" in place of organizational change efforts. Our language shifted, in a direction and with a speed, that surprised us. To reflect our insider knowledge of the world of ethics programs in the defense industry, we spoke of "ethics hotlines," "fraud, waste, and abuse," and the "defense industry initiative." Before we knew it, the "feminist executive" had faded in our memories and was filed away for "future research."

The role of language in coopting participants has been vividly portrayed in Cohn's (1987) study of the world of defense intellectuals. In a world where men (almost exclusively) spend their days matter-of-factly strategizing about "limited nuclear war," "clean bombs," "counterforce exchanges," and "first strikes," Cohn assumed the role of participant observer to ask the question: "How could they talk this way?" To gain legitimacy in the system, she learned to speak the language of insiders. As Cohn learned the language, she became less shocked by the cold-bloodedness of the talk, and eventually engaged by it:

> The words are fun to say; they are racy, sexy, snappy. . . . Part of the appeal was the power of entering the secret kingdom, being someone in the know. . . . Few know, and those who do are powerful. . . . When you speak it, you feel in control. (Cohn 1987, p. 704)

The more proficient she became in the language, the easier it became to talk about nuclear war and the more difficult it became to speak as a critical outsider. As her language shifted to "defense-speak," the referent shifted from people to weapons. Human death became "collateral damage."

> I found that the better I got at engaging in this (insider) discourse, the more impossible it became for me to express my own ideas, my own values. I could adapt the language and gain a wealth of new concepts and reasoning strategies—

but at the same time the language gave me access to things I had been unable to speak about before, it radically excluded others. I could not use the language to express my concerns because it was physically impossible. This language does not allow certain questions to be asked or certain values to be expressed. (Cohn 1987, p. 708)

Thus, the power of language was not in the ability to communicate technically, but rather in its capacity to rule out other forms of talk, thought, and identity.

The temptation to defer radical commitments adds another pressure toward cooptation, as we learned in our own experience. Our ethics officer study was intended as a short deferral, but we strayed from our original concern further and for longer than we planned. Early invitations to talk about this topic at conferences took us deeper into this line of research, which forced us to learn more, which led to more opportunities and papers, which generated more knowledge and questions to be researched. Such is the course of a "research stream." Compromise behaviors create environments that require more of the same behaviors (Weick 1979).

Like other compromise solutions, the strategy of deferring radical commitments until a foothold is established seems reasonable. From the tempered radical's perspective, it might seem less risky to advance more threatening agendas from a position of power and security. She might be tempted to wait and collect what Hollander (1958) calls "idiosyncrasy credits" by initially conforming to and exemplifying the organization's norms. Later, when she accumulates enough credibility, trust, and status, she would "spend" these credits to reshape organizational norms. However, this deferred radicalism may stall the change effort in two ways. First, when "later on" arrives, the tempered radical may have lost sight of her initial convictions. Second, it may become impossible to tell when "the moment" has arrived to cash in credits. It is always tempting to wait until one has yet more formal power and security and can *really* effect change.

As individuals wait longer to disclose their identities and agendas and spend more time investing in their careers, it becomes more difficult to resist cooptation on material, psychological, and political grounds. Ferguson (1984) doubts that women can transform traditional bureaucracies from within them:

They (liberal feminists) hold out the hope that once women have made their way to the top, they will then change the rules: "When they get to be dealer—they can exercise their prerogative to change the rules of 'dealer's choice' ". . . . They see women as the hope for humanizing the work would and convincing men of the need for change. By their own analysis, this hope is absurd. After internalizing and acting on the rules of bureaucratic discourse for most of their adult lives, how many women (or men) will be able to change? After succeeding in the system by those rules, how many would be *willing* to change? (Ferguson 1984, pp. 192-193)

In addition, it becomes difficult for the tempered radical to turn her back on, or even criticize, those who were part of her career success. Individuals confront extreme backlash and resentment when they suddenly speak out against injustice after years of quietly tolerating it. Anita Hill is a compelling recent example. Reactions are particularly severe if the people involved have succeeded in the system. They are asked: "If the system is so sexist, why has it treated you so justly and well?" "If you have been quiet in the past, what's the motive for your sudden fuss?" Fear of such accusations cause many to silence their frustrations indefinitely.

Deferral poses one source of cooptation. Tempted radicals can also be coopted by the process of tempering their emotions to appear rational and cool-headed, to be "the reasonable feminist." Hot-tempered emotion fuels a tempered radical's desire and impetus for change, but this hot side of the emotional balancing act may often lose out to the cool organizational persona, particularly because real, spontaneous emotional expression is far from the norm in most organizational contexts (Mumby and Putnam 1992). Again, our project may be illustrative. We have tried to make this paper, in form and content, an expression of our own tempered radicalism. As such, we have struggled with the balance between making it legitimate for publication and making it true to the lived experience. As we read and re-read interview transcripts, we began to think of our allies and colleagues as "data." In our effort to get the paper published, part of the "balance," we consistently have "over-tempered." Our tempered radical began to appear as a highly rational strategist who at every turn attempts to reach a balance, appeal to multiple constituencies, and optimize impressions.

Many of our tempered radical colleagues complained that our description missed the essence of the experience: the heat, passion, torment, and temper that characterize the experience of being a tempered radical. Some argued that in our effort to construct a theory about tempered radicals, we over-categorized and overrationalized the phenomenon and, in doing so, unwittingly made our protagonist and paper complicit in maintaining traditional constraints. Other reviewers, however, complained that the paper lacked a coherent theoretical strategy, was not sufficiently grounded in a single literature, and was too inconsistent in its style. The interweaving of self-reflective narrative and theory in this paper represents our ambivalent and somewhat unsatisfying response to this problem. As we tried to satisfy some readers, we inevitably lost others. This very experience heated up the frustration of tempered radicalism for us.

Emotional Burdens

As sociologists and psychologists remind us, ambivalence generates anger plus a variety of powerful, unpleasant emotions, which also contribute to the difficulty of sustaining this posture. Among others feelings, a tempered radical's ambivalence may result in guilt and self doubt (Weigert and Franks 1989), which arise when people cannot live up to their own ideals (Goffman 1963). An assistant to the Chancellor of a major university revealed to us her continuing anguish:

> There are qualified people who get turned down (for tenure) just because they are women. And my job is to make sure that doesn't happen. Sometimes I feel like I have hit a grandslam, but my team was already behind by seven and so . . .
> there's no victory for me and there's no victory for her. There's only the lingering feeling in both of our minds that I didn't do it good enough. If I had just done a little more or done it a little better, done a little differently, played my cards a little better or viewed it from a slightly different angle or made a slightly different argument. . . .I find that it is impossible for me to suffer enough to absolve myself when we get done. It's extremely difficult for someone to deal with that because my energy has nowhere to go. And so I find myself flagellating myself in most extraordinary and creative ways when the problems are institutional and it didn't matter what I did. . . . The pressure I feel because I know the pain that they are in. I don't sleep.

For those with a history of being outsiders, the self-doubt arising from ambivalence can be particularly debilitating, as illustrated in this depiction of Black students' experiences:

> Students who strive to assimilate while covertly trying to remain engaged with Black experience suffer extreme frustration and psychological distress. . . . Maintaining this separation is difficult, especially when these two contradictory longings converge and clash. . . . On the surface, it may appear that he has coped with this situation, that he is fine, yet his psychological burden has intensified, the pain, confusion, and sense of betrayal a breeding ground for serious mental disturbance. (hooks 1989, pp. 67-68)

One tempered radical says, "It is corrosive to constantly feel disrespected by the system. . . . It has been a struggle for me to feel good about myself in the face of collegial disapproval and disrespect." Another interviewee admitted that she continually worked in an environment in which "people act as if I am not here." If sustenance for tempered radicals comes from artfully working the system to make changes, this feeling of being devalued can make them wonder whether they are effective and whether it is worth carrying on. Many choose not to and leave, including those who might be important contributors to the organization (Kolb and Williams 1993).

Several features of tempered radicalism can produce stress. Tempered radicals frequently experience role conflict and role ambiguity, which can lead to stress and strain (e.g., Kahn et al. 1964). The tedious rate at which change occurs further frustrates tempered radicals, many of whom report periodic battles with burnout. Because tempered radicals must learn to suppress or temper emotions at times or, worse, hide their identities, they may feel additional stress and frustration from "bottling it up" (Bell 1990, Coser 1979, Worden et al. 1985). As symbols of a marginalized cultural community, they may also worry about how their performance will affect others in their cultural group (hooks 1989; Kanter 1977).

We do not want to end this section on such a pessimistic note. In addition to the pain of loneliness, guilt, self-doubt, and shaky self-esteem, some tempered radicals also report feeling authentic as a result of having a "rather unorthodox, complex identity" (McIntosh 1989), and feeling encouraged by others who can relate to the complexity of their commitments (Gilkes 1982, hooks 1989). We turn now to a discussion of strategies that help tempered radicals effect change and simultaneously sustain their ambivalent identities despite the pressures described above.

STRATEGIES OF CHANGE AND AMBIVALENCE

In general, tempered radicals create change in two ways: through incremental, semi-strategic reforms and through spontaneous, sometimes unremarkable, expressions of authenticity that implicitly drive or even constitute change. In this section, we discuss two change-oriented strategies—small wins and local, spontaneous, authentic action—and discuss how they relate to change, with the additional benefit of sustaining tempered radicals' identities and purposes. The other two strategies we discuss—language styles and affiliations—work in the reverse fashion. They are directed at authentic identities, but also implicitly provoke and redefine change.

The process and politics of change in organizations has been addressed extensively in a variety of literatures, including work on radical change and community organizing (e.g., Alinsky 1972), innovation (e.g., Frost and Egri 1991, Kanter 1983), "championing" (e.g., Howell and Higgins 1990, Kanter 1983), upward influence (e.g., Kipnis et al. 1980, Mowday 1978), "issue selling" (Dutton and Ashford 1993), and impression management (e.g., Goffman 1959, Rafaeli and Sutton 1991). These literatures issue prescriptions that might be useful to the tempered radical as change agent. However, none of these literatures focuses on how problematic and painful identity politics are for the change agent, in part because they do not assume a change agent who is dissident with the organization's fundamental premises. Steering a course between assimilation and separatism is a central and defining issue for the tempered radical.

The tempered radical bears some semblance to the boundary spanner role described in the organizational literature (Pfeffer and Salancik 1978, Scott 1984, Thompson 1967), who must bridge two organizations that have different goals and resources. The tempered radical is different from this classic boundary spanner in the important sense that part of her core identity is threatened by or threatening to the dominant coalition of either or both of the organizations. Even so, tempered radicals may usefully employ some of the strategies of traditional boundary spanners, such as buffering the core aspects of their function in the organization from their change agent role (tempered radicals may be found in roles that are not explicitly chartered to deal with change) or creating bridging strategies with critical external groups.

The change agents in the organizational literature generally do not have broader visions of change in mind. Although terms like "revolutionary" and "deep" are sometimes used to describe change, those terms rarely refer to system change that challenges the embedded assumptions of the status quo (Alinsky [1972] and Frost and Egri [1991] are exceptions). In our review of strategies for tempered radicals, we refer occasionally to these literatures but also break with them.

Small Wins

A small wins approach (Weick 1984, 1992) addresses several problematic aspects of tempered radicalism and seems to be a viable strategy for change and identity maintenance. First, small wins reduce large problems to a manageable size. Big, unwieldy problems produce anxiety, which limits people's capacities to think and act creatively (Weick 1984). A colleague created a small win recently when she convinced the dean of a business school to delay the start of the tenure clock until new recruits' dissertations were complete. (For a variety of systemic reasons, women begin jobs before completing dissertations more frequently than men.) While this policy change goes only a short way toward ending gender-based discrimination, it is a tangible first step with potentially large ramifications.

Second, small wins can be experiments. They may uncover resources, information, allies, sources of resistance, and additional opportunities for change (Weick 1984). Small wins often snowball as they create opportunities and momentum for additional small wins. Weick argued that the real power of small wins as a strategy for social change comes in the capacity to gather and label retrospectively a series of relatively innocuous small wins into a bigger "package" that would have been too threatening to be prospectively adopted. For example, a multipronged work and family policy could have been envisioned in the 1970s but might have been too sharp a departure and perhaps even too radical a label to propose then. However, a gradual accretion of different aspects of the program—from flex-time to on-site child care—has resulted by the 1990s in many companies (almost a quarter of a representative national sample) having or discussing what are now labelled "work/family programs" (Osterman 1994). A series of small wins is "less likely to engage the organizational immune system against deep change" (Frost and Egri 1991, p. 242).

As experiments, small wins act as a system diagnostic. With relatively minor visibility, risk, and disruption, small wins can test the boundaries of an organization's capacity for change. Even "small losses" can be a source of discovery (Sitkin 1992). Alinsky (1972) warned that reformers could miss change opportunities not only by "shooting too high" but also by "shooting too low." The tempered radical never really knows what too high means until she steps over the line or what too low means until she learns of opportunities lost. Moreover, the line between too much and too little is constantly shifting.

Third, a small wins approach encourages picking battles carefully. Tempered radicals possess a limited amount of emotional energy, and they have access to limited legitimacy, resources, and power. The Chancellor's assistant described this problem:

> I have to choose very carefully when I'm going to go against the party line. . . . Like when there's a woman up for tenure and she's been turned down I'm the last person to comment before it goes to the Chancellor. I have to decide who to fight for. Because if every time a woman comes along who's been turned down I say, "Oh my God, what a horrible injustice" then I won't have any credibility with the Chancellor. So I have to take my shots carefully when it's close, because the Chancellor is a very choosy constituent.

Of course, often the tempered radical does not have a neat menu of battles from which to select rationally. To quell rage even temporarily in a way that feels inauthentic can be neither desirable nor possible. The tempered radicals we most admire are those who have been able to draw courage from their anger and sometimes pick battles with fierce drive and reckless abandon.

Fourth, small wins are therefore often driven by unexpected opportunities. To be poised to take advantage of opportunities, the tempered radical's vision of the specific course of change must be somewhat blurry. Relatively blurry vision and an opportunistic approach enable an activist to take advantage of available resources, shifting power alliances, lapsed resistance, heightened media attention, or lofty corporate rhetoric to advance a specific change (Alinsky 1972, Martin et al. 1990). We are reminded of a story told by one tempered radical of another. After receiving an invitation to a corporate Christmas party to which spouses and significant others were invited, a lesbian executive (who had not yet come out at work) informed her boss that she was going to bring her girlfriend. Her boss refused to accept this guest. Enraged, she took the issue (along with samples of corporate rhetoric about diversity) to the CEO, who welcomed her guest and "talked to" her boss. Born out of rage and frustration, this woman's courageous act turned out to be a significant intervention that produced real and symbolic change in the organization.

While a small wins approach can help a tempered radical push change while maintaining her identity, we should point to some risks associated with the small wins approach. First, tempered radicals in high positions may lose sight of the fact that, for lower level employees, some changes may be urgent, or the order of changes may matter a great deal. Although it may not matter in the long run which type of change comes first, employees may be desperate for child care solutions, but able to live quite easily without a policy about delayed partnership reviews.

Second, being driven solely by opportunity may mean that tempered radicals follow, rather than lead, change. They may achieve only those small wins that were there for the asking. Efforts that are too tentative or small may set a change process backwards by making people feel an issue is closed—"OK, we have a day care facility and have solved the 'work/family problem.' " Small wins may distract people from a more fundamental issue, provide a premature sense of completion, or steer a change effort off course.

Even taking these cautions into account, the small wins approach is attractive. Immediate action means that commitments are not being deferred. The accumulation of small wins changes the organizational landscape for later battles, as "outcomes of current political activity form the basis of the future deep structure of interaction" (Frost and Egri 1991, p. 282). Furthermore, as the organization gradually changes, the tempered radical's alignment struggles also shift. The only way for the tempered radical to locate the appropriate degree of resistance is to push continuously against the limits and keep the organization in flux. Smircich's notion of aligning as ongoing, local actions avoids reifying the organization and its limits:

> There isn't really "an organization" out there that I am aligning myself to, rather my actions of aligning are doing organizing for myself and others. . . . [The orga-

nization is not] some independent hard separate reality, imposing itself on us, somehow disconnected from the very patterns of activity from which it is constituted. (Smircich 1986, pp. 6-7)

Because it involves continuous pushing, a small wins approach sustains the tension between what it means to be an insider and what it means to dissent.

In our discussions with tempered radicals, we have heard of few instances in which tempered radicals who "pushed too hard" were not given a "second chance," even if they did push beyond what was organizationally appropriate. If small wins are used as an experiment, then successive tactics can become bolder and better attuned to the environment. An advantage for the tempered radical of being an insider is precisely to learn the dynamics of the local system and be able to act more confidently within it. As several tempered radicals have reminded us, enacting and celebrating small wins help sustain tempered radicals.

Local, Spontaneous, Authentic Action

A second way that change takes place—local, spontaneous, authentic action—is less strategic than small wins. It happens when tempered radicals directly express their beliefs, feelings, and identities. For example, a female surgeon explained how she changed her work environment by behaving more authentically. When she treated each member of her surgical team with respect and displayed compassion toward patients on her rounds, she demonstrated an alternative style of professional behavior. Her treatment of nurses in the operating room modeled new ways for the residents to behave toward nurses and may have helped alter the nurses' and residents' expectations of how teams share power and how surgeons should treat nurses. By acting in a way that was simply authentic, she created resistance to the authoritarian model that others on her team had taken for granted.

Acting authentically, as simple as it sounds, counteracts many of the disadvantages of sustaining ambivalence that we discussed earlier. The tempered radical who behaves authentically, even if this means inconsistently, may not feel dissonant. She and others may be able to accept her ambivalence as complexity (in the person and situation) rather than as insincerity or hypocrisy. The authenticity with which she behaves minimizes the possibility that she will experience feelings of fraudulence, self-doubt, or guilt.

Language Styles

Earlier we described how tempered radicals, forced to adopt the language of insiders to gain legitimacy, risk losing their outsider language and identity.

In this section, we describe some strategies that can be used to counter the cooptive power of insider language. First, speaking in multiple languages and to multiple constituencies can help. While it is easy to imagine how one might speak different languages to different constituencies (e.g., academic to academic audiences, applied to applied audiences), it is harder to see how one might speak multiple languages to the same constituency. For example, some individuals choose to do "diversity work" because of their commitment to social justice, their identification with a marginalized group, and their insights into the dynamics of disadvantage and privilege. Those who work in corporations learn to speak the language of insiders: in this case, to talk about diversity in "bottom line" terms (e.g., recruitment and retention in a changing labor market, innovations born of diverse approaches, access to a broader customer base). However, tempered radicals may be most effective if they speak to each constituency in both languages. They do not channel their language so that business people hear only bottom line rationalizations, nor so that community organizers hear only the social justice reasons for proposed changes. Unexpected internal allies can be discovered in using the language of social justice inside the corporation.

The tempered radical might counter the cooptive power of insider language by using her insider knowledge and facility with the language to deconstruct it and then reconstruct alternative worlds. A few scholars in the management field have begun to deconstruct the traditional discourse in an attempt to expose assumptions, question what has been left unsaid, dislodge the hegemony of the traditional texts, and make room for alternative conceptions of organizing and management (e.g., Calás 1987, Calás and Smircich 1991, Gray 1994, Kilduff 1993, Martin 1990, Meyerson 1994). As a provocative illustration of this genre, Mumby and Putnam (1992) deconstructed the concept "bounded rationality" and then used this deconstruction to reconstruct organizing in terms of "bounded emotionality."

A linguistic strategy that helps avoids cooptation by harnessing the dominant language is captured in the metaphor of jujitsu, a martial art in which the defender uses the energy of the attacker against itself. Tempered radicals can effect change by holding those in power to their own rhetoric and standards of fair play. In our study of corporate ethics officers, we observed this "linguistic jujitsu." Lower level employees appropriated the language of ethics to bolster their claims for more ethical treatment. This tactic worked particularly well in those companies that defined ethics broadly in terms of "treating each other fairly, with dignity and respect." Once such language was publicly espoused by management in ethics training sessions, employees could use it to push for more responsive and accessible grievance channels and other changes consistent with "fairness, dignity, and respect." Managers' fear of losing credibility persuaded them to be responsive to claims that invoked their own language (Scully and Meyerson 1993).

Affiliations

Another approach tempered radicals may find helpful is to maintain affiliations with people who represent both sides of their identity. Almost all of the tempered radicals we interviewed emphasized the importance of maintaining strong ties with individuals, communities, or groups outside of their organization. These outside affiliations act as sources of information, resources, emotional support, and, perhaps most important, empathy. Affiliations with communities, organizations, and people help mitigate against the difficult emotions associated with ambivalence. Affiliations help keep the tempered radical from suppressing her passion and rage and from acting in a way that makes her feel fraudulent or guilty. They keep her fluent in multiple languages.

The tempered radical's understanding of oppression and injustice can only be preserved by continuing to identify with outsiders. Identifying as an outsider reminds her of her own privilege as an insider (Worden et al. 1985). Bell (1990, p. 463) argues that a Black woman professional can access her bicultural experience as a source of inner strength and empowerment," giving her a feeling of spiritual, emotional, and intellectual wholeness." Affiliations help tempered radicals guard against losing their ability to speak as outsiders. For example, hooks (1989) cautions Black women against losing sight of how their minds have been "colonized," and furthermore, warns against viewing identity politics as an end in itself rather than as a means to an end. Ties to the community are part of "the struggle of memory against forgetting" (hooks 1989).

In our own experience as organizational scholars we have learned to treasure our outside affiliations. For example, our ties to women's studies programs and women's political organizations have served as sources of emotional and intellectual vitality. Our ties to friends and colleagues who are more radical in their approaches have sustained our ambivalent course by encouraging our commitments and nurturing our radical identities. We know two or three people who have taken more radical courses, and we try to imagine them reading our papers. Imagining as well as receiving their feedback helps us to sustain our commitments. Outside affiliations can also provide a sense of independence. One tempered radical claimed that his outside activities as an activist had become a crucial source of self-esteem when he felt alienated from his profession.

In addition to outside ties, connections to like-minded people inside the organization are a source of sustenance. Sometimes tempered radicals are hard to find precisely because their public personae are tempered. Reformers who think the system needs only minor changes and tempered radicals engaged in small wins en route to more massive changes may be difficult sometimes to distinguish. However, sometimes tempered radicals find each other and can build coalitions. Some tempered radicals report that they experience joy and connection because they have a strong sense of community inside as well as outside the organization (e.g., Gilkes 1982, Worden et al. 1985). Even if membership and energy are in flux, there may be a collective momentum that outlives individuals' lulls. In a study of collective action inside organizations (Scully and Segal [1994]), one member of a grassroots coalition reported its importance to her for maintaining organizational and personal attention to diversity issues:

> [The diversity issue] tends to peak and valley. It's not consistent energy, even from the grassroots. I think it goes up and down. I think because of the grassroots efforts, it hasn't been dropped. . . . The grassroots efforts have been instrumental even during the lower periods in bringing it back up to a peak, so I don't think you can do without the grassroots efforts.

We have seen each other through peaks and valleys and benefited from our long-standing collaboration on this project and on projects that grew out it. When one of us felt confused or pulled by the tension inherent in our ambivalent stance, the other could help redefine the tension in terms of excitement or challenge. We did "cooptation check-ins" by phone. When we listened to each other talk about our joint project, we could hear the other's, and sometimes our own, language. We could hear in each other the changes in how we described and thought about our project. We should admit, however, that despite our efforts to keep each other on course, we sometimes failed and became complicit in each other's "digression." Yet, we can without hesitation recommend collaborating with another of like heart and mind.

CONCLUSION

This paper has focused on the tempered radical as an internal change agent quite different from those more commonly portrayed in the literature. Although tempered radicals face many of the same challenges, they also confront unique challenges associated with their ambivalent identities and their broader definition of ultimate change. This paper contributes to the literatures on change from within organizations by introducing a fundamentally different type of change agent than the protagonists of these other literatures. We hope that this paper also gives tempered radicals a kind of legitimacy, inspiration, and sense of community.

The labor of resistance may be divided among those who push for change from the inside, from the outside, and from the margin, each effort being essential to the others and to an overall movement of change. The importance of maintaining affiliations with colleagues and friends who are more and less radical than oneself may be crucial for tempered radicals, not only as a means to sustain their ambivalent course, but also as a way to make their struggles collective. Tempered radicals may be playing parts in movements bigger than themselves and their organizations. In the course of effecting change, they are helping prepare for bigger changes that more radical outsiders may be better positioned to advance. Tempered radicals can also support insiders who push for big changes from positions of power. Thinking in terms of a collaborative division of labor among activists helps resist the counterproductive tendency, particularly among liberals and radicals, to judge who is being the best and most true advocate for change.

Our effort to recognize tempered radicals comes at a crucial time. Those who do not neatly fit—mostly white women and people of color—have been fleeing mainstream organizations at a high and costly rate (Cox 1993). Some leave because they can no longer tolerate the seemingly glacial pace of change, others leave because they are tired of being devalued and isolated, and still others leave simply because they no longer have the energy to "play the game." This exodus has serious repercussions for organizations.

Tempered radicals represent a unique source of vitality, learning, and transformation. Particularly as organizations attempt to become more global, multicultural, and flexible, they must learn to nurture those organizational members that will push them through a continuous transformation process. As the tempered radical's own survival depends on transforming the organization to achieve alignment, so too the contemporary organization may well depend on aligning with new voices and players in a diverse, global environment.[1]

NOTE

1. Tempered radicals often cannot find each other. If you identify yourself as a tempered radical, and if you are interested in creating links among us and mobilizing isolated activist, please send email to either author (fmeyerson@gsb-peso.stanford.edu or scully@mit.edu).

REFERENCES

Alinsky, S. D. (1972), *Rules For Radicals,* New York: Vintage Books.

Bell, E. L. (1990), "The Bicultural Life Experience of Career-Oriented Black Women," *Journal of Organizational Behavior,* 11, 459-477.

Bem, D. J. (1972), "Self-Perception Theory," in L. Berkowitz (Ed.), *Advances in Experimental Social Psychology,* New York: Academic.

Calés, M. B. (1987), *Organizational Science/fiction: The Postmodern in the Management Disciplines,* Unpublished doctoral dissertation, University of Massachusetts, Amherst, MA.

———— and L. Smircich (1991), "Voicing Seduction to Silence Leadership," *Organization Studies,* 12, 567-601.

Cohn, C. (1987), "Sex and Death in the Rational World of Defense Intellectuals," *Signs: Journal of Women in Culture and Society,* 12, 4, 687-718.

Collins, P. H. (1986), "Learning from the Outsider Within: The Sociological Significance of Black Feminist Thought," *Social Problems,* 33, 6, 514-532.

Coser, R. L. (1979), "Structural Ambivalence and Patterned Mechanisms of Defense," *Training in Ambiguity: Learning Through Doing in a Mental Hospital,* New York, Free Press.

Cox, T. (1993), *Cultural Diversity in Organizations: Theory, Research Practice,* San Francisco, CA: Berrett-Koehler.

Culbert, S. A. and J. McDonough (1980), "The Invisible War: Pursuing Self-Interest at Work," in J. Frost, V. F. Mitchell and W. R. Nord (Eds.), *Organizational Reality: Reports from the Firing Line,* 202-211.

Demo, D. H. (1992), "The Self-Concept over Time: Research Issues and Directions," *Annual Review of Sociology,* 18, 303-326.

DeYoung, K. (1988), "Jackson is Symbol to Some U.K. Blacks and Sellout to Others," *London Herald Tribune,* 1.

Dutton, J. E. and S. J. Ashford (1993), "Selling Issues to Top Management," *Academy of Management Review,* 18, 3, 397-428.

Ferguson, K. E. (1984), *The Feminist Case against Bureaucracy,* Philadelphia, PA: Temple University Press.

Festinger, L. (1964), *Conflict, Decision and Dissonance,* Stanford, CA: Stanford.

Foy, N. (1985), "Ambivalence, Hypocrisy, and Cynicism: Aids to Organization Change," *New Management,* 2, 4, 49-53.

Frost, P. J. and C. P. Egri (1991), "The Political Process of Innovation," in B. S. Staw and L. L. Cummings (Eds.), *Research in Organizational Behavior,* 13, Greenwich, CT: JAI, 229-295.

Gecas, V. (1982), "The Self-Concept," *Annual Review of Sociology,* 8, 1-33.

Gilkes, C. T. (1982), "Successful Rebellious Professionals: The Black Woman's Professional Identity and Community Commitment," *Psychology of Women Quarterly,* 6, 3, 289-311.

Goffman, E. (1959), *The Presentation of Self in Everyday Life,* New York: Doubleday.

———— (1963), *Stigma,* Englewood Cliffs, NJ: Prentice Hall.

———— (1969), *Strategic Interaction,* Philadelphia, PA: University of Pennsylvania.

Gray, B. (1994), "A Feminist Critique of Collaborating," *Journal of Management Inquiry,* in press.

Harrigan, B. L. (1977), *Games Mother Never Taught You: Corporate Gamesmanship for Women,* New York: Warner Books.

Hasenfeld, Y. and M. A. Chesler (1989), "Client Empowerment in the Human Services: Personal and Professional Agenda," *The Journal of Applied Behavioral Science,* 25, 4, 499-521.

Hochschild, A. R. (1983), *The Managed Heart,* Berkeley, CA: University of California.

Hollander, E. (1958), "Conformity, Status, and Idiosyncrasy Credits," *Psychological Review,* 65, 117-127.

hooks, b. (1984), *Feminist Theory from Margin to Center,* Boston, MA: South End Press.

——— (1989), *Talking Back: Thinking Feminist, Thinking Black,* Boston, MA: South End Press.

Howell, J. M. and C. A. Higgins (1990), "Champions of Technological Innovation," *Administrative Science Quarterly,* 35, 2, 317-341.

Jackall, R. (1988), *Moral Mazes: The World of Corporate Managers,* New York: Oxford.

Kahn, R., D. Wolfe, R. Quinn, D. Snoek and R. Rosenthal (1964), *Organizational Stress: Studies in Role Conflict and Ambiguity,* New York: Wiley.

Kanter, R. M. (1977), *Men and Women of the Corporation,* New York: Basic Books.

——— (1983), *The Change Masters,* New York: Simon and Schuster, Inc.

Kilduff, M. (1993), "Deconstructing Organizations," *Academy of Management Review,* 18, 1, 13-31.

Kipnis, D., S. M. Schmidt and I. Wilkinson (1980), "Intraorganizational Influence Tactics: Explorations in Getting One's Way," *Journal of Applied Psychology,* 65, 440-452.

Kolb, D. and S. Williams (1993), "Professional Women in Conversation: Where Have We Been and Where Are We Going?" *Journal of Management Inquiry,* 2, March, 14-26.

Krieger, S. (1991), *Social Science and the Self: Personal Essays on an Art Form,* New Brunswick, NJ: Rutgers.

Lenski, G. E. (1954), "Status Crystallization: A Nonvertical Dimension of Social Status," *American Sociological Review,* 19, 405-413.

Marris, P. (1975), *Loss and Change,* Garden City, NY: Anchor.

Martin, J. (1990), "Deconstructing Organizational Taboos: The Suppression of Gender Conflict in Organizations," *Organization Science,* 1, 339-359.

Martin, J., M. Scully and B. Levitt (1990), "Injustice and the Legitimation of Revolution: Damning the Past, Excusing the Present, and Neglecting the Future," *Journal of Personality and Social Psychology,* 59, 281-290.

McIntosh, P. (1989), "Feeling Like a Fraud: Part Two," Paper presented at the Stone Center, Wellesley College, Wellesley, MA.

Merton, R. K. (1976), *Social Ambivalence and Other Essays,* New York: Free Press.

Meyerson, D. E. (1994), "From Discovery to Resistance: A Feminist Read and Revision of the Stress Discourse," Working Paper, University of Michigan, Ann Arbor, MI.

Mowday, R. (1978), "The Exercise of Upward Influence in Organizations," *Administrative Science Quarterly,* 23, 137-156.

Mumby, D. K. and L. L. Putnam (1992), "The Politics of Emotion: A Feminist Reading of Bounded Rationality," *The Academy of Management Review,* 17, 3, 465-486.

Osterman, P. (1994), "Explaining the Diffusion of Employer-Based Benefits: The Case of Work/Family Programs," unpublished paper, Sloan School of Management, MIT, Cambridge, MA.

Park, R. E. (1928), "Human Migration and the Marginal Man," *American Journal of Sociology,* 33, 881-893.

Pfeffer, J. and G. R. Salancik (1978), *The External Control of Organizations,* New York: Harper and Row.

Rafaeli, A. and R. I. Sutton (1991), "Emotional Contrast Strategies as Means of Social Influence: Lessons from Criminal Interrogators and Bill Collectors," *Academy of Management Journal,* 34, 749-775.

Reinharz, S. (1992), *Feminist Methods in Social Research,* New York: Oxford University Press.

Scott, W. R. (1984), *Organizations: Rational, Natural, and Open Systems, 2nd ed.,* Englewood Cliffs, NJ: Prentice Hall.

Scully, M. and D. Meyerson (1993), "The Separation of Law and Justice: The Implementation of Ethics Programs at Two Companies in the Defense Industry," *Employee Responsibility and Rights Journal,* 6, 4.

———— and A. Segal (1994). "Passion with an Umbrella: The Mobilization of Grassroots Activists in Organizations," unpublished paper, Sloan School of Management, MIT, Cambridge, MA.

Shklar, J. N. (1984), *Ordinary Vices,* Cambridge, MA: Belknap.

Sitkin, S. (1992), "Learning Through Failure: The Strategy of Small Losses," in B. Staw and L. L. Cummings (Eds.), *Research in Organizational Behavior,* 14, Greenwich, CT: JAI, 231-266.

Smircich, L. (1986), "Can a Radical Humanist Find Happiness Working in a Business School?" Paper presented in the symposium. *Alignment in the Development of Social Science-Towards a New Role for Organizational Development,* Annual Meetings of the Academy of Management, Chicago.

Stonequist, E. (1937), *The Marginal Man,* New York: Russell and Russell.

Sutton, S. E. (1991), "Finding Our Voice in a Dominant Key," unpublished paper, University of Michigan.

Thompson, J. D. (1967), *Organizations in Action,* New York: McGraw-Hill.

Warner, J. (1993), "Mixed Messages," *Ms* 4, 3, November/December, 20-25.

Webster's New World Dictionary (1975).

Weick, K. E. (1979), *The Social Psychology of Organizing,* Reading, MA: Addison-Wesley.

———— (1984), "Small Wins: Redefining the Scale of Social Problems," *American Psychologist,* 40-49.

———— (1992), "Wisdom in the 90s: Adaptation Through Small Wins," Hale Lecture #4, University of Michigan, Ann Arbor.

Weigert, A. and D. D. Franks (1989), "Ambivalence: A Touchstone of the Modern Temper," in D. D. Franks and E. McCarthy (Eds.), *The Sociology of Emotions,* Greenwich, CT: JAI.

Worden, O., M. Chesler and G. Levin (1985), "Racism, Sexism, and Class Elitism: Change Agents' Dilemmas in Combatting Oppression," in A. Sargent (Ed.), *Beyond Sex Roles,* 2nd ed., St. Paul, MN: West Publishing Co., 451-469.

14

The Virtues of Closet Qualitative Research

ROBERT I. SUTTON
Department of Industrial Engineering Management,
Stanford University

Qualitative research now enjoys considerable legitimacy in the organizational studies literature. Qualitative data were crucial in developing early perspectives like the human relations school (Roethlisberger and Dickson 1939) and institutional theory (Selznick 1949). Support for qualitative organizational research waned by the late 1960s. Qualitative methods were often portrayed as primitive tools compared to modern, scientific, and quantitative methods like survey research, analyses of archival data, and experiments. By the late 1970s, interest in the support for qualitative research began to build again. A growing number of organizational researchers argued that qualitative methods were well-suited for building theory and writing rich descriptions. And some argued that quantitative research was often so fraught with investigator bias, sampling error, and measurement error that it was not more scientific than qualitative research.

John Van Maanen's 1979 special issue of the *Administrative Science Quarterly* on qualitative methods marked and helped facilitate this increased legitimacy (see Van Maanen 1983). It encouraged experienced researchers to reconsider unflattering views about qualitative methods, and it encouraged doctoral students to do such research. The issue has a strong effect on assumptions about qualitative methods in my doctoral program at The

University of Michigan. I was taught during my first year in the program that quantitative research was scientific and qualitative research was not. I began to unlearn this lesson at a gathering where 50 or so faculty and students— almost all of whom were quantitative researchers—met to discuss Van Maanen's special issue. I was appalled that these quantitative researchers all seemed to support qualitative methods. I was one of the few researchers to speak out against these "messy and unscientific" methods; I was rebuked by Joe White (now Dean of Michigan's Business School) for being narrow-mined, detached from organizational life, and ignorant of the value of qualitative data for theory building.

Joe White's comments stung at the time. But his logic, the special issue, and, later, support from J. Richard Hackman and Robert Kahn, led me to appreciate and use qualitative methods. Many of us who were doctoral students studying organizational behavior at that time subsequently used qualitative methods throughout our careers and have been rewarded for doing so, including Deborah Ancona, Stephen Barley, Jane Dutton, Kathleen Eisenhardt, Connie Gersick, William Kahn, Gideon Kunda, and Anat Rafaeli. Senior scholars who once conducted only quantitative research, but now use qualitative methods as well, include Janice Beyer, Keith Murnighan, Karlene Roberts, Jerry Ross, and Barry Staw. My dissertation advisor, Robert Kahn, conducted quantitative survey research for over 40 years before publishing his first qualitative study at 75 years of age (Kahn 1993).

There are still corners of the organizational literature where qualitative methods lack legitimacy. Journals that appear to follow norms for nonclinical psychological research, like *Journal of Applied Psychology* and *Organizational Behavior and Human Decision Processes,* have yet to publish qualitative research. I also know some researchers who still dismiss qualitative methods as "unscientific." But I know more researchers who are unfairly biased against survey methods. We work in a low paradigm field with little consensus about how research ought to be done and what theories are best (Pfeffer 1993); this lack of consensus means that almost any method or theory will lack legitimacy in some corners.

Participant-observation studies, case studies of single organizations, and qualitative comparisons across individuals, groups, and organizations are now published routinely in *Organization Science (OS), Academy of Management Journal (AMJ),* and the *Administrative Science Quarterly (ASQ).* At *OS,* the editors have written two editorials calling for a move to nontraditional research topics and methods; both express support for qualitative methods (Daft and Lewin 1990, 1993). At *AMJ,* although far more quantitative than qualitative papers are still published, an article with qualitative data has received the best paper award five times during the last decade. At *ASQ*, two of the five editors who make publication decisions—Steve Barley and Keith Murnighan—have published papers with qualitative data in the journal. I have also published qualitative papers in *ASQ* and, during the four years I was an associate editor at *ASQ*, I wrote acceptance letters for nine papers that contained qualitative data.

Nonetheless, although it is now legitimate to publish qualitative papers in most top organizational research journals, the theme of this essay is that there are still circumstances when qualitative research is best treated as a closet activity. My aim is to show that there are times when original qualitative data are crucial for developing an author's ideas, but it may be best—at least from some vantage points—to conceal or downplay the role that such evidence played in developing the ideas. I will show that there are times when closet qualitative research can be justified, even glorified, because it leads to better papers. I will show that there are other times when qualitative research is a closet activity because our norms about what is adequate scholarship are too restrictive or because some editors, reviewers, and journals remain unfairly biased against qualitative research. In such cases, authors may decide—or be required—to hide or downplay their qualitative data if they wish to publish the ideas inspired by such evidence.

I've learned about the virtues of closet qualitative research from trying (and often failing) to write and publish a mix of quantitative, qualitative, and conceptual papers in the organizational literature during the past decade or so. These trials and errors have led me to publish about a dozen papers that were inspired and guided by original qualitative data, but where these data were not mentioned or were de-emphasized. I've found four circumstances when authors, their audiences, or both parties may benefit from treating qualitative research as a closet activity. These are: (1) when weak qualitative data lead to good insights; (2) when describing the qualitative research reduces the quality of the writing; (3) when an outlet does not publish "empirical" papers; and (4) when writing for an audience that remains biased against qualitative research.

This essay focuses on my work because, given this is a closet activity, it is hard to know when and how others have done it. But I do use a few examples of closet qualitative research that colleagues have told me about. And I draw on Cialdini's (1980) chapter on full-cycle social psychology. He explains how qualitative data were used in the "scouting" phase of several quantitative articles even though these qualitative data are not mentioned in these articles. The remainder of this essay explicates the four circumstances where qualitative research may best be treated as a closet activity.

1. WHEN WEAK QUALITATIVE DATA
LEAD TO GOOD INSIGHTS

Qualitative research is well-suited for theory building. Most quantitative methods require that variables be identified, precisely defined, operationalized, measured, and coded, with these criteria usually specified before data collection begins. Cialdini (1980), Eisenhardt (1989), Glaser and Strauss (1967), Mintzberg (1979), and Van Maanen (1983) suggest that, as a result, quantitative methods more narrowly constrain what the investigator will learn about and provide less inspiration and guidance for developing new theory. In contrast, these and other authors contend that qualitative methods allow more flexibility in what variables and processes are encountered and examined. This flexibility means that qualitative methods provide more chances to learn information that is independent of or in contrast to existing theory.

When the goal of qualitative research is theory development, the "significance test" for assessing its quality may seem like it should be restricted to whether or not new, interesting, and logical insights are developed. Concerns about whether or not design and analysis are rigorous enough to confirm such insights may seem irrelevant. After all, the intended product of such research is new insights, not a test of those insights. The open-ended and flexible methods that seem best suited to discovering new insights may seem to be poorly suited for testing the reliability, validity, and generality of those insights. Yet the degree to which many organizational scholars will find the outcome of theory building research to be persuasive is not influenced by just the strength of the theory. Norms for evaluating the outcome of qualitative research are influenced by the standards used to establish generalizability, validity, reliability in quantitative research. Eisenhardt (1989), Glaser and Strauss (1967), and Miles and Huberman (1984) all emphasize that qualitative research should be systematic rather than impressionistic. They propose guidelines about the amount and kind of qualitative data to gather, how to code such information, and how it should be analyzed to provide grounding and credibility for theory.

Norms for systematic qualitative research encourage theorists to think carefully about the definitions of constructs or processes, logical links between constructs or processes, links between theory and evidence, and the extent to which the theory generalizes beyond the sample used to generate it. Systematic approaches do lead to new theory. Connie Gersick (1988), for example, used years of research, hundreds of hours of listening to tapes, and careful analysis to develop her interesting and influential group development model. Systematic collection and analysis of qualitative data has also helped my co-authors and me develop new ideas, explicate the logic supporting our arguments, and provide interesting examples in the dozen or so papers we've written on topics ranging from organizational death (Sutton 1987) to the good-cop, bad-cop technique (Rafaeli and Sutton 1991).

These norms mean that insights are more convincing to most of us when they are grounded in lots of qualitative data. Rich qualitative data are indispensable when an author's goal is to produce interesting and detailed descriptions of organizational life. I am not convinced, however, that there is a particularly strong relationship between the amount of data gathered or other indications of the "rigor" with which qualitative research is done and the quality of the resulting insights. Weick (1989) suggests that the "disciplined imagination" required for building good organizational theory results from an iterative process of trial-and-error thinking. This process of "mental testing" may be triggered and guided by a large pile or a small scrap of qualitative data. The quality of such thinking may, as Weick implies, depend more on the rigor of the thinking process that occurs inside the researcher's head rather than on the rigor with which the stimuli are collected or the number of stimuli collected.[1] I've noticed examples—in my own work, in papers that I edited at *ASQ,* and doctoral committees that I've served on—where much carefully collected and analyzed qualitative data led to nothing new or interesting, just to a bunch of old, boring, and logically flawed assertions. In contrast, I've noticed instances where a speck of qualitative datum triggered sparkling insights, especially in writings by Goffman and Weick. I've also generated new insights from tiny bits of qualitative data or qualitative research that is poor given current standards for good qualitative research. I've learned to think of qualitative data as stimuli that can guide and inspire new ideas, even when the data are so weak that they do not provide much grounding for those new ideas.

When good insights come from qualitative research that will be perceived as incomplete or poor, it may be a good time to publish the insights, but to omit or downplay that the insights were derived from original qualitative data. At least given current norms for qualitative research, the weak data are likely to distract the reader from the insights and cause the reader to question the validity of the insights. Consider the following examples.

It might have looked silly (or at least undermined the persuasiveness of our logical arguments) if Anat Rafaeli and I had explained that many ideas for our conceptual papers on expressed emotion (Rafaeli and Sutton 1987, 1989) were derived from the unplanned questions that we asked during restaurants and other service transactions. For example, Anat once interrogated a waiter at Postrio, one of the most trendy restaurants in San Francisco, about the range of tips he got, what emotional expressions helped him get big tips, and how big a tip he expected from us. Anat and I made no advanced plans about what questions we would ask or who we would ask them to, and we kept no field notes. Yet we often discussed these experiences when writing up our ideas about expressed emotions in organizations. Because we maintained no records about the data we collected, it would have been difficult to write a method section or even a meaningful footnote describing what we did. And, if we had done so, at least given the norms that most of us are socialized to follow, it would have undermined the legitimacy of the resulting ideas.

Cialdini (1980, p. 22) describes how, when he worked at Ohio State, he spent a Saturday morning puzzling over a consistent, but not quite statistically significant, effect in an attitude change experiment. He was still trying to decide how to get an extra half-point effect on a seven-point scale when he went to a football game later that day:

> So engaged, I moved towards my seat, mostly oblivious to the behavior around me. Not for long, though, because the Ohio State team had left the dressing room and had begun to run out in the field, *merely* to run out in the field. The crowd was up and shouting. . . . A large group of fans repeatedly roared "We're number one!" while thrusting their index fingers upward. I recall quite clearly looking up from thoughts of that additional half-unit of movement on a seven-point scale and realizing the power of the tumult around me. "Cialdini." I said to myself, "I think you're studying the *wrong* thing."

This incident is not mentioned in the research that it inspired about how undergraduate football fans "bask in reflected glory" when their teams win games (Cialdini et al. 1976). Nor do I think that it should appear. A statement something like "this research began with 47 seconds of unplanned observation by the first author" might not constitute adequate grounding by even the most liberal standards. I doubt that Cialdini and his co-authors would have been allowed to describe this datum in the *Journal of Personality and Social Psychology (JPSP),* and if they had, it may have undermined the legitimacy of their arguments.

Jeffrey Pfeffer became interested in organizational politics early in his career, when a senior faculty member claimed that the power of their academic department could be increased by teaching more students. Pfeffer told me that he and Gerald Salancik did an informal qualitative study of local resource dependencies that showed teaching more students would reduce rather than increase departmental power; their evidence indicated that teaching more students would lead to no more financial resources and teaching was viewed as having less prestige than research in the school. This modest study guided Pfeffer's initial ideas about power and politics. But it is not mentioned in the books that he wrote on the subject because more persuasive data were gathered and found in published sources to support his ideas (Pfeffer 1981, 1992).

Another form of closet qualitative research entails acknowledging that weak research was done, but downplaying how much it influenced the resulting insights. I did this in a paper on photography and the reconstruction of bygone emotions (Sutton 1992). I asserted that taking, editing, and assembling photographs and describing them to others facilities positively biased selective recall among Disney visitors, even those who were grouchy or bored (Sutton 1992). This paper reads as if I gathered a bit of qualitative data, but the ideas were derived primarily from existing scholarly and popular writings. I must admit, however, that my central insights about the role of photography in remembering and forgetting resulted from one visit. The academic and popular articles that I found later, and cited so heavily, presumably made my assertions more convincing to the audience. But my central insights and supporting logical arguments changed little after this visit. I buried my thin qualitative methods in one sentence in a long footnote. If I had revealed the impact of these weak data on the theory development process, I suspect that my ideas about photo-reconstructed memories would have had less credibility.

Perhaps we ought to change our field's norms so that when suspect qualitative data inspire good ideas, this evidence can be included in the text. These less restrictive norms are already reflected in some book chapters. For example, a footnote indicates that John Van Maanen drew heavily on his work experiences at Disneyland in the late 1960s to write portions of an essay for *Research in Organizational Behavior* approximately 20 years later (Van Maanen and Kunda 1989). Some of the newer journals in our field also seem to allow authors to acknowledge they are drawing on qualitative data that are suspect by more traditional standards. It was probably more acceptable to reveal my weak qualitative data in the Disneyland paper that I published in the new and "nontraditional" *Journal of Management Inquiry* than it would have been in a more staid journal like *AMJ* and *ASQ*.

Regardless of what these norms should be, however, the standards currently used in many top journals mean that authors who have good ideas inspired by thin or otherwise suspect qualitative data can only have the benefit of publication—and readers can only benefit from these ideas—if the data are not mentioned or are downplayed. Some readers may argue that such omissions are unethical "deceptions," that authors should always disclose the sources for their ideas. These omissions might, however, be justified as the lesser of two evils when doing so averts unfair bias that will result in the rejection of sound ideas. Furthermore, authors can never "disclose" every event that occurred during a quantitative or a qualitative study because journals have limited space and readers have limited time and attention. As I argue next, such omissions can be justified, even glorified, when doing so results in more interesting and persuasive papers.

2. WHEN DESCRIBING QUALITATIVE RESEARCH
REDUCES THE QUALITY OF THE WRITING

The belief that writing style is an essential, even *the* essential, feature of a scholarly paper is currently fashionable in many corners of the social sciences.[2] Regardless of whether one believes that the writing is the only important part of a scholarly paper, the most important part, or just one important part, there is agreement that scholarly papers are less likely to be published, or if published, less likely to be read or cited, if they are not sufficiently well-written to hold their readers' attention (Becker 1986, Van Maanen 1989). Linda Pike, *ASQ*'s managing editor, suggests that good academic writing is really good storytelling:

> Storytellers refine a story over time as they tell it to different audiences and see their listeners' reactions. The primary interest is in keeping their listeners' interest. In revising their story repeatedly, they strengthen the story, drop digressions that made their readers fidget, clarify confusions that cause wrinkled brows, and expand on parts of the story that piqued their listener's interest. Most important, they strive to tell a story that satisfies a listener's need for coherence: The story has a beginning, middle, and end. A well-told story captures listeners' attention and makes them want to listen. A well-crafted journal article should do the same. (Pike 1994, p. 1)

Building on Pike's argument, even when an author is writing for an audience that supports qualitative research and when the research is of reasonable quality, there are times when, to tell the story in a manner that will capture and hold the reader's attention, it is best to downplay or avoid mentioning that qualitative data shaped the ideas. Tom D'Aunno, Rick Price, and I did this in a quantitative paper on isomorphism and external support in drug abuse treatment organizations that we published in *AMJ* (D'Aunno et al. 1991). This article was first submitted as two papers, one on isomorphism and the other on external support in drug abuse treatment organizations. Richard Mowday, *AMJ*'s splendid editor, asked us to combine them into a single paper. The original paper on external support contained quotes from a qualitative study of nine organizations. It had been conducted in conjunction with the quantitative survey research that was the primary focus of our article. As we went through the process of combining the two papers into one, however, all original qualitative data were deleted because they hampered the story that we were trying to tell. Some bits of data were interesting and relevant but made a long paper even longer, some were interesting but distracted the reader from our conceptual arguments, and some were boring. As a result, we downplayed the data so much that, although we acknowledged that they helped us develop our ideas, none are left in the published article. The paper is better to read as a result. Similarly, Anat Rafaeli and I published a research note that focused on quantitative data from grocery stores where she had done extensive ethnographic work (Rafaeli and Sutton 1990). This qualitative work is acknowledged in the paper and discussed at several points, but we had to downplay the role these data played in developing our ideas to write a brief research note that flowed well.

Closet qualitative research might be especially useful for coming up with new ideas to make discussion sections more interesting. The discussion section is where authors can go beyond their data and suggest interesting implications. It is also where researchers can explain unexpected findings and suggest boundary conditions for their theory and data. Qualitative data can fuel such creative thoughts. But revealing that such new data were gathered may bore, distract, or irritate the reader. I've never intentionally done a qualitative study for a discussion section. But I once was trying to think of the disadvantages of expressed positive emotion for a discussion section when a colleague called and, without prompting, said something like "I've got to stop being so nice to people. I can't get any work done. When I growl at them, they leave me alone." I didn't put this quote in the paper. But it inspired me to write that grouchy employees may be more productive because they are interrupted less often (Staw et al. 1994, p. 65). If the discussion section had included this qualitative datum and an explanation of where it came from, our arguments might have been less persuasive because they were based on a single data point. And even if we had conducted a thorough qualitative study, it might have been best to avoid mentioning it because justifying and documenting a new study so late in the paper might have ruined the flow.

3. WHEN AN OUTLET DOES NOT PUBLISH ORIGINAL "EMPIRICAL" PAPERS

About 20 years ago, officials of the Academy of Management decided to publish one journal for empirical papers with original data (the existing *Academy of Management Journal*) and a second journal for conceptual papers with little or no original data. This second journal, the *Academy of Management Review (AMR),* is now among the most widely cited outlets in the organizational studies literature (Johnson and Podsakoff 1994). Labeling papers as either "empirical" or "non-empirical" is easy in most cases, but this distinction can cause difficulties when theory is based partly on original data and partly on existing literature. Independently of merit, papers that fall into this void have occasionally proven to be inappropriate for either journal; they don't contain enough original data for *AMJ* but contain too much original data for *AMR*.

I had a paper early in my career that *AMR* declined to publish, in part because it contained too much original data. I had another paper that an *AMR* editor told me not to submit because it contained too much original data. And other colleagues have struggled with the overlap between *AMJ* and *AMR*. Stephen Barley submitted a paper to *AMR* that was sent back because it had too much data. He then submitted it to *AMJ;* it was then rejected despite strong theory because the data were too weak. It is easier not to reveal that some data were collected than to collect more data. So, even when the ideas in papers that I write for *AMR* are shaped by original data of reasonable quality, I don't admit or downplay the role of such evidence. Leonard Greenhalgh, Anne Lawrence, and I published a propositional inventory on workforce reduction strategies in *AMR* (Greenhalgh et al. 1988); several propositions were inspired or refined on the basis of six case studies conducted by a class that I was teaching. The paper was influenced much more strongly by existing literature than by these case studies. We did not mention these original data, in part, so that our paper would not fall into the void between *AMR* and *AMJ*. We did cite one case as a Stanford working paper in the reference section; by doing so, we helped maintain the illusion that no original qualitative data had been used in developing the propositions.

This is not meant as a criticism of *AMJ* or *AMR;* this split generally works well. And I've always found the editors to behave sensibly when papers do fall into this void.[3] The point is that many outlets—not just Academy of Management publications—classify papers as either "empirical" or "conceptual." When theory is developed on the basis of a mix of original qualitative data and existing writings, it may be impossible to publish the resulting insights in a purely "theoretical" outlet if the author reveals the important but partial influence of the original qualitative data. Authors who submit papers to *Psychological Bulletin* may face the same problem because the editorial statement indicates that it only publishes integrative review papers and that only small amounts of original data can be included. In such cases, to get a paper published, or to please readers who don't expect to see original data in an integrative theory or review piece, it may be best to not mention that qualitative (or quantitative) data were gathered, or to de-emphasize its role in developing the paper.

4. WHEN WRITING FOR AN AUDIENCE THAT REMAINS BIASED AGAINST QUALITATIVE RESEARCH

I emphasized at the outset that low par digm development in the organizational area means that any approach, including qualitative methods, will lack legitimacy in some corners. Qualitative methods are, for example, sometimes dismissed by traditional experimental psychologists and econometricans as lacking rigor. An experimental social psychologist once urged me to reject a qualitative paper submitted to *ASQ* primarily because "This is not science." Authors who write for outlets and subfields where such biases are prevalent may be forced to treat their qualitative research as a closet activity if they want to gain legitimacy as scholars and to publish their ideas.

I talked about closet qualitative research for nearly ten years before writing this essay. The inspiration to write it finally came when a doctoral student told me that she planned to do case studies to enhance the theory in her quantitative thesis. The student then told me that, because her advisor was biased against such methods, the case studies would not be mentioned in the thesis, and she intended not to tell the advisor or any other member of her dissertation committee that this work had been done. My first thought was to urge the student to stand up to her narrow-minded advisor. But I then realized that the advisor was unlikely to change her mind, the student would suffer, and it would be partly my fault. I also realized that I'd be hypocritical to press for a confrontation. I too have used closet qualitative research when writing for audiences that I thought were biased. My first sole-authored article reports correlations between stress and strain in 200 schoolteachers (Sutton 1984). Many of these stressors were derived from talking to the teachers who helped us gather these data. I do not mention the qualitative data in this paper because, when I first drafted it, I believed that such soft data had no place in the scientific process. By the time I found a journal that would publish the paper, I appreciated qualitative methods but believed that the reviewers were biased against qualitative methods, so I kept these qualitative data in the closet. Similarly, beyond our desire to write well, a secondary reason that we downplayed the role of the qualitative data in our article on isomorphism and external support (D'Aunno et al. 1991) was that we believed that at least one reviewer was biased against qualitative research.[4]

Cialdini's writings indicate that he used closet qualitative research in his article on the "low-ball procedure" in *JPSP* (Cialdini et al. 1978). Cialdini's (1980) later chapter on full-cycle social psychology describes his participant-observation research as an automobile sales trainee; part of his training involved watching how salespeople persuaded customers to buy cars. He observed that "throwing a low ball" was a common technique: "The customer was given a price figure substantially below the amount at which the salesperson ever intended to sell the car. . . . Once the customer had made the decision for a specific car (and had even begun completing the appropriate forms) the price advantage was deftly removed" (1980, pp. 32-33).

Cialdini's 1980 chapter goes into detail about how his participant-observation research helped him identify the "low-ball" technique, judge it to be effective, and develop ideas about why it was effective. But the introduction to his 1978 *JPSP* article does not indicate that the article was inspired and guided by this participant-observation research. The introduction states that social psychology should look to natural settings for generating new hypotheses, offers references to popular writings including *Consumer Reports* to support assertions that the low-ball tactic is widespread, and provides a detailed description of how the "low ball" is used to sell cars. The text on page 464 of the 1978 *JPSP* article about the low-ball technique closely parallels the text on pages 32 and 33 of the 1980 chapter. The main difference is that the *JPSP* text does not say that this information came from Cialdini's participant-observation (or from any other original qualitative research). The discussion does finally imply—but does not quite come out and say—that the research was guided and inspired by original qualitative data:

> At the outset, we described a sequence for the investigation of compliance-related factors that was designed to increase confidence in the ecological validity of these factors. The sequence suggests that a researcher should begin with a period of observation, perhaps even participant observation, of the procedures, techniques, and tactics that are regularly used in natural compliance settings. . . . Variables, so selected, should then undergo experimental investigation to determine their reliability, generality, and theoretical relevance. The present research used such an approach to examine the low-ball technique, a tactic commonly used to produce compliance in sales settings. (Cialdini et al. 1978, pp. 474-475)

The paper never says what kind of qualitative data were gathered or how these data were used to guide and ground particular assertions. These authors may have left Cialdini's qualitative research as a closet activity before submitting the paper or deleted mention of this research in response to editorial suggestions. Regardless, I believe that it was concealed because participant-observation research was viewed as lacking rigor by most researchers who edited, refereed, wrote for, and read *JPSP* at that time. I applaud Cialdini and his coauthors for stretching—but not quite violating—these norms. If they had presented a detailed description of Cialdini's qualitative methods and described it as a primary source of their ideas, I suspect it would have been more difficult, or even impossible, to publish the paper. And those bold assertions about the value of ecological observation, as they put it "even participant observation," might never have been published in *JPSP*.

If Cialdini and his colleagues submitted a paper to *OS, AMJ,* or *ASQ* showing that their insights were based on participant-observation research, doing so would likely increase the legitimacy of their assertions among most authors and reviewers. But there are still some reviewers at these outlets, and especially outlets like *JAP* and *OBHDP,* who would have a more positive reaction if such qualitative data were omitted, obfuscated, or de-emphasized.

CONCLUSION

I began this essay by asserting that there is now widespread support for qualitative methods. I hope that the legitimacy of qualitative research will continue to increase so that good qualitative research need not be hidden because others are unfairly biased against it. And, in my core discipline of psychology, I hope that norms change so that openly qualitative papers can be published in *JAP, JPSP,* and *OBHDP* someday.

Even if this little fantasy comes true, however, there would be a place for closet qualitative research. An underlying theme of this essay is that even if qualitative research had full support in every corner of the organizational sciences, and every corner of the wider behavioral sciences literature, there would still be circumstances where it would be best to do it but not admit it. More generally, all researchers encounter circumstances where they believe that, in order to practice their craft well, it is best not to reveal certain steps that occurred during their research to the reader. Gary Alan Fine (1993) shows in his article "Ten Lies of Ethnography" that being honest and candid can do ethical harm, reduce the quality of the research, reduce the quality of the writing, and harm the researcher's reputation. This theme also seems applicable to quantitative research. I've been toying with writing a sequel to this essay called "The Virtues of Closet Quantitative Research." I have more experience with closet qualitative than quantitative research. But I've realized that, between my own experiences and stories I've heard from colleagues, I might be able to scrape together enough examples for a sequel that follows the structure of this essay. I can't find any examples where closet quantitative research was used to improve ideas in the discussion section or because the audience was biased against quantitative research. But I suspect that I could dig up examples if I started looking around.

Closet qualitative and quantitative research will always have a place in the organizational studies literature because, as Linda Pike (1994) argues so well, good scholarly writing tells a story that captures the readers' attention and interest. Keeping some of the research in the closet is one way that authors can avoid creating bored, irritated, and cynical readers. More broadly, many of the steps required to do good scholarly writing play a role like scaffolding does in the construction of a building. You need to use it to make something that is beautiful and useful. But if it is left as part of the finished product, the beauty and utility will be difficult for others to see.

NOTES

1. I am also not convinced that collecting qualitative data from many people, groups, or organizations usually helps researchers support claims that their insights can be generalized beyond the authors' sample. Regardless of whether qualitative researchers use a large or tiny sample, they almost never have a sample that is representative of a known population. The use of convenience samples means that most qualitative research cannot support claims that findings can be generalized (Kish 1965). There is no reason to believe, for example, that findings from a convenience sample of one-thousand organizations are any more or less representative of a known population than findings from a convenience sample of one organization. I should also add, however, that most quantitative field studies use convenience samples and suffer from this drawback as well.

2. For examples of literature on the social sciences as writing, see Becker (1986), Clifford (1988), Rabinow and Sullivan (1979), Richardson (1990), and Van Maanen (1989). The recent debate between John Van Maanen (1995) and Jeffrey Pfeffer (1995) in *Organization Science* is partly a reflection of and a reaction to this emphasis on the importance of writing in the social sciences and to related work on narrative as a form of knowledge (Bruner 1986). Van Maanen's (1995, p. 135) "Style as Theory" provides a compelling argument for the importance of writing persuasive text, asserting that "Rather than mirroring reality, our theories help generate reality for readers." Pfeffer's (1996) is also persuasive, arguing that, while writing is important, many of our best theorists do more than induce belief and generate reality in reader's minds, they develop objectively replicable, teachable, and transferable concepts and methods. Both authors agree, however, that good writing is important in the organizational studies.

3. William Kahn's (1990) paper on business ethics suggests that some *AMR* papers can contain substantial amounts of original data: it states that it is based on 32 interviews that he conducted. This paper was published in *AMR* rather than *AMJ* because its purpose was to develop a research agenda rather than to test or develop theory.

4. One of the reviewers of this paper expressed concern that, because I am a tenured professor (rather than a vulnerable novice like this student), by describing how I choose to conceal my qualitative data in the face of such bias, "It seems to me that you perpetuate this kind of bias and bullying rather than arguing against it." This comment upset me because I have no desire to perpetuate bias against qualitative research: I've fought against it as an editor, reviewer, author, and dissertation committee member. I've withdrawn qualitative papers from journals because I wouldn't change them to meet the demands of biased editors, and I've made enemies of several colleagues because I argued so vehemently that their biases were misguided and destructive. The fact remains, however, that novices and senior scholars are similar in that they sometimes face this choice of whether to fight bias or hide their qualitative data; there are costs to battling with people who are biased against qualitative research, and those costs may not be worthwhile in every instance.

REFERENCES

Becker, H. (1986), *Writing for Social Scientists,* Chicago, IL: University of Chicago Press.
Bruner, J. (1986), *Actual Minds, Possible Worlds,* Cambridge, MA: Harvard University Press.
Cialdini, R. B. (1980), "Full-cycle Social Psychology," in L. Bickman (Ed.), *Applied Social Psychology Annual,* Beverly Hills, CA: Sage Publications.

————, R. J. Borden, M. R. Walker, Thorne, S. Freeman, and L. R. Sloan (1976), "Basking in Reflected Glory: Three (Football) Field Studies," *Journal of Personality and Social Psychology,* 34, 366-375.

————, J. T. Cacioppo, R. Basset, and J. A. Miller (1978), "Low-ball Procedure for Producing Compliance: Commitment Then Cost," *Journal of Personality and Social Psychology,* 36, 463-476.

Clifford, J. (1988), *The Predicament of Culture,* Cambridge, MA: Harvard University Press.

D'Aunno, T., R. I. Sutton, and R. L. Price (1991), "Organizational Isomorphism and External Support in Conflicting Institutional Environments: The Case of Drug Abuse Treatment Units," *Academy of Management Journal,* 34, 636-661.

Daft, R. L. and A. Y. Lewin (1990), "Can Organization Studies Begin to Break Out of the Normal Science Straight Jacket? An Editorial Essay," *Organization Science,* 1, 1-10.

———— and ———— (1993), "Where Are the Theories for the 'New' Organizational Forms? An Editorial Essay," *Organization Science,* 4, 1-4.

Eisenhardt, K. M. (1989), "Building Theories from Case Study Research," *Academy of Management Review,* 14, 532-550.

Fine, G. A. (1993), "Ten Lies of Ethnography," *Journal of Contemporary Ethnography,* 22, 267-294.

Gersick, C. J. G. (1988), "Time and Transition in Work Teams: Toward a New Model of Group Development," *Academy of Management Journal,* 31, 9-41.

Glaser, B. and A. Strauss (1967), *The Discovery of Grounded Theory: Strategies for Qualitative Research,* London: Wiedenfeld and Nichols.

Greenhalgh, L., A. T. Lawrence, and R. I. Sutton (1988), "Determinants of Workforce Reduction Strategies in Declining Organizations," *Academy of Management Review,* 13, 241-254.

Johnson, J. L. and P. M. Podsakoff (1994), "Journal Influence in the Field of Management: An Analysis Using Salancik's Index in a Dependency Network," *Academy of Management Journal,* 37, 1392-1407.

Kahn, R. L. (1993), *An Experiment in Scientific Organization,* MacArthur Foundation Occasional Paper, Chicago, IL: MacArthur Foundation.

Kahn, W. A. (1990), "Toward an Agenda for Business Ethics Research," *Academy of Management Review,* 15, 311-328.

Kish, L. (1965), *Survey Sampling,* New York: Wiley.

Miles, M. B. and A. M. Huberman (1984), *Qualitative Data Analysis,* Beverly Hills, CA: Sage Publications.

Mintzberg, H. (1979), "An Emerging Strategy of 'Direct' Research," *Administrative Science Quarterly,* 24, 580-589.

Pfeffer, J. (1981), *Power in Organizations,* Marshfield, MA: Pitman.

———— (1992), *Managing with Power,* Boston, MA: Harvard Business School Press.

———— (1993), "Barriers to the Advance of Organizational Science: Paradigm Development as a Dependent Variable," *Academy of Management Review,* 18, 599-620.

———— (1995), "Mortality, Reproducibility, and the Persistence of Styles of Theory," *Organizational Science,* 6, 681-686.

Pike, L. J. (1994), "Writing as a Storyteller's Art," presented at the 1994 National Academy of Management Meetings, Dallas, TX.

Rabinow, P. and A. Sullivan (Eds.) (1979), *Interpretive Social Science,* Berkeley, CA: University of California Press.

Rafaeli, A. and R. I. Sutton (1987), "The Expression of Emotion as Part of the Work Role," *Academy of Management Review,* 12, 23-37.

—— and —— (1989), "The Expression of Emotion in Organizational Life," in L. L. Cummings and B. M. Staw (Eds.), *Research in Organizational Behavior,* 11, Greenwich, CT: JAI Press, 1-42.

—— and —— (1990), "Busy Stores and Demanding Customers: How Do They Affect the Expression of Positive Emotion?" *Academy of Management Journal,* 33, 623-637.

—— and —— (1991), "Emotional Contrast Strategies as Means of Social Influence: Lessons From Bill Collectors and Interrogators," *Academy of Management Journal,* 33, 623-637.

Richardson, L. (1990), *Writing Strategies: Reaching Diverse Audiences,* Newbury Park, CA: Sage Publications.

Roethlisberger, F. G. and W. J. Dickson (1939), *Management and the Worker,* Cambridge, MA: Harvard University Press.

Selznick, P. (1949), *TVA and the Grass Roots,* Berkeley, CA: University of California Press.

Staw, B. M., R. I. Sutton, and L. H. Pelled (1994), "Employee Positive Emotion and Favorable Outcomes at the Workplace," *Organization Science,* 5, 51-71.

Sutton, R. I. (1984), "Job Stress Among Primary and Secondary Schoolteachers: Its Relationship to Well-being," *Work and Occupations,* 11, 7-27.

—— (1987), "The Process of Organizational Death: Disbanding and Reconnecting," *Administrative Science Quarterly,* 32, 542-569.

—— (1992), "Feelings About a Disneyland Visit: Photography and the Reconstruction of Bygone Emotions," *Journal of Management Inquiry,* 1, 178-287.

Van Maanen, J. (1983), *Qualitative Methodology,* Beverly Hills, CA: Sage Publications.

—— (1995), "Style as Theory," *Organization Science,* 6, 133-143.

—— (1989), "Some Notes on the Importance of Writing in Organization Studies," *Harvard Business School Research Colloquium,* Boston, MA: Harvard Business School Press, 27-33.

—— and G. Kunda (1989), "Real Feelings: Emotional Expression and Organizational Culture," in L. L. Cummings and B. M. Staw (Eds.) *Research in Organizational Behavior,* 11, Greenwich, CT: JAI Press, 43-104.

Weick, K. E. (1989), "Theory Construction as Disciplined Imagination," *Academy of Management Review,* 14, 516-531.

15

Critical Issues in Organization Science

A Dialogue, Part 2

JOHN M. JERMIER
College of Business, University of South Florida
STEWART R. CLEGG
Faculty of Business and Technology, University of Western Sydney

DIRECTIONS

John: A second thing I would like to do in this interview, Stewart, is explore some more general philosophical issues that are relevant to developing a science of organizations and organizing. This is a very interesting time to be a student of organization science as the most fundamental questions are being raised about the nature of both organizations and science. Something that has crossed my mind often, especially lately, is that the field of organization science points toward social processes and social practices, namely organizations and science, neither of which exist in the meaningful sense that once constrained, bounded and defined them. At the margins they are in the process of radical transformation. Take the concept of organization, for example. We have networks, we have information technology and computers, remote work stations, and are ascending to a level of spatial disarticulation previously never achieved. Perhaps the essence of organizations doesn't even exist in the way that we thought before, in concrete material forms. How do you theorize adequately an organizational world that is changing like this? Today, what is an organization?

Stewart: In Scotland, in the most remote part of the Orkneys, there are people who have chosen to live in crofts who control through their computer terminals the flow of traffic in the shipping lanes in Hong Kong. I'm not sure there is any singular necessity attached to the category "organization" anymore. However, discursively, if we continue to talk about something called organization, then we're constituting it as existential, as existing. Yet, this is to say that discursively we continue to constitute it in very many changing ways. Some of the very many changing ways in which we constitute it, in what Giddens calls the "double hermeneutic," have an impact on the ways in which agents out there in the world do their jobs, actually go about doing organization.

Organizations are historically constituted, they're historically evolving, they're socially constructed and they're socially changing all the time. In our analytic abstractions we fix various more or less pervasive representations of them, that get fixed discursively for periods of time. They become the predominant pathways to understanding. However, no concept of social reality is eternal. We're not dealing with the solid unchanging material world that some of us might think our natural science colleagues and the other faculties deal with. We're dealing with a matter that is much more fluid. It is much more unstable and uncertain, not in the sense of being chaotic, because many organizations achieve the status of highly routinized phenomena—that is a way in which we recognize some of them. But it's a kind of rolling routinization. There is routinized drift and change and transformation . . .

A central metaphor has to be of organizations not as solid stable matter, not as things that are recurrent, eternal, essential verities, not as things that are fixed categorically once and for all, but as entities that are socially constructed and socially changing. And, the changes interconnect dialectically with the kinds of representations and observations that people like us are involved in making. Organizations are the effect, in part, of an ongoing conversation. They' a discursive effect of the kinds of conversations that go on inside organizations, go on between organization theories and organizations, go on between organization theories and consultants, consultants and corporations, governments and organizations, employee bodies and organizations and a myriad of other bodies. To have the notion that there is something out there that is like a piece of masonry that a professional licensed mason whom we call an organization theorist can chisel and design until it's perfect, well, it seems to me to be nothing so much as part of a self-aggrandizing professional project. It bears very little relationship to the way in which organizational phenomena ordinarily and discursively get constructed. It may build a bridgehead against some more imperialist disciplinary tendencies, such as the economists, in the Business School world of social science. It is not evident that the views that I am advancing here would be fashionable in many

Business School contexts. There the notion of theorist as analogous to a doctor often is proposed. But, of course, this is a misguided analogy. One's liver, as far as one is aware, may have a problem if one regularly abuses it, but it does not give literal "voice" in the decision process one has concerning what to consume or not to consume until such a stage as the damage is done. The medical metaphor for organization and management theory founders on an unwarranted organicism.

John: Prior to a session yesterday, I heard a colleague talking about this issue of the reality of organizations. She made reference to Karl Weick's view (or at least a view he might not be too far from) in suggesting that the organization leaves when the people leave on the subway at night. Any comments?

Stewart: Well, it does some of both things. Certainly some aspects of some organizations leave when the people leave on the subway at night, but they come back to work the next day and usually they haven't radically changed overnight. They carry the same sorts of disciplinary mechanisms, the same sorts of institutional framing with them, which produce the very material routines that we experience as a reality of the organization. The truth of the matter lies in neither position entirely. A very good example of that is to look at organizations that have been constructed from blueprints in the most adverse kinds of contexts and situations. The establishment of monasteries for instance, particularly in colonial situations, as Jon Miller's work demonstrates, is a very good example. There was plenty of documentation about how to go about setting up a Jesuitical institution. So it could be done even in the most adverse and inhospitable ecological and social climates. A climate where you're literally under siege by the surrounding population; nonetheless it could be done through the usual ways in which organizations make systematicity. Through procedural manuals, through rules, through routines, through disciplinary mechanisms that are both tangible and real and written down and formal and some of which get instilled into the very fiber, what the monks called the soul, of their members. In that respect I think those organizations are no different from organization today.

Remember Etzioni's categories, the different kinds of organization power and compliance structures, and the model of structural balance across the diagonal? Much of recent organization theory, particularly of the more evangelical kind, the sort of stuff that sells well in the marketplace, looks to be a concerted attempt to move the calculative/remunerative relationship to one that is more moral and remunerative. The employee gets pushed toward having a moral relationship with the organization. One thinks of the literature by Deal and Kennedy on Corporate Cultures, of Ouchi's Theory Z, of Peters and Waterman's *In Search of Excellence*. The whole excellence literature is a very interesting example of the phenomenon. Now that moral commitment is something that can walk out of the office door but, according to this genre, if you're successful in creating it, it walks onto the subway in the evening and right back in the next day. Such theory seeks to provide the conditions for its own truth.

John: The other aspect of organization science that seems to be in radical flux is the very meaning of science itself. In fact, one of the reasons *Organization Science* came into existence was to provide an outlet for work underwritten by alternative social philosophies and research paradigms. This is reflected in the journal's editorial statement: "The term 'Science' in the journal's title is interpreted in the broadest possible sense to include diverse methods and approaches. The editors believe that creative insight often occurs outside traditional research approaches . . ." At this point, for many people, it does seem that structural functionalism and the varieties of positivism are not supplying the kind of comfort and compelling definitions of the nature of the social world and social research that they once did.

Stewart: Well, they're not necessarily abandoned. Many colleagues, probably a majority, continue to work within a framework that is primarily functionalist. The assumptions that they make about the nature of the phenomena and how to appropriate knowledge of those phenomena are only loosely constrained by what critics would often call logical positivism. I think that it is important not to use those words in derogatory ways. Where a problem presents itself is in the supposition that in doing organizational research, or any other kind of research, one is necessarily in possession of a royal road to truth. All other approaches, all other ways are heretical, should be excommunicated, not given tenure, kept outside the prestigious academies or whatever the disciplinary mechanisms are. There is a sense in which one is expected to knuckle down to orthodoxy, like it or not. But, we do live in a pluralist world, intellectually. In the academy, in organization theory, the resolute claims to articulate theoretical perspectives that would be anathema to forms of functionalist analysis are well established. The piper is at the gates of a new dawn of scientificity where what counts is only what can be counted has already been sidelined. The gates are wide open. The hordes are already inside the gates and it's too late to shut them. However much the puritans might want to exclude those voices, the voices are there and I don't think they're going to go away.

There is a question of politics. The plurality and the spread of other ways of addressing organizations is now very rich. It is part of the diversity of the field. It's part of what makes it continue to be a more interesting place in which to work than I think it was twenty or even ten years ago. Twenty years ago I don't think there were many dissenting voices; they were very marginal. I know. I think that there are more now, to such an extent that it's not clear where orthodoxy is any longer. I think we should point to the highly plural nature of the ways in which we approach organizational theorizing. We should take a pragmatic orientation toward it. For some kinds of issues, for some kinds of questions, some kinds of methods and some kinds of techniques are probably going to do the job best. Partially, this is because of the nature of the questions they ask. Other traditions will use other techniques and ask other questions. Some insights come from all of these, I think.

John: I don't imagine that your conclusion from this would be that because we have and want pluralism, we can be assured that all approaches are equally productive or that all researchers working within all approaches are going to be equally productive in their contributions. It seems we still must attempt to establish good standards in each research tradition within each of the paradigms. These standards should allow us to differentiate the better and exemplary work from that which is not as good. Without this, there would be no coherent research enterprises or even programs and it seems our research would be plagued by tremendous inefficiencies.

Stewart: Yes, I think that is absolutely right. A problem is if the canon of legitimacy of one tradition becomes the gateway or conduit through which all must pass. That means then that if the journal, *Organization Science,* is true to its masthead, there is a sense in which it must be dealing with the post-modernist conception of what constitutes science. That is a conception of science that is not just rooted in any one set of empirical procedures, any one set of techniques for collecting and manipulating data, any one set of theoretical categories for conceptualizing and organizing that data, any one set of theories for generating issues in terms of debate.

There is no reason why the term science should not be as appropriate to these changed conditions as it appeared to be to conditions of more ideological consistency that might have prevailed once upon a time. Just as the nature of social reality is something that is constructed, that shifts and changes by the things people do, so science changes. Science is what scientists do. It's not what Popper or some other philosopher of science tells them they should do. One thing that comes through very clearly from those empirical studies of science that sociologists have made, people like Law and Callon and Latour, is this: they established that what scientists do and what scientists say they do and what philosophers of science say they should do are very different phenomena. I have colleagues at the University of Bath, for instance, which has been particularly strong in the empirical sociology of science, who have succeeded in revising the conditions under which the science curriculum is taught in the Science Faculties in the University. There has been reformation through the insights of the empirical sociology of science. If sociologists are able to do that kind of reform in the Science Faculties, I don't see why we can't achieve the same kinds of reform in the Organization and Management Theory curriculum.

We have a bizarre situation. We have defenders of a "scientific" faith, or at least an "orthodoxy" who use a Popperian creed that is clearly nonscientific, moralistic and prescriptive. They presume to uphold a standard that claims to be value-free and scientific, yet the terms that raise this standard conform to none of the things that the standard claims to license. Organization theory suffers and sustains forms of foolishness in the philosophy of science with a vengeance that is scarcely credible in the context of the claims that advance it. The empirical reality of a natural science's practice and the practice of natural scientists is not one informed by such moral philosophy. It admits of very much more contingent, local and situational considerations, much less than the paradigm totalization that we might think. In some areas of social science, such as organization theory, there are theorists who work with the intellectual equivalent of the Inquisition on the grounds of procedures that are hardly more scientific than those that once determined hereticism. Amazingly, they claim scientificity in consequence!

John: Is there a commonality between Popperian falsificationism and the pluralists or the postmodernists or the deconstructionists? Certainly, there are radical differences among these philosophies, but a parallel seems to be that for none of them is the project of building and developing theories and other systematic thought structures ever finished.

Stewart: That is a good insight and one that I had not thought of before. There are obviously differences. Popper's view is, as Lakatos clarified it subsequently, that the hard core slowly accumulates. I guess what the postmodernists would suggest is that there is probably not just a single hard core that is accumulating, but a plurality of diverse hard cores, each of which is seeking to configure intellectual, theoretical and empirical spaces in its own image. Organized science is a battleground. We've known this much at least since Watson and Crick's account of the double helix. If that is true of molecular cell biology, it's equally true in organization theory and any other field of social science and its application.

In our social science, we are doing what people do in organizations every day. That is we try to use whatever capacities and resources we can recruit to ourselves; we try to configure the terrain in which we operate in such a way as to enable these capacities and resources to be mobilized. We seek to enroll and recruit others to the design that we make. The problem is, of course, that they're all doing the same thing, and that is what makes social life so complex, so messy, so nasty at times, and so interesting. Social science is no different from everyday life, only it produces involvement in its games that is more collective and public than in many other spheres of activity.

16

"Soul Work" in Organizations

PHILIP H. MIRVIS
Sandy Spring, Maryland

I came to my first community building workshop in the late 1980s rather skeptical about the whole idea. The previous five years I'd spent researching a book on cynicism in American life: people's inclinations to act primarily out of self-interest and to view other's motives with mistrust and suspicion (Kanter and Mirvis 1989). Data told part of my story: Over twentysome years pollsters showed Americans losing faith in government, business, and most every institution. My own surveys found them doubting their neighbors and the goodness of human nature.

The other part of the story was my own. As a teen in the 1960s, I had been fired by ideals of making a better world. But in the death of the Kennedys and King was a little bit of me. The bloodless body counts in Vietnam, the lies in Watergate, followed by two decades of high-level shenanigans and cover-ups, had doused me with disillusionment about the workings of the nation-state. Ongoing urban flight and decay, the break up of so many families, the breakdown of most civic institutions, and the onset of mass downsizing, free agent management, and such in business had dimmed by hopes of creating community on a more everyday plane. All of this, plus the "swim with the sharks" ethic of the 1980s, made me somewhat edgy about getting together with strangers to "break bread."

Still, I was agreeable when a good friend of mine, a business executive and civic leader, invited me to join him at the workshop. He thought it might deepen my work in companies where I help people give voice to their values and organize around their vision of effectiveness and well-being (Mirvis 1996). This is good work, in theory, but often constrained in practice by people's doubts and fears, their inability to communicate openly with one another, and by short-term profit pressures that allow their companies to rationalize incivility in the name of the "bottom line."

The workshop was being run by the Foundation for Community Encouragement (FCE) and its founder, M. Scott Peck. Peck (1978, 1987, 1993) is a prophet to legions who have read his multi-year bestseller about spiritual awakening, *The Road Less Traveled.* He is also an activist and organizer; following publication of *The Different Drum,* he put his moneys and energy into forming FCE, whose volunteer leaders teach principles of community building and peacemaking in large group workshops and consult with organizations—religious, civic, and commercial—that want to operate as a community.

To prepare myself for the plunge, I skimmed Peck's writings and was taken with his model of the "stages" of community making, particularly the notion that "emptiness" precedes the creation of *true* community. From my experiences in training groups, as well as with some task forces and teams in organizations, this sort of breakthrough typically follows a struggle over leadership or control of the agenda (cf. Slater 1966). The "storming" gives way as a group examines and works through power issues and thence *organizes* itself, a phase of group development called "norming" (Tuckman 1965). Peck proposes a different method of working this through: Emptying entails vulnerability and requires active surrender of one's leadership, goals, issues, and, interestingly, collective appeals to organization. Build community, he counsels, and then set your agenda. Sounded interesting.

By comparison, Peck's "spiritual" slant, wherein he equates messages from the unconscious with grace and likens the experience of community to a miracle, seemed rather woolly and more than a touch messianic. I conjured up images of people meditating, chanting, or, worst yet, thanking everyone for sharing. Not to belabor, I arrived at my first workshop with plenty of preconceptions and, as the saying goes, lots of baggage. Turned out to be handbags in comparison; the 100 or so others in attendance were carrying steamer trunks.

At Quaker meeting, members take about 45 minutes or so to "empty" themselves—of everyday thoughts and feelings as well as their most profound pleasures and pains—to make room for the "inner light." Evidently they have it down because we spent over a day at that workshop unburdening ourselves. After a brief prototypical spell in what Peck calls "pseudo-community," wherein a few people told the group about themselves or what they hoped to find in the workshop, we entered a period of chaos. Here, in traditional group dynamics theory, power struggles begin and, in psychodynamic terms, the bowels metaphorically come into play (Bennis and Shephard 1956). We instead operated like a "recovery" group and heard tales from alcoholics, abused spouses, workaholics, spouse abusers, children who had loved parents who did everything but love them, all amidst lots of weeping. Hey, I thought, mashing my teeth, can we lighten up? "Any joy here?" I eventually asked. "Yes," said one, "and now let us get back to work."

Welcome to witnessing. And letting it in and sitting with it. New stuff for action-oriented, ready-for-a-power-struggle me. Always quick to conceptualize, my mind was mush. Furthermore, the group seemed shapeless and wasn't taking any direction. So this was emptying. Naming this phase gave me some comfort. Then I recalled the Zen Buddhist teaching to the effect that understanding a ritual is no substitute for participating in it. I paid attention, and my ears opened . . .

One man's story about growing up with an alcoholic parent jarred me. My mom was an alcoholic, but the family was slow to grasp it and not very skilled at working with it. Neither was mom. Then a tale of job failure caught my attention. Not my story, but I knew the anger and self-doubt in the voice. Finally, I talked about "going native" in my studies of cynicism and how my wariness was preventing me from being "fully present." Nothing heavy. Why was I tearful?

Consciousness—of the self and other—are two cornerstones on which to build community. Be aware of yourself and what moves you, Peck advises, and what inhibits you and causes you to crawl into a shell. But such self-awareness comes from gaining consciousness of the "other": from seeing others fully, listening to their stories, and comprehending their lives and circumstances. This is, at root, the stuff of personality formation, whereby children differentiate themselves from the world around them, and thence the architecture of relationships, wherein our separate selves come together (Fromm 1956, Klein 1959). The connection to community is in *seeing ourselves in the other and the other in ourselves.* Meanwhile, projection, stereotyping, intellectualization, over-identification—all the so-called defense mechanisms (see Freud 1965) that inhibit this connection and reinforce self-reference—were coming to life in my mind and to light in the workshop. So this is what I had to let go of . . .

I began afresh really tuning in to people's stories. And paying deeper attention to myself in doing so. The range of my receptors increased and new ones switched on. Stimuli were coming through via my head and heart and even my hands. Slowly then surely my past life was being accessed in fast forward. Others' stories were triggering trace memories and forgotten emotions.

There was my mom, and my family, and my friends in my mind's eye, and my own pains. And I was connecting to those of the others in the workshop.

Now these kinds of emotions and experiences are common among attendees of twelve-step programs and self-help groups where empathy, understanding, and ultimately connection emerge from "relating" to another's life story and sharing your own (cf. Buber 1965, 1970). In such forums, however, people share a common addiction or affliction. Here the sources of hurt, rejection, or disappointment in one's self were many and varied. What did we have in common? Only what Peck calls a universal "fear of disarming ourselves."

Then someone commented about predilections to be "pain junkies," not directed at anyone specific but to the group as a whole. We chewed over the idea of healthy versus unhealthy pain and what constituted "legitimate" suffering in a "broken world." And we also began to exchange puns and laugh. Happy moments pulsed through from my past, too. This, I guess, marked our movement into a new phase of group development.

Over the next day, the group looked less to Peck and the workshop facilitators as role models or targets for disaffection. A collective letting go of these expectations gradually gave the group a rhythm and together we forged the means to manage ourselves. People were saying the right thing, to each other and to the group as a whole. They were also group guardians, reaching out to the silent who wanted to speak, and letting the talkative know when the group could gain most from their silence.

"Group consciousness" is a third cornerstone of community. It requires paying attention to the parts *and* the whole (cf. Bateson 1972). Our workshop group was gaining a new and fluid organization as we attended to our collective dynamics and shared responsibility for building relationships. Now I'd experienced this simultaneous awareness of the forest-and-trees in other group encounters and lived it in out-of-doors workshops when helping teammates across a stream or up a mountain. This capacity to "see the system" while operating within it seems to develop when groups immerse themselves deeply and repetitively into their experience, much as in therapy (Smith and Berg 1987). This proved a comforting explanation at the time; it put psychologic to my feelings of communion.

Late in the workshop I was resting on the floor, close to Peck's feet. Suddenly, "religious" images dammed (or damned) up in my psyche began bursting forth. I imagined myself as the apostle Paul being thrown from his horse as a phrase circled the air above me: "Many are called, but few are chosen." The spell was broken when a voice inside me boomed: "Who does the choosing?" I suddenly wondered: God? Me?

Years of religious baggage were lifted for my inspection: overly-friendly priests and too-distant nuns, fear of hellfire and guilt over disappointing

Jesus. Peck reminds that spirituality is *not* the same as religion, but here the naming did not provide much comfort. Neither did the recognition that people's identities and anxieties outside of a system have a way of creeping into their experiences within it (cf. Alderfer 1966). Still, I wasn't troubled, hepped up, or even hung up by the recollections, nor was I crafting fine distinctions between my rejection of God "out there" and willingness to apprehend God "within." I was just, well, peaceful.

Now I know about the power of suggestion, and how this can all be explained in the male psychodynamics of transference: me a little guy in the big hands of God the Father cum Scott Peck. And I'm not talking about being born again. But *something* was happening. And not only to me. People around me sounded thoughtful and poetic. We together were in sync and working well. Suppressed conflicts were surfaced. And many of our manifest disagreements were rapidly resolved. The group seemed to be blessed . . .

The final cornerstone of community is to organize in harmony with what William James (1902) calls the "unseen order of things." People who work with groups and organizations without otherworldly reference simply call it alignment (Harrison 1983). But, aligned toward what? Mission, vision, values: these were my prior referent points in working with organizations. Love? You see that in business, too, and surely in relationships. But aligned with the Spirit? A metaphor, I reasoned, of *these* people in *this* setting.

Three months later my mom died: lung failure following exploratory surgery that diagnosed her as having a difficult-to-treat cancer. In the course of a few days after the surgery, she was resuscitated once and got to say her goodbyes to me and my brother and sisters. And we to her. We also spent our time sorting out the meaning of her living will with doctors and medical ethicists and, even more so, sorting things out among ourselves. We worked through hyper-rationality, estrangement, anger, sorrow, and exhaustion. And we did it well.

Now to what extent events and circumstances are dictated by chance or law is a source of profound speculation among philosophers and theologians, scientists and lay people. On this matter, Peck is a believer in serendipity. His is a universe where the dice roll in cycles both vicious and virtuous. On this subject, I can only say that I was unusually prepared to be with my mother at her death bed, and to reach out to my family, in a manner most serendipitous.

COMMUNITY DEFINED

So far, I've used the term "community" without defining it. It may help to say what it does *not* mean in this discussion. For example, community does not refer here to a physical place, like a neighborhood, workplace, or gathering spot. Nor does it connote necessarily a social space, or affiliation, such as a political party, family, or reference group. As a starting point, see in the root word "common" notions of sharing, mutual obligation, and commitment that link people together (Bellah et al. 1985, McMillan and Chavis 1986). This yields, insofar as a person is concerned, what Seymour Sarason (1974) terms "the psychological sense of community" and encompasses the emotive experience of feeling close to others, being connected to them by reciprocity or empathy, and even of living at least some of your life with and through them.

But what of a community's collective character? Ties that bind, such as shared values, congruent interests, cohering rituals, and a common purpose are sociological indicators. To this, those who study ongoing communities add concepts like caring, support, mutual aid, and trust (cf. Kanter 1972, Bellah et al. 1991, Wuthnow 1991, Putnam 1992). But are Communitarians, Unitarians, or Rotarians any more communal than, say, Libertarians, Branch Davidians, or Wall Street traders in these regards? Much depends, in Peck's formulation, on the degree of consciousness and intention that motivates their collectivity.

This brings up the component of "unity" in community. Contemporary sociologists speak of this as the "solidarity" people experience with community members or their collective sense of "we-ness" (Etzioni 1993). Charles Horton Cooley (1922), a forebear of today's community-minded sociologists, characterized it as the "fusion of personalities into a larger whole." Peck espouses this same holistic concept but configures it in a "group mind." This speaks to the need for community members to consciously embrace unity and to inquire deeply and periodically into their reasons for doing so. He questions, for example, the "blind trust" sometimes found in cults and mindless followership that can mark bands of "true believers." Peck also believes that the *exclusivity* found in groups that are caring, supportive, and helpful to their own kind but unresponsive and even hostile to others counterfeits their claims to community.

The objection here is that those who would unite on the basis of like minds, a similar heritage, or a common enemy may be side-stepping the struggle essential to fusing with "unlike" others (cf. Friedman 1983). True community, in Peck's terms, is born of *inclusiveness* and comes into being as a group *transcends* differences. John Gardner (1995) terms this "wholeness incorporating diversity." In this light, community is understood as a "process," rather than a psychological state or sociological condition. Thus it can be experienced in a weekend workshop among strangers as well as in the daily life and doings of ongoing groups, organizations, and other intentional communities.

BEHIND COMMUNITY BUILDING EXPERIENCE

A group from 50 to 75 meet to participate in one of FCE's community building workshops. The first session begins with a reading of the "Rabbi's Gift," an apocryphal story of a 12th century monastery restored after a wise, old rabbi advises that one of the monks, but unknown which one, is the "messiah." Then silent reflection. What follows is a group's unique wending through the stages pseudo-community, chaos, and emptiness described earlier. The creation of community is itself emergent, not itself predictable, programmable, or reducible to precise formula, nor a function simply of the collective effort of high-minded people with good intentions. In the community building experience, however, Peck and FCE leaders assert that the process cycles and deepens through frank and intimate communication.

Their counsel: Be open, inquire deeply, be realistic and authentic, and bring things to light mindful of the moment. These timeless truisms about how to talk, listen, and be with others were refined by human relations researchers decades ago and are taught today by management educators, school teachers, the clergy, and healers of all types, usually through experiential exercises. What FCE adds is the Quaker-like injunction that people be "moved to speak": to wait to be moved before speaking and, importantly, to speak when so moved. This takes skill at listening to one's inner self and courage to speak from the heart.

There is, broadly, something new in how we think about and construct communication exercises that is by no means unique to FCE. The "dialogues" studied at MIT (Isaacs 1993), the "appreciative" inquiries at Case Western Reserve (Cooperrider 1990), and the "sociotherapy" groups of Patrick DeMare et al. (1991), to name but a few examples, all incorporate traditional human relations techniques and experiences but derive from a different set of assumptions about group development and social organization.

For instance, drawing from the tenets of humanistic psychology in the 1950s and 1960s, many human relations trainers stress the importance of dealing directly with "here and now" behavior and regard interpersonal feedback as key to the "helping" relationship (cf. Bradford et al. 1964). Indeed, to heighten self-awareness in sensitivity training, people are encouraged to "mirror" their reactions to other's behavior and, in some circles, to offer interpretations. By comparison, participants in community-building workshops are advised to speak to the "group as a whole" and urged to self-reflect, and be aware of their filtering and judgments, all in service of emptying oneself of what gets in the way of truly hearing another person. The idea, as expressed by William Isaacs (1994) with reference to dialogue groups, is that by "observing the observer" and "listening to your listening," self-awareness of thoughts, feelings, and experiences, past and present, seep gently into consciousness.

In turn, the notion of offering Rogerian-type counseling in a group—to help people see themselves more clearly through questioning or clarifying—is discouraged. In FCE's lingo, this equates to "fixing," a worthy aspiration that has to be emptied in order to experience oneself and others more fully. On this point, it is worth noting that Peck, an MD and psychotherapist by training, in no way equates community building with group therapy. Nor does he see it as an especially fertile medium for personal growth. The focus in FCE workshops is on collective development and interpretive comments, if offered at all, are aimed at the group as a whole (cf. Bion 1961).

Still, there are obvious parallels between the dynamics in therapy or encounter groups and in community building workshops. Community building groups, for example, are just as apt to express dependency on leaders, to engage in fight-and-flight, to form pairing relationships, and to manifest the myriad unconscious conflicts that surface in other kinds of group encounters. But the intent is not to "work through" these dynamics by confronting them directly. Rather, the group serves as a "container" to hold differences and conflicts up for ongoing exploration. This keeps "hot" conversation "cooled" sufficiently that people can see the "whole" of the group mind. This facilities development of group consciousness by counteracting tendencies toward "splitting" in group dynamics whereby people identify with "good part" of their group and reject the "bad part." This container resides in what some call the "quantum universe" (Wilbur 1984, Talbot 1986). From the study of particle physics, it is believed that observation of a particle influences the quantum field around it, meaning literally that observing affects the observed (Capra 1976, 1982). David Bohm (1986), the physicist whose theories stimulated development of the dialogue process, generalized the point to human communication and gatherings. By simultaneously self-scanning and inquiring with a group, in his view, people create a connective field between observer and observed. By "holding" this field, in turn, a group can "contain" both energy and matter, and investigate more fully what it is producing. And in uncovering this "tacit infrastructure," some theorists believe, lay the possibility of creating new collective dynamics.

Here is where FCE's principles apply. At the start of a workshop, aspirations are set to welcome and affirm diversity, deal with difficult issues, bridge differences with integrity, and relate with love and respect. In this sense, community building advances by the "positive values = positive action" equation that guides groups involved in appreciative inquiries. At the same time, FCE leaders are admonished that they cannot "lead" a group to community. They may be "moved" to empty themselves of feelings, or to commune with a coleader, and these may serve as a stimulus and example to a group that has had enough of fighting or fleeing and is ready to examine some new behavior. Leaders, and anyone else present, are also free to call a group into silence, slow discussion down, or offer up thoughts for contemplation, the sorts of things that lend themselves to what Bohm (1989) describes as "superconductivity" in a group: where the electrons, or in this case the elements of the conversation, move as a "whole" rather than as separate parts.

It is plausible to think of the heightened group consciousness in community building workshops in the psychodynamic terms of bisociation: people reclaiming "split off" ideas, feelings, and subgroups and reconstituting the group-as-a-whole. But what of the spiritual connection with the "unseen order of things?" Testimonials abound about the creative breakthroughs that groups experience in Outward Bound programs, when engaged in sports and the arts, in meditation and therapy, and in other mediums where the experience of wholeness translates into creative insight or action or both. These are labelled "flow" experiences (Csikszentmihalyi 1990) and attributed to the harmonious co-evolution of mental and material forces (cf. Bateson 1979).

Several variants of the "new science" speak to this dynamic. The order to be found in chaos, for instance, revolves around an aptly named "strange attractor;" Margaret Wheatley (1993), among others, suggests that its human equivalent is *meaning*. Theories of transpersonal psychology are, so to speak, on the same wave length. But, to Peck, Willis Harman, founder of the World Business Academy, and others like them, such notions of an implicate order come from the field of inquiry known as "spiritual science" where, it is presumed, mind and matter co-evolve and interpenetrate.

As novel and scientific-sounding as these ideas might seem, they can be found in ancient Buddhist tracts and other tenets of "eastern" thought and in many indigenous peoples' ways of understanding the world. They have also reached the west over the centuries in novels, poetry, and arts, in the words of mystics and deeds of heretics. In testimony to its timelessness, it is customary to say that this kind of knowledge is inspired or revealed, rather than invented or discovered. Perhaps the source is a muse, or a spirit, or some other "unseen" force?

In an evocative essay, Diana Whitney (1995) describes spirit variously as energy, as meaning, and as epistemology. Her illustrations come from Native American traditions, Chinese medicine, the myths of the new science, and the musings of organizational scientists trying to make sense of the forces that impinge on themselves and those they study. In many cultures, she notes, spirit is also sacred. This moves us from the realms of philosophy and metaphor to matters of faith. It is clear enough that the world's great religions, as well as more personal or idiosyncratic ones, offer different ways of apprehending and expressing their revealed truths. Yet the comparative study of religions suggests that all have, at their core, a near universal means of accessing spiritual knowledge. It is this that Willis Harman (1988) calls their "perennial wisdom."

Peck and FCE are adamant that community building is *not* religion and that its rules are by no means sacred. Religion is about answers, so they say, spirituality is about questions. Yet the experience of making community is described as transcendent: a term that means literally to "climb over" or, more colloquially, to achieve a "peak experience" or find one's "higher self" (cf. Maslow 1954, 1968). William James, speaking of the common core of revelation, says we find "MORE" of that quality "which is operative in the universe outside of (ourselves)."

Sit easy with James' capitalization and the mountain-top imagery: Buddhism teaches that we can find "more" when approaching everyday tasks like sweeping the floor, washing the dishes, and working in the work-a-day world whenever we are especially "mindful" (Hahn 1990, 1993). The paradox here is that emptiness may be essential to mindfulness and vice versa. Whether it is this embrasure of yin and yang, or of paradox broadly, or simply, as physician Bernie Siegel (1986) put it, a miracle, it seems to me that what dialogue groups, appreciative inquiries, and community building workshops offer, in much the same way as do tribal kivas and Quaker meetings, is that near-universal *medium for accessing spiritual knowledge and becoming our better selves.*

SPIRIT IN ORGANIZATION LIFE

However we characterize the experience of community and its spiritual dimensions, it is plain enough that vast numbers of people, from all walks of life, are searching for new relationships, attachments, and "something more" in their individual and collective lives. That this yearning is being felt in the workplace is not surprising. People are spending more of their time working and number among closest friends their coworkers (Schor 1991). Lacking continuity and connection in so many other settings, many naturally look to their organization as a communal center.

The problem is that organizations seem far less hospitable to community making than in the recent past. From post-WWII to the early 1980s, the American workplace, corporate and governmental, was a relatively stable and secure setting in which to develop a career, make friends, give and get social support, and participate in purposeful activities larger than one's self. Today's workplace, marked by multiple changes in ownership and large-scale layoffs, more internal movement and individual job hopping, and increasing numbers of people on temporary assignment or working part-time, is riven instead by fear, pressure, and impermanence. What are the prospects, then, of making community and finding spirit amidst these spoils?

They seem to be growing: Over 100 employees of the World Bank gather together at 1:00 pm every Wednesday and discuss the potential of "soul consciousness" in their organization (*Business Week* 1995); Boeing has had poet David Whyte (1994) stir 500 or so of its top managers with recitations from his volume on "the preservation of the soul in corporate America"; and Tom Chappel, CEO of a health products company and proponent of running a prayerful business, is in demand on the lecture circuit. These are but a few examples of how people are searching for and finding community at work today (cf. Cox 1993).

It's easy enough to dismiss "soul work" in business as marginal and gatherings of this sort as "feel good" palliatives. A closer look, however, reveals many different ways in which community and spirituality are making their way into organization life and have something to offer, to both practice and theory.

Leading From Within

One place to locate this new emphasis is in contemporary models of leadership and leadership development. It wasn't too long ago that "situational leadership" was in vogue and executives were advised to make their leadership style "contingent" on the situation. By comparison, Robert Greenleaf's (1993) notion of "servant leadership," Max Depree's (1989) accounts of "artful" practice, Stephen Covey's (1990) "principle-centered" approach, and Abraham Maslow's (1965) prescient writings on "eupsychian" management all speak, in one way or another, to a leader's inner sources of inspiration and outward embodiment of ideals. Why this emphasis on leading from within? In his account of "leading minds" throughout history, Howard Gardner (1995) makes the observation that "it is the particular burden of the leader to help individuals determine their personal, social, and moral identities." Leaders accomplish this, he finds, by relating "identity stories" about their life struggles and how they resolved their own identity issues. Note, in support of this point, how many autobiographies of business executives have been published these past several years not to mention a few volumes of their business-related poetry.

Shell Oil has incorporated this general thrust into its leadership development agenda. As part of its "Leaders Developing Leaders" program, Jerome Adams, head of Shell's Learning Center, has had the top 200 executives record their life histories and career experiences to identify sources of personal passion and meaning. The executives, guided by myself and commu-

nity artist Maggie Sherman, also fashioned a plaster cast of their face and
decorated it with symbols of their life journey and leadership transformation in Shell. The decorated masks, and stories behind them, were shared with
colleagues and today appear in offices throughout the corporation. Interestingly, Shell's top ten executives helped to "prime the pump" by telling
their own identity stories and participating in mask making. In turn, the 200
shared their masks and stories in a subsequent program aimed at middle
management.

It should be remembered that McGregor's (1960) influential writings of
thirty-five years ago urged managers to probe their own "Theory X versus Y"
assumptions. Thereafter, a science of self-assessment emerged, exemplified
by Schon's (1983) studies of "reflective practitioners," Argyris's (1982,
1985) approach to uncovering motives behind actions (right/left hand col-
umns), and a myriad of self-scoring personality tests, type indicators, and
competency evaluations. Nowadays, however, development-minded leaders
are returning to simpler and more timeless approaches—prayer, meditation,
journaling, and spiritual retreats—methods traditionally classified under
"care for the soul" (cf. Moore 1991). Furthermore, in lieu of power lunches,
executives are attending prayer breakfasts, such as the one hosted by the First
Tuesday Club in Boston that typically includes the CEOs of Digital, Gillette,
the Bank of Boston, and Raytheon, along with the heads of smaller outfits.
Finally, my impression is that many more leaders, at every level in organizations, are joining support groups, involving themselves in mentoring relationships, and going to conferences where they engage in "inner work" and
contemplate the meaning of what they do with fellow searchers.

Meaning in Work

Work itself is also being rediscovered as a source of spiritual growth and
connection to others. Recall laments about the "blue-collar blues" or "white-
collar woes?" Thirty years of study has shown that the components of fulfilling work—producing a "whole" product or service, and finding variety,
autonomy, and challenge in tasks—can be modeled, measured, and trans-
lated into work fit for human capabilities. As a result, many job designs once
based on scientific management principles are being enriched and close
supervision is giving way to self-managing teams. But does intellectually
enriched work truly satisfy the heart and make the human spirit soar?

Studies of artisans and craftspersons, inventors, wordsmiths, and other
creative types, not to mention scientists, athletes, and musicians, find them
immersed in their tasks, carried away or elevated to new heights, envisioning
a creation in its fullness (Koestler 1964, Arieti 1976). For a time, scholars
attributed these experiences to something "intrinsic" to work, as though it

were present without the worker and absent context (Herzberg et al. 1959). Now, this is understood in a web of relationships: in the interplay of person and material, and in a larger context that makes it more or less meaningful (cf. Mirvis 1980).

Perhaps these "relational" qualities of work are easiest to find among people who care for people. Doctors, for instance, diagnose, cut, and drug but their "laying on of hands" is vital to curing. In the same way, the treatment of mental illnesses centers on the relationship between therapist and patient. To generalize the point, some scholars contend that empathy, support, and caregiving are the prime ingredients of truly meaningful work (Kahn 1993, Fletcher 1996).

On this matter, research by Michael Learner (1996) finds that what middle-class blue- and white-collar workers bemoan most is the absence of love and care in the workplace and any connection between their jobs and larger purpose in life. What are organizations doing today to help people meet their meaning needs in the workplace? There are a growing number of firms whose statements of vision, mission, or purpose lift up the value of work products and services and speak directly to employees' dignity and self-worth. In the best of cases, employees at all levels have had the chance to shape or affirm these visions or craft one for their own work areas.

On a communal scale, companies are holding community building workshops, dialogues, and appreciative inquiries, as well as countless teambuilding programs that offer a regimen of human relations training, time and space for reflection, and maybe a ropes course, river raft, or some other "opening up" experience. The close bonds forged are well documented along with gains in team performance (Beinecke 1994). Interestingly, social service is increasingly a part of team building in companies like Ameritech, Ford Motor Company, and General Electric. Noel Tichy has designed a variety of such "service learning" experiences wherein employees help to rebuild inner-city housing, assist in clinics and orphanages, or counsel those in need. What's it all about?

It is, according to Tichy, a means to get people in touch deeply with themselves, their teammates, and the human condition around them. Naturally, there is some crabbing about the "relevance" of such experiences and the "transfer of training" back to the workplace. Anita Roddick (1990), founder of the Body Shop and innovator in this regard, counters that one can "find the spirit in the world through (social) service." She adds a pragmatic point: "You educate people by their passions. . . . You want them to feel that they are doing something important, that they're not a lone voice. . . . I'd never get that kind of motivation if we were just selling shampoo or body lotion." Beyond its benefits to the business, it is the social significance of this kind of work that connects people's employment to their larger purpose in life.

Goodness in Groups

Scholarly papers on work groups usually begin with a discussion of the Hawthorne studies and commentary on how productive norms developed in the bank wiring room once management showed its human face (cf. Cartwright 1951, Hackman and Suttle 1977). As an alternative, Charles Hampden-Turner's (1971) analysis focuses on people's liberation from mindless rules, dawning consciousness of their powers and responsibilities, followed by consensual commitment to look out for one another and do the job right. In his view, the women in the bank wiring room became a "self-managing" work group.

The broader Hawthorne studies have become a parable for organizational scientists over the years, reinterpreted by every generation to affirm their view of how the world works. Some contend that it was changes in the lighting that led to increased productivity; others point to management's empowerment of workers; still others to the feminine impulse to bond and work together. My question: Could the struggle with chaos and emptying of resentments, fears, and learned limits have helped to unleash collective creativity in the bank wiring room? And could, perhaps, we be referring to "something more" when we talk about the "Hawthorne" effect?

It is the researcher's job to parse out variables and identify their unique contribution to collective life. I remember well my own eye opening about our field's peculiarly anti-social psychology when administering a questionnaire to production workers at a plant in Bolivar, Tennessee in the mid-1970s. They had formed into work teams, with the assistance of Michael Maccoby, and busied themselves learning problem-solving skills. The workers also set up a "school" to teach each other how to read, improve the yield of their gardens, balance checkbooks, handle problems with their kids, and deal with other chores at the intersection of work and life. Our questionnaire measured concepts like social distance, participation in decisions, communication patterns, conflict resolution, and such. Maccoby asked me which questions measured group "spirit?" I was at a loss to answer.

The "Principles of Community" developed at Carlisle Motors, a multi-location auto dealership in west Florida, asks employees to "relate with love and respect" and to be "open to Spirit." Several community building workshops among staff are credited with "breaking down the walls" between the sales force and back office and with humanizing working relationships throughout the auto dealership. Taking its principles to market, the dealership has adopted a "fair and simple" approach to auto pricing, that eliminates "haggling" and the disadvantages incurred therein by women and minorities in new and used car purchases. Buyers can also return their cars with "money back" to sales people who now work on salary rather than commission.

Profits-per-car are down, but volume has soared. According to Scott Wilkerson, CEO, this is simply a matter of "living the principles." I would hypothesize further that as people relate to each other with love and respect, and strive to be open to Spirit, their aspirations to produce "something more" at work are awakened.

Company as Community

The distinction between company and community blurs in firms like the Body Shop, Ben & Jerry's and other so-called "companies with a conscience" that have a dual bottom line: doing good and doing well. Over the past several years, the case has been made that such firms can juxtapose social responsibility alongside the profit motive and still achieve commercial success (cf. Scott and Rothman 1992, Ray and Rinzler 1993). What is interesting for the present purpose is the impact on employees. Employees at Ben & Jerry's register extraordinary high ratings of job meaning, camaraderie with coworkers, and trust in management in their biennial survey. Interestingly, however, neither material rewards nor these psychosocial factors are the prime predictors of job satisfaction and commitment to the organization. Rather it is pride in and support for the firm's "social mission" that best differentiates between the most- and least-fulfilled employee. This social mission is reflected in the firm's products and marketing and is brought to life in countless acts of social service undertaken by Ben & Jerry's employees. One result, regularly recorded on surveys and in group discussions, is that many employees have, in effect, "found themselves" through their employment in the company. In addition, many report that they have had their "consciousness raised" as a result of their involvement in social and political issues and several attest to having "learned compassion" through their social service work in the company.

The theme of company = community is also being expressed today in the myriad of good works being undertaken within firms today to advance social welfare and justice. Studies find that companies that are leaders in employee training, work enrichment, and progressive human resource management take the lead in valuing workforce diversity and promoting work/family balance as well (cf. Mirvis 1993a). At one time, schools, families, and other community institutions provided leadership and the necessary supports in these regards. Nowadays, the best-managed companies are taking on these communal responsibilities. Furthermore, they are often doing so through employee task forces and committees, literally taking on a communal governance structure to do the human community's business.

This reminds that there is a *process* side to running a business like a community: Robert Bellah and colleagues (1991) contend that constant attention

to purpose, marked by inquiry into what is going on and face-to-face participation by people in decisions, are earmarks of the "civil" organization. Communal processes are being introduced into companies in the form of search
conferences, town meetings, and the like (cf. Schindler-Rainman and Lippitt
1980, Wiesbord 1992, Bunker and Alban 1992). Carrying this further, a "soul
committee" was formed at Lotus Development Corporation to revitalize the
software maker's originating spirit in light of ongoing layoffs and competitive market pressures. Digital Equipment undertook a variation of the theme
(Greenfield 1996). And top executives at Shell Oil join together to explore
"leadership as being" and regularly host dialogues throughout the company
where personal values are compared with corporate directions. This process,
which has people dig into their hearts and bring what they find into communal
conversation, is very much a part of the "work" in these organizations (cf.
Gozdz 1996, Shaffer and Anundsen 1993).

DESCRIBING THE INDESCRIBABLE

I have seen Richard Hackman at a loss for words. He was leading a seminar
at the Kennedy School at Harvard about his research at People Express air-
lines. Talking through a model of the developmental stages of high performance organizations, he opined that *something* had led People Express to
move swiftly and fluidly through the typical crises encountered by start-up
businesses that center on leadership and competition among subgroups in the
organization. There were lots of hypotheses about how market and organizational dynamics might have "sped up" the developmental process but, when
pressed, Hackman talked about *indescribable* processes and moods in the
company that seemed to create an alignment of energy and yield timely decisions and actions. What is more, he confessed, he felt himself "caught up" in
these and no longer had an objective view of how the company worked.

I've had my own problems trying to talk about community in business
without sounding silly or sliding into cynicism. At another FCE gathering,
following two days of building community, we discussed applications of the
experience to the management of business. I began with all sorts of caveats
and cautions about the inhuman aspects of human relations training and how
T-groups and other social technologies had proved faddish and ineffective as
means of organization change. Still, with all the interest in corporate culture,
and with managers growing comfortable with the idea of organizing around
vision and values, and, especially, with working people thirsting for community at work, it seemed to me that it was worth exploring how we might build
community in companies.

"Bullshit," a leading management writer and advisor in attendance shouted, cutting through it all. I lacked realism and was pie-eyed to think that community building had anything to do with the central mission of business: to make money. Worse, conducting workshops in business would be akin to preparing "lambs for the slaughter." So there I was, facing the stereotypical nay-sayer and the whole of the military-industrial complex. My initial retorts were scarcely civil. Then, suddenly, I saw my own shadow and called for a moment of silence and reflection.

Self-reference in a social system is difficult to describe. But in the group, to use Peck's terms, we seemed to recycle through chaos to emptying to civil community in that quiet time and space. I do remember hearing birds in the distance. The discussion picked up again, but it was no longer between two male buffaloes cum management experts. Others chimed in. Defensiveness gave way to heartfelt statements and listening. We two supposed experts never really found common ground. (What do you expect, miracles?) But the group discussion was elevated and more than a few left the gathering bound-and-determined to move organizational behavior in their companies in some new directions.

FOR GOD AND COMPANY?

To an extent, Ben & Jerry's and the Body Shop, like Levi Strauss, Hershey, Corning Glass, and many other "values-led" businesses reflect their found-er's personal values. There are also examples of companies whose principles explicitly express their leader's spiritual grounding. For instance, many of Digital Equipment's egalitarian policies can be traced to founder Ken Olsen's religious beliefs; the same is true of Cummins Engine whose longtime chair-man J. Irwin Miller is a proponent of "ethical culture." And Max Depree, for-mer head of Herman Miller, not only writes about the moral and spiritual sources of leadership, he also welcomes countless visitors who come to benchmark his company's communal practices and culture.

One executive who is unabashed about using "God language" is C. William Pollard, Chairman of ServiceMaster, whose corporate objectives, carved in a marble wall at headquarters, begin with the aspiration "To honor God in all we do." Pollard contends that this gives employees a "reason for being and doing." He asserts that faith in God gives leaders a moral compass and is not shy about debating stockholders on, say, the relationship between God and profits. He also encourages employees to discuss "what's right and what's wrong" in decisions they make on their jobs. The intent is summed up in one of ServiceMaster's leadership principles: "We have all been created in God's image, and the results of our leadership will be measured beyond the work-place. The story will be told in the changed lives of people."

Is Pollard unique? As a person, of course. So is the head of Mary Kay Cosmetics who attributes her company's success to the principles of "God first, family second, and career third, giving women a chance to keep their lives in proper perspective." Yet a recent *Forbes* survey of *Fortune* 500 executives finds that over two-thirds regularly worship at church or synagogue. Is ServiceMaster's pledge of service to God without precedent? The Atlanta-based Fellowship of Companies for Christ numbers over 500 firms around the U.S. while the California-based Full Gospel Fellowship sponsors 3,000 chapters in nearly 100 countries.

The foregoing raises troubling questions about who has access to these leadership networks and to what extent nonbelievers are at a disadvantage in these companies or even welcome at all? Certainly the CEOs cited above are all Christians and the associations of like-minded business people primarily involve Boston Catholics and Congregationalists, Midwestern Lutherans and Methodists, Bible Belt Baptists, and born-agains on the west coast. In turn, there have been many cases where employees have suffered discrimination in hiring, promotion, or access to important social circles because they did not subscribe to the religious tenets of the leaders of their enterprise.

Pollard (1996) speaks to this directly in his book *The Soul of the Firm* and points to a top leadership team composed of Christians, Muslims and Jews. As to other misuses of spirituality in organization, my colleagues in FCE urge me to "trust the process." I do so, but with caveats and cautions.

CAVEATS AND CAUTIONS

There are good reasons to be careful when doing community building in the business world. Obviously the culture and climate in many organizations are antithetical to community building and openness to the Spirit. That said, proselytizing about religion or using spiritual beliefs to exclude others undermines the requirement for inclusiveness. Still some organization members regard conversations of the sort found in community building workshops to be invasive of their privacy and feel a subtle coercion to reveal something about their own private lives. Furthermore, others view "loose talk" about spirituality, soul, and other things sacred as inappropriate in a secular setting. It is crucial, therefore, to *secure people's informed consent* before subjecting them to this kind of experience and to ensure that they can opt out without prejudice or harm (Mirvis 1993b). It is also worth noting that all manner of corporate consultants, helpers, and healers are out there peddling their own variant of community building and spiritual enrichment. The upshot? Buyer beware.

There is also potential danger when community takes hold in a business. The indescribable feelings that Hackman reported can also be called indoctrination. Pundits have gone so far as to say that People Express practiced "Kool Aid Management," likening its demise to Rev. Jim Jones' cult in Guyana that ended in enforced mass suicide. By all accounts, the airline's employees willingly embraced its management principles, including the high-minded aspiration of "making a better world." Nonetheless, critics assert that this sort of testimony is itself evidence of the pervasiveness of corporate mind control (see *Time* 1986, Bennet 1986, Prokesch 1986).

The introduction of spirituality into the mix raises the stakes. There are, for example, documented cases of companies that proselytize employees with specific religious doctrine (Nash 1996). And cases of corporate programs wherein employees, exposed to "New Age" ideas about consciousness and the cosmos, felt their own brand of faith compromised (*Newsweek* 1987). Thus the tendency in public education, as well as in most private venues, has been to erect a wall between, say, church and state, faith and reason, the spiritual and secular. Needless to say, this makes thoughts and feelings about the spirit "undiscussable" in most organizations.

At the same time, human resource specialists, whether incorporating workforce diversity or reaching out to employees in their fullness, stress the importance of engaging the "whole" person at work (Kahn 1992, Hall and Mirvis 1996). The idea of "seeing" a system-as-a-whole is taking hold in corporate plants, offices, and boardrooms. *To the extent that we acknowledge people as spiritual beings, and are at least open to an "unseen order" in the world around us, it seems to me that the drive to create wholeness must take account of people's spiritual life and its collective potential.* Certainly there are voices making the case for open discussion of faith, gods, spirituality, and religion in public schools and civic forums (cf. Carter 1994). How can we not, they argue, if we are to tend to our community? I would make the same case for businesses that strive to be communities.

Yet I've also argued that if companies turn into "total communities" there is some risk that people will become "lost" in the oceanic mood and lose sight of the world beyond the boundaries of their firm. Why worry about preschool education when your company provides for your children's needs? Why make community with your neighbors when you are called to do so at work? Why even go to church when your company's spiritual gatherings have a lot more sizzle? On this count, I am heartened by Carlisle Motors reaching out to its customers, by Ben & Jerry's setting up ice cream "partnerships" with community groups, by the Body Shop's attentiveness to the animal and natural environment, and by many other examples of companies who find "something more" to do with the community impulse than just taking care of their own. As organization scientists, we can turn a cold, objective eye on this search for spirituality and quest for community in business and see it as a monster sure to get us in the end. Why then are growing numbers of organizational scientists welcoming it?

SPIRITUALITY AND COMMUNITY IN ORGANIZATION SCIENCE

Some of the reasons are because our own institutions and belief systems are breaking down, connection and meaning have become more elusive for many of us, and we are part and parcel of the larger postmodern social process that surrounds us (cf. Habermas 1971, Etzioni 1988, Hawley 1993). As evidence of our field's search for something more, consider the ferment in organization sciences occasioned by feminism, multiculturalism, and environmentalism. This search has led scholars to form into subgroups of women, people of color, and environmentalists within the Academy of Management, to join a society to advance socioeconomics, to advocate for the "politics of meaning," and go "on line" in many and varied "electronic communities."

In addition, many practitioners—line managers, human resource specialists, consultants, and workers at every level in companies—are bringing matters of faith and spirit into public discourse. I counted more than 30 conferences that addressed spirituality and business through their whole program or in segments in 1996. Add to this all the rage around "learning organizations" where it is presumed that heightened consciousness—of the self, others, and the system as a whole—undergirds a learning community (Kofman and Senge 1993). Furthermore, Senge (1990) himself hints at the spiritual foundations of this in his appendix on a Euboric "sixth discipline."

But can organization scientists consider seriously the idea that companies can be organized along the lines of an "unseen order" or, what theologian H. Richard Niebuhr (1963) calls, in words that appeal to my ears, the "universal community . . . whose boundaries cannot be drawn in space, or time, or extent of interaction, short of a whole in which we live and move and have our being." In his deeper reflections, Gregory Bateson (1979) posits that social systems are gifted with wisdom. Some who go deep within themselves believe that we humans have "tacit" knowledge of universal community and can co-create a new order in our collective lives in line with it (cf. Polanyi 1969, Chopra 1989). This is the utopian aspiration for business outlined by Harman and Hormann (1990) in *Creative Work*. They make the point that the "central project" of laborers and leaders in the Middle Ages was construction of great churches in honor of their god. It shifted as god moved from the center of the universe and earthly science and material pursuits defined who we are and why we work. Today they wonder if a new central project for civilization might emerge from our new consciousness and new appreciation of what is the center of our existence. Peck (1993) hopes so in concluding *A World Waiting to be Born:* "Utopia may not be impossible to achieve after all."

Where to go with all of this? One option is to take the concept of community-in-organizations seriously and inquire into it (cf. Rothschild-Whitt 1979). Surely it is worthwhile for postmodern scholars to deconstruct this concept and assess whose interests are served by organizations introducing spirituality into their modus operandi. At the same time, it would also be useful to work together with colleagues in theology, utopian studies, and the spiritual sciences to understand how their disciplines understand these things and think about them in the business world. Such inquiry could yield more popular books like *Jesus, CEO* (Jones 1995) and works like *Spirit at Work* (Conger et al. 1994) that combine ideas from the organizational sciences with those of several spiritual traditions.

Field research also beckons: consider studying the cultures of Service-Master and Hewlett Packard. Both have strong, entrepreneurial cultures and transmit values through storytelling about their founders and heroes; yet one emphasizes faith in God and the other stresses perseverance and cooperation. Or simply take a closer look at faculty meetings where Meryl Louis (1994) finds, at least in one case, the principles of community at work.

Second, there is the exploration of your own voice on these matters. To this point, the best writing on the subject at hand comes from Parker Palmer, Max DePree, John Gardner, and M. Scott Peck: all practitioners in the best sense of the word. William Torbert, Jean Bartunek, Peter Vail, and Mary Ann Hazen are among the few organizational scientists who have spoken directly to matters of community and spirit over the course of their scholarly careers. I can envision, however, an outpouring of ideas and creative dialogue as we plumb our own depths and consider seriously what it would mean to be organized in line with "universal community."

Finally, we can do our collective work in new ways. Consider some examples:

- A conference on "Working with Spirituality in Organizations" in Scotland in 1990 (Snell et al. 1991);
- An Academy of Management symposia on "Organizations as Spiritual Settings" in 1991 (*Journal of Organization Change Management* 1994);
- A gathering of practitioners and scholars in Massachusetts in 1993 to discuss spirituality and leadership (leading to Conger et al. 1994);

- A conference on "Global Organizational Change," sponsored by the Academy of Management and Case Western Reserve, that intermixed talks on theory and strategy with sacred readings and tribal dancing.

Even as our interest in all of this increases, a new community of business people and scholars is taking shape. Its members meet at gatherings like Bretton Woods and successor sites, join the World Business Academy, an off-shoot of the Institute of Noetic Sciences, participate in FCE programs and conferences, and put their energies into reforming the curricula taught to management students or start "alternative" business schools. In turn, new voices emerge in volumes like *Community in Business* (Gozdz 1996) and familiar ones take on an unfamiliar but pleasing tone, as in Bolman and Deal's (1995) *Leading with Soul* and Quinn's (1996) *Deep Change.*

Who knows where this will take us? Likely as not, to a place we know but have never been before.

REFERENCES

Alderfer, C. P. (1966), "An Intergroup Perspective on Group Dynamics," in J. Lorsch (Ed.), *Handbook of Organizational Behavior,* Englewood Cliffs, NJ: Prentice Hall.

Argyris. C. (1982), *Reasoning, Learning, and Action,* San Francisco, CA: Jossey-Bass.

——— (1985), *Strategy, Change, and Defensive Routines,* Cambridge, MA: Ballinger.

Arieti, S. (1976), *Creativity,* New York: Basic Books.

Bateson, G. (1972), *Steps to an Ecology of the Mind,* New York: Chandler.

——— (1979). *Mind and Nature: A Necessary Unity,* New York: Dutton.

Beinecke, R. H. (1994), "Assessing the Economic Impact of Personal Development Programs," in F. Heuberger and L. Nash (Eds.), *The Fatal Embrace? Assessing Holistic Trends in Human Resources Programs,* New Brunswick, NJ: Transaction.

Bellah, R., R. Madsden, W. Sullivan, A. Swinder and S. Tipton (1985), *Habits of the Heart,* New York: Harper & Row.

———, ———, ———, ——— and ——— (1991), *The Good Society,* New York: Knopf.

Bennet, A. (1986). "Airline's Ills Point out Weaknesses of Its Unorthodox Management Style," *Wall Street Journal,* August 11.

Bennis, W. G. and H. A. Shephard (1956), "A Theory of Group Development," *Human Relations,* 9, 415-437.

Bion, W. R. (1961), *Experiences in Groups,* London, UK: Tavistock Publications.

Bohm, D. (1986), *Wholeness and the Implicate Order,* London, UK: Ark.

——— (1989), *On Dialogue,* David Bohm Seminars, Ojai, CA.

Bolman, L. and T. Deal (1995), *Leading with Soul,* San Francisco, CA: Jossey-Bass.

Bradford, L. P., J. R. Gibb and K. W. Benne (Eds.) (1964), *T-Group Theory and Laboratory Method,* New York: Wiley.

Buber, M. (1965), *Between Man and Man,* New York: McMillan.

——— (1970), *I and Thou,* New York: Scribner.

Bunker, B. B. and B. T. Alban (Eds.) (1992), "Large Group Interventions," *Journal of Applied Behavioral Science,* 28, 4.

Business Week (1995), "Companies Hit the Road Less Traveled," June 5.

Capra, F. (1976), *The Tao of Physics,* New York: Bantam.

―――― (1982), *Turning Point: Science, Society, and the Rising Culture,* New York: Bantam.

Carter, S. L. (1994), *The Culture of Disbelief,* New York: Basic Books.

Cartwright, D. (1951), "Achieving Change in People: Some Applications of Group Dynamics Theory," *Human Relations,* 4, 4, 381-392.

Chopra, D. (1989), *Quantum Healing,* New York: Bantam Books.

Conger, J. & Associates (1994), *Spirit at Work,* San Francisco, CA: Jossey-Bass.

Cooley, C. H. (1922), *Human Nature and the Social Order,* New York: Scribner's.

Cooperrider, D. (1990), "Positive Image, Positive Action," in S. Srivastva and Associates (Eds.), *Appreciative Management and Leadership,* San Francisco, CA: Jossey-Bass.

Covey, S. (1990), *Principle-Centered Leadership,* New York: Summit.

Cox, M. (1993), "Business Books Emphasize the Spiritual," *Wall Street Journal,* December 14.

Csikszentmihalyi, M. (1990), *Flow: The Psychology of Optimal Experience,* New York: Harper & Row.

De Mare, P., R. Piper and S. Thompson (1991), *Koinonia: From Hate Through Dialogue to Culture in the Large Group,* London, UK: Karnac.

Depree, M. (1989), *Leadership Is an Art,* New York: Doubleday.

Etzioni, A. (1988), *The Moral Dimension,* New York: Free Press.

―――― (1993), *The Spirit of Community,* New York: Touchstone.

Fletcher, J. (1996), "A Relational Approach to the Protean Worker," in D. T. Hall and Associates (Eds.), *The Career is Dead—Long Live the Career,* San Francisco, CA: Jossey-Bass.

Freud, S. (1965), *New Introductory Lectures on Psychoanalysis,* in J. Strachey (Ed.), New York: Norton.

Friedman, M. (1983), *The Confrontation of Otherness: In Family, Community and Society,* New York: Pilgrim Press.

Fromm, E. (1956), *The Art of Loving,* New York: Harper & Row.

Gardner, H. (1995), *Leading Minds,* New York: HarperCollins.

Gardner, J. (1995), *Building Community,* Washington, DC: Independent Sector.

Gozdz, K. (Ed.) (1996), *Community Building in Business,* San Francisco, CA: New Leaders Press.

Greenfield, H. (1996), "Corporate Community," in K. Gozdz (Ed.), *Community Building in Business,* San Francisco, CA: New Leaders Press.

Greenleaf, R. (1993), "The Leader as Servant," in C. Whitmyer (Ed.), *In the Company of Others,* New York: Putnam.

Griffin, E. (1993), *The Reflective Executive: A Spirituality of Business and Enterprise,* New York: Cross Roads.

Habermas, J. (1971), *Knowledge and Human Interests,* Boston, MA: Beacon Press.

Hackman, J. R. and J. L. Suttle (1977), *Improving Life at Work,* Santa Monica, CA: Goodyear.

Hahn, Thich Nhat (1990), *The Miracle of Mindfulness,* Berkeley, CA: Parallax Press.

―――― (1993), "Awareness: The Consciousness of Community," in C. Whitmyer (Ed.), *In the Company of Others,* New York: Putnam.

Hall, D. T. and P. H. Mirvis (1996), "The New Protean Career: Psychological Success and the Path with a Heart," in D. T. Hall and Associates (Eds.), *The Career is Dead—Long Live the Career,* San Francisco, CA: Jossey-Bass.

Hampden-Turner, C. (1971), *Radical Man,* New York: Doubleday.

Harman, W. (1988), *Global Mind Change,* New York: Warner.

―――― and J. Hormann (1990), *Creative Work,* Indianapolis, IN: Knowledge Systems, Inc.

Harrison, R. (1983), "Strategies for a New Age," *Human Resource Management,* 22, 209-235.

Hawley, J. (1993), *Reawakening the Spirit in Work: The Power of Dharmic Management,* San Francisco, CA: Berrett-Koehler.

Herzberg, F. B., B. Mausner and B. Synderman (1959), *The Motivation to Work,* New York: Wiley.

Isaacs, W. N. (1993), "Dialogue: The Power of Collective Thinking," *The Systems Thinker,* 4, 3.

——— (1994), "Dialogue, Collective Thinking, and Organizational Learning," *Organizational Dynamics.*

James, W. (1902), *The Varieties of Religious Experience.*

Jones, L. B. (1995), *Jesus, CEO,* New York: Hyperion.

Journal of Organizational Change Management (1994) 7.

Kahn, W. A. (1992), "To Be Fully There: Psychological Presence at Work," *Human Relations,* 45, 4, 321-349.

——— (1993), "Caring for the Caregiver: Patterns of Organizational Caregiving," *Administrative Science Quarterly,* 38, 4, 539-563.

Kanter, D. L. and P. H. Mirvis (1989), *The Cynical Americans,* San Francisco, CA: Jossey-Bass.

Kanter, R. M. (1972), *Commitment and Community: Communes and Utopias in Sociological Perspective,* Cambridge, MA: Harvard University Press.

Klein, M. (1959), "Our Adult World and Its Roots in Infancy," *Human Relations,* 12, 291-303.

Koestler, A. (1964), *The Act of Creation,* New York: Macmillan.

Kofman, F. and P. Senge (1993), "Communities of Commitment: The Heart of the Learning Organization," *Organization Dynamics,* Fall.

Learner, M. (1996), *The Politics of Meaning,* Reading, MA: Addison-Wesley.

Louis, M. R. (1994), "In the Manner of Friends: Learning from Quaker Practice for Organizational Renewal," *Journal of Organizational Change Management,* 7, 1, 42-60.

Maslow, A. H. (1954), *Motivation and Personality,* New York: Harper.

——— (1965), *Eupsychian Management,* Homewood, IL: Irwin/Dorsey.

——— (1968), *Toward a Psychology of Being,* New York: Van Nostrand.

McGregor, D. (1960), *The Human Side of Enterprise,* Englewood-Cliffs, NJ: Prentice Hall.

McMillan, D. W. and D. M. Chavis (1986), "Sense of Community: A Definition and Theory," *Journal of Community Psychology,* 14, 6-23.

Mirvis, P. H. (1980), "The Art of Assessing the Quality of Work Life," in E. Lawler, D. Nadler, and C. Camman (Eds.), *Organizational Assessment,* New York: Wiley Interscience.

——— (Ed.) (1993a), *Building the Competitive Workforce,* New York: Wiley.

——— (1993b), "Human Development or Depersonalization: The Company of Total Community," in F. Heuberger and L. Nash (Eds.), *The Fatal Embrace?* New Brunswick, NJ: Transaction.

——— (1996), "Midlife as a Consultant," in P. J. Frost and M. S. Taylor (Eds.), *Rhythms of an Academic's Life,* Beverly Hills, CA: Sage.

Moore, T. (1991), *Care of the Soul: A Guide of Cultivating Depth and Sacredness in Everyday Life,* New York: Harper-Collins.

Nash, Laura (1996), Professor at Boston University, working on a book on "Christian-based" organizations.

Newsweek (1987), "Corporate Mind Control," May 4.

Niebuhr, H. R. (1963), *The Responsible Self,* New York: Harper and Row.

Peck, M. S. (1978), *The Road Less Traveled,* New York: Simon and Schuster.

——— (1987), *The Different Drum,* New York: Simon and Schuster.

——— (1993), *A World Waiting to Be Born* New York: Bantam.

Polanyi, M. (1969), *Knowing and Being,* in Marjorie Grene (Ed.), Chicago, IL: University of Chicago Press.

Pollard, C. W. (1996), *The Soul of the Firm,* New York: HarperBusiness.

Prokesch, S. (1986), "Behind People Express's Fall: An Offbeat Managerial Style," *New York Times,* September 23.

Putnam, R. D. (1992), *Making Democracy Work,* Princeton, NJ: Princeton University Press.

Quinn, R. E. (1996), *Deep Change,* San Francisco, CA: Jossey-Bass.

Ray, M. and A. Rinzler (1993), *The New Paradigm in Business,* New York: Tarcher/Perigee.

Roddick, A. (1990), *Body and Soul: Profits with Principles,* New York, Crown.

Rothschild-Whitt, J. (1979), "The Collectivist Organization: An Alternative to Rational-bureaucratic Models," *American Sociological Review, 44,* 509-527.

Sarason, S. (1974), *The Psychological Sense of Community,* San Francisco, CA: Jossey-Bass.

Schindler-Rainman, E. and R. Lippitt (1980), *Building the Collaborative Community: Mobilizing Citizens for Action,* University of California Extension.

Schon, D. (1983), *The Reflective Practitioner,* New York: Basic Books.

Schor, J. B. (1991), *The Overworked American,* New York: Basic Books.

Scott, M. and H. Rothman (1992). *Companies with a Conscience,* New York: Birch Lane Press.

Senge, P. (1990), *The Fifth Discipline,* New York: Doubleday.

Shaffer, C. R. and K. Anundsen (1993), *Creating Community Anywhere,* New York: Tarcher/Putnam.

Siegel, B. S. (1986), *Love, Medicine & Miracles,* New York: Harper & Row.

Slater, P. E. (1966), *Microcosm,* New York: Wiley Interscience.

Smith, K. and D. N. Berg (1987), *Paradoxes of Group Life,* San Francisco, CA: Jossey Bass.

Snell, R., J. Davies, T. Boydell and M. Leary (Ed.) (1991), "Joining Forces," *Management Education and Development,* 22, 3.

Talbot, M. (1986), *Beyond the Quantum,* New York: Bantam Books.

Time (1986), "People Express," January 13.

Tuckman, B. W. (1965), "Developmental Sequences in Small Groups," *Psychological Bulletin,* 54, 229-249.

Wheatley, M. J. (1993), *Leadership and the New Science: Learning about Organization from an Orderly Universe,* San Francisco, CA: Berrett-Koehler Publishers, Inc.

Whitney, D. (1995), "Spirituality as a Global Organizing Potential," Paper delivered at conference on The Organizational Dimensions of Global Change, Cleveland, OH: Case Western Reserve University.

Whyte, D. (1994), *The Heart Aroused,* New York: Doubleday.

Wiesbord, M. (1992), *Discovering Common Ground,* San Francisco, CA: Berrett-Koehler.

Wilbur, K. (1984), *Quantum Questions,* Boston, MA: Shambala.

Wuthnow, R. (1991), *Acts of Compassion: Caring for Others and Helping Ourselves,* Princeton, NJ: Princeton University Press.

17

Bridging Academia and Business

A Conversation With Steve Kerr

PETER FROST (PF): A very important reason for my wanting to meet with you, Steve, and to interview you is the fact that you've had many, many roles in your fine career and they've spanned scholarship, teaching, administration at a university, presidency of the Academy of Management, consulting, and now a management professional job as VP of management development at General Electric. There are very few people in the field who have that breadth and that experience. In my view, this is a time when as management scholars, we need all the help we can get to learn about what's happening in and around organizations in these times of change. I wondered if you could maybe start by telling me a little about the milestones of your career, how you got to where you are now, and then we can talk about some of those experiences and about how you see the links between academia and business and what lies ahead in each of these arenas.

    STEVE KERR (SK): Sure. The quick backdrop, if you want a conceptual underpinning—Michael Driver, a former colleague at USC, talks about career types and labelled me a spiral. This was many years ago. Somebody who has discontinuous careers. I seem to spin out of one thing into another. I'm not sure it's a flattering term but that's how I scored. And nobody I know would take career advice from me, because I really do very little volition-

From "Bridging Academia and Business: A Conversation with Steve Kerr," by Peter J. Frost and Steve Kerr, 1997, *Organization Science, 8,* pp. 333-347. Copyright © 1997, The Institute of Management Sciences. Reprinted with permission.

ally—I seem to be nagged into taking most jobs I have had. So any pattern is purely retrospective attributions.

PF: Sure.

SK: I had begun a corporate career. I was eight years in industry and living in Manhattan. I went to C.U.N.Y., a local school. (They called it the other UCLA, which is the University at the Corner of Lexington Avenue.) I ran into Bob House (currently at Wharton); I was a programmer for Mobil Oil and Bob was a guy who was real skittish about computers. So he basically lured me into—I was just in a part-time MBA program—and he lured me into the doctoral program, for his own reasons, as he said. He wanted somebody who knew computers, so he struck a deal where my income in his consulting firm would be the same and I would get my dissertation data, etc., etc. So I ended up doing a doctoral program by being lured into it, away from my career path. I loved university life, and then through his influence I got a job interview at Ohio State, and I was at Ohio State for seven years. House has been a great mentor in my life. From there I went to USC. I was a professor and never meant to be a department head, but the department kind of ganged up on me and asked me to take the department chair, so I did that for a while. Then Warren Bennis and Jim O'Toole cornered me and said: "the dean, Jack Steele, is tired, he needs help, there's no associate dean, you're the only one he trusts, you gotta do it."

So I got nagged into being an administrator—that's how I became a dean. I would never have gone to L.A. if I'd known they were planning to turn me into an administrator. I ended up as dean of faculty for four years, and then GE started what *Fortune* magazine called the biggest cultural change in the history of corporate America, a radical transformation of a $60 billion dollar (at that time) corporation. Twenty-four faculty were selected. They were all pedigree except me. They were all, you know, Wharton and Michigan and Columbia and Harvard, but they needed somebody in the west because there was one GE business in the west. So they selected me to run the nuclear business Work-Out program.

I got the best job in the world: an easy job disguised as a hard job. Welch and company thought that nuclear would be a very hard one to do, because they're the most regulated business in the GE family and for other reasons. But in fact the people there were wonderful, and the more I told people it was easy the more they thought I was being modest. So by 1990, Jack Welch needed a showcase, an organization doing its Work-Out program very well. He needed to show it was working. Some of the ones he was counting on *weren't* working that well in the beginning, and here was nuclear, so they brought me into the big centre stage of GE. It was the Boca Raton meetings, where the top 500 people get together. And it wasn't so much, I thought at the time, about how well I was doing but the message was, if nuclear can do it, *anyone* can do it! So I went in and described it. Two businesses there had just removed their first Work-Out consultant. They heard what I did and invited me in, and by 1992 and 1993, I was working 200 days a year for General Electric, and I was on leave from USC. Then the University of Michigan offered to let me do a visiting professorship in an intensive way: 10 weeks, and later 12 weeks solid. I was living with the students in the executive residence building, but during the rest of the time I was free to do my consulting.

So this was, as you said, an introduction to consulting. Again, it just happened, I never signed on to do that either. When we signed on for GE they said: "give us 25 days a year," which was all I had to spare as dean. But it turned out that it just kept growing and growing, and again, it was by inches. I never really made a commitment to change my life, it's just, I looked up one day and I found I was doing this thing a lot. And then it ended with my predecessor in the Crotonville position leaving, and Welch called me. I remember I was in Dow Brands consulting, in Indianapolis, and Welch called and said, "Help me build an applicant pool." And later it turned out I *was* his applicant pool. I had *no* idea I would be offered it. I had *no* thought I would take it. I did turn it down for a while, but the chairman of GE is a very irresistible salesman. If he wants something, at the end of the day you've given it to him.

And so, in cameo form, that's my career. I was, as you said, involved in the Academy. I have been president, I guess seven years ago. And in my USC career I also ended up directing the doctoral program for several years. I even was interim director of the entrepreneur program for a year. And it helped me—I've never had a job I didn't learn from. And that's part of the reason— I mean, I *have* lurched through life, people nag me and I take things. But I think I would have learned not to do it if I'd had a bad experience. And that's why I said that you carry your life satisfaction with you, more or less. I mean some jobs are below the cut, and nobody could find joy in them, but I've never had a job that poor. I've enjoyed every place I've lived, and I've enjoyed every place I've worked. So I do have a very interesting job now, and it's enough like what I've done so that there's tremendous transferability of learnings.

PF: What sorts of things would you highlight in the job at the moment?

SK: What I do now? There are several types of activities in GE. First, I have an office in Crotonville, and in fact I have a house in Crotonville that comes with the job. Crotonville is the GE Leadership Development Facility. It's gotten a lot of celebrity in the press; *Fortune* calls it the "Harvard of Corporate America." I assume that's flattering. [*Laughter*]

Crotonville is responsible for all the leadership programs that are *centrally* done in GE. A great deal of training in GE is done within the businesses, and isn't within my bailiwick. There are a set of courses designed to provide functional education. So these people come in, some are 22 years old, some have graduate degrees but many are undergrads. We put them through two years of training. They take a lot of resources, more than they give back in the first two years. They have weeks at Crotonville for courses, but they also have typically four rotations in different assignments, and they're very, very attractive by the time the two years have gone by. In fact, we always have to guard against attrition.

PF: You're training for competitors?

SK: Yeah, but obviously it's still worthwhile for us to do it, and most stay. So there are a number of courses tied to that, and later, provide an advanced functional education: advanced HR, advanced finance, and so on. So that's a trail of courses. There's a second trail that corresponds to people's career stage—that's under my bailiwick. From a new manager to an experienced manager, to the first time you have a general manager's responsibility, to when you have a global responsibility. And we don't proact; the businesses send people in, but it's known through GE at what career points it pays. And actually, this is part of it. GE does more thoughtful succession planning than any company on the planet, probably.

PF: Has that been historically true, or has it only been since Jack Welch took over?

SK: No, no, I think it's been true over time. *Built to Last* [James Collins & Jerry Porac, Harper Business, 1994] has chapters on companies that have made it, that have lasted through the twentieth century. And their major point is that the key to GE's success has been succession planning and leadership development. They mention Crotonville. But a lot of it's the succession. In fact, they make the point that it's a misbelief that Jack Welch came riding in from the outside on his white horse, to save the company. He didn't ride in from the outside; GE was his first full-time job. And their point is that, therefore, GE made Jack Welch as much as Jack Welch has made GE. And it's been the succession planning. You know, the case is well known, of how Reg Jones picked a successor, the whole notion of how Welch was selected.

And so the current Chairman of GE, Welch, certainly maintains a tradition. There's a senior level person whose full-time job it is to do succession. So in any event, that's the answer. It's a very, very thoughtful approach. And by the way, it's not just training. GE is willing to move people into jobs that might not make sense for the company, for the organization, in order to enrich the person.

PF: For example?

SK: Well, it's spooky how much Welch knows. The guy's incredible. In fact, I used to work with Andy Siegler, when he was chairman of Champion, and who's on the GE board. And Andy said, "I run a smaller company than GE, and I couldn't begin to have the in-depth knowledge of people that Jack does." So, for example, in these review sessions, Jack knows *intimately* the career paths of more than a thousand employees in GE. More than a thousand. So he'll have a typical review session (called a session C). For example, he'll say, "I thought we agreed that Hawkins was going to have field experience. What's he still doing in the home office?" "Well, Jack, this project came up. . . ." And he's there, "I don't care what happened. This guy *has* to be in the field." Or "He hasn't yet been in a short-cycle business. How are we gonna groom him if he doesn't get into that?" Or "He has not yet been in a consumer business. Why isn't he moving to Lighting?"

PF: So he's keeping that big picture in front of people?

SK: It's a giant chessboard. He's got all these businesses, so you can give people almost any experience, in every country, in every business. You want short cycle or long, you want union or non-union, you cut the pie any way, GE's got businesses. And that's interesting, but the real interest is the GE willingness, starting with the chairman, to put people in a position because it's the right professional growth experience for that person. And they don't say, "Well, by the way, he may not help this particular generator." That's not the point of it. And so Jack has his test pads, his demonstration projects. And in this giant tableau, it's not all about training, it's about management succession, and always about evaluation; I mean, GE is compulsive about evaluation. Session C is the formal review, but the expression is "Every day is Session C at General Electric." You're always on trial.

PF: And what are they looking for in the evaluation? Just straight performance, or are there also process aspects?

SK: Both. Jack is adamant that we're a big company that has to walk small, think small, talk small. Speed is everything. We've gotta be able to move quickly. You know, there's none of this paralysis of analysis. Just trust the people and put the ball in play. And if it doesn't work, we'll do something else. But the big sin is to do nothing. Don't sit. Problems get worse if you don't act—take your best shot. You know, if your decision made sense, given the data base you had at the time, you won't be hanged for it. If you made a bad decision and anyone could have foreseen it, nobody's very forgiving at GE. We don't tolerate mediocrity. But the point is, we understand that was your data base. Given that, I would have made the same decision—wrong decision, move away, get on with life. And that's very, very interesting. And if you don't attack people, they don't become defensive. I'm not taking back what I said. It's very evaluational—extremely so. But it's not playing "gotcha!" you know. It really is a lot of "look at the process" stuff, where they ask "did you make your numbers or not?" and "did you exhibit the values (which is a process) or not?" And if you don't make the numbers, but your process was right, your values were right, we'll give you another swing.

The third type of courses are tailor-built to fit GE initiatives.

It's funny, you know, Jack, he was really lauding the place—luring me to come, you know: "what a great place," which of course it is. And then when I get there he says: "You have got problems!" [*Laughs*] "What do you mean *I*'ve got problems?" He said: "You've got people who come in from universities. They don't know us, but they think they can help us. They teach . . ." (He used accounting as an example, but it didn't have to be accounting, it could have been anything.) He said: "He comes in, he teaches accounting, he's been doing it for twenty years, if he doesn't know us, how can he help us?" His point was, this is a *leadership* institute. Leadership is helping the business and helping the business leader achieve the corporate priorities. They call them the *initiatives* in GE. So he said: "Always be tailoring your courses to fit to the GE initiatives." And the initiatives are very robust. For example, productivity, globalization, quick market intelligence (QMI), which we got from Walmart, the notion of being in constant touch with your markets. The problem is, you don't have a professor of QMI out there, you *do* have professors of accounting. So it immediately got more difficult for me because we don't have an in-house faculty; we source our talent from the outside.

That's a big plus, but also a minus—you can almost be paralysed. You know, you're not limited to what you're capable of doing, you could do *anything*. And all Jack says is "honor the initiatives. Always help people achieve the initiatives." So that's the third type of course I do—it's not tied toward functional expertise, it's not tied toward career stage, it's tied toward what's needed at a given time. We fell in love a few years ago with demand flow technology, which is essentially a build-to-order instead of build-to-inventory. You do it right, inventory turns go great and working capital drops—it's wonderful. But it has intricate training—a lot of training associated with it. As you do quality, it is the same thing, a lot of training. You gotta think about how you source this stuff. And you've got academics, you've got consulting firms, and so on. So there's a whole third type of course which is tailor built to fit particular initiatives. And these always change over time, so I'm always running around trying to build programs. That's the third leg of the stool of what I do in the way of education.

PF: That's fascinating. It leads to some questions for me, particularly from the point of view of management training using academics. Do we have academics who can cut the mustard in sufficient depth that you can use them? And if this becomes the model for other organizations, could they reach out and source in from universities, or are we as academics far from the "helpfulness" mark?

SK: We have found academics to be the largest single source of talent. Clearly they are excellent at the functional courses—that's leg one. At the career stage courses, we know—we think we know—what kind of content we want. I should add that two out of the three of these executive course sequences—there are three courses they take—two of them have traditionally been international, four-week programs of which most are spent abroad. So some of the preparation, if you will, is about international—about globalization. There are people we bring in who do very good work, but some of them are and some are not from academe. We will make use of some independent consultants, but in general we have not had a problem—in fact, we've been very fortunate, because the higher you go, the less clear it is to everybody, certainly including me, what kind of education is needed. To prepare somebody for their first management assignment, I think we know a lot—not everything. To prepare people to assume a global leadership role in business, you know, I have got some ideas, but they're very fragmented.

So it isn't like we nail it down and then bring in Jones from Yale or UBC [University of British Columbia], and he does "the program." It is tremendously interactive, and you've got to get the *right* faculty. So the applicant pool gets smaller as you go higher, but it doesn't take you away from academe. It takes you to some very thoughtful people and they help shape it. Now, the difference is that, I believe, in many universities you shape it around the teaching and knowledge preferences of the faculty. So, you know: "What's the elective course?" "I don't know, what are you good at?" And when we hire somebody, we say, "Well, you can teach your course." Here it isn't about that. So it isn't that they have to bend to us, because we don't have it nailed, the job description. On the other hand, they can't just come in and do, you know, "Jones 101." So there's a lot more play. I think it does challenge the faculty and me.

But still, when all's said and done, we do find academics to be a very appropriate source—there are very good people. And I must say, universities let them off too easy. And as dean, *I* did. You know, I would say, "Well, Ian Mitroff, he's doing crisis management. Great, Ian—teach that! Mike Driver's one of the world's authorities on careers—great, Mike, teach that!" It's easy for the faculty, it's easy for the dean—I didn't stretch people very much. Here, I don't do it because I'm interested in stretching faculty, I'm doing it because I've gotta make the fit. But I've found academics can be much broader than their pigeonhole if you force them to come out of their pigeonhole. Now some won't—some just know A, and if A doesn't fit, you don't hire them.

Not only does Crotonville benefit from employing academics, I think the academics also benefit. Everybody knows that journals are 12 months in review and 12 months in press, and by the time you get it, you're reading two-year-old stuff. But that's not the major delay. At least in the U.S.—maybe I'll generalize to North America—most of the innovations, I think, come out of industry or consulting firms. Academics get in early, write it up, codify the knowledge, share it—a very valuable role, the bee pollinating the flower.

PF: But they're not the seeders at the beginning?

SK: I don't think so. And I'm sure someone would read this and come up with counterexamples and they'd be right. You know, Theory Z came out of Ouchi's stuff and he was an academic at the time. I don't mean there are *none*. But if you pull out ten of the major innovations—and even ten of the silly fads—most start, I think, from some other source than academe.

PF: Is that a function of a lack of connection to what's happening in a speedy way these days, or is that just the way academia works. Or—is there something we should be doing differently?

SK: I think it's some of each. I think that there are inadequate connections between academe and the corporate world. Again, you can't tar everybody—many individuals have one foot in each world very comfortably, and many business schools have very good boards of advisors or counsellors and get the corporate world in and it shapes their curriculum. I don't mean it doesn't happen at all—it's not even rare. But, having said that, I wouldn't go back on what I said—there are still many places with inadequate connections.

It's also the way academe works. One of the major differences I have in a corporate university—I don't have an AACSB, I don't have a curriculum committee, I don't have review committees, I don't have people who are tenured professors. I mean, I would have—dialogues in universities would be, you know, "I want to teach this course." "Well, what are you going to stop?" "Well we'll stop that course." "You can't stop that course." "Why not?" "Ernie teaches that course." "What's that got to do with . . .?" "Ernie's tenured, that's what he teaches. If he doesn't teach that, what will he do?" "Well, nobody takes it." "No problem, we'll make it required." [*Laughs*] That's just an academic dialogue—now people will take it, we've created a demand by making it a required course. And you don't have that dialogue in corporate universities. So, I mean there's much more of a connection—I can do things much quicker. God knows I can get into trouble much quicker! I can put a fad in place and waste everybody's time much quicker. I'm not trying to say bad or good, I'm just responding to your question. It's not just connections—it's that academe gets into trouble much more slowly, but also it gets into innovation at a much slower pace. There's just a lot more review, a lot more people have to touch it as it goes by. So the new important and the silly both get started mostly in industry or in consulting firms, which don't have that (academic) culture.

Now the other point that I want to make, because it's been on my mind since I just became a trustee in the Marketing Science Institute, and I'm real impressed with this approach. We have, in the Academy, we have about a thousand practitioner members. I don't know the exact number. At the Marketing Science Institute, you come representing your institution. And by signing on—it's at your option, you can always say no—but you know your role, among others, is to be a broker. That the academics who join will be looking for research entree, maybe even some expense coverage on research, and they will be coming to you and you will broker the right ones into your firm. It's a lovely model, I really like it. And so, again, part of why this stuff happens—in the Academy, we do have practitioner members, but I don't come here knowing it's my responsibility, and in fact I kind of get grouchy, because I find with my new name tag I'm visited by people who think it would be great if I'd give them money or let them in and so on. And in the Marketing Science Institute I don't resent it because I understand that's my role, to be that kind of a broker. So I think there's more we can do. The people are here now. I mean, HP, AT & T, we're all here, but we're not making the connections adequately. And the faculty who do tug on my sleeve, I mean, I do get cranky, they're feeling funny—it shouldn't be that way, there are ways we can smooth the connections. I don't know if there's any way you can solve the rate of change problem—academe will always move slowly. In fact, there is that old Warren Bennis quote—I think it was Warren—he said "the only thing slower than changing a curriculum is moving a cemetery." That I don't think this will change in my lifetime.

PF: There's one other thing I wonder if you've had some thoughts on. All of what you've described suggests a heightened pace of connection between academia and the business world, through the kind of people you use and how they have to adapt and you have to adapt. In research focussed business schools, if not in the teaching schools, one comes in to learn one's craft, do one's craft, to publish, get established in a career, and to follow one's path this way up through to being a full professor. One implication for me is that it's possible that the people that you're using for GE are the ones who've been through all these steps and are now, in a way, more available. On the other hand, some of the brightest minds may well be the ones of those who are more junior. In many schools such an academic would receive advice *not* to teach at or work with the Crotonvilles of the business world. It would be considered a bad career move, or a pulling away from research where one should be focussing. And I'm wondering if you've experienced that, and what implications it might have?

SK: Yeah. A couple of observations—I think you've made a very good point. First, I don't need to have the advanced rank to establish credibility. So—you're right, if I were to do a demographic on the people I bring in, most of them are senior people who have been through the stages you described, that's true. But it isn't as if, when I would have a person come in for a speaker series at a university, I would necessarily go for a full professor because I need the cachet. That's not true in Crotonville—people trust the process. Now, if I brought in losers they would stop, but that doesn't happen. So it isn't that I *couldn't* go for a bright, young assistant, but having said that, let's get to the more deep causes. When I was program chair at the Academy, which goes back to the Disneyland meeting in '88, I kept some program time to myself. The Divisions were on their own, but when we went into the central program time that I kept, the theme was "The Marriage of Theory and Practice." I had joint reviewers—a reviewer from academe, and a reviewer from the business community. And it was delightful to do interrater reliability checks and see, when a practitioner didn't like a piece, why didn't she? And when an academic doesn't like a piece, what were the reasons? . . . My point is, if people wanted to change attitudes and actions, one of the two things that could change this would be to include practitioners in the practice. It *is* true that a young person should concentrate on establishing a specialty, and that includes research and publishing, and consulting could be diverting. But why is it that when you do your research you go through what are almost exclusively academic reviewers? I mean, look at the mastheads of the major journals. It's not zero. You always have three or four—I'm on seven editorial review boards. They didn't put me on because I was GE, only one is since I've been at GE, but nobody told me I'm no longer suitable. Why couldn't we have a sharp increase in the number of practitioners? Now, the academic would read this and say "well, but you're unusual." You know, I used to publish stuff on psychometrics, I did a Ph.D., I understand it. But that's my point. I'm less useful, because I *don't* use the practitioner lens. I still have trouble thinking of myself that way. Get true practitioners in there, and let them look at a person's work.

Now, you have a right to say "I don't choose to play to that audience," but I mean, *business* schools shouldn't be afraid to go into business. Medical schools—you wouldn't become a doctor without doing internship and residency. Even the clergy wouldn't fail to go out and do a service from time to time. There are very good professions that have practice as a major part of getting ready. I hope it's not instead of research. I hope that when a physician becomes a physician they're up on the latest research on what they're doing. But in addition, they do extensive work in the world of practice. It's not denigrated—it's part of their training. Become an intern, get out there! You can't learn about a field by reading about it, you must get out there. So this notion of being isolated from the world of practice—where is it written that that makes you a better theorist or a researcher? I think we're the only profession that seems to believe that.

PF: If we go back now to your first experiences with the Work-Out, why do you think it worked for you? And what is it about the Work-Out that's sort of generalizable? Is there something about its philosophy that's important? Is there something about the practice of implementing it that's really critical?

SK: Yeah. Both points. And first I'll paraphrase a little bit of Welch. He said: "There are only two kinds of interventions in this world. And the one you choose depends on whether you trust your people." If deep down in your soul you don't trust your people, then you bring in a consulting group. And they push your people aside, they remap your processes, they rewrite your procedures, they build your training manuals, then reluctantly they let your folks back in the building, they teach them the brave new world and off you go. Now, everybody needs consultants sometimes. There are always times when you can't trust your people because there's some specialized expertise out there you need from the outside.

But, having said that, there is intervention type number two: you make the assumption that the people who do a job every day are unusually competent at knowing about that job, and probably even know ways to improve it. If that's so, why do you need an intervention at all? And the answer is, two things get in the way. One is time. In our downsized, delayered universe, people are so hassled it's very hard to think of new ways to do anything. The other is safety. In the average organization, if you *do* come up with a good idea, it's far from obvious that anybody at the top is dying to hear about it. So you go home at night with stuff in your head that would help UBC be more effective, and you don't tell anybody. You got stuff in your head that would help your boss do a better job, and you don't tell him or her. Because it's awkward, maybe even risky. So imagine if you could untap all that energy, give people time and make it safe. So that was the notion of, the underpinning of Work-Out. And then how you do it, the implementation, it's got a thousand ways it rolled out but it all had to do with giving people time and making it safe. Time was easy—Welch said there should be three days. **Three days!** The doubters said "we don't have three days!" Well, you better find three days. Important goals come from the top. Jack always says how you do it is up to you, but get it done. And that's very powerful. I know corporations that thought they were gonna have a uniform dress code, uniform performance appraisal system, uniform this, uniform that. GE understands—you're in a lot of businesses, a lot of countries, you're not gonna legislate stuff out of corporate headquarters. So Jack said: "I understand you've got to tailor it, but I want to be able to recognize it as Work-Out." So that's "give it time." And then we did a number of things to make it safe, from disguising ideas, to having groups recommend it, or having roadblock busters who protected the champions.

The fascinating part of Work-Out—you know, there's nothing new about having groups of people come up with ideas and proposing them to management at the end of the day. The only new feature really was the idea of the champion. In a quality circle experience, low-level people present good ideas to management. They leave, the low-level workers leave, feeling great. Management, on the other hand, came in with 10 great ideas and no time, they left with 14 great ideas and no time. So you had a low implementation rate. The GE notion—and that was Welch's idea, I think the champion, somebody in the group has to *own* that idea, has to make it happen. So you have a low-level clerk or a new hire who's just been charged with making a major policy change in a GE corporation, a worldwide corporation. Oh my God, how could they do it? Well, there was a detailed action plan, and there was also a roadblock buster, who was an 800-pound gorilla whose job it was to protect the champions. So what you had in this Work-Out effort was a revolution plotted at the top, carried out at the bottom—or, actually, at all levels and protected at the top, by the use of these roadblock busters. An interesting balance of power.

PF: I was going to say it's a very sophisticated notion of how politics works in organizations.

SK: And it was built by a sophisticated politician, namely the chairman of GE. When the theoreticians build it—and I know, I would go back, and we had a lot of academics, we would go and try to explain this to academic audiences and nobody was impressed. "Oh that's Theory Z," "Oh that's Quality Circles." And that's right—there's nothing new, in theory. But in *practice,* it was built to work in your average political, time-sensitive, resource-poor corporation. And he made it work.

And the other feature was saying yes or no in real time. That you couldn't say, "well you've given us food for thought, we'll bring this up at our staff meeting back home." You were exposed, you had to say yes or no. Again, that's the GE notion—you might be right, you might be wrong, but for gosh sake do something. The worst sin is to do nothing.

PF: What I hear in what you're saying is that there's a very important message, I don't know whether you'd call it management or leadership policy or if that matters, but an instruction that actually legislates or mandates that people *will* spend time on this particular issue.

SK: Yes. And it was time they didn't have. But there was another key, and again, I tried to do it wrong. My people wouldn't let me—they forced me to do it right and I became a successful model. I didn't want to do small stuff. I wanted to get major stuff, because I was looking at what was happening in the other Work-Out businesses. I'm out there in San Jose, and these other guys are setting up multi-million dollar, fast-balance test facilities, and they're moving all the requisition engineers from New York to South Carolina. And my people were doing the most *piddly* stuff, and I was embarrassed. But the nuclear business—the whole industry, it wasn't GE's fault—had been brutally downsized, so they were afraid that Work-Out really meant more Heads Out. Plus, as I've mentioned, they're the most regulated business. So I didn't have any trust going in. So they were gonna do small stuff. We had this thing called the RAMMPP Matrix, which turned out to be a godsend. RAMMPP stood for the first letter of Reports, Approvals, Meetings, Measures, Policies and Practices. And the question was, could these be done less often? Could they be done with fewer people? Could they be done in a more sophisticated technological way, etc.? So my point is, because they were afraid to do the big stuff, because they were afraid it took out jobs, they did stuff which, it turned out, saved time. They went after RAMMPP. They got rid of reports. They shortened the approval cycle, they made the meetings go away that were useless. So, they went out for—40 people go out for three days, that's 120 days out. That's a third of a man-year, or two-fifths of a man-year. But they saved that in the first meeting. They came back and they had saved for themselves tons of man days—weeks, months.

So I got lucky. I was trying to get them to do what my brothers were doing in the east. But they were afraid to do it, and it turns out they were absolutely right. We called that low-hanging fruit—basically, we found out where the arrow landed, drew a target around it, and yelled "bull's eye!" I never meant for it to happen! And then, the following January, I'm explaining how we went after it all, and it sounded great.

Ultimately, you can't do piddly stuff. Welch talks about a beachhead—he said these hotel sessions were a beachhead. A beachhead is ultimately a worthless hunk of sand—if you don't move off the beach, you get shot. But it's a place you can organize your supply lines, and organize your communication lines, so looking back, that's what we did. We established a beachhead, we went after small stuff, we cleared the weeds so we could then go after the important stuff. And so time became very critical, but we were saving it, not spending it. And when the word of *that* went around, it legitimated the future Work-Outs.

PF: That's an interesting boot-strapping kind of an image. You had to start somewhere.

SK: Yes. And it was absolutely essential to making it work.

PF: That's great. What I want to pick up next is the arena of training. What types of practices, what types of issues were important in preparing people to manage?

SK: If you look at college curricula, you will find 80 percent, 85 percent of what we do in there. But let me say a bit about the most powerful classroom experience I've ever been part of in my 25 years as a teacher. It's called CAP, the Change Acceleration Process at GE.

PF: Let's talk about it.

SK: It's a JIT construct. You know, we could say, "we're gonna teach managing a multi-locational business because it's week five of a syllabus." That's not interesting. Or we could say "you 40 people are here because within three months your businesses tell us you are going to be put in charge of something significantly different than you've ever had before, and we thought you might want to learn how to do it." [*Laughs*] So it's the tee up, it's the timing, it's the bringing together of people from multi-businesses. And because you're GE, you can have all kinds of perspectives. Anyone can do that, but we have so much diversity, of having a person who runs NBC Miami sitting there with a person who is negotiating with China on a delicate turbine deal, sitting in a room with somebody who's building plastics and somebody who's marketing, etc. You can't go to your average class at BU or OSU and pull it together, so some of it's just a GE advantage. Welch comes to virtually every class. The CFO comes, the chief HR officer comes, the vice-chair comes all the time. And they're not just teaching. They're proselytizing and they're listening. My shop is the Broadcast Studio, it's the transmitter and the receiving station for the GE values and the GE culture. So, that part you can't replicate in a university. And it's very powerful. And it isn't motherhood. Welch's sessions in the Pit—and others do as well, but for a large company to have a CEO be that candid . . . I mean, he was telling people the truth about the NBC deal when the public didn't know and the *Wall Street Journal* was getting it wrong but the GE people knew what was happening. I admire his courage. I mean, it's hard to think of 90 people keeping secrets, but Jack just doesn't worry about that. On the record or off, Welch has got tremendous integrity.

So, that's the part that you couldn't replicate. Not the teaching, but the proselytizing, the orientation, the values, the culture, and it's not going in and motherhood. It leads to really interesting discussions where you say, "Look man, what's not negotiable is you're going to be cleaner than clean. You're not going to break any local law, you're not going to break *U.S.* law. I don't care if it's legal there, you can't do it." Having said that, "How on earth can we penetrate those markets," and so on. So it isn't philosophical and clean.

If there's any rap on GE, it has nothing to do with: "They make it up and pretend." There's a deep, deep ethical concern. However, the goals are so high, the demands are so high. Jack always says "show me where C students are more honest than A students." But we really do set standards high. And a person who can't meet them, he has *no* legitimacy, he has no right, but there's the motive to go looking for ways to do shortcuts.

When Welch talks leadership, this isn't out of a textbook. This is a guy who is *living* it. So that's part of what we do.

Another part of what we do is "teach the initiatives." The pilot happened to be the HR program. We used to teach a day on performance appraisal and a day on labor relations and a day on reward systems and a day on training. Now what we might do is in the morning bring in someone who's not HR, who will teach about, let's say, new product introduction. Then in the afternoon you take the HR people and you say, "Okay, you're HR, your tools include staffing, training, rewards, communication, measurement. What do you have in your bag of tricks that could help your business and your business leader do better at new product introduction? For example, are we measuring the right stuff? Are we rewarding the right stuff? Are we training the right things? Are we staffing the right people?" The next morning, in come someone else who's not HR, and the talk is about the Order to Remittance process. What do we know about process flows, and so on. In the afternoon, "Okay, you people in HR, what can you do . . ."

So you see, it's not honoring HR for HR's sake, it's "you're a leader, this is a leadership institute. Your business is faced with meeting these initiatives, what can you do?" Now a month later in come the MIS people. The mornings won't be different. They're still gonna learn about the key GE corporate initiatives, the priorities, but in the afternoon we say "What are your bag of tricks? What can *you* do to help your business achieve new product introduction?" Then in come the finance people, "What can *you* do?" But it's not "Honor the function," it's "Hey, we've got corporate priorities, you're part of a team."

Let me just tell you one more example of what's unique in Crotonville— and maybe universities couldn't do it.

Part of my job is helping to spread Best Practices. Jack Welch may say: "Go down and check this out! Go down to Louisville, they've got the greatest one-team concept, this is what they did." Well, you go down there, and you find stuff that looks idiosyncratic. "Well, it's a short-cycle business." "Well, it's a union site." The trick is—and ultimately any case-writer must face this—what's portable? What's not idiosyncratic to Louisville or to the site or to the fact that they make appliances? What is there that other businesses could learn? And then, how do you package it? How do you put it together as a dynamite learning experience—is it a case? Is it a role play? Should people visit there?

So these are examples of what you can do. And here's another example of something else you couldn't do in a university. It's called a live case. You bring up six people from Louisville, the people that did this wonderful thing. You've got the marketing person, the finance person, you've got the head of the union, you've got an HR person, you've got a Purchasing/Sourcing person, etcetera. They do a 10 or 15 minute teaser, because "I want people to learn how to learn, not just learn." So we fill a room, 80 people from seven different businesses, maybe. They're gonna learn what Louisville did. The Louisville people do a teaser—just enough so you get your arms around it. Now, the Louisville people go to six different rooms.

Each team—the NBC team, the Motors team, the Capital team—huddles. Who goes to what room? What questions are we gonna ask? Then they peel off, and they go for two 45 minute rounds. So at the end of an hour and a half, each person has been in two rooms and has heard two of the Louisville people. But collectively, the NBC team has heard all six. Then they get back and they've gotta triangulate the data. What caused this to happen? What do they do and how do they do it? "Well, the key was, you know, the union was really on-board." "The hell they were! I spoke to the union guy, he said he hated it!" "No, he didn't say that!" And they're trying to wrestle with the different data. Then, when they think they've got their act together, we go back to the big room and the teams report back to Louisville. "Here's what you did and how you did it." And they get feedback, and then, at the end, whoever's running it asks the Louisville team, "what did these guys not think to ask?" "Well you know, they never even asked about sourcing—that turned out to be key." Or "they never thought about what we did . . ." And at the end of the day, seven businesses understand what Louisville did, and with luck they understand what's generic, because that's the final question: "What do we do, how do we use this? We're not in that business, but . . ." And the Louisville people also get some dynamite feedback.

PF: That's fascinating. Let's go back, then, to CAP. What do you think would be important for readers to know?

SK: A little background. Jack Welch said: "Here's how you take your greatest nightmare and turn it into a competitive advantage." The irony here is GE, as much as any one place, gave the world models of centralized planning. Even the old SWOT analysis came out of GE, and while everybody's writing up GE and teaching it, GE is quietly getting rid of most of the centralized planning in the company. And Jack says, "Change is coming so fast, and so discontinuously, that I don't think we can plan for it. I don't know how you forecast it. So what we gotta do is be better at reacting to it. Quick response." Jack's point is that we don't have to be great at managing change, we just have to be a little better than the other guys at managing change. We have to literally outrun our mistakes. So all you gotta do to take the worst nightmare, which is change you can't predict, and turn it into a friend. And the more crazy the world gets, the more it's on your side. So it is about how to turn a nightmare into a competitive advantage.

So, that's the background. Jack hires four people—all outsiders. I'm one. The four of us are charged with building a change model for GE. And the pay is good so we're making this job last. You know, we're reading the change literature about suicide prevention and Alcoholics Anonymous, and how to stop smoking, and Weight Watchers. And what we come up with is this tired, pedestrian model of change. I mean, it's Lewin out of the '40s, it's Schein, it's Beckhardt, it's—Kotter wrote it up recently in HR, it's the same model of change. And we're kind of embarrassed. Not enough to give back the money, but still, we're kind of sheepish. And this is a case where the client makes the consultant feel good. He says, "The trouble with you professors is, you value creativity, right?" And we say yeah, so he says, "As a result, once you guys have done something once, you don't like to replicate, you like to do new stuff." We say yeah. So he says, "As a result, you guys never get good at anything! Because you get excellence by doing it over and over again. Professors never stay around long enough to do it over to get excellent, they're always doing new stuff." So he said: "It's your hangup that it's not new and creative. I don't care about that." I got two questions here: "Is it true?" We said yeah. "And are my people doing it now?" We said, "Not consistently." He said, "Stop apologizing and start teaching." And he made it mandatory that every president of a business, officer of the company, senior executive, like a thousand people, roughly, would come in. And it was seven days of content over a 10 or 11 week period. You gotta come in and do this, he said. And what makes it the most powerful change experience I've ever been a part of? It's not the content.

It's a seven-step model of change. Step one is creating a shared need. Anybody want to call that unfreezing? Lewin did 50 years ago! Shaping a vision, mobilizing commitment, monitoring progress, making change last—everybody has the same model. But Welch said that's OK. In fact, Welch gave us another metaphor—Welch said it's a pilot's checklist. He said you're gonna fly from here to Boston. Is your pilot gonna learn new stuff reading this checklist? Do you *want* your pilot learning new stuff? Hell, no! You'd be terrified! It's not about new stuff, it's about the *discipline of doing it every time.* He says "That's how you should sell this thing. Don't sell it as new, don't apologize because it's not new. It's not supposed to be new. We don't care about new stuff, we want to do it excellently."

So, that's the model. It's an accurate model, it's useful, it's not special. But what makes it special is the top people had to come in, they came in teams, the teams were united by a project. In Welch's terms, the project had to be on a "need to do," not a "nice to do." So it's something of importance to the business. And they may have been natural teams, or they may not have been. For example, one project united the Environmental Health and Safety Officers for each business. They work in different places, they don't normally work together, but they had a common project to work on. And the information presented in modules is no longer than two hours. A typical day of CAP: From 8 a.m. to 10 a.m. maybe we teach Creating a Need and Shaping a Vision. Each module says: what does theory, research, and other companies' Best Practices have to say about how you create a need? Then each team goes into a separate Break Out room, and that's where the real work occurs. Every team has a CAP coach, who knows the model, assigned to their team. They do everything from team process, if it's needed, to helping them understand the model. It's just-in-time learning. They work on their project—are you the only guys in the building, in the company, that believe in this thing, or is there a shared need already? Here's how to tell. We give them lenses, ways to look at the organization to see if they've got a shared need. How do you shape the vision, or do you need shaping? When they say they're ready, come back in, we'll do some more. But in a typical day, from 8 a.m. to 10 a.m. we teach

Creating a Need and Shaping a Vision, then they go off from 10 a.m. until 3 p.m., and including lunch, they work on that. With the help of the coach— how do we get people on board? We've taught them what other companies do, what research says. Then when they're ready to come back in, "Great, let's do the next step in the model." Back they go, they work, in the evening we come in. So what makes it powerful is it's a team. You know, OD 101 says "never send a changed person back to an unchanged environment." Yet 99 percent of the training we do violates that rule. They come in to a program one at a time, you get them all excited, they go back, their work is piled up their desk, their boss doesn't know what to do, and the energy goes to pieces. Here's a team with a project that's a Need To Do, and usually reports to a higher level. They themselves are usually high level, but even if they're not, they report to a high level.

The early results are that CAP is very powerful. People are having much more success in managing change, and it works with any change. It could be small as a new product introduced, or a number, like we're going to cut cycle times or improve inventory turns, or it could be amorphous, such as a workforce diversity project, or how do we improve environmental awareness throughout the corporation? And we tell them, we don't know what the future will be. Next month will be another fad or another major change or another threat. But you are change masters.

PF: You've told me a lot of things about process and about programs at GE. Does the organization, in this incredibly fast-moving arena that you've described, have a capacity to critically reflect? I mean, think about what it's doing, where it's going? If it's laying off a lot of people or if it's preparing and motivating people, as you've said, who are wanting to go out and jump into their work, are the latter group at risk in terms of burning themselves out? Are there ways in which the organization is thinking about itself in a critical way?

SK: There are some. But I fear that those are inadequate. I always remember the old quote from Winnie-the-Pooh. You know, here comes Edward Bear, on the back of his head, down the stairs. And he's thinking, "There's a better way. If I could only stop bumping for a minute I'm sure I could think of one, but I can't." So he keeps on bumping.

I think that's a good question. I don't think we do it enough. Nothing prohibits you from doing that. It's accepted, it's respected. But, in fact, you're not required to do it. The required meetings are meetings of discussion and action. I'm not sure that we spend enough time doing it. I think that you do have the pressure, the hard-driving. There isn't any natural time out, you feel like you don't have enough time to do that. And I fear that we may *not* be reflective enough. We may not be asking the broader questions. That's one thing—in academe, it's more likely to happen.

PF: Although it's not necessarily that it does.

SK: No. And in GE it's not necessarily that it doesn't. What I'm saying, it is more built into the rhythms of academe that I think into the corporate rhythms. In the GE's of the world, you don't ever have to look up. You go home and sleep fine at night, you feel so righteous because you're so tired because you've done so much useful, good work. You don't have that nagging question, unless you give it to yourself or somebody gives it to you.

PF: One other GE-related question that has two parts: I suspect they may have similar answers, though I don't know. In terms of managing diversity, not just diversity of business but people, around gender, around ethnic background, around personal philosophy, around those things: how is that dealt with in GE? The other one is: how does GE deal with environmental issues?

SK: Well, they're key issues. Some types of diversity come easily to GE. For example, you know, Welch challenged the company a few years ago: "We call ourselves a global company but we're not, we're an American business doing business around the world and we've got to get more global. The idea of parachuting in GE locals to run the different countries' businesses—we've got to start using local nationals, we've got to trust the Koreans to manage in Korea, etc., etc." So, I'm building a global Crotonville. I've hired a Chinese Singaporean out of Singapore recently, somebody in Delhi, an Indian local national. I'm looking now at a Japanese for Tokyo. So a lot of that kind of diversity happens of its own accord. I remember Welch, this meeting that happened in Boca Raton years ago. There's a ladies room right outside the major auditorium where we meet. And when GE meets, they paint the word "men" over it, use it as a men's room. The ladies go upstairs. And Jack said, "I'll know we've arrived, in terms of gender, when they can't do that anymore because there are too many women in this room and they've got to use that ladies room." Again, a rich way of saying it. We *track* it meticulously. You know, there *are* women in GE who run businesses. But not enough. So it's pursued. Same thing with Afro-Americans. Some of the things GE does is to, through a fund, give money to the high school. The point being, if you look at the recruiting goals of the top 30 companies alone, it's in the hundreds. And they're fighting for the 100 or so black students coming out, or they end up stealing each other's people. So you may look better, but collectively you haven't helped anything.

PF: Right.

SK: So GE does a lot to support of schools in minority areas, starting with high schools, and we track who goes to college and then give support to go to graduate school—enrich the applicant pools around diversity. Having said that, though, I don't think we're special. I think we are socially responsible in that area. Welch is always asking, when there's an applicant pool, "Who's in that pool? Create a diverse slate." Always pushing for it. But I think most companies do that now. I wouldn't say we're lagging, I wouldn't say we're leading. When they do the progression, it's *much* better. GE has many more minorities and women in key leadership roles. But, when you look at what you want to have, you're not there yet. One good sign is that at least, we win a lot of community awards for helping in the communities.

Environmentally, it's tricky, because some of this, like the Superfund, is retroactive knowledge. I mean, you learn in 1990 that you didn't cover your nuclear sludge in 1980 in a certain way, and now the obligation is you still have to manage it. And it's all above board, but some of this is just, you know, you're in the nuclear business, you're in the plastics business, it's just harder to get this stuff exactly right. The state of the art is still advancing so rapidly.

PF: So what's the message to academics? I know you've noticed the growing interest in the Academy, in this area.

SK: I think that, because you're in a corporation doesn't mean you're a bad person. The old stereotype, "All he cares about is profits," that's mostly silly. I don't find that among my colleagues. But having said that, there's a lot of pressure on numbers. People don't say, "I'm going to hurt the environment because I don't care, I'd rather make my number." It isn't thought of that way. It's just that there's never enough budget. How much money do I spend on research and development to make sure the generator is cleaner? And so people in the specialties have to become continually clearer about what is and is not environmentally sound. Some of the laws that I mentioned the other night, they're bewildering, they're contradictory. I remember Welch saying to the Environmental Officer, "I want us to be cleaner than clean." And he was trying to get up his nerve to say "Jack, you gotta understand. If we're in compliance with *this* law, we are necessarily out of compliance with that one. They require opposite things." So, some of it's about that. Some of it's about making a consumer societally aware. I mean, when the countries of the world began to require environmental standards superior to American law in order to bid. American companies got real interested in advancing environmentally, above what was legally required. Because there were some countries in this world that said, you can't bid unless the noise level is less than X. Or the emission level has to be less than Y. And it may be that you're in full compliance, it's not a case of being unlawful, but all of a sudden you can't get into those markets. People should require that, and withhold support from organizations that don't comply. I think that's key.

So again, we're not guilty of noncompliance, but I think there's incomplete knowledge. And it's the same thing I mentioned earlier on integrity. Nobody winks at that stuff in GE—it's a really reputable place. On the other hand, you got so many things you have to do, there's a limit on money. and unfortunately, the costs of environmental neglect, they're more subtle. If you ever say to somebody "Are you aware . . .?" I don't know one person in fifty who'd go ahead and do the bad thing. But it's lack of awareness. "I didn't do anything to the environment. All I do is make this decision to spend money." "Oh yeah, but by implication, couldn't those dollars have been used to do a cleaner reactor?" "Oh yeah, if you put it that way." So that's what it is. It's honorable people who might do the wrong thing out of lack of awareness. The universities have their counterparts. The faculty member doesn't say, "I'm not gonna keep office hours. I'm not gonna do my guidance counsellor responsibilities, I don't care if the kids grow up without a good model." One out of 50 says that. It's not that. It's just that the signals are there. You've got to do your research, research has got to be done out of the building. You look up and you say: "Oh, I guess I wasn't much of a mentor last year."

PF: I agree with that. Another example it triggers for me is the case of an academic racing to get something ready for class who burns up half a tree stand through photocopying. That could have been avoided if it had been timed in a different way. Or if somebody had thought about it that way, you know, had thought about the tradeoff.

SK: And I think that's most of the neglect. It doesn't make it any—I mean, the tree still dies. I'm not trying to minimize it. We have to do it better. But I think that's the nature of the problem. It's not the stereotyped evil industrialist who doesn't care about the environment. There aren't many evil people running around. I think the people I've met in GE are very much like the people in universities. They may not have as much time to reflect, it's just that the seduction of the numbers you have to make takes over. And that's part of the reward systems. And we're working on it. You have to have environmental standards, that has to be among the numbers set, otherwise it doesn't get measured, doesn't get done.

PF: My last major question for you: Of all the work you've written and published, what have you been most proud of? And it may have been influential or not. It's your call.

SK: *[Laughs]* It's funny you mention that. I always thought it would be a great study to ask people, what are you best known for, and what do you wish? And I think it would be a, you know, on one axis, your degree of pride, and on the other axis, the degree of recognition. I met Richard Hackman, he was getting a lot of celebrity around his job enrichment stuff, for a while, and he couldn't get people to read his groups stuff. And I was experiencing the same kind of thing. Well, to answer your question, the work on reward systems—I really like it. I mean, I think that it's powerful. And I haven't published enough, so some of it's my own fault. The Folly article is best known. In fact, they did a little survey, and most people said oh yeah, it's still true. I guess it's always going to be true. I like that and the other reward systems stuff I've done. I did a piece on integrity, it was a chapter in a book, that I like—and I don't know if people read it.

PF: Where was it published?

SK: It was published as "Integrity in Effective Leadership" in *The Functioning of the Executive* [S. Srivastva, ed., Jossey-Bass, 1988]. I was asked to be a speaker at an integrity conference. So I thought, "I'm a model of integrity." Then I began to read the literature, and I found that I'm doing everything you're not supposed to do. I pointed out that, in the course of being an administrator—I was dean at the time—it seems as though I must violate integrity all the time. And I said, either I'm unintegritous, and I'm just rationalizing that the job makes me do it. Or number two, I lack integrity but so do all of my colleagues, which makes it even worse. Or three, maybe I don't lack integrity. Maybe there's something wrong with the standard definitions of integrity. And I gave examples, appropriating sums. You can't pay moving expenses to job candidates at a public school, but they won't come if you don't pay moving expenses. So you give the candidate a seminar, and the stipend happens to equal his moving expenses. So now you're moving money from one category to another. Or you move it to another category period, where you can't buy it now but you can buy it in a month. So I ended up saying, look, I'm violating all the canons, and I'm saying, I don't know what to do about this thing. You know, if you tell the truth about why someone's being let go, they sue you— you're not allowed to do that.

So I wasn't profound, but I really tried to talk about integrity in everyday life. And I was saying, either we're all getting it wrong, or something's wrong with our definitions. And I didn't go far enough. I didn't say, here's what I would substitute for it. Anyway, that's a piece I really liked.

PF: I suspect that anybody who reads this who has been anywhere in administration would resonate to what you have just said.

SK: And I like very much my work on "Substitutes for Leadership." But it's never had solid empirical support, and I've never wavered in my conviction that it's right. [*Laughs*] And I don't know what that says about anything, including about me. But the underlying logic is that you have to know how to do something, and you have to want to do it, or else performance cannot occur. That's just ability × motivation. And it seems to me that the leader may or may not be a source of those things. If the leader doesn't motivate you, an outside reward system may motivate you, or a peer group may motivate you. And knowledge can come from all kinds of sources. So I said, we're bragging about the .3 correlation, which means we explain nine percent of the variance. We never get curious about the 91 percent unexplained. But if you start at the other end, something has to make you able, something has to make you want to. If the leader hasn't done it, why don't you take the other view and say "what did it when the leader didn't do it?" Let's say a hundred percent—you do want to and you do know how, what did it? And I looked at the other sources. I've never wavered that there's something important there. And I could be flat out wrong, but I think there's probably something in there. So I like that a lot.

PF: Sure. Is there anything that we haven't captured, or something else for your field or for General Electric if you look ahead?

SK: I don't know. I think we've probably covered what I . . . I'll just say it differently. When you put people in different boxes, or different categories, you give them a different perspective, a different fate, a different point of view. The world is getting increasingly diverse. The Academy is more heterogeneous than before and the workplaces are, anyway you want to cut it. If you had everybody the same, you might force diversity. But that isn't the case. To increase further diversity by labelling everybody differently and then treating them that way, I don't think is fruitful. I said this in my academy Presidential speech five years ago, but it hasn't become any less true in my mind or any less relevant—you know, honoring Full Professors, and stigmatizing Clinical Professors. Like calling people Adjunct. And they're *not* Adjunct. They're full time, they cover a huge number of FTE hours. And labelling other people Consultants. I just don't see the point of all that. It seems to me what we want to create is a community of scholars, and among the knowledge you want to obtain is practical knowledge of how to intervene in organizations. Why is it that if I learn a fact about theory, it's good. If I learn a fact that's about consulting, it's bad. It seems to me that knowledge is good and more knowledge is better. And whenever I had authority over other people, I would find out what people did well and give them more of it, and find out what people did poorly and gave them less of it. Why force people with nothing to say to write. I don't *want* people with nothing to say to be in the literature. I'm embarrassed to have my school's name on their paper. So I always worked with teaching tracks, research tracks, service—find out what people like to do and do it well. I don't mean to make it sound like a hobby shop. When I was dean, I would go to the departments and I would say: "You've got 24 people, the average load is four, you're gonna cover 96 courses. That's good, because I've got 96 courses that are going to be offered this year. I also want you to be in the journals, I want you to be active in the associations, I want you to have one third of you marching in Graduation—I'm embarrassed when I'm the only one out there and the parents show up. So collectively, that's what you have to do. I don't have to tell you who's doing what." So, when I try to impose a six course load on a four course mentality, they all get upset. But when you do it this way, a good teacher's thinking, "Hey, I'm not gonna hit the literature, you know I'm not. But I would be willing to do seven courses if you would consider that my full performance and give me a high grade and honor me—my words, but his sentiment—I'll do that." A young guy who hates students—I don't know why people who hate students join universities, but they come!—

says: "Well, if I didn't have to do that teaching crap, I could do five of the eleven articles all by myself." And I would say fine, as long as you have voluntary choice and collectively you meet these requirements, do what you want to do. Do it well. That's what I think there should be more of. This notion of pigeonholing, stereotyping, undergrad versus grad, macro versus micro, required versus elective—all these ways of cutting the pie, you end up with as many different categories as you have people. So I really think we ought to work on it. I used to have a model—I never did it, but I had it in my head—a model of offices on pushcarts. Because I noticed at USC, at least, the departments were not where much energy occurred. The excitement was around programs and centres, where common bodies of work got done. And I thought, everyone should be required to—join a program, join a centre. And if nobody would take you or you didn't know anywhere else, the department was a residual place where you could go.

So I don't know if there's anything in that. There's so much more we're capable of, and this business of labelling each other, it just gets you nowhere.

PF: Nice way to finish. I really do think that's one of the key things we have got to face and resolve in the future. Thank you.

PART IV

CONCLUSION

The chapters in this book have covered a wide territory, yet there is a building block of ideas to help readers clarify their own positions with respect to organization science. Part I started with debates concerning economics versus behavioral approaches to organization studies, and arguments for both single and multiple paradigm perspectives. The second part moved to discourses, broadening the perspective to show how the field is organized, and introduced the self, agnosticism, a historical perspective, and stories of grounded research, to enlarge the reader's perspective. The third part presented dialogues that suggest ways to build bridges and undertake new research directions.

One hoped-for impact of this book is that it encourages readers to take time to look around, to explore the intellectual and emotional territories through which they travel on their scholarly journeys . . . to the "ocean of truth," or at least to other "wells of knowledge." There is much to be learned from and with others as one attempts to map and to understand the phenomena we study in the field of organization science, and we are often blinded to the richness such attention can provide, both to the scholar traveler and to her field.

A young boy traveled across Japan to the school of a famous martial artist. When he arrived at the dojo, he was given an audience with the sensei (teacher). "What do you wish from me?" the Master asked.

"I wish to become your student and become the finest karateist in the land," the boy replied. *"How long must I study?"* *"Ten years at least,"* the Master answered. *"What if I studied twice as hard as all your other students?"* *"Twenty years,"* replied the Master. *"Twenty years? What if I practice day and night with all my effort?"* *"Thirty years,"* was the Master's reply.

"How is it that each time I say I will work harder you tell me it will take longer?" the boy asked. *"The answer is clear. When one eye is fixed on your destination, there is only one eye left with which to find the way."*

—Anonymous

So, as you reflect back on what you have learned from your reading (and perhaps rereading) of the pieces in this book, you might not only ask yourself: "In which direction do I want to go?" and "Which direction(s) am I willing to support: continued debate, integrative discourse, or dialogue and community?" but you might also permit yourself to expand your attention, to open your mind and heart to your experiences along the way. We hope we have provided you with sufficient stimulus and variety to draw you to this way and to have given you enough food for thought to sustain you as you move forward.

—Peter Frost, Richard L. Daft, and Arie Y. Lewin

About the Editors

Peter J. Frost is the Edgar F. Kaiser Chair in Organizational Behaviour at the University of British Columbia. He has been a senior editor for *Organization Science,* and the Executive Director of the Organizational Behavior Teaching Society. He has co-authored a number of books, including *Reframing Organizational Culture, Doing Exemplary Research, Researchers Hooked on Teaching, Rhythms of Academic Life,* and others. Frost has also been recognized for teaching: He received the CASE Canada Professor of the Year Award in 1989, the Financial Post "Leaders in Management Education Award in 1997, and the Academy of Management's "Distinguished Educator" Award in 1998. His recent interest in how emotional pain is handled in organizations has resulted in work about why compassion counts in organizations (in the *Journal of Management Inquiry*), and the role and hazard of toxic handlers (in the *Harvard Business Review*). He relishes time spent with his family, and is an avid movie-goer, bird watcher, and Scottish country dancer.

Arie Y. Lewin is Professor of Business Administration and Sociology and IBM Research Fellow at the Fuqua School of Business, Duke University. He is the Director of the Center for International Business Education and Research (CIBER) and of the recently established Center for Research on New Organization Forms. Lewin has been Program Director for Decision, Risk Management Science at the National Science Foundation (1986-1998); Departmental Editor of *Management Science* for the Department of Organization Analysis, Performance and Design (1974-1987); founding Editor-in-Chief of *Organization Science* (1989-1998); DKB Visiting Professor Keio University Graduate School of Business (Spring 1993); and Visiting Research Professor Institute for Business Research, Hitotsubashi University

(1994–1995). His primary research interests involve the coevolution of new organization forms. He leads a cross-cultural (Germany, Japan, Korea, Sweden, Switzerland, Denmark, the Netherlands, the United Kingdom, and the United States) research consortium—New Organization Forms for the Information Age (NOFIA) involving a longitudinal comparative study of strategic reorientations and organization restructurings. The objective of this research program is to map the emergence and diffusion of new organizational forms and to anticipate the dimensions of these new dominant forms of organization. He is author or editor of seven books, and his research articles have appeared or are forthcoming in many different journals, including *Academy of Management Journal, Decision Sciences, European Journal of Operational Research, Journal of Applied Psychology, Journal of Mathematical Sociology, Management Science, Organization Science, Organization Studies, Personnel Psychology, Policy Sciences, Science, Simulation,* and *The Accounting Review.*

Richard L. Daft holds the Ralph Owen Chair in the Owen Graduate School of Management at Vanderbilt University, where he specializes in the study of organizational change and leadership. Daft received his MBA and PhD from the University of Chicago, is a Fellow of the Academy of Management, and has served on the editorial boards of *Academy of Management Journal* and *Administrative Science Quarterly.* He was the Associate-Editor-in-Chief of *Organization Science* for seven years and served for three years as Associate Editor of *Administrative Science Quarterly.* He has authored or co-authored ten books, including *Organization Theory and Design* (6th ed., 1998) and (with Bob Lengel) *Fusion Leadership: Unlocking the Forces That Change People and Organizations* (1998). He has also authored dozens of scholarly articles, papers, and chapters on the topics of organization design, manager information processing, and organization innovation and change.